PIONEERS FOR PROFIT

Pioneers for Profit

Foreign

Entrepreneurship

and Russian

Industrialization

1885-1913

John P. McKay

THE UNIVERSITY OF CHICAGO PRESS
CHICAGO & LONDON

International Standard Book Number: 0–226–55990–4
Library of Congress Catalog Card Number: 79–103932

The University of Chicago Press, Chicago 60637
The University of Chicago Press, Ltd., London

To Jo Ann

CONTENTS

vii

MAPS

ABBREVIATIONS USED IN FOOTNOTES

A.E., Brussels	Archives du Ministère des Affaires Etrangères, Brussels
A.E., Paris	Archives du Ministère des Affaires Etrangères, Paris
A.N.	Archives Nationales, Paris
B.U.P.	Archives de la Banque de l'Union Parisienne, Paris
C.C.	Correspondance Commerciale (commercial series of the French consular correspondence)
C.I.C.	Crédit Industriel et Commercial, Paris
C.L.	Archives du Crédit Lyonnais, Paris
C.N.E.P.	Comptoir National d'Escompte de Paris, Paris
E.M.	Archives de l'Ecole des Mines, Paris
P.R. MSS	Company records of the Forges de la Providence Russe, Marchienne-au-Pont, Belgium

Note: All dates are given in the order of day-month-year; thus 3–5–1897 means 3 May 1897.

PREFACE

This study investigates the role of foreign entrepreneurship in Russian industrialization between 1885 and 1913. My purpose is to go beyond work on the statistical dimensions of large external investment in Russian industry and to understand the actual processes, mechanisms, and contributions of active foreign entrepreneurship. In doing so I have focused on three distinct problems: the pattern of enterprise and investment as practiced by business leaders of the advanced countries of western Europe before the First World War; the pattern of foreign participation in Russian industry and its influence on accelerated Russian growth in this period; and finally the nature of relations that existed between economically advanced foreigners and relatively backward Russians during development. All of these are related to vexing contemporary problems, and therefore I have gladly run the risks of didactic history.

My work is based largely upon previously unutilized private business archives in western Europe, and of course public archives as well. These archival materials are discussed in the bibliography. They permitted me to study a large number of French, Belgian, and German firms operating in Russia. Published Russian material has proved to be less valuable, but it has been carefully examined and important on occasion. There are two obvious omissions which are connected—most English entrepreneurs and the petroleum industry. Originally I had intended to analyze the petroleum industry, which was dominated by foreigners, and particularly Englishmen. Finally it seemed best to examine the rapid rise of the entire Tsarist petroleum industry in a separate study. I hope to do this at a later date.

Beginning with the examination of a large goup of
foreign entrepreneurs, I have tried to find the foreigner's average performance and to respond thereby
to the criticism that entrepreneurial studies are
often unrepresentative or irrelevant. The dimensions
of entrepreneurship have been presented analyti-
cally in Part I. Part II consists of four carefully
chosen case studies that exemplify and corroborate
key findings in Part I. The analytical chapters of
Part I and case studies of Part II are thus meant to
reinforce each other and sharpen our understanding
of the performance of the representative foreign
entrepreneur.

A word of explanation concerning the problems of
Russian proper names and transliterations is necessary. Within the text I have generally used the accepted English spelling for place names, and I have
transliterated proper names according to the Library of Congress system with slight modifications.
To aid the reader in identifying different enterprises, I have added an appendix of major firms discussed. This appendix gives the original titles of
firms in either French or Russian as well as the
firm's English equivalent as found in the text.

In researching and writing this study I have been
aided and encouraged in many ways by many people.
Although it is impossible to do justice to this support, a few acknowledgements may express my grati-
tude. I would like to thank: the staff of the Interli-
brary Loan Service at the University of California,
Berkeley, for tracking down many obscure volumes;
various archivists and directors in Europe, and especially those of the Crédit Lyonnais and the Banque
de l'Union Parisienne; and the Foreign Area Fel-
lowship Program and Dr. James Gould, for generously supporting my work in this country and

abroad. An earlier version of chapter nine first appeared in *Business History Review,* whose editors kindly granted me permission to use it here. In the academic world I wish to single out for their aid: Professor Olga Crisp of London, my colleagues Professors Ralph Fisher and Benjamin Uroff, Professor Gerald Feldman of Berkeley, and Professor David Landes, my thesis advisor, who gave me invaluable aid and criticism, as did Professor Henry Rosovsky. Professors Landes and Rosovsky first stimulated and then channeled my interest in economic history. They may rightly claim a large measure of whatever credit this study deserves, without, of course, being in any way responsible for its shortcomings. Lastly, I am very grateful for Jo Ann's constant help and encouragement.

Part I

Dimensions of Entrepreneurship

1

INTRODUCTION

1

In the latter part of the nineteenth century the ever widening waves of the Industrial Revolution launched in Great Britain a century earlier broke upon economically backward agrarian Russia with great force. Military defeats and economic stagnation in the 1850s had forced a hesitant feudal society to begin in earnest the arduous task of modernization and industrialization. Then in the 1860s and early 1870s a whole series of developments—such as the emancipation of the serfs, the real beginnings of a railroad system, an expanding internal market, and the creation of a considerable banking system —helped establish the preconditions of modern economic growth. The initial overall effect of these changes was limited, however, and it was a generation before the tempo of industrial progress quickened to revolutionary proportions in the 1890s. After the Russian industrial revolution of that decade (or "big spurt" or "take-off," to use somewhat analogous current terminology), the pace of industrial development marked time during the serious depression from 1900 to about 1908. But it recovered impressively and was probably "self-sustaining" in the second surge, which lasted from 1909 to the outbreak of World War I. The pattern of two great booms broken by a long depression may be seen in table 1.

The rate of growth for Russian industrial production compares favorably with rates of industrial growth in other countries during both their respective industrial revolutions and the years at the turn of the century. Indeed, in the 1890s Russia's rate of

Table 1

ANNUAL GROWTH RATES OF RUSSIAN INDUSTRIAL PRODUCTION, 1885–1913
(In Percent)

Years	Growth Rate
1885–1889	6.10
1890–1899	8.03
1900–1906	1.45
1907–1913	6.25
Average	5.72

SOURCE: Alexander Gerschenkron, "The Rate of Growth of Industrial Production in Russia Since 1885," *Journal of Economic History* 7 Supplement (1947): 149.
NOTE: For the years 1894–99 the growth rate was approximately 9 percent; for 1910–13, approximately 7.5 percent.

industrial growth was perhaps the highest in the world. Even after 1900 it was still higher than rates in the major European countries, as table 2 shows.

At the same time the weight of the large and backward agrarian sector, the rapid rate of population increase, and the very low level of industrial development in 1860 (or 1890 for that matter) meant that Russia remained far behind other industrial nations in 1913 in all per capita comparisons of income or consumption in spite of its industrial achievement after 1885. In 1913 per capita income in Russia was only 101.4 rubles, as opposed to the equivalents of 300.4 rubles in Germany, 460.6 rubles in Great Britain, and 682.3 rubles in the United

States.[1] That rapid growth left Russia poor in absolute and comparative terms probably helps account for the great divergency of judgments concerning the nature of the Russian economy on the eve of the

Table 2

GROWTH OF INDUSTRIAL PRODUCTION IN SELECTED
COUNTRIES, 1860–1913
(In Index Numbers: 1913 = 100)

Year	Great Britain	France	Germany	Russia	U.S.A.	World
1860	34	26	14	8	8	14
1870	44	34	18	13	11	19
1880	53	43	25	17	17	26
1890	62	56	40	27	39	43
1900	79	66	65	61	54	60
1913	100	100	100	100	100	100

SOURCE: *Vierteljahrshefte zur Konjunkturforschung* 31 (1933): 18.
NOTE: Industries included are mining, textiles, ferrous metallurgy, and food processing.

First World War and related historical what-might-have-beens. Those drawing an essentially optimistic interpretation stress (among other things) the relatively high and sustained *rate* of industrial growth as decisive, while pessimists cite the low *level* of development as symptomatic of fundamentally unaltered backwardness in 1913. Thus the arguments of optimists and pessimists often go past each other. They refer to two different sets of facts, and perhaps to different fundamental conceptions of what is important in history.

In analyzing this considerable Russian industrialization after 1885 many investigators have focused

1. Olga Crisp, "Russia, 1860–1914," in Rondo Cameron et al., *Banking in the Early Stages of Industrialization* (New York, 1967), p. 184.

on the primary influence of the state. As Professor Gerschenkron puts it, "The strategic factor in the great industrial upsurge of the 1890s must be seen in the changed policy of the government. . . . Industrial development became an accepted and in fact the central goal."[2] The centrality of the state in Russian economic development in the last years of the nineteenth century almost seems, then, to connect the reforms of Peter the Great with the accomplishments of the commissars in a seamless pattern: Russian economic development was always directed by political authority for political goals.[3] For another respected scholar in an expansive mood the finance minister, Count Witte, who was chief architect of Russian economic policy in the 1890s, even becomes basically "a forerunner of Stalin rather than a contemporary of Nicholas II" or, presumably, John D. Rockefeller. And Russia in the 1890s becomes "the pioneer of all modern experiments in deliberate economic development."[4]

Certainly no one would deny the general importance of active governmental involvement in Russian industrial development in the 1890s. Yet on the basis of Professor Gindin's marvelous study on the State Bank from 1861 to 1892, one might well argue that the decisive change in governmental attitudes really occurred in the late 1860s and early 1870s.[5] Similarly, one may well question whether Witte was a civilized Stalin, and whether economic planning in today's underdeveloped countries is derived from

2. *Economic Backwardness in Historical Perspective* (Cambridge, Mass., 1962), p. 125.

3. Ibid., pp. 145–51.

4. Theodore Von Laue, *Why Lenin? Why Stalin?* (New York, 1964), pp. 52–53.

5. I. F. Gindin, *Gosudarstvennyi bank i ekonomicheskaia politika tsarskogo praviiel'stva, 1861–1892 gody* (Moscow, 1960).

projects formulated by a tsarist finance minister. Indeed, one should. For the role of the state in Russian development in these years is actually quite subtle. And an understanding of that role is extremely important for any study on foreign entrepreneurship.

What in fact did the state do? Three activities stand out. First, it provided high tariff protection for industry—very much like that associated with the contemporary governments of Méline in France, or McKinley in the United States. Second, it accounted for the greater part of new railroad construction, which almost doubled the Russian system from 1889 (18,600 miles) to 1901 (35,000 miles).[6] The government simultaneously bought numerous private companies for top prices, so that by 1901 government roads constituted two-thirds of the total rail network.[7] Third, the government engaged in a vast public relations campaign to enlist support for industrialization at home and abroad.

Of these three activities, only large-scale construction of railroads by the government might seem to be a radical departure from the earlier experience of industrializing countries. Yet, as every undergraduate has been taught for a long time, only Great Britain built its railroads without benefit of extensive state aid. And several continental railway systems, like those of Belgium or Imperial Germany, became essentially state-owned and state-operated by the end of the nineteenth century.[8] At first

6. P. A. Khromov, *Ekonomicheskoe razvitie Rossii v XIX–XX vekakh* (Moscow, 1950), p. 462.

7. Theodore Von Laue, *Sergei Witte and the Industrialization of Russia* (New York, 1963), p. 89.

8. For example, Arthur Birnie's oft-printed *An Economic History of Europe, 1760–1939* (London, Methuen edition, 1962), pp. 41–44.

glance the case for radical government experiment and novel intervention seems exaggerated.

With further investigation it becomes even more so. Surely the model for Stalin and future planners would have seen the state blazing some sort of trail as producer and industrial manager, complete with pilot plants, quotas, and ruthless elimination or control of possible competitors. The Russian state did nothing of the sort. In fact, with the exception of previously mentioned state-owned railroads, almost all of Russian industry remained in private hands. Almost all increase in industrial output came from private enterprise producing for profit within a relatively free market system. And when on occasion the state, as banker of last resort, came to hold an industrial enterprise, like the Putilov Works in the 1880s, or the Kerch Metallurgical Company in the first decade of the twentieth century, it did so reluctantly and returned such plants to private owners as quickly as possible.

One may argue of course that demand is almost always crucial in economic development: where it leads supply will follow. Accordingly, whether Russian demand came mainly from large state purchases, or from some state demand combined with propaganda and public relations adding up to an investment boom, the state would remain crucial. Different societies and their businessmen will invariably respond to increased demand and opportunities for large gain, since alleged differences in social attitudes influencing business activity are largely illusory or inconsequential.[9] Yet even if one accepts

9. This states, admittedly a little baldly, the position of Alexander Gerschenkron in an extremely interesting discussion of the development of entrepreneurial history, which is reprinted in *Economic Backwardness*, pp. 52–71. For the other side, see,

this argument, it is clear that the state only bought goods; it did not produce them. At most, the state embarked upon an important program of public works in an attempt to create adequate effective demand, a demand that could be substituted for the weak private market.[10] In reality, this alleged substitution by the state has also been exaggerated, at least among Western scholars. As a recent study of the period shows, "the specific criticism which can be brought against the Russian government is that only a minute part of its budget expenditures went directly for the purposes of developing the industrial sector."[11] Thus direct railroad construction and subsidizing of private railroad construction, by far the government's most important economically productive activity, totaled little more than one billion rubles between 1880 and 1900, the period of greatest construction. This sum did not exceed government custom revenue from imports of tea, coffee, alcoholic beverages, salt, and herring in these years.[12] Or, to put it another way, the state spent less than 5 percent of its budget during this period on railroad construction.[13] Yet this was by far the largest item for industrialization purposes. Direct subsidies to industrialists were not even a close second.[14]

among others, David S. Landes, "French Entrepreneurship and Industrial Growth in the Nineteenth Century," *Journal of Economic History* 9 (1949) : 45–61, which served as Gerschenkron's point of departure, and the ensuing Landes-Gerschenkron debate in *Explorations in Entrepreneurial History,* 1954.

10. Gerschenkron, *Economic Backwardness*, p. 126. See chapters 3 and 8 for further discussion of government policy.

11. Arcadius Kahan, "Government Policies and the Industrialization of Russia," *Journal of Economic History* 27 (1967) : 466.

12. Ibid., 466–67.

13. Khromov, *Ekonomicheskoe razvitie*, pp. 498–503.

14. Kahan, "Government Policies," p. 467.

Nonetheless, I would argue that government did have a key role in the crucial 1890s. That role was, however, very largely one of public relations, propaganda, and radiation of enthusiasm. If "historians tend often to disregard the existing features of the reality of government policy and to pass judgment on the basis of general pronouncements," [15] their failure is understandable. The public relations campaign was well organized and resourceful. And it had real significance for development, as we shall see later. Yet even so, the Witte system emerges as a wager, though perhaps a safe one, on capitalists and private entrepreneurs.[16] Such a strategy would seem to have much more in common with a market economy than with the command economy of Stalin, or the planned economies of parts of the underdeveloped world, where the state is an important or predominant producer.

The wager on private capital was of course anything but safe. The nearly automatic supply of creative entrepreneurship to increased opportunity in backward countries is all too rare. Many observers have noted, for example, that the price system often does not seem to work in such countries, in part because large groups of the population refuse to alter methods or outlook in the face of changing market conditions. Certainly Finance Minister Witte believed Russia lacked local businessmen who had the incentive and the know-how, not to mention the capital, necessary for accelerated development. He believed there was nothing automatic about the supply of entrepreneurship or knowledge, but that it could only grow gradually hand-in-hand with the growth of industry. And since industry itself was

15. Ibid., p. 464.
16. Von Laue, *Witte,* p. 300.

dependent upon entrepreneurship, industrial know-how, and capital, which were all insufficient, Russia was apparently caught in the vicious cycle of backwardness and slow change. Yet it was precisely in the context of this analysis that the entire Witte system bet on a massive response from private producers. Or more precisely, it bet on private foreign entrepreneurship and its financial resources. Witte himself summed up the matter in 1899 in a secret memorandum for Tsar Nicholas II.[17] "The inflow of foreign capital is, in the considered opinion of the Minister of Finance [i.e., Witte], the only way by which our industry will be able to supply our country quickly with abundant and cheap products. Each new wave of capital, rolling in from abroad, knocks down the excessively high level of profits to which our monopolistic businessmen are accustomed and forces them to seek equal profits through technical improvements which lead to price reductions."[18] This suggests that the state believed it could content itself with creating some real demand and great investment enthusiasm because, although the Russian market was very imperfect and its entrepreneurship inadequate, the international market system of capitalistic Europe and its businessmen was highly responsive to new opportunities. Not only would foreign capitalists enter Russia for high profits, but they would continue to do so even as profits

17. See Witte's secret memorandum to the tsar in March 1899 for the fullest exposition of his system, upon which the foregoing is based, in Akademiia Nauk SSSR, Institut istorii, *Materialy po istorii SSSR,* vol. 6: *Dokumenty po istorii monopolisticheskogo kapitalizma v Rossii* (Moscow, 1959), pp. 173–95. (This very important document has been translated by T. Von Laue in *Journal of Modern History* 26 [1954] : 60–75.)

18. Ibid., p. 184.

fell through increased competition. Thus the sharp rise in demand would not result only in windfall profits for local monopolists. Rather it would elicit such a response and increase in productive facilities that eventual market equilibrium would give both lower prices and lower rates of profit. Therefore Russia's great asset, which would allow it to escape the fatal dilemma of underdevelopment, was a vast *external* pool of entrepreneurship, knowledge, and capital waiting to be tapped.

Here indeed Russian economic policy was striking out in a new direction. But it seems that the ensuing developmental experience had more in common with those of contemporary Puerto Rico or the Ivory Coast than with those of Mao's China or even Nehru's India. The wager on massive response by foreign capitalists to profit opportunities which government helps create is the common strand in these policies. The successes and failures of this truly pioneering experiment in Russia are the subject of our investigation.

2

At this point it is necessary to pause and consider some of the general theoretical questions related to such a developmental plan. First, there is the question of definitions. In the quote cited above, Witte spoke of "foreign capital," which might include *all* foreign investment and not just foreign entrepreneurial investment. At the same time it seems clear that he is referring *primarily* to investment in private corporations and excluding foreign loans to the Russian government. Tsarist and Soviet studies conventionally make the same distinction: analysis of "foreign capital" in Russia focuses on foreign investment in joint-stock corporations; "foreign loans" to the Russian government and its agencies are discussed separately. The term "foreign capital" is approximately equivalent to foreign corporate investment, which will be used often in this study as a less ambiguous rubric.

There is second consideration. Foreign corporate investment does not necessarily mean foreign decision-making power, power normally prerequisite for effective foreign entrepreneurship. Thus the meaningful distinction in current discussion between *direct* investment and *portfolio* investment in corporations operating in foreign countries. The former exercises foreign control based on concentrated foreign ownership; the latter often goes with foreign ownership that is small, or fragmented, or passive, and this ownership pattern may be quite compatible with local management and decision making.[19] In the real world the line between active foreign direction and passive portfolio participation is often unclear, but the conceptual distinction is clear and important. For our purposes foreign entrepreneurship and direct foreign investment are roughly analagous. Both presuppose foreign decision-making capability.

Are there sound reasons supporting an industrialization policy which encourages, or even relies upon, foreign entrepreneurship and direct foreign investment? Or is it more likely that foreign entrepreneurs exert a negative influence, promoting unwittingly (or intentionally) the same backwardness they are intended to cure? If both positive and negative contributions are possible, how may the positive

19. See Wilfred Guth, *Capital Exports to Less Developed Countries* (Dordrecht, Holland, 1963), particularly pp. 27–29; Raymond Mikesell, ed., *U.S. Private and Government Investment* (Eugene, Ore., 1962), pp. 32–187.

be maximized and the negative minimized? To answer these questions fully would require an elaborate analysis of foreign investment, economic development, and even cultural change far surpassing our empirical investigation and historical inclination. Nevertheless an attempt to construct an explicit conceptual framework should provide tools to attack our problem, and it may eventually produce conclusions of interest to many students of economic development and foreign investment, as well as to specialists in European economic history.

It is often claimed that direct foreign investment contributes to development by employing idle resources, such as unexploited mineral deposits or underemployed labor, which usually abound in poor countries. By putting idle resources to work foreign investment adds to both output and income in the host country. The most common explanation of this possibility is the lack of adequate capital for the development of existing resources.[20] First, poor countries have a limited *stock* of capital, and this means that even a high rate of savings provides only modest sums for investment. Second, the *rate* of savings is generally quite low (Rostow's 5 percent), and therefore investable funds barely cover replacement of existing equipment. Capital available for new projects (net capital formation) is heartbreakingly inadequate. Thus an inflow of foreign investment can supplement insufficient domestic savings and permit increased investment leading to more rapid economic progress.

It seems likely, however, that direct investment

20. For example, A. A. Fatouros, *Government Guarantees to Foreign Investors* (New York, 1962), pp. 11–15; Gerald Meier and Robert Baldwin, *Economic Development: Theory, History, Policy* (New York, 1957), pp. 419–27.

responds to more than a shortage of local capital. Albert Hirschman has argued that in poor but developing countries there may be less a lack of savings than a lack of investment ability, which he defines as the ability to direct existing or potentially existing savings into productive investment. The shortage of investing ability is often so acute that total savings actually exceeds total investing capacity and results in frustrated savings.[21] A variant of this argument is found in recent historical studies of early industrialization in continental Europe. These studies stress the importance of financial intermediaries in the far from automatic linking of savings from the traditional agricultural and commercial sectors with farsighted entrepreneurs in the industrial sector.[22] Thus industrial development may be limited in part by an entrepreneurial failure, the failure to join savings and investment opportunity. Foreign businessmen may provide this successful entrepreneurship—precisely the missing agent in backward areas. Then their example and the expansion of the modern sector itself may create a large and previously missing supply of local entrepreneurship.

This is another reason to believe that inadequate local entrepreneurship is as crucial as inadequate local savings in direct foreign investment. If a shortage of capital were the determining factor, domestic entrepreneurs would borrow funds from abroad —either indirectly through local banks with access to foreign credit, or directly through the sale of corporate securities—and carry out investment

21. Albert Hirschman, *The Strategy of Economic Development* (New Haven, 1958), pp. 35–39.
22. Cameron et al., *Banking in the Early Stages of Industrialization*, particularly pp. 6–14 and 150–56.

themselves. Development would then advance with massive foreign portfolio investment in stocks and bonds and very little foreign entrepreneurship. The large-scale borrowing of the United States during the nineteenth century, for example, would seem to follow this pattern.

It is of course true that local businessmen might not have equal access to foreign capital sources. But better promotional techniques, better knowledge, and better results—in short, better entrepreneurship—can lessen this disadvantage. And this was probably truer in the nineteenth century than today, since most foreign capital then went abroad as portfolio rather than as direct investment. Similarly, a shift from direct investment to portfolio investment in a given country over time suggests a continuing (or developed) need for foreign capital qua capital, and the formation of adequate domestic investing capacity, as Hirschman suggests.[23]

But here we must add the fact that a large portion of contemporary direct investment also flows between advanced countries, often in both directions. Apparently, these advanced countries lack neither capital nor entrepreneurship. Capital markets and financial institutions function actively; rates of investment and net capital formation are high; and there is a large and growing pool of businessmen who share the society's general commitment to continued development. Yet direct investment takes place on a massive scale; witness, for example, American investment in Europe in the last decade.

In these circumstances a principal cause and contribution of direct investment seems to be the establishment of superior technology in the host country.

23. Hirschman, *Strategy,* pp. 38–39.

Superior technology permits more *efficient* use of employed resources, rather than the use of idle ones, so that any given output per capita is obtained from smaller inputs of resources. This greater efficiency frees some resources to boost output in other activities.[24] By raising productivity, more efficient techniques also promote lower production costs and hence lower prices. This in turn means cheaper products for consumers and obvious welfare benefits, as well as cheaper inputs for existing or potential manufacturers, which may result in a whole new series of investment opportunities.[25] (Of course, superior technology may also require expensive, capital-intensive investment or nonexistent investing capacity, or both. But this need not be the case, especially if technical improvements are closely guarded by a few powerful enterprises.) In general, it would seem that the greater the gap in techniques, the greater the potential benefit from improved technology through foreign investment for the capital-importing country.

Most discussions by "bourgeois-liberal" economists, upon which the foregoing considerations are based, admit that these potential benefits of direct foreign investment which we have distinguished are far from automatic. A country runs real risks in accepting, much less courting, foreign businessmen. One risk is primarily economic, the other political.

Economically, there is the danger that direct foreign investment will not integrate itself into the domestic economy but rather will remain a small ad-

24. Eric Lampard, "The Social Impact of the Industrial Revolution," in Melvin Kranzberg and Carroll Pursell, Jr., eds., *Technology in Western Civilization,* 2 vols. (New York, 1967), 1: 305–6.

25. Mikesell, *U.S. Investment,* pp. 140–44.

vanced island in a sea of backwardness. This is particularly likely to occur with investment of the "colonial" type, which is often concentrated in mines and plantations.[26] In the best of circumstances the gains from such enclave investment go primarily to the capital exporter and his country, since the enclave exists as an integral part of the capital exporter's economy. The enclave exports its output and thereby provides cheap inputs for the industrialized country. It gives the industrialized country an outlet for investment, manufactured goods, and even agricultural products. It employs highly paid foreign technicians to run sophisticated equipment, and it may conscientiously avoid hiring hard-to-train local labor whenever possible. In short, the foreigner's failure is colossal: there is no fundamental change in the backward local economy.

In the worst of circumstances something happens, but it is mostly bad. Not only does foreign investment *establish* a dual economy, but it *maintains* that economy in order to maximize its profit.[27] The more advanced foreign sector actually thrives on pervasive backwardness elsewhere, or so the argument runs. For example, local tariff protection to foster domestic manufacturing could threaten the enclave's source of cheap equipment and would therefore be unacceptable to foreign investors. Or the training of local personnel could require expensive

26. H. W. Singer, "The Distribution of Gains between Investing and Borrowing Countries," *American Economic Review* 15 (1950) : 473–85.

27. See, for example, Maurice Dobb, *Economic Growth and Underdeveloped Countries* (New York, 1963), pp. 17 ff., and Ragnar Nurske, "International Investment To-day in the Light of Nineteenth Century Experience," *Economic Journal* 64 (1954): 744–58, for a Marxian and a non-Marxian discussion of the problem of dualism.

and unwanted investment in education at the very least; more probably it would create attitudes critical of the traditional "feudal" society or of the foreign presence. Or long-term planning might be impossible because the economy is lopsided and dependent on violent fluctuations in commodity prices and exchange earnings. One could go on and on.

Thus direct foreign investment must do more than supplement inadequate savings or provide investing capacity, or even establish superior technology. All three of these contributions, which we have considered, are compatible with enclave investment and limited total development. This means that really beneficial foreign investment must powerfully affect the entire domestic economy and make things happen there. To realize its full potential it must therefore educate, change attitudes, and infuse a missing dynamism. Such dynamism goes beyond "present static comparative advantage and this is perhaps precisely why manufacturing industries are so universally desired by underdeveloped countries; namely, that they provide the growing points for increased technical knowledge, urban education, the dynamism and resilience that goes with urban civilization, as well as the direct Marshallian external economies."[28] If this tall order were met, foreign investment might indeed serve as the catalyst to start or greatly accelerate development. Certainly it is with such expectations that conscientious officials today, like Witte yesterday, seek foreign investment, and it is this ideal arrangement they hope to approximate.

Such high hopes impose heavy obligations. Foreign businessmen will probably be required or expected to make large and perhaps unforeseen ex-

28. Singer, "Gains," p. 476.

penditures of the social-overhead type for schools,
housing, transportation, etc., to make local manufacturing possible. Then initial difficulties of construction and management may well be complicated by
training tasks which are likely to postpone the pay-
off period on already unexpectedly large investments. If, on the other hand, fortune smiles quickly
and warmly, an unwritten (or written) code of good
conduct often enters the picture. Profits should be
reinvested to contribute to further domestic capital
formation and growth, and not simply be drained
away. Ideally, subsequent investments would link
backward to substitute domestic for foreign suppliers, or link forward to further processing of local
output, as the foreign impact continued to be felt.

How, then, may one judge whether foreigners
make this beneficial impact on the domestic economy? The presence of substantial manufacturing investment and the willingness to assume large social-overhead investment would both suggest such
an impact. We shall look for these and other indexes
of impact in this study. Thus, if at first technical and
managerial abilities were scarce domestically,
greater use of local personnel in top positions of
foreign firms could mean this key bottleneck was
easing. Similarly, an increased supply of domestic
entrepreneurship would be another telltale sign of
impact. Evidence for this could be domestic businessmen rising to meet new investment challenges
and gently or not so gently easing foreigners into a
subordinate role. (This might go with the shift from
direct entrepreneurial investment to passive portfolio investment discussed earlier.) Beneficial influence upon the labor force, another important dimension, might raise wages, increase the level of skills,

and create a more responsive labor supply. In some or all of these ways harmful enclave investment can be avoided.

There is a second, essentially noneconomic set of apprehensions concerning foreign investment. Foreign ownership and economic power must not curtail the host country's effective political sovereignty. This consideration is important today, and it has always been so for independent nations. It seems safe to say that nations today instinctively feel that real political independence is a prerequisite for honorable and hence bearable modernization, a modernization including much more than the important component of economic development. If the choice must be between either foreign domination with rapid growth or national integrity with slower economic progress, few nations will hesitate to pick the latter. Honest differences of opinion over what actually constitutes effective sovereignty are possible, but the existence of such sovereignty is not negotiable.

A related noneconomic apprehension is that foreign investment may exacerbate some of the unavoidable problems of modernization and industrialization. Foreign participation might, for example, inject rabid xenophobia into already difficult labor relations, turn hard-pressed local businessmen into discontented radicals, foster dissension in the bureaucracy, etc. In short, problems of social stability would be heightened.

This question of social stability is probably more serious than that of political independence, but both foreign businessmen and local officials should understand why this is so. Industrialization is profoundly revolutionary—one author likens it to an earthquake [29]—and it demands sacrifice and creates discontent which can be minimized but not avoided. If foreigners truly become agents of industrialization, they must expect some hostility—earthquakes are frightening. Thus the greater the impact and therefore the potential long-term benefits, the greater the immediate dislocation and the need for intelligent private and official action.

To summarize, we have seen how foreign entrepreneurship may both aid and impede a country's economic development. Additional capital, increased investment ability, and superior technology are major potential contributions. At the same time enclave investment and political domination must be avoided, and ideally a powerful impact should infuse a missing dynamism into the entire local economy. If this goal is achieved, then unavoidable social tensions will require both sympathy and action.

It is also possible and desirable to examine foreign investment from a quite different viewpoint, the viewpoint of the individual foreign firm. Such analysis is related to microtheory, or the theory of the firm (in this case the foreign firm), just as our discussion of direct investment in the total economy was related to macrotheories of general economic development. How, we ask, does private foreign investment take place and earn profits, profits essential whatever the contribution to the domestic economy may be? This microquestion may be crucial not only for foreign firms but *even* for political leaders of the host country. For once these leaders have given private enterprise an important place in their developmental policy, in the belief that private foreign investment in manufacturing is normally bene-

29. Robert Heilbroner, *The Great Ascent* (New York, 1963), pp. 128–32.

ficial, their principal problem becomes the attraction of such investment. (Occasional foreign irregularities can be disciplined as such cases arise.) To attract this investment requires better understanding of the behavior of foreign enterprise. This is our second area of concern.

A very suggestive analysis of the "foreign investment process" by an Israeli economist begins at this point: (well-behaved) foreign investment is, a priori, beneficial for an independent developing country; therefore, what is the foreign investment process, and how does one direct it toward his nation? [30] That an Israeli economist should fasten on this neglected side of the question is understandable. Similarities in the goals and results of early private philanthrophy and of subsequent profit-orientated investment in Israel clearly exist. One suspects that the dangers of foreign control through foreign ownership seem quite manageable when put against international political realities. But in other, less specialized cases, countries (not to mention lagging regions of the domestic economy) are more concerned with *securing* outside investment than with *evaluating* its performance in terms of unattainable perfection. Here Russia's pioneering experience should be particularly instructive.

Foreign businessmen are even more willing to assume their own benevolence and to focus on practical questions of investment and management. Their major concern is long-term profit maximization as local development proceeds. This is no easy task. Thus as we analyze foreign firms we shall try to discover their major advantages and disadvantages,

30. Yair Aharoni, *The Foreign Investment Decision Process* (Boston, 1966). I found this book stimulating and helpful. There is a good bibliography.

and to see how these change as the foreign firm expands and the local economy goes forward. Then it may be possible to tie our micro- and macroanalyses together, and to suggest to what extent foreign private profit and local public benefit are mutually antagonistic or mutually interdependent. That is the ultimate question.

3

To return to the case at hand, there is no doubt that foreign investment in Russian industry was considerable throughout much of the entire postreform period. Witte's predecessors and successors generally encouraged foreign investment, which began to quicken with the first intensive building of railroads from about 1865 to 1874 and culminated in the foreign surge into Russian banking before the First World War. Since the incidence of foreign investment in Russia was always striking, a number of scholars have attempted to establish the statistical dimensions of these investments in Russian industry.[31] Such studies tell us surprisingly little about the character and quality of foreign participation, but they do at least quantify foreign stock ownership. And they serve as a point of departure for an examination of foreign entrepreneurship.

31. The principal studies are P. V. Ol', *Inostrannye kapitaly v narodnom khoziaistve dovoennoi Rossii* (Leningrad, 1925), and *Inostrannye kapitaly v Rossii* (Petrograd, 1922); L. Ia. Eventov, *Inostrannye kapitaly v russkoi promyshlennosti* (Moscow, 1931); L. Voronov, *Inostrannye kapitaly v Rossii* (Moscow, 1901); V. S. Ziv, *Inostrannye kapitaly v russkoi gornozavodskoi promyshlennosti* (Petrograd, 1917); B. Ischchanian, *Die ausländischen Elemente in der russischen Volkswirtschaft* (Berlin, 1913); I. I. Levin, *Germanskie kapitaly*, 2d ed. (Petrograd, 1918); A. Crihan, *Le capital étranger en Russie* (Paris, 1934); A. Krimmer, *Sociétés de capitaux en Russie impériale et en Russie soviétique* (Paris, 1934).

The best-known and most comprehensive examination of foreign investment, or "foreign capital," in Russian industry was made by P. V. Ol'. This talented reactionary statistician and bitter Witte critic made the quantification of foreign ownership of Russian industry his lifetime work.[32] Thus among the students of foreign capital only Ol' estimated the flow of that capital into corporations operating in Russia under either Russian or foreign statutes for the entire nineteenth century. Other scholars have contented themselves with stock estimates of foreign participation for a given year. A Soviet scholar, Eventov, subsequently added the yearly figures of the minister of finance on total capital of all corporations, foreign and domestic, after 1888. Thus he determined the percentage of foreign ownership of common stock of corporations in Russia from 1888 to 1916. These important estimates are combined in table 3.

Assuming for the moment that estimates by Ol' are fairly accurate, several initial findings stand out. First, foreign capital was important during the entire period to be covered by this study. Never less than one-fifth of the total common stock capital of all corporations operating in Russia, it rose to more than two-fifths of the total on the eve of the First World War. Second, the latter half of the 1890s saw a definite quickening of the tempo of foreign investment, which rose from about one-quarter of the total in 1894 to three-eighths of the total in 1900. Third,

32. Verstraete, the French consul at St. Petersburg, noted in 1900 that Ol', who was part of "the clan of Witte opponents where he distinguishes himself by the ardor of his attacks," had finished his study but doubted it would pass the censor. The initial work of Ol' was finally published in expanded and revised form by the Soviets in the early twenties. A.N., F 30, no. 344, Verstraete to Delcassé, 4–1–1900.

Table 3

FOREIGN CAPITAL IN CORPORATIONS AND BANKS OPERATING IN RUSSIA
(In Millions of Rubles) [a]

Year	Foreign Common Stock [b]	Dividends on Foreign Common Stock (In %)	Foreign Bonded Debt [c]	Total Foreign Capital	Total Common Stock, Foreign and Russian	Percentage of Total Common Stock Owned by Foreigners
1860	9.7	7.7		9.7		
1865	16.3	6.7		16.3		
1870	26.5	9.5		26.5		
1875	74.1	6.3	4.6	78.7		
1880	92.0	7.3	5.7	97.7		
1881	109.6	6.5	5.7	115.3		
1882	120.0	6.7	5.7	125.7		
1883	133.0	6.2	4.9	137.9		
1884	136.9	6.5	7.6	144.5		
1885	147.3	6.3	12.2	159.5		
1886	159.1	6.8	14.2	173.3		
1887	160.9	6.8	16.2	177.1		
1888	178.3	6.5	17.3	195.6	662	27
1889	179.4	7.1	18.9	198.3	704	25
1890	186.2	6.4	28.5	214.7	734	25
1891	198.2	6.1	32.6	230.8	791	25
1892	201.6	6.4	33.9	235.5	831	25
1893	203.3	7.2	35.2	238.5	850	24
1894	209.7	7.8	35.3	245.0	900	23
1895	244.0	8.9	36.1	280.1	954	26
1896	321.4	7.5	47.7	369.1	1,200	27
1897	378.9	7.2	63.3	442.2	1,381	27
1898	476.4	7.4	87.3	563.7	1,538	30
1899	644.1	5.8	117.8	761.9	1,879	34
1900	761.9	4.8	149.1	911.0	2,030	37
1901	814.3	3.8	161.0	975.3	2,192	37
1902	815.1	3.9	167.1	982.2	2,281	36
1903	828.5	4.1	178.8	1,007.3	2,304	36
1904	850.8	4.0	171.6	1,022.4	2,432	35
1905	849.6	3.8	187.8	1,037.4	2,391	35
1906	905.1	3.9	183.2	1,088.3	2,517	36

Table 3—*Continued*

Year	Foreign Common Stock [b]	Dividends on Foreign Common Stock (In %)	Foreign Bonded Debt [c]	Total Foreign Capital	Total Common Stock, Foreign and Russian	Percentage of Total Common Stock Owned by Foreigners
1907	945.4	4.3	189.5	1,134.9	2,632	36
1908	988.7	4.3	198.6	1,187.3	2,772	36
1909	1,026.7	5.1	216.3	1,243.0	2,809	36
1910	1,125.6	5.8	232.5	1,358.1	2,983	38
1911	1,287.9	6.5	247.4	1,535.3	3,346	38
1912	1,482.0	7.2	257.2	1,739.2	3,601	41
1913	1,700.6	6.8	259.2	1,960.1	4,091	41
1914	1,856.4	4.0	268.7	2,125.1	4,311	43
1915	1,939.3	5.3	266.6	2,205.9	5,085	38

SOURCE: Cols. 1–4, P. V. Ol', *Inostrannye kapitaly v narodnom khoziaistve dovoennoi Rossii* (Leningrad, 1925), pp. 12–13. Cols. 5–6, L. Ia. Eventov, *Inostrannye kapitaly v russkoi promyshlennosti* (Moscow, 1931), p. 17.

a. All figures are converted into rubles equaling 1/15 imperial, or the ruble established officially in 1897, which equaled 2⅔ gold francs. (Before 1897 the ruble officially equaled 1/10 imperial [4 gold francs]. This "gold" ruble was only a unit of account, however, and all normal transactions were in fluctuating "paper" rubles which were not convertible into gold.)

b. Par or face value.

c. Long-term funded debt, not including bank or short-term loans.

while there was certainly no liquidation of foreign holdings after 1901, the foreign portion increased only slightly from then to the First World War. Thus it seems that there was a period, the late 1890s, when foreign capital was most significant—precisely the years of Witte's wager on foreign capitalists and Russia's most rapid industrial growth.

The case for these conclusions on foreign participation is strengthened when one excludes banks, in-

surance companies, and commercial firms and focuses upon specifically industrial corporations.
These data, processed by Eventov, but based upon
the data of Ol', are presented in table 4.

Table 4

FOREIGN AND RUSSIAN COMMON-STOCK CAPITAL IN
RUSSIAN INDUSTRY, 1880–1916
(In Millions of Rubles)

Year	Total Capital	Foreign Capital [a]	Percentage of Total Owned by Foreigners	Foreign Capital as Percentage of New Capital
1880	280	48	17	
1890	443	114	26	41 (1880–1889)
1893	509	136	27	33 (1890–1892)
1900	1,401	628	45	55 (1893–1899)
1903	1,534	691	45	47 (1900–1902)
1906	1,620	761	47	81 (1903–1905)
1909	1,834	840	46	37 (1906–1908)
1914	2,807	1,322	47	50 (1909–1913)
1916	3,747	1,431	38	12 (1914–1915)

SOURCE: Eventov, *Inostrannye kapitaly,* p. 20.
a. Bonded capital is excluded.

Since this study is concerned with foreign entrepreneurship in Russian industry, table 4 is more
relevant for our purposes than table 3. Table 4
shows clearly that foreign industrial participation
was relatively small in the early 1880s. (This is
because early investment in railroads and banking
weighed heavily as a portion of total investment
until that time.) Then there was clearly an accelera-
tion of foreign investment after 1893, when foreign
investment really began to pour in. Table 4 also
shows that if, in fact, foreign participation in all
Russian corporations continued to rise after 1909,
investment in industry accounted for very little of
that increase.

The enormous importance of foreign capital in the crucial years of rapid growth is particularly clear when one computes the foreign share of new capital formation of industrial enterprises (measured by new common stock at par value) in the different periods, as I have done in column 4, table 4. Foreign investment thus accounts for a huge 55 percent of new capital formation of industrial enterprises operating in Russia in the years from 1893 to 1900. And the foreign portion was higher the closer one came to 1900. In the key sector of mining and ferrous metallurgy, for example, foreign capital accounted for 22 percent of total new capital during 1896, 38 percent during 1897, and 67 percent during 1898.[33]

Ol's data, supplemented by Eventov's, provide that unbroken line of estimates so dear and valuable to statisticians. But how accurate are these figures, and what are their limitations? It is necessary to remember that even the most careful estimates of foreign capital contain a margin of error, for several reasons. Almost without exception shares were not registered but were in the anonymous bearer form. The movement of such bearer shares is extremely difficult to follow. Another factor to consider is that the nationals of one country sometimes deposited their shares with custodians in another country. French investors, for example, often left shares of non-French companies with Belgian banks to avoid French income taxes. Or, in some cases, Russian owners deposited their shares with banks or agents in western Europe, especially if the principal market for the given security was there. Thus even the meager records on where coupons were paid are sometimes misleading. Certainly all estimates are at best just that—estimates.

33. Akademiia Nauk SSSR, *Materialy*, 6:218.

At the same time estimates by Ol' have been widely used, and investigators with quite different biases toward foreign investment in Russian industry have found them the most useful.[34] Nor are the estimates of Ol' out of line with other available independent estimates, as may be seen in table 5.

Table 5

ESTIMATES OF FOREIGN CAPITAL IN CORPORATIONS
OPERATING IN RUSSIA
(In Millions of Rubles)

Year	Investigator	Common Stock		Stock Plus Bonded Debt of All Corporations
		Excluding Banks	Total	
1890	Ol' (a)	156	186	216
1900	Voronov (b)	691	—	—
	Verstraete (c)	758	—	—
	Witte (d)	—	—	1,000
	Ol' (a)	715	762	911
1914	Kristmann (f)	1,340	—	—
	Ziv (e)	1,282	1,532	—
	Ol' (a)	—	1,856	2,125
1916–17	Ol' (g)	1,749	1,984	2,242

SOURCES: (a) P. V. Ol', *Inostrannye kapitaly v narodnom khoziaistv dovoennoi Rossii* (Leningrad, 1925), p. 11.
(b) L. Voronov, *Inostrannye kapitaly v Rossii* (Moscow, 1901), p. 22.
(c) Maurice Verstraete, "Les capitaux étrangers engagés dans les sociétés industrielles en Russie," *Congrès international des valeurs mobilières*, 5 vols. (Paris, 1900), 4 no. 111: 10–28. For France, Belgium, Germany and Great Britain only. Includes bonded debt, excludes banks.
(d) P. A. Khromov, *Ekonomika Rossii perioda promyshlennogo kapitalizma* (Moscow, 1963), p. 153.
(e) V. S. Ziv, *Inostrannye kapitaly v russkoi gornozavodskoi promyshlennosti* (Petrograd, 1917), p. 123.
(f) Kristmann, "Russkaia promyshlennost' pered revoliutsiei," *Yezhegod. Komin.*, 1923, p. 334. As quoted by P. I. Lyashchenko, *History of the National Economy* (New York, 1949), p. 714.
(g) P. V. Ol', *Inostrannye kapitaly v Rossii* (Petrograd, 1922), pp. 8 ff

34. Eventov, *Inostrannye kapitaly*, pp. 17 ff.; Von Laue, *Witte*, p. 287; Krimmer, *Sociétés en Russie*, p. 126.

Although there is a high degree of agreement in
the estimates, one finds that those of Ol' are somewhat higher than the others, particularly for the last
years. In view of these differences and of findings
made in the course of this investigation, it seems to
me that Ol' slightly overestimates foreign investment in Russia (though he feels that if he errs, it is
in the other direction).[35] One reason for this is that
Ol' undoubtedly overestimates foreign participation
by assuming that, with few exceptions, all companies incorporated abroad were wholly foreign-
owned, which was certainly not the case, as we shall
see. Similarly Ol' seems to exaggerate the extent to
which entirely Russian corporations were able to
peddle minority interests to passive foreign investors between 1910 and 1914. Thus, though Ol' is very
thorough in his estimates, it is well to remember
that actual foreign ownership of Russian industry
was probably somewhat less than the foregoing tables suggest.

The rush into foreign investment came from four
leading industrial nations of western Europe:
France, Belgium, Germany, and Great Britain. Significant differences in the timing and extent of investment by nationality are shown in table 6, which,
again, is based on the data of the indefatigable Ol'.

Among these differences one may note the abrupt
inflow of Belgian investment, an inflow which was
very strong in the 1890s and weak both before and
after. On the other hand, the French and the Germans had more even patterns. And clearly the English and the North Americans were latecomers. English capital, in fact, more than tripled from
£3,918,000 in 1910 to £12,744,000 in 1914.[36]

35. Ol', *Dovoennoi Rossii,* pp. 8–9.
36. Eventov, *Inostrannye kapitaly,* pp. 28–29.

Investment by nationality may also be compared with investment by industrial sector. Using Eventov again, it is possible to ascertain the foreign share of

Table 6

FOREIGN CAPITAL BY NATIONALITY IN ALL CORPORA-
TIONS OPERATING IN RUSSIA (BONDED DEBT EX-
CLUDED)
(In Millions of Rubles)

	1880	1890	1900	1915
France	26.8	61.4	210.1	594.4
Great Britain	29.0	29.8	102.8	491.5
Germany	29.8	68.8	197.4	399.0
Belgium	1.7	17.1	220.1	230.4
Other	4.2	9.1	31.5	224.0[a]
Total	91.5	186.2	761.9	1,939.3

a. This figure includes 114,000,000 rubles of U.S. investment.

a given sector for bench-mark years. (Banks, insur-
ance, transport, public utilities, construction, and
trading companies are again excluded by Eventov.)
This material is grouped in table 7.

If we take the very detailed breakdown given by
Ol' for separate foreign nationality groups by major industrial sectors in the year 1916–17, and compare his findings with those in tables 3-7, we have
the basic statistical outlines of foreign capital in
Russia before the Revolution (see table 8).

Several points stand out. Although foreigners
held more than 60 percent of all capital in mining
and metallurgy as well as in engineering and machinery in 1915 (table 7), there were important differences in emphasis by nationality. The French and
Belgians dominated in steel production, with 79 percent of all foreign investment in this industry in the
year 1916–17. And an examination of tables 6 and 7

Table 7

GROWTH OF FOREIGN AND RUSSIAN CAPITAL IN MAJOR RUSSIAN INDUSTRIES, 1880–1915
(In Millions of Rubles)

Note: In the original, braces group **Mining, metallurgy** with **Engineering, machinery** for the 1880 Total (69.0) and (%) (41), and for the 1915 Total (1,700) and (%) (63). These combined figures are shown in the Mining, metallurgy row below.

	1880 Total	1880 Foreign	(%)	1890 Total	1890 Foreign	(%)	1893 Total	1893 Foreign	(%)	1900 Total	1900 Foreign	(%)	1915 Total	1915 Foreign	(%)
Mining, metallurgy	69.0	22.9	41	85.8	55.7	65	100.9	61.0	61	472.2	343.8	72	1700	740.8	63
Engineering, machinery		5.4		27.8	13.9	50	32.7	16.4	50	177.3	125.6	71		322.7	
Cement, ceramics, glass	5.0	0.2	4	6.7	0.2	3	9.1	0.2	2	59.1	26.6	45	129.9	185.7	14
Lumber				3.3	0.2	6	8.1	0.2	2	17.8	7.8	44	74.4	24.3	32
Chemicals	10.5	1.6	15	15.6	6.4	41	17.1	9.4	55	93.8	29.3	31	173.2	70.8	41
Food processing	82.4	6.7	8	87.6	7.5	8	94.8	8.0	8	158.3	11.4	8	447.8	34.6	8
Leather processing	3.9	3.0	75	7.3	3.1	43	6.6	3.1		16.5	5.9	35	54.2	14.5	26
Paper	?	0.4		11.4	1.1	9	14.3	1.1	7	31.8	6.1	20	93.2	19.9	20
Textile	109.0	7.8	7	197.6	26.0	13	225.9	37.0	16	373.7	71.4	20	729.2	155.0	21
Total	279.9	48.0	17.6	443.1	114.1	26	509.5	136.4	27	1,401.5	627.9	45	3,402.0	1,401.3	41

Source: Eventov, *Inostrannye kapitaly*, pp. 22–23.

shows that this inflow of French and Belgian investment in the steel industry was concentrated between

Table 8

FOREIGN CAPITAL BY INDUSTRY AND NATIONALITY,
1916–17 (INCLUDES BANKS, EXCLUDES BONDED DEBT)
(In Millions of Rubles)

Industry	France	Great Britain	Germany	Belgium
Mining, metallurgy	259.6	280.2	54.2	97.0
Petroleum	51.1	164.3	3.0	6.8
Gold	4.5	30.7	1.5	5.1
Coal	78.5	4.2	16.6	18.0
Steel	108.0	13.6	30.3	60.8
Engineering, Machinery	144.5	27.9	83.8	30.7
Steel fabricators	28.3	1.5	3.0	0.3
Machinery Makers	30.2	6.5	17.2	3.1
Electrical Equipment	1.2	2.0	32.1	—
Banks	133.3	25.7	84.7	2.5
Textile	47.1	59.8	40.5	8.8
Chemicals	31.6	1.4	31.5	8.7
Local utilities, building	25.7	16.5	68.5	62.6
Streetcars	3.2	—	0.8	24.7
Electric lighting	14.6	—	48.9	31.9
Food processing	5.7	18.3	9.6	0.7
Lumber	5.3	10.7	0.2	—
Cement, glass	3.8	—	0.9	10.3
Trade	3.5	8.3	2.8	—
Transport	1.5	0.6	6.0	—
Insurance	1.0	0.9	3.0	—
Paper, pulp	1.0	3.5	17.0	—
Animal products	0.4	10.0	2.1	2.0
Total	644.1	463.7	404.8	234.7

Source: P. V. Ol', *Inostrannye kapitaly v Rossii* (Petrograd, 1922).

1894 and 1900. Equally striking is the English role
in the oil and gold-mining industries. English investments in petroleum accounted for 73 percent of all

petroleum investments, and for 58 percent of all their investments in Russia. And English investment constituted 73 percent of all foreign investment in the gold-mining industry. Thus 71 percent of all English investment was in extractive industry. The English orientation toward extractive industry and the export of raw materials meant that English investment was the most "colonial" in its character. (This is one reason why it would be best to consider general English entrepreneurship as part of a study of the Russian petroleum industry at a future date.)

The place of Belgian investment in local utilities is another instance of national peculiarity. Almost all streetcar companies were not only foreign but also Belgian. This specialization in streetcar construction helps explain the large Belgian role in electric lighting, which was often undertaken in conjunction with the electrification of horse-drawn tramways. The Belgians shared this leading position with the Germans, who, as the leading producers of electrical equipment, were closely tied to electric utilities. German investment was also very strong in chemicals, a position that was shared with the French. The upswing of German investment in this industry did not await the 1890s but began strongly in the 1880s.

This brings us to a last important point to be drawn from the existing statistical data. This concerns the regional distribution by nationality. Here the best data are those prepared for 1900 by Maurice Verstraete, the French consul at St. Petersburg. They are presented in table 9.

The national differences by industry thus had their counterpart in differences in regional concentration. Clearly the French and the Belgians played the dominant foreign role in the new industrial area of southern Russia. (Belgian concentration was the more marked, since French investment was also significant in both Poland and the Urals area.) German investment was concentrated in areas contiguous to the German Empire, either in Poland, the Baltic

Table 9

FOREIGN CAPITAL IN RUSSIAN INDUSTRY BY REGION IN 1900 (DEBT INCLUDED, BANKS EXCLUDED)
(In Millions of Francs)

	France *a*	Belgium	Great Britain	Germany
South	275.2	550.0	33.7	29.1
Poland	106.3	32.0	3.8	92.6
Center (Moscow area)	71.5	106.2	4.3	24.0
North & Baltic	42.6	43.2	33.4	82.6
Caucasus	42.4	43.9	146.8	20.0
Urals	104.7	43.4	12.6	—
Siberia	12.4	4.0	—	—
Finland	—	2.8	—	—
Turkestan	—	1.8	—	—
No specific region	37.2	7.0	10.0	12.8
Total	692.4	831.0	235.5	261.0

SOURCE: Verstraete, "Les capitaux étrangers."
a. Verstraete believed about 100,000,000 francs of Belgian capital was held by French investors.

provinces, or the St. Petersburg area. The Baltic provinces excepted, these were all "old" industrial areas which grew gradually, as did the German investment in them. The Caucasus was the chosen field of English investment.

These regional preferences fit the division by industrial sector analyzed above. The dominant position of France and Belgium in southern Russia was due to their position in heavy industry—steel, coal, and metal processing—which grew very rapidly in that area in the 1890s. The German preference for the North went with its predominance in chemicals and electrical equipment, which in general were manufactured in the old established industrial areas. And as table 9 suggests, the first great surge of English investment went into the Baku oil industry from 1896 to 1900 and was matched by another surge into other Caucasian oil fields from 1908 to 1914.

Further refinements concerning the timing, size, nationality, sectoral preferences, and regional distribution are possible, but they would not modify significantly the basic statistical picture. Let us therefore summarize these data and our preliminary conclusions. And with our earlier conceptual discussion in mind, let us see which questions remain unanswered.

1. Foreign investment was very important in the Russian economy before 1914. Quantitatively it accounted for approximately 50 percent of new capital formation in industrial corporations between 1893 and 1914. In 1914 foreigners held at least two-fifths of the total nominal capital of corporations operating in Russia. Such large and continuous inflows suggest that Russia lacked adequate funds for accelerated development, whatever else may have been present or missing.

2. Foreign investment was distributed throughout the economy and was not confined to enclave investment. Investment in petroleum and precious metals there was, but manufacturing investment in heavy and light industries working for the domestic market clearly predominated. Such investment could not be sealed off from the domestic economy, and as a result it could very well have carried a powerful impact.

3. In spite of considerable diversity in time, place, and origin, one may tentatively identify a crucial, typical pattern of foreign investment after 1885. Chronologically, the period from 1893 to 1900 stands out as the period of greatest inflow. This coincides with the large role of foreign capital—usually French or Belgian—in mining and metallurgy, particularly in the new southern industrial area, during this period. Therefore, to understand the central core of foreign entrepreneurial activity in Russia, one should probably focus on the 1890s chronologically, mining and metallurgy by industry, the French and the Belgians by nationality, and the South by region. This is the most typical pattern, although other types and geographical areas of investment should be considered, as a control for checking our findings on the foreign investment experience.

4. Existing statistical data suggest a major foreign impact. The nature of that impact remains obscure, however. The incontrovertible fact of large-scale foreign investment does not support the polemical generalizations that often follow: that foreign enterprise was responsible for Russia's fairly rapid industrial development before 1914; or that this same enterprise exploited Russia ruthlessly. (Previous studies indicate, however, as was shown in table 3, that the average rate of return on foreign investment normally varied from 4 to 7 percent, and hardly amounted to the "colossal profits" of orthodox Marxist-Leninist analysis.)

5. The briefs for and against foreign investment are quite slender, for good reason. There is a paucity of information on the actual behavior of foreign enterprise in Russia. One needs to know what foreigners did if one is to judge their contribution.

Active creative entrepreneurship might well have
been essential to rapid growth, just as passive parasitic investment might well have harmed the economy. In the light of our present knowledge neither
case is very convincing. More importantly, one feels
that such generalizations are probably simplistic
clichés based on limited understanding of foreign
entrepreneurship. Furthermore, statistical data tell
even less about the foreign entrepreneurial process,
one of our major concerns.

The foreigner's place in Russian industrial development before 1914 is part of a larger problem. In a
world hungering for economic development, what
role may the foreigner from an economically advanced area play in poor lands? If that role is potentially large, what methods should the foreigner use
and what are his chief assets? How may the foreigner's contribution change over time? Surely there is
much to learn from the Russian experience, where
there were so many cases of foreign enterprise and
activity in different industries and by different nations. Surely there are insights into the relationship
between advanced and backward nations as the
waves of industrialization continue to spread in one
of the great dramas of modern times.

2

ENTREPRENEURS: SOURCES
AND TYPES

In this study more than two hundred firms operating in Russia with varying degrees of foreign participation were examined. Although some of this participation was passive and clearly did not involve foreign decision making and therefore entrepreneurial (direct) investment, the vast majority of the firms had active foreign business leadership at some stage in their development. In spite of countless variations, systematic empirical investigation revealed recurrent patterns of foreign entrepreneurship, patterns which may be grouped into three ideal types.

1

The first and most readily apparent entrepreneurial type was the major west-European industrial firm which founded an affiliated Russian enterprise. The term *affiliated* is used advisedly. With few exceptions the parent firm was not the sole or even the majority shareholder of the separate corporation operating in Russia. But it generally provided the driving creative force, the entrepreneurship, for the allied firm which it founded, promoted, and managed. With a broad distribution of ownership among small investors and speculators, a large minority position gave the parent firm continuous control and decision-making authority. This pattern of direct corporate investment characterized a large number of the foreign firms.

Certainly most major Russian metallurgical concerns in which foreigners played an active role were associated with an important foreign metallurgical enterprise. This was particularly true after 1885, although this pattern existed earlier in Russian Poland and northern Russia to some extent.[1] One of the founders of the famed Huta-Bankova Steel Company in 1877 in Poland, for example, was Eugène Verdié of the Forges et Aciéries de Firminy in the Loire Valley.[2] Verdié acted for both himself and Firminy in this Polish venture. In the same year a St. Petersburg ironmaster of Scottish origin, George Baird, called upon another leading steel producer of France's Loire area, the Terrenoire Company, to form the Alexandrovskii Steel Company. This new company was to supply an order of 30,000 tons of steel rails from the Russian state. Three years later in November 1880 Baird teamed up with two other metallurgical firms from the Lyons area, Marrell Brothers of Rive-de-Gier and the Forges et Aciéries de la Marine et des Chemins de Fer of Saint Chamond, to found the Usines Franco-Russes (Baird). This new company modernized a second Baird property, a small shipyard that worked primarily for the Russian navy.[3]

The French were not alone in this early period. In 1883 Heinrich Kamp of the large Westphalia Union

1. Brandt, *Inostrannye kapitaly,* 2:28–43, shows that this was the case in Polish metallurgy, for example.

2. This firm is discussed in detail in chapter 11.

3. A.N., 65 AQ, K 4, Société Russe des Aciéries d'Alexandrovski, Annual Reports, 25–5–1881, 24–5–1882; *Le Pour et le Contre,* 19–8–1894; C.L., Usines Franco-Russes, dossier; *L'Information,* 8–10–1910.

was a founder of the St. Petersburg Iron and Wire Works, the result of the merger of the Westphalian firm's Russian subsidiary and another firm.[4] German metallurgical firms also founded a number of subsidiaries in Russian Poland in the early 1880s, most of which were rather small.[5] These examples, as well as others, suggest that strong parent companies generally stood behind most foreign-associated steel makers.

An analysis of steel producers in southern Russia confirms this impression. Between 1888 and 1900 fourteen major producers were built, and all but one, the Briansk Ironworks Company, had foreign entrepreneurial investment. Of the remaining thirteen foreign steel companies in southern Russia, every one was closely associated with a non-Russian parent. In every case this parent steel producer supplied technical aid necessary to build and usually to manage its Russian affiliate. No other characteristic was universally shared, although with one exception the foreign parent was also a major steel producer of some renown and importance. In at least nine cases these parent firms supplied important, if al-

4. See the detailed unpublished study, or étude, dated December 1904, on this firm, Société des Laminoirs et Tréfileries de St. Petersburg (Obshch. St. Peterburgskikh zhelezoprokatnogo i provolochnogo zavodov), by the Etudes Financières section of the Crédit Lyonnais. Hereafter such unpublished studies, which are filed under the French name for the firm in question at the Archives of the Crédit Lyonnais in Paris, will be identified by company and date of completion. Thus subsequent citations of this study will read: C.L., Laminoirs de St. Petersburg, Etude, December 1904. Consult the Bibliography for discussion of archival sources. Major steel and coal firms are listed in the Appendix.

5. There are several discussions of German entrepreneurs in Poland in the early 1880s, all on approximately the same level of concreteness. They do not permit a detailed study of those firms, most of which were private family affairs. See Ischchanian, *Ausländischen Elemente*, pp. 103–7, 143–45, 161–75.

ways minority, portions of the necessary joint-stock capital. Normally the parent was also to receive a share of profits for a period of time as remuneration for purely technical as well as managerial aid. In only two instances did the foreign steel company combine with an existing Russian steel producer in a new venture. In several cases, however, the parent had a partner of some sort, usually a major bank, either foreign or Russian.

It is well known that the founding of the South Russian Dnieper Metallurgical Company in 1888 was due in part to the initiative of the Société John Cockerill, Belgium's leading industrial establishment.[6] The Donets Steel Company at Druzhkovka (1892) was purely and simply a subsidiary of the Huta-Bankova, a French firm and the leading steel company in Poland. The parent company subscribed half of its subsidiary's stock and offered the other half to its own shareholders. The Donets-Yur'evka Metallurgical Company, a major steel producer, was founded in 1895 at the beginning of the great rush of foreigners into the Donets partly at the initiative of a leading Silesian producer, the Friedenhütte. The Friedenhütte combined with a Russo-German firm, the above-mentioned Iron and Wire Works of St. Petersburg, in this common venture.[7] The Kramatorskaia Metallurgical Company, a latecomer among Donets steel producers, was founded in 1899 by Fitzner and Gamper to convert their existing boilermaker factory in southern Russia into an integrated steelworks. Fitzner and Gamper, a union of German and Swedish metallurgical interests, had originally

6. See chapter 9.

7. See the very complete dossier of unpublished studies, annual reports, and brochures on the Société Métallurgique du Donetz-Yourievka at the Crédit Lyonnais.

established themselves in Poland in the early 1880s in response to higher tariffs.[8]

Four smaller specialized steel companies created in southern Russia in the late 1890s were closely associated with Belgian parents. The Olkhovaia Blast Furnaces Company at Uspensk was founded at Brussels in April 1896 by the Halanzy Steel Company. Halanzy received all the 5,000 founders' shares, which were entitled to 25 percent of all dividends in excess of 5 percent per annum, while Halanzy's directors and shareholders themselves were the primary initial subscribers of capital shares. (Halanzy's own precarious financial situation precluded a direct investment in the Russian subsidiary.) [9] Olkhovaia produced only pig iron; the Konstantinovka Sheet Mills Company only rolled sheets, and it was in fact the La Louvière Company of La Louvière, Belgium, adapted to the Russian environment. Initially, Alexis Isidore was the manager and director of both firms, while one of the two founders, Alfred Piérart of La Louvière, subscribed 2,000 capital shares of 250 francs each and divided the founders' shares.[10] The Chaudoir Tube Works at Ekaterinoslav was, as its title suggests, closely linked to Georges Chaudoir's plant in Belgium.[11] In this city the Ekaterinoslav Steel Company was also located, and its principal shareholder

8. C.L., Société Métallurgique de Kramatorskaia, Etudes, February and September 1904; Brandt, *Inostrannye kapitaly,* 2: 41, 60; Levin, *Germanskie kapitaly,* p. 65.

9. C.L., Haut Fourneaux et Usines de l'Olkovaia, August 1904; A.E., Brussels, no. 2902, sec. 1, Olkovaia; *L'Echo de la Bourse,* 11–12–1902.

10. A.N., 65 AQ, K 58, Société des Tôleries de Constantinovka, Articles of Incorporation and Annual Reports.

11. A.E., Brussels, no. 2902, sec. 1, S. Boeye, Voyages d'inspection à Ekaterinoslav, 7–11–1912.

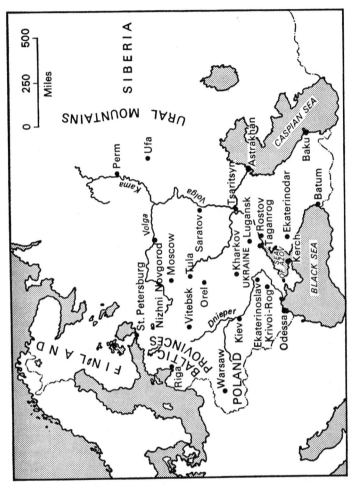

EUROPEAN RUSSIA IN 1914

(40 percent initially) was the Bruges Steel Company.[12]

Two important integrated southern steel producers on the Sea of Azov are also examples of direct investment by leading Belgian parent firms in partially owned affiliates. The Russian Providence Company (1897) was initially a branch of the Forges de la Providence of Marchienne-au-Pont in the Charleroi basin, one of the chief Belgian steel companies.[13] The Taganrog Metallurgical Company, incorporated under Russian law in June 1896, was a combined effort of two allied firms from Liège, Belgium. One was a large integrated producer, the Société d'Ougrée, and the other was a specialist in sheets and forms, the Société des Tôleries Liègeoises. Of the original 12,000 shares Ougrée took 5,420 shares while Tôleries Liègeoises took 1,300 shares for itself and for another party.[14]

Foreign attempts to revitalize older producing areas followed the same pattern. The Tula Blast Furnaces Company, for example, founded at Brussels in October 1895, was unusual in attempting to operate in central Russia, which was both the oldest and most decadent of Russian metallurgical areas. Quite predictably, however, it was a subsidiary of the Société Métallurgique d'Espérance-Longdoz of Liège. Espérance-Longdoz was to receive a typical special remuneration for its technical aid—15 percent of all profits exceeding 6 percent for eleven years. It offered 40 percent of Tula's capital stock of five million francs to its own shareholders, while managers and directors of the parent firm took

12. A.E., Brussels, no. 2902, sec. 1, Société des Forges et Aciéries d'Ekaterinoslav, Articles of Incorporation.
13. C.L., Société de la Providence Russe, Etude, December 1898.
14. *Moniteur des Intérêts Matériels*, 19–7–1897.

much of the rest.[15] Subsequently the pig iron produced by this first venture was finished as high-grade corrugated-iron roofing sheets by a second Espérance-Longdoz creation. This was the Tula Rolling Mills Company, which was founded in December 1899 and in which the home firm had a 40 percent participation of 2,000,000 francs.[16] The presence of a strong parent firm is thus a salient characteristic of foreign-controlled enterprise in the Russian steel industry. And it will be remembered that quantitatively and probably qualitatively this was the industry in which total foreign investment was most significant.

The strong parent firm also stood behind foreign participation in the allied railway equipment and metal processing industries. If again only those firms containing undeniably active entrepreneurship are considered, and if cases of passive portfolio investment are excluded, this was apparently the universal case after 1890. The Upper Volga Railway Equipment Company, incorporated under Russian law in 1897, was founded by Dyle and Bacalan, a leading constructor of railway equipment in both Belgium and France.[17] A second constructor of railroad cars, the Southern Ural Metallurgical Company (1898), was founded in part by Ateliers Germain, another producer for railroads.[18] The two constructors of locomotives with active foreign participation dating from this period were closely

15. L. Willem and S. Willem, "Histoire de la Société Métallurgique d'Espérance-Longdoz" (unpublished manuscript, 2 vols.), 2:380–83; A.E., Brussels, no. 2902, sec. 1, Société des Hauts Fourneaux de Toula, Russie Centrale.

16. Willem and Willem, "Espérance-Longdoz," 2:395–98.

17. C.L., Société du Matériel de Chemin de Fer du Haut-Volga, Etude, May 1904; Economist français 26 (1898) : 225; Semaine financière, 1898, p. 123.

18. A.N., 65 AQ, K 165, Société Métallurgique du Sud Oural, Articles of Incorporation.

linked with a parent firm. The Hartmann Machine
Company at Lugansk (1896) was tied originally to
Gustav Hartmann and his firm in Chemnitz, Ger-
many.[19] The Russian Locomotive and Mechanical
Construction Company, also known as the Bouhey
Company in France, was founded and directed in
part by a French machine tool producer, the Société
Bouhey of Paris, and its president and chief share-
holder, Phillippe Bouhey.[20]

It is well known that leading German electrical
constructors, primarily Siemens and Halske, Siemens and Schukert, and the Allgemeine Elektri-
zitäts Gesellschaft, dominated this industry in Russia through wholly or almost wholly owned Russian
subsidiaries.[21] Few know, however, of the less successful activities of another world-famous firm—the
Westinghouse Company of Pittsburgh, which operated in Russia through a French subsidiary.[22]

Although the textile industry was always the chosen field of the native Russian bourgeoisie, foreign
participation in the industry was significant, if
quickly assimilated. And the tradition of Baron
Knoop, the German clerk from Bremen who built a
textile empire with techniques learned in England,
was continued on a modest scale in this period by
leading textile firms from western Europe.[23] In the

19. C.L., Société Russe des Usines de Construction de Machines
Hartmann, Etudes, August 1898 and January 1904.

20. A.N., F 30, 340, Société Russe de Construction de Locomotives et Mécaniques. Hereafter cited as Construction de Locomotives et Mécaniques [Bouhey].

21. Levin, *Germanskie kapitaly,* p. 64; Ziv, *Inostrannye kapitaly,* p. 26.

22. A.N., 65 AQ, G 470, Société Electrique Westinghouse de
Russie, Articles of Incorporation and various clippings.

23. Knoop, connected with the catchy popular saying, "No
church without a *pop* [priest], no mill without Knoop," has attracted the attention of various economic historians. See Ischcha-

Polish textile industry five firms were directly linked to leading Belgian and French parent firms. All four of the French firms were from Roubaix, the French Manchester, and three of them were associated with the Motte family, the most famous spinning family of French Flanders. Paul Desurmont, Motte et Compagnie, société en nom collectif, established a wool spinning mill at Lodz in 1890. La Czenstochovienne, incorporated at Roubaix in 1899, was a leading cotton spinner at Czenstochowa under the presidency of Eugène Motte. The following year Motte, Meillassoux et Coulliez also founded a wool spinning mill at Czenstochowa. Another French firm, the Cie Générale des Industries Textiles Allart, Rousseau of Roubaix, was active in wool spinning at Lodz from 1878. Peltzer and Son, the leading wool spinners of Verviers, was active in Poland after 1887. The five major French firms employed 10,000 workers in 1910.[24] French and Belgian firms were in fact latecomers to the Polish area, where the textile industry had grown very rapidly after 1830 with small German firms and partnerships providing the bulk of the entrepreneurship.[25]

It is significant that outside of Poland each of the four important French or Belgian textile firms founded in those hectic boom years of 1898 and 1899, for which this investigator found fairly good material, was closely connected with a parent firm, and a parent firm of some repute. In 1899 a leading French textile manufacturer incorporated its Russian branch as a public company to facilitate an

nian, *Ausländischen Elemente,* pp. 178–80; Krimmer, *Sociétés en Russie,* p. 121.

24. A.N., F 30, no. 344, French Industry in Poland, De Coppet to Quai d'Orsay, 18–2–1911.

25. Ischchanian, *Ausländischen Elemente,* pp. 39–41, 161–73.

increase of capital for the construction of a second mill in Moscow. Business was profitable and rapidly expanding.[26] A second firm, the Belgian Vitebsk Linen Company, was founded in 1898 by four linen-producing firms of Belgium and France.[27] Another linen producer, the Kostroma Linen and Cotton Company, was due in part to the initiative of the Etablissements Gratry of Lille and its president, Jules Gratry, as well as of two Belgian spinners, Firmin Gérard of Brussels and Nicolas Navaux of Verviers.[28] The Russo-French Cotton Company, incorporated at Paris in 1898, was a joint effort of leading spinners of northern and eastern France,[29] In addition, two latecomers to Russian textiles, founded in the boom before the First World War, were initiated by Western firms. The Société Cotonnière de Dedovo, incorporated at Epinal in 1911, was founded by Paul Cuny and the Groupe des Filatures de la Vologne. The Société de la Soie Artificielle de Myszkov (Brussels, 1911) was formed by Etablissements E. Crumière, which claimed to possess an improved process for treating cellulose and producing rayon.[30]

There were many other examples of foreign firms establishing partly owned affiliates in Russia. Per-

26. The parent firm was the Société de Schappe de Lyon, while the Russian subsidiary was the Société de Schappe en Russie, also incorporated at Lyons. A.N., 65 AQ, H 235, Société de Schappe en Russie, Articles of Incorporation and Annual Reports.

27. A.N., 65 AQ, H 93, Articles of Incorporation and clippings on the subsequent reorganization.

28. A.N., 65 AQ, H 153, Manufactures de Lin et de Coton de Kostroma, Articles of Incorporation and Annual Reports.

29. C.L., Société Cotonnière Franco-Russe; *Opinion financière,* 11–12–1913.

30. C.L., Soie Artificielle de Myszkov, Articles of Incorporation; A.N., 65 AQ, H 82, Société Cotonnière de Dedovo, près Moscou, Articles of Incorporation and press clippings.

haps a glance at the glass and ceramic producers as well as chemical companies may suffice, however. In both industries dynamic foreign participation was considerable. In the glass industry the Donets Glass Company (1895) was a joint undertaking of Marie-mont Glass and Hamandes Glass, both respectable Belgian firms, while the Roux Mirror Works of Belgium founded the Lakash Mirror Works in 1898.[31] One leading Belgian brick and ceramic producer even founded three subsidiaries in three years in the Donets. As its first venture, this firm, the Société des Terres, Plastiques et Produits Réfractaires de Seilles-lez-Ardenne et Bouffioulx, took a small plant from Vladimir Pleshev at Ekaterinovka, which was renamed the Nadine Company and incorporated under Russian law in 1895. Two more companies followed in 1896 and 1897.[32]

As for fine chemicals, every casual observer has noted the dominant position occupied by branches of German firms in tsarist Russia. Among others, Badische Anilin und Sodafabrik, Friedrich Bayer und Kompagnie, A. G. für Anilin Fabrikation in Berlin-Treptow, Moskau Farbewerke, and Schering were particularly important with their closely held subsidiaries.[33] The foreign impulse is also seen in Lubimov-Solvay, the leading firm in heavy chemicals to 1914.[34] The Russian Dynamite Company, the first company to produce dynamite in Russia, was a sub-

31. A.E., Brussels, no. 2902, sec. 3, Société des Verreries du Donetz à Santourinovka; Société Belgo-russe pour la Fabrication des Glaces à Lakasch.

32. Ibid., sec. 4, Société Nadine des Produits Réfractaires et Céramiques du Donetz à Ekaterinoslav; Société Krinitchaia des Produits Réfractaires et Céramiques du Donetz; Société des Produits Réfractaires et Céramiques de Wladzimirovka.

33. A.N., F 30, no. 1091; Levin, *Germanskie kapitaly*, p. 64.

34. L. F. Haber, *The Chemical Industry during the 19th Century* (Oxford, 1958), pp. 138–42.

sidiary of a leading French producer, while a second leading firm represented the international Nobel Syndicate.[35]

Thus it is clear that direct investment by leading foreign corporations was a major source of foreign entrepreneurship in Russia between 1885 and 1914, and particularly in the 1890s, when both foreign investment and economic advance were greatest. With the exception of the branches of German chemical and electrical equipment companies, the parent firm generally took only a minority interest sufficient for effective control in a publicly held corporation. This means that the presence of direct corporate participation and entrepreneurship is not immediately self-evident in the corporate title and has often been missed, although a detailed examination of foreign firms soon reveals this presence.

2

The second type of foreign entrepreneur was the individual promoter. Despite many particular differences, the members of this group generally shared common characteristics. The promoter had the ability both to perceive Russian investment opportunity and to secure capital from abroad. He usually engaged both his own capital and that of friends and associates in his ventures, but, like that of parent firms, his was almost invariably a minority participation. In contrast to leading firms, the individual promoter was often active in several companies, if only for brief periods of time.

Many promoters were foreign businessmen who

35. C.L., Société Franco-Russe de Produits Chimiques et d'Explosifs (Dynamite Russe), Articles of Incorporation; Etudes, May 1905 and January 1911; *Revue Cottet*, 18–12–1896; *Actualité Financière*, 23–5–1913.

resided permanently in Russia and were active in
Russian industry. These men had acquired a profound knowledge of local conditions while retaining
ties with their home countries. They were ideally
suited to promote the marriage of local resources
with the techniques of leading foreign firms and the
capital of foreign banks and stock exchanges.

Two Frenchmen, Jules Goujon and Léon Gautier,
both long-time residents of Moscow, were such intermediaries. In 1872 Goujon founded an enterprise to
produce drawn wire, which was subsequently incorporated as the Moscow Metallurgical Works in 1883.
The Wogan Bank of Moscow and a number of
French as well as English, German, and Russian
capitalists participated in the company; but Goujon
remained the undisputed boss until 1909. He was
described as "one of the oldest and best known
Frenchmen in Russia, which he understands
completely." [36]

Presenting Russian projects to French capitalists
was another activity of this aggressive entrepreneur. In 1896 Goujon assembled plans for a vast
metallurgical complex. The projected company
would produce pig iron in the Urals, in Perm province, and then refine and process that pig iron into

36. C.L., Société de l'Usine Métallurgique de Moscou, Etudes,
February 1905 and July 1911; *L'Information*, 9–10–1905;
Science et Industrie 8 (April 1924) : 118–19. Goujon was also a
very large stockholder in the Soieries de Moscou, formed in 1881
to merge the works of the heirs of P. Goujon, first founded in
1833, and those of another Frenchman (A. P. Moussy) dating
from 1871. Apparently, then, the Goujon family had been active
in Russian industry since the early part of the century. The family reflects both the foreign origins of much of the Russian business class and the tenacious preservation of ethnic identity without assimilation. C. Giraud et Cie was another silk producer of
French origin which was very important in the Russian silk industry.

steel on the River Volga near Kazan. These plans were examined by a study company representing a French syndicate also formed in 1896 to seek out Russian affairs. The syndicate contained "the highest industrial and financial aristocracy" of France —Schneider and Company (Creusot), de Wendel and Company, Demachy and F. Seillière, and the Banque de Paris et des Pays Bas. The following year the syndicate used Goujon's plans as the basis for the Volga-Vishera Mining and Metallurgical Company with a share capital of 9,275,000 rubles (25,000,000 francs).[37]

Fifteen years later Goujon was still presenting metallurgical projects to French entrepreneurs and financiers. He came close to finding the necessary financial and technical support for at least two very large ventures. In 1912 he had an option, which was not exclusive, to buy the bankrupt Kerch Metallurgical Company from the State Bank. In December 1913 he had an exclusive three-month option with Dreyfus and Company to buy Hughes's New Russia Company. Both options were presented unsuccessfully to the Banque de l'Union Parisienne among others.[38] Perhaps Goujon had more time for promotion after 1909, when the Wogan Bank forced him to accept a secondary role at Moscow Metallurgical Works.[39]

Léon Gautier, a French iron merchant in Moscow, had long considered the possibility of founding a

37. A.N., F 30, no. 343, Verstraete to Delcassé, 31–3–1899, 25–3–1901; *Le Pour et le Contre*, 6–2–1898; C.L., Société Minière et Métallurgique de Volga-Vichera, Rapport . . . sur l'affaire apportée par M. Goujon, Maitre de Forges à Moscou.

38. B.U.P., Russie, no. 219, Affaires Métallurgiques en Russie, Darcy to B.U.P., 8–12–1911, 12–10–1912; C.L., New Russia Company, Note, 4–12–1913.

39. C.L., Usine Métallurgique de Moscou, Note, 3–6–1911.

major metallurgical establishment in Tula province to supply the Moscow market. The disadvantage of Tula's low-grade (45 percent) phosphoric ore would be outweighed by a nine-kopeck per pud transport advantage over Donets pig iron in the Moscow market. In 1895 Gautier succeeded in interesting Armand Stouls, the director-general of Espérance-Longdoz of Liège since 1886, in these mineral deposits. This led to the formation of the previously mentioned Tula Blast Furnaces Company in October 1895. Gautier originally had 400 hectares of mining concessions for the new firm, and he subsequently negotiated other concessions totaling 6,000 hectares. He was also sales agent until 1901, when disagreements with Espérance-Longdoz forced him to retire.[40]

Top employees of existing foreign firms also sought to found their own firms and become independent entrepreneurs, in addition to performing their normal tasks. Etienne de Manziarly, who had entered Sinçay's South Russian Rock Salt and Coal Company in the 1880s and had become the company's director-general in Russia, was one example of foreign management in one stage providing entrepreneurship in the next. In 1896 Manziarly negotiated a thirty-six-year lease of 2,300 hectares with the representatives of the Dolinskii heirs, who were minors. Situated in the northern part of the Donets on the Debaltsevo-Popasnaia line and containing reserves of about six million tons of coal, the property was worked on a small basis until October 1900. Then Manziarly incorporated his holding under

40. C.L., Haut Fourneaux de Toula, Etudes, December 1898 and January 1905; Willem and Willem, "Espérance-Longdoz," 2:379–94; A.N., 65 AQ, K 242, Annual Reports, 3–10–1899. 1–10–1901.

Belgian law as the Irmino Coal Company. Manziarly had secured the support of the Länderbank, or Banque des Pays Autrichiens, which was incorporated in Austria, had important branches in Paris, London, and Prague, and was always a leading underwriter of foreign enterprise in Russia.

The capital stock of Irmino—named after Manziarly's wife—was 4,000,000 francs; the bonded debt was for an equal amount at 4 percent, amortizable in thirty years. All the stock and 1,000,000 francs of the bonds went to the founders. Since 3.4 million francs paid for the concession, a full 1.5 million francs went for the "expenses" of incorporation. Thus the concession, only a thirty-six-year leasehold, cost 1,500 francs per hectare, or more than most coal companies in the Donets paid per hectare of fee-simple property. To top it off, the company paid a royalty of 0.20 francs per ton—or five times what the Ekaterinovka Coal Company paid as royalty for the highest quality coking coal. The firm was grossly overcapitalized because the Irmino Company, Manziarly's creation, had paid much too much for its property—Manziarly's original contribution.[41] Such inflation suggests why salaried employees turned to creation and promotion if they could.

Manziarly, like Goujon and Gautier, was typical of foreign promoters in that he moved easily in many different business and national environments. Having noted that Irmino was "a private affair" of Manziarly, who was also director of the South Russian Rock Salt and Coal Company, the French consul in Kharkov volunteered that "this conduct is

41. C.L., Société Houillère d'Irmino, Etudes, February 1905 and September 1909; *Moniteur Belge*, 8–11–1900; A.N., F 30, no. 343, Irmino.

strange and not very scrupulous according to opinion in the Donets, where people do not have a thin
skin by any means. . . . At Kharkov Manziarly has
the reputation of being a skillful businessman of the
Avdakov type [the commercial director of the Société Générale's Rutchenko Coal Company], caring
well for his interests and poorly for those of his
shareholders. His nationality is uncertain. Born in
France of a Hungarian father and an Austrian
mother who was born in France, he calls himself
French at Paris, Slav in Russia, and Austrian at
Vienna, following the necessities of his well-under-
stood self-interest. A clever operator who always
knows how to feather his nest—such is the general
judgment here." [42] On the basis of this appraisal,
the French minister of finances refused to grant
Manziarly and the Länderbank permission to list
Irmino on the Paris Exchange in 1901 and again in
1905. Listed at Brussels, but very unsuccessfully
placed, Irmino performed indifferently financially
until 1911, when it practically merged with the
South Russian Rock Salt and Coal Company. (Sinçay's company bought 8,225 of the 10,000 Irmino
shares as well as the land Irmino had originally
leased to 1932.) Thus Manziarly's attempt at individual promotion ended inconclusively as a division
of the French firm, where he himself had risen to
board member and chief subordinate of Sinçay in
the Paris office after 1905. [43]

Besides permanent foreign residents who occasionally promoted affairs, there were temporary
foreign residents permanently promoting new ven-

42. A.N., F 30, no. 343, Irmino, Rabut, vice-consul at Kharkov,
to Delcassé, 8–5–1905.
43. C.L., Société des Sels Gemmes et Charbonnages de la Russie Méridionale, Etude, August 1912. Hereafter cited as Sels Gemmes.

tures, at least during the years of the great company boom from 1895 to 1900. One such was Felicien Maes, "a Frenchman of very doubtful nationality," and a "speculator who has made a specialty of creating shares abroad for later sale in France at a premium." [44] In the late 1890s he was a founder or a promoter of several important companies: the Makeevka companies (both coal and metallurgical); two other coal companies, the Irmino and Pobedenko Coal Companies; two mining firms in the Krivoi-Rog region; the Omnium Russe; and at least one streetcar firm (Cie Russe-française de chemins de fer et de tramways). In all these affairs Maes was a link between Russian property holders, bankers, and dignitaries on the one hand, and Western banks (usually the Société Générale of Paris and the Länderbank) and leading Western corporations on the other.

Some of these promotional activities were organized through the Société Financière Russe of Brussels, whose principal director was Maes. This firm was an engine for speculation stoked by projects from Russians with properties to sell and geared in part to the needs of Russians with wealth who were participating in new foreign companies. Hector Legru, one of the Société Générale of France's representatives in Russia, was a board member; but generally the Société Générale seems to have used the Société Financière Internationale of Brussels, of which Legru was president, as screen and agent for Russian activities of doubtful morality. [45]

44. A.N., F 30, no. 338, Cie Russe-française de Chemins de Fer et de Tramways, mission at St. Petersburg to Quai d'Orsay, 19–5–1900.

45. A.N., 65 AQ, L 344, Société des Charbonnages de Pobedenko, Articles of Incorporation; Ak. Nauk SSSR, Trudy lenin-

Maes's task and technique are seen in two mining ventures. In late 1894 he helped negotiate an option to purchase 10,600 hectares containing coal deposits and to lease 3,200 more from the Ilovaiskii heirs for 6,000,000 rubles (16,000,000 francs). On the basis of this option Paul Laurans and Maurice Hachette, delegates of the Paris branch of the Länderbank, formed a Belgian company of 6,000,000 francs in 1895 which was immediately superseded by a Russian firm of 2,500,000 gold rubles (10,000,000 francs). In the first company Maes subscribed 2,000 shares worth 1,000,000 francs in his own name and represented ten Russian businessmen and bureaucrats for 340 more.[46]

Maes again performed his function of linking French capitalists and Russian proprietors in another Belgian company, the Iron Mines of Rakhmanovka-Krivoi-Rog. Maes's first step again was to negotiate options to purchase or to lease mines at the Krivoi-Rog. These included a twenty-six-year lease on lands of the Rakhmanovka peasant commune. The commune was to receive a royalty of 1.5 kopecks per pud of ore mined as well as the right to transport ore to the Krivoi-Rog railroad station for an additional 1.5 kopecks per pud. Another lease for thirty-six years with a landowner named Tsibuka called for a royalty of 0.75 kopecks per pud of ore.[47] For his options Maes received 4,500 participation

---

gradskogo otdelenie instituta istorii, *Monopolii i inostrannyi kapital v Rossii* (Moscow, 1962), pp. 378–79.

46. A.N., 65 AQ, K 69, Société de l'Industrie Houillère et Métallurgique dans le Donetz (Anciens Etablissements Ilovaisky), Articles of Incorporation.

47. C.L., Mines de Fer de Rakhmanovka-Krivoi-Rog, Etude, March 1903; A.N., 65 AQ, L 829, *Notice pour acquérir les mines et concessions de la maison G. Emeryk.*

shares (*actions de jouissance*), entitled to one-third of all super dividends above 5 percent on capital shares. These participation shares were no doubt distributed among insiders from the Société Générale of Paris and the Länderbank, who were to float the shares directly or indirectly, and Russians like Isidore Kon, director of the Azov-Don Commerce Bank, for whom Maes subscribed 500 capital shares.[48] Again in November 1898 Maes also tried—unsuccessfully—to interest Stouls of Espérance-Longdoz in furnishing technical assistance to develop iron deposits and steelworks in the Caucasus.[49]

Another promoter was Fernand Schmatzer, an Austrian engineer and director of the Société Austro-Belge de pétrole, who lived in Brussels. He played a role in the formation of at least four firms. He was founder and president of Vladimirovka Refractory and Ceramic Products in the Donets, and he served as an intermediary between the Ekaterinoslav Works of Esau and Hantke and Bruges Steel Works to form the Ekaterinoslav Steel Company.[50]

Schmatzer was also the promoter behind two of the larger foreign coal companies, Prokhorov and Rykovskii.[51] The Prokhorov Coal Company is indeed an example of promotion by an individual who moved easily between several national groups. The company was formed to exercise an option which Schmatzer had negotiated for 960 desiatinas—1,050

48. *Annex du Moniteur Belge,* 24–1–1898, 25–1–1898.
49. Willem and Willem, "Espérance-Longdoz," 2:395.
50. A.E., Brussels, no. 2902, sec. 1, Aciéries d'Ekaterinoslav. This was in effect a subsidiary of the Metallfabrik Hantke, Warsaw, itself a branch of the Oberschlesische Eisen-industrie.
51. See chapter 10 for a detailed study of the Rykovskii Coal Company.

hectares—of producing coal lands in the Don Cossack Territory, Taganrog district. According to the option, an initial advance was required to pay off all previous debts and to stand as the unique first mortgage on Mr. Prokhorov's property. Schmatzer further agreed to pay 1,072,000 rubles—5,000 rubles down and the balance in six months—for the land and ten small, poorly equipped mines producing 140,000 tons in 1894. Schmatzer thus had six months to find backers; if he failed he would lose only his 5,000-ruble down payment, since the mortgage represented real value. Schmatzer found backers, and Prokhorov was subsequently incorporated with 5,500,000 francs of capital stock and 1,500,000 francs of bonds. Schmatzer received 1,050,000 francs in shares for his option, of which 1,000,000 francs were placed in a separate blocked account by the new company pending the Russian government's authorization of the Belgian firm and the transfer of clear title to the properties.[52]

A vigorous policy of expansion brought prosperity to Schmatzer's creation until coal prices collapsed in 1901. Production increased almost threefold from original levels (to 404,000 tons in 1901), 132 Coppée coke ovens were installed, and dividends averaging 8 percent of invested capital were paid through 1899. Prokhorov's shares were the object of lively speculation on the Brussels Exchange, and they sold for a high of more than 1,000 francs— twice their par value. Subsequently losses were heaped up, bringing new management in 1901 and reorganizations and new capital in 1905 and 1909. The original shares and bonds were almost total

52. C.L., Société des Charbonnages de Prokhorov, Etude, January 1899; ibid., Articles of Incorporation.

losses.[53] Few investors were to remember Fernand Schmatzer and his Russian coal companies without remorse.

3

Clearly, large west-European corporations which established affiliated Russian operations and aggressive individual foreign promoters who were intimately acquainted with Russian business conditions were two key sources of entrepreneurship. There was also a marked tendency for corporate investment to dominate in the most sophisticated industries, such as metallurgy, electrical equipment, and chemicals, while individual promoters were associated with less complex mining operations in which initial negotiations with Russian owners were crucial. One would thus explain the sources of entrepreneurship in terms of comparative advantage and specialization: individual corporations had techniques; individual promoters had skill for negotiations.

This was certainly part of the pattern of foreign entrepreneurship in Russia as far as the origins of individual foreign companies in Russia were concerned. But as the sample of firms grows and as one examines corporations founded at different times, a third major source of foreign entrepreneurship emerges slowly, hesitantly, and always somewhat incompletely. Not only does one find a single corporation or individual founding a single Russian enterprise, but one distinguishes a small number of closely knit, though informal, foreign units which were quantitatively very important. Each of these units was responsible for the establishment and management of several enterprises in Russia, all of which bore the stamp of the single unit or "group" that oversaw and coordinated policy.

These groups usually originated with a single venture. They then grew in size and complexity as the initial investment revealed further opportunity, or as it called for complementary investment to sustain the original project. Thus for the most part the major French and Belgian groups had their origins well before the great boom of the 1890s, and these groups remained after the boom collapsed. The wild surge of company formation in the 1890s was the crest of a great wave which had been slowly building and which continued to rush forward after 1900, though with diminished force. The activities of the Société Générale of Paris show the formation of a major group taking place over a number of years. (The growth of the Bonnardel Group, perhaps the largest and most successful coordinated unit of foreign enterprise, is examined in detail in chapter 11.)

The Société Générale of Paris was unusual in its early years among the great deposit banks of France. Closely linked to important industrialists initially, it often operated almost as a *banque d'affaires,* or investment bank, until after 1900. Paulin Talabot, the polytechnician-manager of the P.L.M. Railroad Company, used his directorship on the Société Générale (1865–85) to secure support for his extensive industrial activities—the Charbonnage de la Grand'Combe, Mines de fer de Mokta-el-Hadid, and the metallurgical companies Saut-du-Tarn and Denain-Anzin. Another *chef d'entreprise,* Joseph-Eugène Schneider of Le Creusot, who served as president of the Société Générale from

1864 to 1867, as well as Edward Blount, a banker specializing in railroad affairs, reinforced this early industrial orientation of the Société Générale.[54]

This orientation toward investment banking spilled over into foreign activities. In 1872 the Société Générale undertook the construction of two canal lines in northern Russia and also leased coal properties in southern Russia. These rich but undeveloped coal properties on the new Mariupol-Yuzovo Railroad, which were leased for thirty years from the Mandrikina and Rutchenko families and later totaled 8,000 hectares, were then developed intensively by the Société Générale through a subsidiary, the Société Industrielle Franco-Russe.[55] From only 13,000 tons in 1875, production rose to 74,000 tons in 1880, 165,000 in 1885, 362,000 in 1890, and 432,000 in 1895.[56] In 1899 Rutchenko was the fourth-largest producer in Russia. In 1905 it was the largest.[57]

With each great European investment boom the Société Générale expanded its Russian interest. In the boom of 1879–81 the Société Générale took a large participation in Talabot's creation of enormous industrial significance, the Krivoi-Rog Iron Company, and it was the principal underwriter of the above-mentioned Usines Franco-Russes. Apparently both represented short-term minority participations.[58] Yet they show the continuing interest in

54. *Société Générale, 1864–1964* (Paris, 1964), pp. 22–36.

55. Ibid., p. 68; A.N., F 30, no. 328, Dorizon, Director of the Société Générale, to the Minister of Finances, 5-1-1897.

56. C.L., Société Minière et Industrielle de Routchenko, Etude, August 1897.

57. Brandt, *Inostrannye kapitaly*, 2:116; Comité pour l'Etude des Questions d'Intérêt Commun des Mines et Usines du Midi de la Russie, *Circulaire*, no. 234, 1-7-1908, in A.E., Brussels, no. 2907.

58. *Société Générale*, p. 68; J. B. Silly, "Capitaux français et

Russia and the development of contacts long before either the political alliance or the Russian government's development schemes of the 1890s. The long intermezzo between the creations of 1881 and those beginning in 1895 may be explained by the slight or nonexistent profits of the Rutchenko mine to 1894, despite the rising output. Even after good profits from 1894 to 1896 the St. Petersburg experts of the Crédit Lyonnais estimated that "in general the affair is very mediocre." [59]

When increased profits and broad speculative interest by foreigners in Russian shares clearly emerged in the mid-1890s, the Société Générale was ready. In 1895 it helped underwrite 14,000,000 francs of first-mortgage bonds for the Makeevka Coal Company, a venture led by an old Société Générale working partner, the Länderbank; these bonds were issued to complete payment for the mines and properties purchased from the Ilovaiskii heirs by the newly formed company. Less than two years later the Société Générale took the initiative in building a gigantic steel producer (the Makeevka Steel Company) on these coal deposits. The bank also subscribed a large portion of the capital. [60] At the same time the Rutchenko coal property was given its own identity as a Belgian company and capitalized at 16,000,000 francs. [61] With a capital of 25,000,000 francs the Société Générale then formed a

---

sidérurgie russe," *Revue d'histoire de la sidérurgie* 6 (1965): 31 ff.

59. C.L., Routchenko, Etude, August 1897.

60. C.L., Société Générale des Hauts Fourneaux et Aciéries en Russie, à Makeevka, Etudes, August 1904 and August 1910. Hereafter entitled Aciéries Makeevka.

61. C.L., Routchenko, January 1899; A.N., F 30, no. 328, excerpts of two reports from Verstraete to the Quai d'Orsay, n.d., and 8–5–1897.

Belgian holding company, the Société Générale de l'Industrie Minière et Métallurgique (Omnium Russe), to group its Russian participations together. As the title implied and as the public knew, the Société Générale was morally and financially committed to this Omnium Russe, as the new holding company was familiarly called.[62]

The Société Générale subscribed half the Omnium's capital—capital which was immediately used to buy 99 percent of Rutchenko's outstanding shares and about 50 percent of the Makeevka Steel Company from the bank. These participations totaled 23,000,000 francs, or more than 90 percent of the Omnium's share capital. The Société Générale then floated 15,000,000 francs of first-mortgage bonds for the Omnium. This was to permit purchases of other shares to give the Omnium a semblance of diversification, as well as to help obtain original subscribers. The Omnium purchased one to two million francs of shares in three different coal mines from the Société Générale's French and Belgian associates in Russian affairs. These were the Makeevka Coal Company, the Société Golubovka-Berestovo-Bogodhoukovo, and the Pobedenko Coal Company. Two million francs were taken in the Iron Mines of Rakhmanovka-Krivoi-Rog Company, supposedly to assure Makeevka Steel its iron ore, and 1,000,000 francs were taken in the Russian Dynamite Company. (The founders of this firm, the Barbier brothers, normally did their banking with the Société Générale.) These purchases by the Omnium were tied to the purchase of shares in the Omnium itself, as an examination of the list of subscribers shows.

62. A.N., F 30, no. 340, Omnium Russe, Articles of Incorporation, 26–2–1897; ibid., Annual Report, 10–10–1900; *Economiste Européen*, 7–12–1897.

The Société Générale's associates, like the Société Générale itself, traded their Russian investments for Omnium shares, which were to be placed with the public in order to relieve a number of entrepreneurs of their creations in one fell swoop.[63]

This portfolio remained essentially unchanged until the 1911–14 boom, as did, apparently, the Société Générale's own large holding in the Omnium. Then the sales of the Rutchenko Coal Company to the Briansk Ironworks Company and of majority ownership in Golubovka Coal to the Donets Steel Company, combined with reorganizations of both Makeevka companies, permitted the long-desired liquidation of the Société Générale's venture in Russian entrepreneurship "in the least disastrous conditions."[64] In these ventures the Länderbank was a trusted auxiliary of the Société Générale, either through its Paris or Brussels offices, or even its main office in Vienna.

Some other groups were small, consisting of only three or four firms and unified through the leadership of the directing manager. Two such groups suggest the general pattern. The South Russian Rock Salt Company (Paris, 1883) was directed for twenty-two years by Ludovic de Sinçay. Ludovic was seconded by his brother Edgar as technical engineer until 1905, when Edgar finally succeeded Ludovic as managing director. As a director of the Comptoir National d'Escompte and as an industrialist and scion of a famous industrial family, Ludovic de Sinçay drew support from the upper reaches of French banking and industrial circles. In 1894 the president of the Comptoir d'Escompte, De-

63. See A.N., 65 AQ, K 193, for the Articles of Incorporation, Annual Reports, and press clippings.
64. Ibid., Annual Report, 1912.

normandie, headed this Russian producer, while Hachette of the Länderbank and Anciens Etablissements Cail, as well as a Mirabaud and a Stern, sat on the board of directors. Demachy and F. Seillière, long-standing member of the Haute Banque, was the firm's banker.[65] Such support was a valuable asset for Sinçay, who directed current operations and managed as his judgment dictated.[66]

Until 1896 the mining of rock salt in the Bakhmont district of Ekaterinoslav was the South Russian Rock Salt Company's principal business. After initial problems Sinçay succeeded in merging two smaller Russian companies into his firm, which became the dominant salt producer in the Bakhmont district. Then in 1896 the firm added coal to its name and activities. Capital was doubled to 20,000,000 francs, and 10,000 hectares of coal concessions were leased for thirty years from the peasant communities at Shcherbinovka at the extreme northwest corner of the Donets Basin. The company then sank mines equipped to produce 500,000 tons annually.[67]

At least three other coal mines were subsequently associated with this firm: Manziarly's Irmino Coal Company, the General Coal Company, and the Nikitovka Coal Company. All three firms faltered after 1900. The Länderbank was to aid Manziarly, already

65. A.N., 65 AQ, L 3321[1], Société des Sels Gemmes et Soudes Naturelles de la Russie Méridionale, *Notice* (Paris, n.d. [1894 or 1895]). The company changed its name slightly in 1896. See Rondo Cameron, *France and the Economic Development of Europe* (Princeton, 1961), pp. 355–60, 382–84, for the extensive entrepreneurial activities of Louis St. Paul de Sinçay in the Belgian Société des Mines et Fonderies de Zinc de la Vieille-Montagne and in Germany.

66. C.L., Sels Gemmes, Etudes, January 1899, January 1900, and August 1912.

67. Ibid., as well as Annual Reports and clippings in A.N., 65 AQ, L 3321[1-2].

mentioned above, in passing his shares to rentiers, but the crisis nullified this plan. In 1911 Sinçay's firm bought the land Irmino leased and held 75 percent of that firm's shares. The Nikitovka Coal Company was also a leased property, which had been founded by the foreign directors of Gorlovka Coal Company. This company, which was adjacent to Sinçay's company's property, was caught short by the crisis, and its directors preferred to sell out to the strong Sinçay Group. The General Coal Company, a creation of Belgian industrialists, met a similar fate. Edgar de Sinçay represented these four firms in the coal syndicate (Produgol).[68]

The ambitious projects of the Belaia Coal Company, founded in 1896 by Eugène Carez, a wealthy Belgian industrialist, quickly blossomed into visions of an entire industrial park. The coal company's initial goal was to transform a barren 4,200-hectare property in the Donets, scarred only by a few abandoned peasant pits, into a large coal (400,000 tons yearly) and coke (70,000 tons) producer with two deep mines and a hundred coke ovens.[69] Then in 1898 Carez and his associates formed a cement company to operate on their property, as well as an ephemeral mining company (Skalevatka Iron Mines) to search for iron deposits needed by the fourth company, the Belaia Blast Furnaces Company, founded in April 1899. This last firm's capital of 10,000,000 francs built two large furnaces, and both steel mills and rolling mills were contemplated. A fifth affiliated firm produced explosives in this industrial complex, a complex knit together by eight kilometers of railways, eleven kilometers of telephone wires, and the

68. See A.N., 65 AQ, L 117, L 222, and L 314.
69. *Rapport sur la mission en Russie par MM. Hardy et Michot en Juin 1896* (Paris, 1896), in C.L., Charbonnages de Bielaia.

activities of 3,500 people. All these companies, with a total capital of 30,000,000 francs, were producing by 1900 when depression hit. Unfortunately, they had cost structures permitting profits only under boom conditions. Endless complex reorganizations brought almost total loss to shareholders, although the plants continued to produce.[70]

In summary, at least three different types of foreign entrepreneurs participated in Russian industrial expansion after 1885. There were individual Western firms which established wholly owned subsidiaries, or more commonly, partly owned affiliates. These affiliated Russian firms, patterned after the parent firms and bound closely to them, bore a striking resemblance to the branch plants of contemporary direct investment. Second, aggressive individual promoters, often long-time residents of Russia, also initiated investment. In contrast to parent firms, which usually focused upon a single Russian affiliate, individual promoters often played a key but ephemeral role in several enterprises. A third force was the groups linking together several powerful and interrelated companies. Each group coalesced around a focal point—an important entrepreneur, a bank, or even a foreign industrial center.

But this is only a beginning. Our discussion of types has revealed enterprises in which two or even all three varieties of entrepreneurship were simultaneously present. Might not all types be linked together in the entire process of foreign investment? Was there perhaps a generalized model of foreign investment behavior, a model in which the three types may be considered separate but interrelated agents with conceptually distinct functions? It is

70. See the dossier at the Crédit Lyonnais, as well as A.N., 65 AQ, L 47, for details and documentation.

our thesis that such a generalized model of foreign entrepreneurship existed; that this model revolved around a definite investment strategy; and that all three entrepreneurial subgroups were functionally necessary and interdependent within the general model. The next chapter will examine this model and the unifying strategy.

3

THE BASIC STRATEGY

1

A student of the growing literature on direct foreign investment often searches in vain for a single primary goal of entrepreneurs in foreign lands. The tariff factory, the export of new (or even old) capital equipment, the creation of captive markets for the parent firm—these are but a few of many factors cited.[1] The anticipated rate of return, the layman's "high profits," appears as one factor, but perhaps not the essential one.[2]

Our study also indicates the multiplicity of motivation in foreign investment, a multiplicity reinforced by the presence of at least three distinct entrepreneurial types. Nonetheless, it seems safe to agree with contemporary observers that the crucial factor for foreign entrepreneurs was the high rate of *anticipated* profit, without concurring with the Marxist assumption, then and now, that such profits were normally attained as a matter of course.[3] Other

1. See, among others, Aharoni, *Foreign Investment Process;* Mikesell, *U.S. Investment;* and Donald Brash, *American Investment in Australian Industry* (Cambridge, Mass., 1966), pp. 34–52.

2. Mikesell notes, for example, that the current return on United States private foreign investment is little higher than the domestic return. *U.S. Investment,* p. 67.

3. G. von Schulze-Gävernitz, *Volkswirtschaftliche Studien aus Russland* (Leipzig, 1899), pp. 274–76, 304–5; Marcel Lauwick, *L'industrie dans la Russie méridionale, sa situation, son avenir* (Brussels, 1907), p. 37; P. A. Khromov, *Ekonomika Rossii perioda promyshlennogo kapitalizma* (Moscow, 1961), pp. 125, 151; Ia. I. Livshin, *Monopolii v ekonomike Rossii* (Moscow, 1961), pp. 141–42; V. I. Lenin, *Sochineniia* (Moscow, 1941), 2:93.

considerations were involved, but they were subordinated to large entrepreneurial profits, as a few of many possible examples show.

When French promoters first tried to form a foreign coal company to buy Ilovaiskii's Makeevka lands in 1881, they anticipated profits of at least 10 percent on total capital; the promoters of the General Coal Company in 1900 expected immediate profits of 7 percent on stock capital of 10,000,000 francs and 25 percent within three years.[4] Another long report on properties at Belaia in 1896 calculated probable profits from large metallurgical works at 2,700,000 francs on an investment of 13,000,000 francs—more than 20 percent.[5] This is not unlike the ''20 to 30 percent on invested capital'' that the Société John Cockerill expected and subsequently received from its pioneering venture of 1888. (See chap. 9.)

By themselves, differences in the prime interest rates prevailing in Russia and western European countries could hardly account for profits of this magnitude, or explain entrepreneurial investment. The average interest rate paid by the Russian government on its gold loans, which were generally held abroad, fell from a moderate 5.08 percent in 1885 to 4.71 percent in 1888, to 4.19 percent in 1894, and to 3.86 percent in 1898.[6] By the end of the century the

4. *Notice sur le Bassin Houiller du Donetz (Nouvelle Russie)*; *Constitution d'une Société pour l'achat des propriétés et des houillères Ilovaisky* (Paris, 1882), in A.N., 65 AQ, K 69. *Rapport sur les Mines de Houille et d'Anthracite 'Zolotoié et Bokovsky' en Russie Méridionale de la Sté Houillère du Donetz, Koreniff et Chipiloff* (Liège, 1900), in C.L., Cie Générale de Charbonnages.

5. *Rapport par Hardy et Michot*, pp. 30, 40.

6. Schulze-Gävernitz, *Volkswirtschaftliche Studien*, pp. 554–57; Olga Crisp, "Russian Financial Policy and the Gold Standard at the End of the Nineteenth Century," *Economic History Review* 6 (1953): 171.

Russian government paid little more than the German government for its money, and only slightly more than the French. Furthermore, the interest rate differential decreased, as comparison with the average interest rate paid by the French government on the nominal value of its debt shows: 1885, 3.56 percent; 1890, 3.45 percent; 1895, 3.22 percent; and 1900, 3.21 percent.[7] This meant that the Russian government paid on the average 42 percent more than the French government for money obtained by gold loans in 1885, and only about 20 percent more at the turn of the century. Thus prime interest rate differentials were moderate, and most importantly, they decreased concurrently with the rapid increase in direct foreign investment. Had such differentials been of primary importance, foreign investment would have tended to decline rather than to increase greatly as it did.

Much more important for entrepreneurs was the increased marginal efficiency (or profitability) of capital, which rose in the boom of the 1890s and again before 1914. It would be hard to say by how much marginal profitability rose, but estimates by Ol' of average return from dividends paid on all foreign capital provides a rough, though dampened-down, indicator. (See table 3.) After averaging a rather consistent 6.5 percent in the 1880s, average return moved in steady jumps to an all-time high in the period under study of almost 9 percent in 1895, and it remained above 7 percent through 1898. Similarly, after falling to less than 4 percent in 1905–6, average return on foreign investment rose again to about 7 percent in the years 1911–13.

Increased marginal efficiency of capital in these

7. Edmond Théry, *L'Europe économique et financière pendant le dernier quart de siècle* (Paris, 1900), p. 16.

periods was not limited to Russia but occurred throughout Europe in conjunction with broad cyclical expansion. J. H. Clapham, for example, concluded that "the industrial revolution began in France about 1895," and he cited the threefold increase in the annual formation of new corporations in the 1890s as supporting evidence.[8] There was another spurt of French company formation after 1906. In Russia, as in other countries, increased profitability facilitated the pursuit of entrepreneurial gains.

Profit on total capital was only half the story in any event, for the entrepreneur's profit was not the shareholder's return but rather a handsome multiple of that return. This important fact is often overlooked. Generally our very large sample suggests that entrepreneurs, or insiders, earned large percentage returns on their own capital even if their firms were only modestly successful. Although this may have been particularly true in Russia, there is every reason to believe this followed the normal pattern of late nineteenth- (and probably twentieth-) century entrepreneurship within the capitalist system. The entrepreneur, unlike the shareholder, had many sources of profit and expected a good return from each of them: the capitalization of technical know-how, the sale of preparatory investigations, high salaries and bonuses, employment for friends and relatives, profits from underwriting the firm's financial operations, and others.

The manipulation of these numerous sources of profit often bordered on malfeasance. For example, some directors were said to ask for reimbursement of considerable expenses involved in travel from

8. J. H. Clapham, *The Economic Development of France and Germany, 1815–1914*, 4th ed. (Cambridge, 1936), pp. 240, 397.

western Europe to Russia, or from St. Petersburg to the Donets, from each of the several companies they represented.[9] The padding of expenses by director-entrepreneurs was endemic; the directors at the Rykovskii Coal Company who took sizable personal commissions on stocks and bonds floated by their company were only following a general pattern. In addition, directors were invariably entitled to a 10 to 15 percent share of all profits in excess of 5 or 6 percent, in accordance with the terms of the articles of incorporation. And these *tantièmes* were considerable for successful companies.

Entrepreneurs and founders were also able to use capital structures that gave them very great leverage. The various mechanisms of leverage, which are examined more closely in chapter 6, might be most simply summed up as the extensive and constant recourse to borrowed money at each stage of the venture. This meant that the rate of profit of the insider, whether parent firm, individual promoter, or group, was a multiple of that obtained by stockholders.

The entrepreneur's aggressive use of borrowed money in highly leveraged capital structures meant that access to organized capital markets, the stock exchanges, was of crucial significance, especially for Belgian and French firms of the 1890s.[10] Correspondingly, almost all these entrepreneurs apparently made two implicit assumptions. First, they needed the support of speculators and passive investors, without whom little was possible.[11] Second, if a

9. A.N., F 30, no. 343, Rabut to Delcassé, 1–7–1904.
10. Levin, *Germanskie kapitaly*, p. 56.
11. This is well documented in a series of articles on Russian companies in the fairly reliable *Semaine Financière*, 1898, pp. 102–3, 142–43, 1036; and 1899, pp. 23, 267–68, 750–51, 970.

venture was possible, the quantity of capital involved was seldom a stumbling block. Indeed, it seems that fairly large companies were preferred, and small affairs seldom considered. There were certain semifixed costs of foundation and operation —business trips, studies, negotiations, underwriting, graft, etc.—that were best spread over a substantial capitalization, as three of many possible examples show.

The Ural-Volga Company noted shortly after it began operations that a medium-sized steel company typically encountered sales problems in Russia because it lacked a complete line of products. ''In addition, in an enterprise like ours the choice of technical and administrative personnel is the essential factor for success. And in a period of great prosperity, men of top quality are rare and expensive. They are equally necessary whether we produce 60,000 or 120,000 tons.'' [12] When the Bonnardel Group's Kama Steel Company considered entering the bitterly competitive railway-equipment field in 1897, it thought of obtaining an enormous government order for 80,000 freight cars worth 280,000,000 francs to be delivered over twenty years by a new firm capitalized at 25,000,000 francs. Such size would reduce the payment of one million francs to Russian vendors of this contract to quite manageable proportions.[13] Size also counted in purely financial operations. The underwriting of 38,000,000

12. A.N., 65 AQ, K 168, Société Métallurgique de l'Oural Volga, report to special stockholders' meeting, 23–2–1899.

13. The Russian vendors, probably bureaucrats and financiers, were also to receive a commission of about 4 percent as the contract was actually executed—an additional 11,000,000 francs over twenty years. C.L., Société des Forges et Aciéries de la Kama, Projet d'établir un atelier de construction de wagons, June 1897, and accompanying letters.

francs of preferred shares for the Briansk Company in 1906 by Thalmann, the Banque de l'Union Parisienne, and the French Société Générale required on-the-spot technical studies by French engineers costing 80,000 francs.[14]

2

Why did businessmen think that there were big profits to be made in Russian industry at the end of the nineteenth century? What factors were present as entrepreneurs went on to analyze specific projects and opportunities? In short, how was information on potential entrepreneurial gains, which was necessary for investment decisions, transmitted to busy businessmen far from Russia?

Active Russian cultivation of a favorable investment image was one very important factor in interesting foreigners in Russia. As was noted in chapter 1, the Russian government, and particularly Count Witte, assigned foreign businessmen a crucial role in its strategy of development. Therefore the government, through a vast public relations campaign, tried to convince foreigners that Russia was a golden investment opportunity. This campaign was perhaps the government's principal contribution to development after 1885.

From the late 1880s on the Russian government distributed French translations of the annual state budget, which contained optimistic projections, through E. Hoskier et Cie, bankers in Paris. Sumptuous volumes were prepared for world fairs, like the 1893 World's Columbian Exposition at Chicago, or the Paris Exposition of 1900.[15] Even specialized

14. B.U.P., Russie, no. 47, Briansk, undated note from Sauerbach, Thalmann et Cie.

15. Russia, Ministerstvo Finansov, Departament zheleznodorozhnykh del, *The Industries of Russia,* 5 vols. (St. Petersburg, 1893); Commission Impériale de Russie à l'Exposition Univer-

periodicals were supported, such as the evanescent English language *Russian Journal of Financial Statistics,* which was published at St. Petersburg in 1900 and 1901. In 1895 the French consul Verstraete shrewdly concluded that speculation, with which he included the formation of new corporations, was "partly the work of the Russian government flaunting its protectionist regime. It is certain that the very considerable orders given by the state without interruption to industrialists and financiers to encourage new factories have nourished speculation, and if such measures continue, so will the speculation." [16] Not that the diplomatic representatives of France were unsympathetic. Verstraete himself helped educate French businessmen and investors in the ways of Russian opportunity with two exceptionally competent contemporary studies on Russian industry.[17] His colleague Sauvaire, the French consul at Odessa, also contributed with a long report on the Donets, which was published in part first in the *Moniteur officiel du commerce* (3–10–1895), and then widely reprinted by the financial press.[18]

Several key points stood out in this economic propaganda. High tariff protection was central because it eliminated foreign competition in the large domestic market, particularly for metallurgical products.[19] "The Russian ferrous metals industry

---

selle de Paris, under the direction of V. I. Kovalevsky, *La Russie à la fin du 19e siècle* (Paris, 1900).

16. A.N., F 30, no. 344, Verstraete to Hanotaux, 23–10–1895.

17. *La Russie industrielle* (Paris, 1897), and *L'Oural* (Paris, 1899).

18. A.N., F 12, no. 7173, Sauvaire to Hanotaux, Le Bassin du Donetz, 27–8–1895. Criticisms of Russian bureaucratic and commercial practices were carefully deleted in the printed version.

19. "The protectionist regime grows stronger daily and creates around this immense territory of the tsars an impassable wall for products from Europe. . . . It forces us Frenchmen to consider

has entered a period of great prosperity because of government and private construction, particularly railroads," wrote the French consul in Warsaw in 1896. "And in spite of tariff reductions after the treaty with Germany, the level of protection is quite adequate for the iron industry." [20] In the face of numerous uncertainties, the fundamental assurance of no outside competition within Russia was very important to foreign businessmen.

Not only was the market protected, but it was large and growing. The limited development of the Russian railway network assured demand, in view of the government's desire to build railroads aggressively. And this demand for metallurgical goods meant derived demand for other industries and general prosperity. Dozens of examples of this reasoning might be cited, but a quote from a confidential French diplomatic report, which might have been lifted from the day's financial press, is representative. "The tendency to borrow money in France for railroad construction seems certain to continue. There is a visible tie between building railroads, industrial prosperity in Russia, and even the definite success of the monetary reform, since prosperity draws foreign capital into Russia in search of manufacturing profits." [21]

The Russian government also cultivated the

---

investment in Russia itself." So wrote J. Belin, vice-consul in St. Petersburg, in the preface of his five-hundred-page unpublished report, "La Russie Industrielle," which was intended to serve as a "practical guide to investment opportunities." A.N., F 12, no. 7014, September 1892.

20. A.N., F 12, no. 7176, note from Warsaw, Production sidérurgique de Sosnowice, 29–10–1896.

21. A.N., F 30, no. 333, Verstraete to Delcassé, 1899. See also *Semaine Financière*, 1898, pp. 102–3; *L'Economiste Internationale*, 2–4, 18–5, 25–5, and 1–6–1895.

image of unshakable stability and financial orthodoxy that was so important for business confidence
and long-term commitments. Witte's establishment
of the gold standard in a series of steps between
1894 and 1897, which guaranteed the repatriation of
profits at a fixed rate of exchange, was but the cul-
mination of Vyshnegradskii's persistent efforts to
balance Russia's international accounts and to accu-
mulate gold reserves between 1887 and 1892.[22] Witte
was well aware of the symbolic importance of putting Russia on the gold standard. He hoped foreign
observers would henceforth more easily recognize
Russia's underlying economic progress and invest
on a massive scale.[23]

Similarly Witte's widely publicized, if often challenged, assertions of balanced budgets throughout
his administration, which again continued Vyshnegradskii's policy, helped create a favorable image.[24]
The unprecedented string of surpluses in the "ordinary" budget after 1888, in spite of deficits in the
"extraordinary" budget, became a key piece of evidence for those publicizing "the immense financial,
economic, and commercial development of
Russia."[25] And every foreign bondholder was a potential shareholder who might be reached through

22. C. Skalkovsky, Les Ministres des Finances de la Russie,
1802–90 (Paris, 1891), pp. 271–325; Crisp, "Financial Policy,"
pp. 161–65.

23. Witte's memorandum to the State Council of 14–3–1896,
quoted by P. P. Migulin, Reforma denezhnogo obrashcheniia v
Rossii i promyshlennyi krizis (Kharkov, 1902), pp. 112–22; A. P.
Pogrebinskii, Ocherki istorii finansov dorevoliutsionnoi Rossii
(Moscow, 1954), pp. 117–18; Levin, Germanskie kapitaly, pp.
26–27.

24. Pogrebinskii, Ocherki, pp. 90–92.

25. Preface to E. Hoskier et Cie's annual Les finances de la
Russie (Paris, 1891) for 1891; Pogrebinskii, Ocherki, pp. 87, 175.

the optimistic prefaces of the minister of finance to the annual budget.[26]

These themes of official and semiofficial propaganda, which created a certain awareness of Russia among big businessmen, also reached small investors. The series of articles in the *Economiste International* in early 1895 which predicted "a magnificent development" and "universal reknown for the great wealth of this inexhaustible region" was but one of many echoes.[27] And the listing on stock exchanges of companies operating in Russia, which were then discussed in the financial press as a matter of course, helped bring Russia within the investor's normal purview. Thus some businessmen first reacted to the intensive speculative demand for Russian securities on foreign exchanges after 1895, and only second to actual opportunities in Russia.[28]

Another source of information was declining exports. Declining exports to Russia due to increased tariffs often compelled firms with important Russian sales to consider direct investment. This was particularly true in the 1880s, especially for companies from Germany, which had always been Russia's main source of imports.[29] The Bayer Chemical Company, for example, traced its decision to build chemical works in Moscow to the tariff of 1882, and other German chemical firms acted for the same reason.[30]

26. See, for example, the discussion of Witte's Budget for 1900 in Edmond Théry's *L'Europe économique,* pp. 266–68.

27. 2–9–1895.

28. "La campagne sur les valeurs industrielles russes," *Semaine Financière,* 1899, pp. 267–68.

29. Levin, *Germanskie kapitaly,* pp. 66–68.

30. Farbenfabriken Bayer, "Geschichte und Entwicklung der Farbenfabriken vorm. Friedrich Bayer & Co. Elberfeld in den ersten 50 Jahren," unpublished history (Leverkursen, 1909), pp. 265–69; personal communication, 11–5–1966, from Badische Anilin & Soda Fabrik; Haber, *Chemical Industry,* p. 142.

(All German dyestuff producers in Russia were extremely profitable, and they certainly reaped the entrepreneurial profits they sought.)[31] Cockerill invested in southern Russia, to compensate in part for the loss of Russian sales. The tariff also encouraged some French and Belgian firms which had never exported to Russia successfully to invest there as a means of tapping a closed market.[32]

All these sources provided foreign businessmen with information on Russian opportunities. But surely the success of foreign businessmen already in Russia was the decisive signal. The unwitting might be fooled, or the disinterested aroused, by glowing imagery or political sentimentality; the sophisticated business leaders of western Europe demanded more. For these decision makers a few terse lines from the balance sheets of potential competitors told the Russian story with unsurpassed eloquence. And when they saw astonishing financial success smiling on fortunate pioneers, they were quick to anticipate similar results. The Belgian consul at Odessa summed up this pattern in 1894 when he wrote that "the prodigious success of some firms has bowled over the business world completely. Everyone moves toward Russia now."[33] Again and again examination of the chronology of foreign investment in various industries shows a pioneer reaping high profits followed by a rush of competitors who soon pushed the rate of return downward

31. Haber, *Chemical Industry*, p. 142; Badische, personal communication, 11–5–1966.

32. A.N., F 12, no. 7175, Rapport sur l'industrie métallurgique en Russie, Birle to the French Ambassador at St. Petersburg, 22–10–1892.

33. As quoted by the French consul at Odessa, 7–12–1894, F 12, no. 7173. Both consuls feared that "many people will regret later this excessive optimism."

to that of the "normal" level of the "average" firm.

In metallurgy, the Société John Cockerill's South Russian Dnieper Metallurgical Company (1888), which was paying 10 percent on its capital in 1891 and 40 percent in 1895, was almost directly responsible for the spate of Belgian followers. According to one close observer, "One must attribute to Cockerill's phenomenal results the great part played by Belgians in the rapid development of industry in the South."[34] In coal mining the Société Générale's Rutchenko Coal Company had the field almost to itself while it limped along financially from 1873 to 1893, even though its production skyrocketed from 13,000 to 400,000 tons.[35] Excellent profits from 1894 to 1896 corresponded precisely with the first influx of foreign coal companies, which continued until 1901.[36] In 1897 an English firm succeeded brilliantly at Baku with the Taguieff Oil Company. The English were previously uninterested in the Russian oil industry, but this success elicited so many followers that by 1898 an unbiased contemporary could speak of a general English take-over.[37] Of 75,000,000 rubles

34. A.E., Brussels, no. 2908, report of H. Henin, consul at Ekaterinoslav, 1–7–1903.

35. The second important foreign venture dated from 1892 when the Banque Internationale de Paris took control of Gorlovka. C.L., Routchenko, Etude, August 1897.

36. Ibid.

37. A.E., Brussels, no. 2901, sec. 3, Belgian consul at Odessa, 20–4–1898. "One year ago some English capitalists bought the properties of Taguieff, the Tartar Midas of Baku, for 5,000,000 rubles. These capitalists soon sold these properties for 2,500,000 rubles to another English company which was exceptionally lucky, bringing in two enormous gushers immediately. The properties are now evaluated at 20,000,000 rubles. This gain, realized with extraordinary rapidity, quickly attracted more English capital and wild speculation." There is a large literature on English investment in Russian petroleum, but this is probably as

invested by foreigners in the Russian oil industry from 1898 to 1903, 85 percent was of English origin.[38] There were at least two other oil rushes at Grozny and Maikop after foreign operators opened these less important Caucasian fields.

Large entrepreneurial profits also had regional ramifications. First, the successful pioneer exerted a great impact on firms in his native region. They knew the pioneering firm, competed with it successfully at home, and assumed they could do as well abroad. This reinforcement of investment decisions also increased (in the short run at least) the likelihood of success for close-knit groups, like Belgian capitalists. "Belgian capital is in the hands of industrialists having reciprocal interests. . . . The solidarity of these interests becomes effective automatically and gives the Belgians an audacity in Russia which we French rarely display."[39]

Second, large entrepreneurial profits, primarily in metallurgy, focused the attention of foreign industrialists in other industries upon the South in general. In response to this increasing interest, Hanotaux, the French minister of foreign affairs, asked the consul at Odessa for a special detailed report on industrial possibilities in the Donets. Hanotaux was informed that "our countrymen can find in this region a useful and remunerative outlet for their activity and capital; the example of those French companies which first gave the signal for the development of the Donets is still worth following." In addition to mining and metallurgy, this consul

accurate a short description of its origins as any. I hope to analyze in detail this participation, as part of a general study on the prerevolutionary Russian oil industry.

38. B. Akhundov, *Monopolisticheskii kapital v dorevoliutsionnoi bakinskoi neftianoi promyshlennosti* (Moscow, 1959), p. 45.

39. A.N., F 12, no. 7176, French consul at Antwerp, 6-2-1897.

noted, naval shipyards, armaments, and railway equipment were promising fields for large enterprises. There were also opportunities for small firms. "For example, there are very few iron mongers of the Ardennes or Loire type, who would find a large market in the area for locally-made products." [40]

Outside the Donets, but in the South, Odessa became a chosen city for Belgian entrepreneurs. In 1899, ten of the city's twenty-nine corporations were foreign and eight were Belgian. The Odessa Tramway Company, founded in 1883 and earning almost 20 percent on its capital in 1899, had apparently helped attract the other Belgian firms to Odessa after 1895, although none was very successful. [41] It is not completely facetious to suggest that if a developing country wishes to obtain massive direct foreign investment its efforts should be directed toward creating a few profitable opportunities for foreigners. The only condition need be annual publication of profit and loss figures.

3

Aggressive huckstering of general Russian opportunity by propagandists and occasional spectacular profits created the critical minimum level of interest in Russian investment among an increasing number of foreign business leaders. But this willingness to consider Russia was only a first step along an intricate path leading toward actual investment. Vague,

40. A.N., F 12, no. 7173, Sauvaire to Hanotaux, Le Bassin du Donetz, 30–7–1895.
41. "Mouvement maritime, industriel, commerciale d'Odessa en 1899," *Rapports commerciaux des agents diplomatiques et consulaires de France,* 1901, no. 23, p. 23.

general interest next had to be focused on specific projects, which were presented by various initiating forces.[42]

One initiating force was the foreign consul. He often spontaneously provided information on investment opportunities along with his reports on trade and commerce. He might, for example, send samples of minerals for analysis. At the request of a Russian landowner the French consul at Odessa forwarded samples of Krivoi-Rog iron ore for analysis at the Ecole des Mines of Paris in 1882. Similarly, a small piece of mica from Archangel among Belgian diplomatic archives testifies to a possible investment opportunity, as the Belgian *Bulletin commercial* duly reported in September 1912.[43]

Consuls announced concessions for which businessmen might compete, or tariff changes opening new opportunities. Thus Berdiansk, Feodosiia, and Sebastopol were reported to be seeking concessionnaires for streetcar lines or electric power plants in 1896.[44] Verstraete reported the impending switch to premiums for naval constructors from existing tariff protection, which had failed to create a Russian-built merchant marine. "French industrialists . . . establishing modern shipyards on the Black Sea would have an excellent chance of rapid success."[45] Representatives of the Bonnardel Group evidently

42. I wish to acknowledge once again my debt to Yair Aharoni's *Foreign Investment Decision Process,* particularly pp. 49–121; also, Clark C. Spence's *British Investments and the American Mining Frontier* (Ithaca, N.Y., 1958), particularly pp. 51–76.

43. A.E., Paris, C.C., Odessa, vol. 12, Jacquemin to Quai d'Orsay, 10–2–1882; A.E., Brussels, no. 2901, sec. 3, note, 31–8–1912.

44. A.E., Paris, C.C., Odessa, vol. 14, reports, 8–4–1896 and 5–4–1896.

45. A.N., F 12, no. 7175, Le capital étranger pour la construction navale, 9–6–1897.

agreed, for they competed unsuccessfully with industrialists from Liège for the deep water harbor of Nikolaev, where the Nikolaev Shipyards Company was established in 1897.

Consuls also forwarded appeals from foreign landowners, as two examples from the foreign-dominated glass industry show. In 1886 Captain Ilunskii, a large landowner near Nizhnii-Novgorod, asked the French embassy to aid him in finding French capitalists capable of building a glassworks on his property. Ilunskii agreed to retain a sizable financial interest.[46] In 1895 a court official named Beklemishev requested aid from the Belgian consul in his search for foreign entrepreneurship capable of transforming and managing his very small glass plant, founded in 1872.[47] Surprisingly, the Lakash Mirror Company followed this appeal—surprisingly, because the multitude of appraisals and appeals from consuls apparently brought few tangible results. How does one explain this? It was mainly because projects submitted were vague and incomplete, which meant that proper evaluation was impossible without further investment of money and time.

Without doubt most companies originated with projects initially submitted to Western entrepreneurs by business associates active in Russia. Banks in Russia, like the Crédit Lyonnais with branches in St. Petersburg, Moscow, and Odessa, tried to match Russian projects with foreign businessmen, partly as a courtesy to major Russian clients. In 1892, for example, the Odessa branch of the Crédit Lyonnais dispatched reports on a functioning coal mine in

46. A.N., F 12, no. 7172, note, undated [1886], given to the French consul at Moscow.

47. A.E., Brussels, no. 2902, sec. 3, Société Belgo-russe à Lakasch, note of 14–9–1898.

Ekaterinoslav province which the Russian proprietor, an important customer of the bank, was extremely anxious to sell. The Crédit Lyonnais was to
receive a commission of 10 percent of the shares of
any subsequent company.[48] Similarly, the assistant
director of the Moscow branch forwarded reports
on iron and coal properties from Siberian owners in
1900, while the St. Petersburg branch forwarded reports from the Department of Mines concerning gold
mines on the auction block in 1896.[49]

Investment banks continually received propositions. In 1909 the Banque de l'Union Parisienne,
which was very active in Russia, was approached by
a Mr. E. Steiner of Mulhouse. Steiner had an option
on the Russian patents for rayon production of the
Vereinigte Glanzstoff Fabriken of Elberfeld, Germany, and wanted to use them. The Elberfeld firm
stipulated in the option granted Steiner that any
Russian company founded would be capitalized with
at least 3,000,000 rubles, of which one-third would go
to the German company for its techniques. Steiner
claimed he had one-half the necessary capital and
sought the rest from the Banque de l'Union Parisienne. Although the German firm was extremely
prosperous, and had very profitable affiliates in
France, Austria, and Great Britain, the bank decided after due consideration that the fee for admittedly excellent patents and licenses was excessive.
Steiner then suggested a venture based on French
and Italian patents of 1890 and 1908. His argument
that "the guarantees of success would be less, but
we would need two, not three, million rubles" failed

48. C.L., Agence d'Odessa, letters to the main office in Paris of
14–7, 27–7, and 13–8–1892.
49. C.L., Agence de Moscou, letter to Paris, 15–3–1900; C.L.,
Société Russe de l'Industrie de l'Or, note, January 1896.

to persuade the bank's directors.[50] The project was finally dropped.

Of these associates or businessmen in Russia, however, the single most important initiating force at this first step was the individual promoter. Like foreign promoters, who were considered in some detail in chapter 2, certain Russian businessmen seem to have specialized in presenting foreign entrepreneurs with Russian projects. We know less than we should like about these men, but the activities of a few provide some insights.

Two brothers, Alexis and George Goriainov, participated in the formation of several foreign firms. Both men were apparently rich, and they were certainly influential: Alexis was plant manager of the Briansk Company's southern steel mills, and George was formerly a high-ranking government mining engineer. One or the other participated in the following foreign firms in the 1890s: the Keramika Brick Company, the Lugansk Lamp Company, the Ekaterinoslav Steel Company, the Dubovaia-Balka Mining Company, the South Russian Mechanical Engineering Company, the Kerch Metallurgical Company, the Donets Stamping Company, and no doubt others.[51] In almost every case, they subscribed a sizable portion of the new firm's capital for both themselves and Russian investors. Occasionally they provided negotiating skills. George Goriainov negotiated with a peasant commune for high quality white clay to be used for bricks, then ceded his rights to the Keramika Brick Company "without profit or loss" in return for part of the founders'

50. B.U.P., Russie, no. 66, Soie artificielle en Russie.
51. See the dossiers on these firms at the Crédit Lyonnais; in A.N., 65 AQ, K 118, L 807, M 387; and in A.E., Brussels, no. 2902, secs. 1–4.

shares entitled to 10 percent of profits above 5 percent for ten years.[52] George Goriainov was also a top manager of the South Russian Mechanical Engineering Company, and both brothers worked closely with the firms of the Bonnardel Group in the late 1890s.[53]

Another free-wheeling promoter was the banker A. K. Alchevskii, general director of the Kharkov Commerce Bank in the 1890s. Before ending his life in despair in 1901 as his bank crashed, he appeared as an important initial participant in several foreign firms, most notably the Donets-Yur'evka Metallurgical Company.[54] Often an important underwriter, he subscribed, for example, one-sixth of the initial 1,200,000 francs of one subsidiary of the Seilles-lez-Ardenne Brick Company.[55] It is absolutely clear that he was important initially in a second major steel producer, the Russian Providence Company, as both top troubleshooter in Russia and underwriter (30 percent of total capital).[56]

Finally, note F. E. Enakiev, engineer and businessman. In 1895 he helped present the Société Générale de Belgique with the project that became the very successful Russo-Belgian Metallurgical Company. Always a member of that company's board, Enakiev presented the Société Générale de Belgique (and its ally the Banque de l'Union Parisienne) with the concession that became the North Donets Railroad Company in 1907. He subsequently presented other projects and ideas and was one of

52. A.E., Brussels, no. 2902, sec. 4, Keramika.
53. See chapter 11.
54. C.L., Donets-Yourievka, Etude, April 1905.
55. A.E., Brussels, no. 2902, sec. 4, Produits réfractaires à Krinitchnaia.
56. P.R. MSS, Délibérations du Conseil, various meetings in 1897 and 1898.

this foreign group's leading free-lance promoters.[57]

These Russian promoters fulfilled at least three important functions. First, they were the link between the graft-ridden, concession-laden bureaucracy on the one hand and foreign capital and technology on the other. "It would be excessively difficult to receive large orders for locomotives to be built in Russia without a partnership [*association*] with Russian groups," wrote the French military attaché in St. Petersburg in 1896.[58] The consul at Odessa was more precise. "As you know, government orders in this country are submitted for public bidding only as a matter of form. To obtain concessions it is necessary to be on the spot, to ask, to bargain, and to make sacrifices to the right people." [59] These promoters also linked Russian landlords and aristocrats, who were disdainful of business but avid for its gains, with Western entrepreneurs. Finally, these promoters moved easily and effectively among various foreign groups to obtain the best bid in a competitive market. Like clever merchants, they spread their glittering wares in the market place and then coaxed, cajoled, and bargained with the ancient practices of the bazaar—practices that made them fully a match for rich, technically oriented modern shoppers.

All the above sources of initiation were external to given enterprises in western Europe. Another initiating source, which became increasingly impor-

57. Akademiia Nauk SSSR, *Materialy*, 6:755; B.U.P., Russie, dossiers on the Chemins de Fer du Nord-Donetz (nos. 37–42); Société des Embranchements de Chemins de Fer (nos. 205–8); and Syndicat des Affaires Russes (no. 239).

58. A.N., F 12, no. 7175, Locomotives, Moulin to Quai d'Orsay, 1–1–1896.

59. A.N., F 12, no. 7176, note on Tramways d'Ekaterinodar, 13–3–1897.

tant as major foreign investment groups developed, was the trusted personnel of the different groups stationed in Russia. These agents not only supervised existing enterprises, but they also received and sought new investment proposals. They were also responsible for screening these projects and for submitting those with promise to their groups.[60]

These initiators, both foreign and Russian, sought, not an immediate investment commitment, but rather a decision to investigate. Their planning was accordingly only preliminary, in order to economize on management time and money, although they did treat all principal questions. These questions included rough evaluations of natural resources, a crude market study, estimates of costs and capital requirements, anticipated profits, and possible sources of capital and technical expertise. (The initiator's natural resources were usually only a short-term option on land or mining rights.) At this point other entrepreneurs, such as leading foreign firms or investment banks, either decided to investigate seriously or declined on the basis of the initiator's information.

A special study group might even be formed for further investigation, although interested businessmen more normally operated within existing organizations. In 1897 a group of industrialists and financiers including Le Creusot and Demachy formed a study group to investigate Russian metallurgy in general, and in particular the Goujon project that became the Volga-Vishera Company.[61] In late 1911 the Banque de l'Union Parisienne and its associates

60. Some of these agents are considered at greater length in chapter 5.
61. A.N., 65 AQ, K 257, Rapport fait par Bouvard et Babu; *Le Pour et le Contre*, 6-2-1898.

formed a special study group to investigate very promising Siberian coal mines. This group was an offshoot of the Syndicat des Affaires Russes, a semi-permanent study group formed by, among others, the Banque de l'Union Parisienne and Thalmann et Cie in February 1912 to screen investment projects. Most of these projects were suggested by the Banque de l'Union representative in St. Petersburg, Pierre Darcy.[62]

Initiators needed to sell their schemes aggressively. One excellent example illustrating the general process was the Kachkar Gold Company, founded in Brussels in 1897. This company purchased producing gold mines in the Urals (Orenburg province, Mias district) from a Russian proprietor, Podvinstev, who had obtained large but decreasing profits since 1880. Accustomed to living in princely luxury, Podvinstev became heavily indebted as his revenues fell, and thus, like many an aristocrat with marketable properties, he saw the surge of foreign interest in Russian industry as a godsend.[63]

Podvinstev turned first to a major French mining company, the Société des Bormettes, which had previously served him as technical consultant.[64] The Bormettes Company sent an engineer to reexamine the mines. This engineer then prepared a report which became part of the preliminary package, since Bormettes agreed to serve as the future firm's

62. B.U.P., Russie, no. 329, Syndicat des affaires Russes.

63. C.L., Société des Mines d'Or du Katchkar, report of Blanc from Irkust, September 1902. See Carl Joubert, *Russia As It Really Is* (London, 1905), pp. 39–42, for a telling contemporary observation on the aristocrat's salesmanship.

64. C.L., Katchkar, letter to Etudes Financières, Paris, from the Marseilles agency, 23–10–1896. This letter noted that Bormettes "has an excellent reputation, exploits it mines skillfully, and its shares of 100 francs par value are at 830 francs."

"technical consultant" but wisely sought capital elsewhere.[65] The Crédit Lyonnais was uninterested, as its Marseilles Agency had anticipated, but Albert Roux, the president of Bormettes, eventually succeeded in convincing two bankers with famous names, Michael Ephrussi and Robert Oppenheim, to support the venture.[66]

Podvinstev sold his properties skillfully. He received 8,000,000 francs (of the initial capital of 12,000,000), of which almost one-half was in shares. According to Blanc, the foreign group "needed to pay only half that sum, if they had known the truth about Podvinstev's financial situation. The mines would have still been quite fully priced."[67] A good measure of Podvinstev's success was due to the connivance of local bankers, bureaucrats, and mine owners, whom Podvinstev bribed into collusion or silence.[68] Ephrussi and Oppenheim naturally hastened to sell their shares to the public, but with limited success.[69] The firm never paid dividends regularly, and it was finally reorganized in 1912. By that time at least one-half of the original capital had been irretrievably lost.[70]

4

Once an entrepreneur was seriously interested, he almost invariably sent a mission of engineers to

65. C.L., Katchkar, letter of 31–11–1896.
66. C.L., Katchkar, Articles of Incorporation; Etude, September 1902. In returning the first Bormettes project to its Marseilles agency, the Etudes Financières at Paris noted discreetly on 31–11–1896 that "we believe information has been obtained which does not agree with that of M. Chevalier [Bormettes's engineer]." The bank's engineers in Russia crossed and recrossed the country for just such information, which proved highly reliable once again.
67. C.L., Katchkar, Etude, September 1902.
68. Ibid.
69. A.N., 65 AQ, L 1611.
70. C.L., Katchkar, Etude, December 1912.

Russia to examine the project in depth, just as Roux of the Société Bormettes did in the Kachkar venture. The resulting examination was normally technically oriented and focused on conditions of production. But this focus was always linked directly with economic analysis of costs and profits. Indeed, countless studies at the Crédit Lyonnais and elsewhere suggest a literary genre with a uniform theme: techniques determine costs, which in turn determine anticipated profits and thus investment decisions.

The formation of this mentality was an integral part of an engineer's training. Graduating students of the Ecole des Mines at Paris proved their worth by carefully analyzing existing enterprises, sometimes located in Russia, as a sort of thesis.[71] One excellent student, Paul Chapuy, demonstrated his ability to analyze steel and coal operations in Russia on his senior thesis trip in 1887. Chapuy principally visited the Krivoi-Rog Company, Hughes, and Rutchenko. Hughes alone, "who had almost closed for good in 1885," was "rather rude and refused to furnish any precise information."[72] The author's flair and precision, as well as an obviously strong interest in Russia, suggest that the Banque de Paris et des Pays-Bas exercised fine judgment when it later promoted Chapuy to handle technical investigations of Russian companies in which they were interested.[73]

71. These reports, which are preserved in the Archives of the Ecole des Mines, Paris, often deal with industrial operations in foreign countries. As such they are an important, if neglected, source for nineteenth-century economic history. I examined all the studies concerning Russia.

72. Paul Chapuy, Journal de voyage, 1887: Russie, Bassin du Donets, student senior thesis, E.M.

73. B.U.P., Russie, no. 37.

Such technical-economic studies were central to foreign entrepreneurship in the late nineteenth century, as a few of many examples show.[74] In 1896 two Belgian engineers examined coal concessions situated on the Belaia River in the northern Donets Basin, twenty-four kilometers from Lugansk, for Eugène Carez and his group.[75] Their method was typical. First came geological analysis. Since Belaia's 4,000 hectares had never been systematically exploited, the engineers extrapolated from conditions existing on the contiguous properties of Prince Dolgorukii. Reserves were then estimated at twenty-five million tons, much of which was judged excellent coking coal on the basis of subsequent tests at the Denain Steel Company in France.[76] Passing over the labor question—"the valley is relatively well-populated with four small villages"—the engineers discussed the equipment and costs necessary for modern coal and coke facilities. An analysis of the market then permitted them to estimate future profits. A complementary report on future steelworks followed. It also estimated costs and anticipated profits for a complete range of metallurgical products in great detail. The entire report was subsequently printed, obviously as a promotional aid. But with the exception of its questionable evaluation of market conditions, it seems honest: coke was indeed good, but only if washed; limestone at Belaia was poor, though excellent nearby, etc. Upon this generally favorable report, the Belaia firms were based.

74. See, for example, *Société Générale*, pp. 20, 44.

75. The French consul had noted in 1895 that these concessions were for sale. A.N., F 12, no. 7173, Le Bassin du Donetz, Sauvaire to Hanotaux, 30–7–1895.

76. *Rapport par Hardy et Michot.*

The General Coal Company bought an existing Russian company after reports of at least three Belgian mining experts.[77] Again this study followed the classic pattern, as the author moved from evaluations of reserves and coke quality to estimates of costs and prices, and then to a statement of required investment and anticipated profits. Rigorous analysis of existing methods, suggestions for their improvement, and a timetable for increasing production completed the analysis of these functioning mines.

Changes in control of existing coal companies gave rise to the same type of study. Thus the Comptoir Nationale d'Escompte de Paris used its engineers to restudy the Rykovskii Coal Company in detail before taking the firm firmly in hand for a brief period.[78] Another example was the Makeevka Coal Company, for which we have evidence of several studies in connection with possible changes of ownership. In 1881 a French engineer first surveyed the vast properties and producing mines of a Russian named Ilovaiskii.[79] In the first half of this report Monin placed the project in its general setting: the quality and quantity of Donets coal; the belated, crucial development of railroads; markets and prices; and measured but enthusiastic predictions of the area's ''great future.'' The second section of the

77. *Rapport sur les Mines "Zolotoié et Bokovsky."* This brochure digested "a very detailed technical study of Alfred Navez, mining engineer and director of Charbonnages du Poirier at Montigny sur Sambre, Belgium," as well as followup reports on accounting practices by Le Jeune, "previously director of the Toretskoe Mines" in Russia, and on techniques by Emile Desvachiez, director-general of Mines de l'Est du Liège.

78. See chapter 10.

79. Monin, *Notice sur . . . des houillères Ilovaisky.*

twenty-two-page printed report turned to Ilovais-kii's lands and mines: the owner's financial problems; reserves and quality of coal; methods and costs of exploitation and possibilities for expansion and economy; and finally estimates of investment and profits. The project was apparently abandoned only because of the crash of 1881.

These properties were studied again in 1895 by engineers attached to the Länderbank prior to their sale to a Franco-Belgian firm. Copies of these studies were not found, but one of two careful examinations made in 1903 was. The Makeevka Coal Company had fallen into default on its first-mortgage bonds and was seeking to avoid bankruptcy through an arrangement with its bondholders. To ascertain the suitability of the company's proposals, the bondholders sent a French mining expert named Barrillon to evaluate the mines with management's blessings. A very long analysis of equipment and mines—piece by piece, shaft by shaft—concluded with detailed suggestions for essential investments to increase production, reduce costs, and establish a viable affair.[80] This report was in part used by Makeevka's management, men of the Société Générale and Länderbank, to beat off a bid from the Bonnardel Group's Ekaterinovka Coal Company for cash purchase which had the support of a dissident group of Makeevka bondholders from Geneva.[81] Ekaterinovka's bid was of course also based on another careful examination which had concluded that the company's properties were rich and its managers

80. Report of Léon Barrillon, unpublished, n.d. [May 1903], in A.N., 65 AQ, K 71¹.
81. Ibid., Syndicat des Porteurs d'Obligations 4% Makeevka, Meeting, 2–6–1903.

incompetent. This unflattering judgment was duly leaked to Ekaterinovka's allies in the financial press.[82]

The extensive foreign participation in Russian streetcar companies shows the serious technical study as well as other previously mentioned factors. The streetcar companies, normally Belgian, were all based upon concessions from Russian municipalities to operate either horse-drawn tramways in the early 1880s or, more importantly, electrically powered trams from 1890 onward. Almost invariably entrepreneurship involved the following steps. First, representatives of leading Belgian equipment makers, who were on the industry's technological frontier and were very disposed to foreign investment, received leads from Russian businessmen (or city councilmen). Then promising opportunities were investigated thoroughly. Finally after more negotiating a concession was perhaps granted and a separate firm was founded to exploit it. By 1911 this process resulted in twenty-three Belgian streetcar companies in Russia with annual revenues of 38,000,000 francs.[83]

A Belgian engineer, Edouard Denis, apparently representing the Empain interests, operated according to the general pattern in April 1892 when he secured an option from the municipal administration of Tashkent to form a streetcar company in

82. See *Le Globe*, 5–10–1905, for a long excerpt. This excerpt has the incisive, biting tone of an Etude from the Crédit Lyonnais. This conjecture is perhaps reinforced by the unexplainable apparent absence of any studies on either Makeevka Coal or Ekaterinovka at the Crédit Lyonnais. Perhaps the study was sent out and never returned.

83. *Vestnik Finansov*, 25–3–1913. There were ten Belgian tramway companies in 1903. Several gave "excellent results." A.E., Brussels, no. 2908, sec. 4, report by Henin, 1–7–1903.

their city. Denis then asked Edouard Otlet, a Belgian who had formed several Russian tramway companies, as well as Lazare Poliakov, a member of the famous Jewish rail and banking family, to share his initial expenses, 79,000 francs, and those of a further detailed study. This study was charged to an engineer named Montagne, the director of Otlet's companies at Tiflis and Kazan. Denis, Otlet, and Poliakov each had one-third of the venture. After Montagne appraised the concession as "passable but not brilliant," Poliakov and Otlet stipulated that Denis's original concession be modified to permit Jewish personnel. This was clearly impossible, since the concession stipulated a Russian rather than a Belgian corporation, and Denis charged this was a pretext to avoid paying their share of the costs.[84] After various complicated negotiations, another concession was granted to Denis, and this formed the basis of a Belgian corporation four years later.

Sometimes the Belgians bought concessions or options on concessions which skilled Russian operators had already negotiated. This was the case with Otlet's Moscow Company (where a Gorchakov brought the concession), the Bialystok firm, Tramways of Nikolaev, Tramways of Kursk, and doubtlessly others.[85] A trip by a Crédit Lyonnais expert through eastern Russia in August 1898 also throws light on the process. Baron du Marais noted that the horse-drawn, Russian-owned Saratov Tramway Company was for sale. The affair was potentially interesting if a lighting concession could be tied to streetcar electrification—and if one were careful

84. A.E., Brussels, no. 2818, Tramways de Taschkent, letter from Denis, 2–4–1892.
85. See A.E., Brussels, no. 2818, for material on these firms

with Golubev, Saratov's president, "who is excessively cunning and with whom one must not deal without very careful consideration."[86]

The history of the Russo-French Cotton Company illustrates the importance of high-quality preliminary studies which carefully link technical questions to economic considerations. Three cotton spinners—G. Badin and R. Offroy of Barentin and Malaunay (Seine-Inférieure), and Roger Douine, previously of Troyes—traveled extensively through Russia in early 1898.[87] The men sought to determine current profits and future prospects in general, "the most profitable weights of thread and types of wovens" in particular, and to choose a plant site after visiting Poland, Reval, St. Petersburg, Moscow, and even Baku and Petrovsk in the Caucasus. The group visited firms employing a million spindles (a seventh of the Russian total); were cordially received by Witte and the minister of commerce and industry, who both gave information and promised support; and met numerous *chefs d'entreprise,* directors, brokers, merchants, and bankers.[88]

They did their work well. They concluded that the industry's prosperity showed little sign of weakening, since both population and per capita consumption of cotton goods were growing. At the same time output per factory had dropped, because new laws forbade night employment of vitally needed women and children. High-quality products ["beaux articles façonnés"] demanding special skills offered the greatest opportunity, and this was to be the new

---

86. C.L., Tramway de Saratov, Etude, August 1898.

87. They themselves were aided by earlier studies of A. Badin and the famed Dollfus groups of eastern France. See *Etude sur l'industrie cotonnière en Russie* (Paris, 1898) in C.L., Société Cotonnière Russo-Française.

88. Ibid.

firm's chosen field. As for location the French spinners hesitated between the Baltic port of Reval,
closest to imported American cotton and possessing
excellent labor, and Petrovsk in the Caucasus, near-
est to the domestic producers of Central Asia and
residual fuel, before finally picking the Moscow
area. Crude oil and Russian cotton would take the
cheap water route along the Volga with only short
railroad transshipment. Since land and labor were
too expensive in Moscow itself, these enterpreneurs
selected a site at Pavlovskii-Posad, sixty kilometers
to the northeast on the Nizhnii-Novgorod line. There
is little doubt that this careful planning contributed
to the success of the firm, which paid dividends of 5
and then 6 percent until the outbreak of war.

When the reorganization of faltering firms became the principal activity of foreign entrepreneurs
from 1900 to 1909, technical studies still followed the
decision to investigate. The Banque de l'Union Parisienne, for example, dispatched a group of engineers
in August 1905 to examine the Russian Providence
and Taganrog Companies in order to evaluate a contemplated merger of these steel companies. Their
long report concluded that a merger was desirable
because each plant could subsequently concentrate
on fewer products.[89]

As metallurgy revived before 1914 the Banque de
l'Union Parisienne, ever a power in Russian metallurgy, was receptive to investigation of an option on
coal deposits in the Kuznetsk Basin in central Siberia. As outlined by Darcy, the bank's agent in St.

89. The 170-page Rapport sur un mission dans le Sud de la
Russie, dated 26–8–1905, contained several pieces. The project
apparently foundered upon incomplete data on Taganrog's cost
structure, which the general director (Trasenster) released in Belgium and in Russia. This study was found only in the archives
kept by the Providence Belge, Marchienne-au-Pont, Belgium.

Petersburg, a man named Trepov had secured an option from the emperor's Cabinet for really excellent concessions.[90] Demand for coal was assured by the Siberian Railroad. Much more intriguing for the French bankers was a related scheme to link this coal with Ural iron ore in a vast Siberian steel complex—Stalin's first five-year plan in miniature. The Banque de l'Union Parisienne, which had previously considered sending a group of engineers to this region in 1911, jumped at this solid proposition.[91] With its associates it allotted 200,000 francs to a study group for a thorough on-the-spot investigation. Five engineers led by the director of the bank's Ural-Volga Steel Company then examined the project in detail and reported very enthusiastically. But with the international storm gathering, the Banque de l'Union Parisienne very reluctantly deferred action.[92]

A final illustration of crucial technical studies comes from the naval defense industry, where many sought and few found large entrepreneurial profits

90. B.U.P., Russie, no. 103, Charbonnages de l'Altai, telegrams and letters, 27–, 29–, 30–12–1911, 2–1–1912. Although it was impossible to identify this man precisely, it seems certain he was a member of the Trepov family whose members held a number of very high government positions during this period. The most famous member of the family was General Dmitrii Trepov (1855–1906). Governor-general of St. Petersburg and associate minister of interior, Trepov was a key man in the Revolution of 1905. For an unflattering judgment see Sergei Witte, *The Memoires of Count Witte* (New York, 1921), pp. 225–26, 326–31.

91. C.L., Mission d'étude dans la région de l'Altai, summer 1911.

92. Trepov required an initial commitment of at least 100,000 francs as evidence of serious intentions regarding his option. If a company were subsequently formed, Trepov and his cohorts would receive shares worth 5,000,000 francs from a total capitalization of 25,000,000 francs, plus 200,000 francs in cash. The emperor's Cabinet would still own the deposits and would receive ½ kopeck per pud of coal raised. B.U.P., Russie, no. 205, Procès verbaux of the Syndicat pour les Affaires Russes, 12–4–1912, 9–12–1912.

before 1914. Two careful examinations in 1911 of the Crichton Shipyards at St. Petersburg had convinced a French shipbuilder, the Société des Chantiers et Ateliers Augustin Normand, that massive transformation of the St. Petersburg shipyard was possible and potentially very profitable.[93] As everyone knew, Russia was embarking upon a great modernization and expansion of her navy, which included the addition of new torpedo boats and submarines. With the Nevskii Shipyards the only existing competitor at St. Petersburg and this projected leap in demand, Crichton seemed assured of large orders *if* it could transform old and inadequate shipyards to meet the fleet's rigid technical specifications.

Assuming orders for nine torpedo boats at approximately 5,300,000 francs each, the engineers of Société Normand further assumed costs equal to those of French yards, provided necessary equipment was properly installed and utilized. The crucial question was the cost of such new equipment, and this point formed the bulk of the study. The engineers decided 6,000,000 francs would be ample. The directors then added 2,000,000 for purchase of old yards, two for working capital, a million for the Société Normand's expertise, and a final one and one-half million for bankers' profits—a total of 13,000,000 francs. Estimated profits of 10,000,000 francs on nine torpedo boats left a 16 percent return on total capital during the first five years.

The Société Normand's appeal to the Crédit Lyonnais for help in underwriting the new firm's capital also contained guarantees of future technical support. The Société Normand pledged that it would

93. C.L., Etude sur l'opportunité d'acheter et de transformer le Chantier Crichton.

remain as technical consultant after it had directed modernization of the shipyards, and that it would supply the new firm with a skilled director and all the necessary technical personnel—even foremen and skilled workers—for as long as they were needed.[94]

5

We are now ready to interpret our data by suggesting a general pattern, a general model, of foreign entrepreneurship in Russia.

This general model contained, first of all, a common investment strategy, a strategy clearly seen in the on-the-spot studies. The work of engineers, these reports were tailored to provide the data needed by foreign executives interested in Russian opportunities. All these engineering reports on existing plants, like those on Crichton, Moscow Rubber, Odessa Cement, and Lakash Mirror, as well as many others discussed or omitted, noted without exception many technical failures.[95] In fact, it seems certain that foreign engineers believed that indigenous Russian industrial techniques were poor and inadequate. Reports on existing Russian-owned coal mines were harsh, even contemptuous, as were those on Russian gold mines. Imputing technical backwardness to Ural steel producers was proverbial among foreigners, partly because it was proverbial among Russians themselves. Thus from the viewpoint of industrial technology, able foreigners were convinced that Russia lagged far behind the West with obsolete or inadequate practices. The existence

94. Ibid., Note Annex.
95. Since these assumptions are analyzed in detail for the steel and coal industries in southern Russia in chapter 4, illustrations in this chapter are taken primarily from other industries.

of such a technological gap is a theme connecting reports handed decision makers.

This gap provided the opportunity for private profit. Introduction of improved technique, which might also require improved management, could potentially reduce costs of production (or permit increased production at constant costs) and lead to substantial entrepreneurial profits. Thus the engineers of the Roux Mirror Company typically recommended a complete overhaul of Beklemishev's old mirror works in Riazan province. All these measures were adopted by the Belgo-Russian Mirror Company of Lakash, the surviving firm. (The large and expandable new plant with an initial capacity of 75,000 square meters of mirror glass fixed and polished a mirror in four and three hours, respectively, as opposed to forty and thirty hours previously. Roux also installed an advanced leveling system.) [96] The French consul at Odessa provided another example of the standard feeling in his appraisal of rich phosphate deposits in Bessarabia. These neglected deposits could be very profitable, he thought, if rudimentary mining methods were replaced by modern cost-reducing techniques.[97] In brief, advanced industrial technology was the means to big profits.

Western engineers almost invariably acted as if they believed that their advanced industrial technology could be transplanted to Russia in its highly developed form without significant modification. Indeed, there is little evidence that foreign engineers and technicians seriously considered alternatives to their customary art. Advanced technology was a given, and there was simply a right way and a

96. A.E., Brussels, no. 2902, sec. 3, letter of 14–9–1898.
97. A.N., F 12, no. 7173, French consul at Odessa, 26–2–1902.

wrong way of doing things. Capital and labor requirements were in turn fixed by the technology fixed in the engineer's mind. The Russo-French Cotton Company, for example, planned to build an additional cotton mill in two stages in 1910 in accordance with international prospects for technical progress in the industry. "Our first efforts will concentrate uniquely on the 40,000 spindle spinning mill . . . since an essential change in spinning technique seems unlikely for many years." The purchase of weaving machinery would be postponed, however, since automatic looms were promising—or threatening—to revolutionize weaving. "We must follow very closely this progress and install these new processes the day they have proved themselves in every way." [98] Foreigners would seek to stay on the international technical frontier in Russia, but they looked outside the country for experimentation and innovation. Generally, the tendency toward technical rationality was strongest in the 1890s, when plants were most often built from scratch or extensively renovated and foreigners who did bother to consider capital-labor ratios had little trouble convincing themselves that labor was relatively expensive. (See chapter 8.)

Strong foreign activity in Russian gold mining before 1914 shows these factors operating. Technique and organization were crude and proprietors lacked capital and know-how for further development, according to foreign observers. [99] "The gold industry is undergoing a crisis. This is because the alluvial deposits have been exhausted and there is no equipment to exploit the ore veins. The general

98. C.L., Sté Cotonnière Russo-Française, Extraordinary Meeting of Shareholders, 15–1–1910.

99. A.E., Brussels, no. 2901, sec. 6, Note sur les mines d'or, 1911.

opinion is that the gold industry must transform itself and abandon its primitive methods of merely washing gold-bearing sand. Instead, the industry must use scientific methods for mining ore and chemical treatment." [100] In the 1890s Ural owners were still contracting with local prospector-entrepreneurs who worked deposits they uncovered for shares. This permitted passive proprietors to avoid furnishing either capital or skill. But Russian prospectors stole ore relentlessly, and they also lacked equipment and scientific training. [101]

Foreign entrepreneurs planned to change all this. They planned systematic exploration and deeper mines with powerful pumping and extracting machinery. They also planned to treat crushed ore with the latest chemical methods, particularly the cyanide process which had been perfected in South African mines and which was assumed to be applicable in Russia. In 1901 there were only four cyanide plants in the Urals and none in Siberia. [102]

The cyanide method also meant that ore previously treated by amalgamation could be profitably reprocessed. Thus the first major investments of the Kachkar Gold Company in the Urals were two cyaniding plants, and an English firm founded in 1901 planned to concentrate on this chemical retreatment of old ore. [103] English mining interests active in South Africa also entered the Lena Gold Company in 1908, where they supplied expertise as well as capital and reaped enormous success. [104]

100. A.N., F 30, no. 344, Industrie de l'or en Russie, Verstraete to Delcassé, 10–4–1901.

101. C.L., Katchkar, September 1902.

102. *St. Peterburgskie vedomosti,* 12–3–1901 (old style) Copy in A.N., F 30, no. 344, Industrie de l'or.

103. C.L., Katchkar, Etude, September 1902.

104. Lord Harris, president of the Consolidated Goldfields of

Engineers in their studies and entrepreneurs in their subsequent decisions apparently assumed that the implantation and management of advanced industrial technology was their essential function, their raison d'être. The engineers of the Société Normand were to modernize old shipyards; those of Roux were to build modern glassworks. Most engineers were in effect investigating how they would provide technical aid for private profit—or exploit the West's technical superiority, according to Russian critics who saw the same phenomenon in a different light.[105] This technical aid, this ''non-material capital'' to use Levin's term, deserved (or received) handsome compensation, as the Société Normand's fee of 1,000,000 francs correctly suggests.[106] Perhaps this close tie to advanced technology explains why foreigners concentrated on new (chemicals, electrical equipment) or unmodernized (metallurgy, mining, etc.) industries, where the technological gap was greatest, even if these industries did not always pay the highest rates of return.[107] Foreign decision makers considered nontechnical aspects of course, particularly the situation in capital markets and commitments for underwriting. But generally they

---

South Africa, and Lena director, mentioned in 1909 that ore was now lifted from the mines by electric elevators, which had replaced horse-driven windlasses—the normal power source in Siberia. Eighteen miles of railroad had also been built by the company. A.N., 65 AQ, L 1294, Lena Goldfields, Annual Report, 1909.

105. *Moskovskie vedomosti,* 31–8–1895 (old style), complained, for example, of an alleged unwillingness of the foreigner to teach his processes to Russian employees. "The foreign capitalist must bring us not only money, but what is more important, he must share his scientific knowledge, experience, and industrial skill." See below.

106. Levin, *Germanskie kapitaly,* p. 46.

107. Ischchanian, *Ausländischen Elemente,* pp. 138, 270–72.

believed, and rightly so, that money was available for good projects.

It has been suggested that the existence of this technological gap created a tension between reality and possibility in the minds of Russian policy makers.[108] No doubt this was true. But such a general and ill-defined feeling might have had limited consequence without the concrete investment-producing tension and excitement that came from a well-conceived report on a *particular* investment opportunity. There the gap and the promise stood out boldly for people who had the capacity to respond with genuine investment decisions.

This is related to the entrepreneurial types we have distinguished, and which constituted foreign entrepreneurship in the broad sense. The individual promoter, like the Russian government, had a generalized awareness of the technology gap. But in most cases (the coal industry was an important exception) the individual promoter's role was limited to initial investigations. He did not have the technical expertise to pass final judgment on a specific investment project and to build and then operate sophisticated equipment. This was precisely what the foreign firm could and did do with great regularity. It could test the generalized perception of backwardness in a specific instance as it supplied investment-making and profit-earning capacity. Subsequently, the groups, which developed out of a successful venture, routinized the tasks of promoters who sought and assembled opportunities and of firms that evaluated and implemented them. They built up their own permanent agents and engineering capacity to carry further foreign investment forward as a matter of course.

108. Gerschenkron, *Economic Backwardness*, p. 8.

4

ADVANCED TECHNOLOGY IN
STEEL AND COAL

According to our model of foreign entrepreneurship, foreign businessmen believed that their advanced industrial technology was their primary asset in their pursuit of large profits. A detailed analysis of technical considerations in the foreign-dominated steel and coal industries, with particular reference to southern Russia, provides additional support for this interpretation. It is also possible to see to what extent foreigners gained the profits they sought in two major instances. A study of these industries also provides evidence concerning the macroquestion of whether or not foreigners had a pervasive impact upon the entire Russian economy, along some of the lines indicated in chapter 1.

1

The fusion of coal and iron ore to produce first iron and then steel in quantity for railroads and machinery—Schumpeter's railroadization—was one of the central technological relationships underpinning economic growth in the nineteenth century. The long absence of such a relationship in Russia was certainly associated with the lack of pervasive industrial development before the end of the nineteenth century. A hearty newcomer under Peter and a lusty youngster under Catherine, eighteenth-century Russian metallurgy, which for a considerable period led the world in the production of pig iron, failed to come of age and adopt the methods of the industrial revolution. In the nineteenth century the famed producers of the Urals stagnated with charcoal-iron techniques and servile labor until 1861. With free labor they did no better.

In the face of such technical and psychological blocks the government encouraged new producers in both northern Russia and Poland to build modern steel-making facilities to process imported pig iron in the 1860s and 1870s. After these efforts proved successful, the government promoted the substitution of domestic pig iron from southern Russia for imported pig iron. This in turn led foreign entrepreneurs to establish a vast integrated steel industry in southern Russia, the most exciting and the most important economic achievement of Russia's fin de siècle industrial surge. This achievement was consolidated and extended in the next decade and a half. By 1908 the entire steel industry had regained its 1900 level of pig iron production, and it then expanded more than 60 percent to reach its prewar high in 1913. It is against this background that foreign investment strategy and impact may be analyzed.

From the 1870s onward foreign entrepreneurs consistently provided technical expertise to realize the profit potential of modern steel making in backward Russia. Three early foreign ventures in each of the three major producing areas outside southern Russia show this clearly. When the Huta-Bankova Steel Company, which is examined in detail in chapter 11, took Plemiannikov's Polish ironworks in 1877, there were four small blast furnaces, seventeen puddling furnaces, nine reheating ovens, an average-sized rolling mill, and two small mills with the various accessories. In short, the plant made iron products in small quantities, and perhaps puddled steel. There were neither Bessemer converters nor Siemens-Martin open-hearth furnaces; nor were there mills capable of rolling steel rails. Yet the making of steel and the rolling of rails were precisely the new firm's purpose. This purpose required complete technical reorganization. Vastly improved methods were subsequently rewarded with high profits and brilliant success.

The Société de Terrenoire, a leading French steel producer of the Loire Valley, provided technical aid to another important enterprise at the same time. In 1877 Terrenoire combined with George Baird, a St. Petersburg shipbuilder of Scottish descent, in founding the Alexandrovskii Steel Company, to which it supplied all plans and techniques, to fill an order for 1,800,000 puds (29,500 tons) of steel rails which the government had just awarded to Baird. Using an abandoned, unsuccessful, government-operated carding factory, which the new company purchased for one-fourth the original cost, the experts from Terrenoire installed Martin furnaces and rolling mills to transform English pig iron (first Cumberland, then Cleveland) into twenty-four-foot steel rails. According to the management the results were perfect both quantitatively and qualitatively,[1] and at least one impartial observer agreed.

The directors of the firm were always French engineers who seem to have kept abreast of technical progress.[2] Thus the plant was using cheaper phos-

1. A.N., 65 AQ, K 4, Aciéries d'Alexandrovski, Annual Report, 25–5–1881; *Le Pour et le Contre*, 19–8–1894.
2. The first director was Eugène Beau, previously director of the Société des Aciéries de la Marine at St. Chamond; he was seconded by F. Walton, the chief technical director, who was previously an engineer with Terrenoire. In 1892 the director was O. Murisier, an engineer from the Ecole Centrale. See the detailed and laudatory discussion of the Russian firm and its French tech-

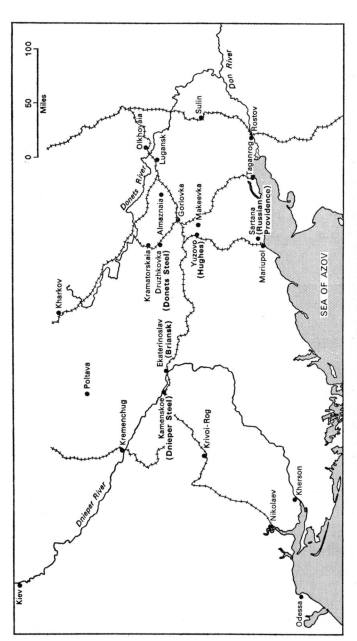

THE SOUTHERN INDUSTRIAL REGION IN 1914

phoric pig iron by 1881, three years after Thomas-Gilchrist's great discovery permitted the use of such pig iron in Bessemer converters. Using Terrenoire patents, Alexandrovskii pioneered in unpitted steel (*acier sans soufflures*) which was required for heavy artillery shells and was preferred for boilers.[3] The development of the Russian firm actually paralleled that of the French parent. The parent became a producer of specialty and military products after the advent of cheap Lorraine steel. By doing so, it developed techniques which permitted Alexandrovskii to make a similar shift from rails to specialties in the face of competition from the expanding steel and rail producers of the Donets.

A third French venture in steel making was a Lyonnese creation founded in the Urals in 1879, the Franco-Russian Ural Company. This enterprise combined the technical direction of Charles Barrouin, general director of the Société des Forges et Aciéries de St. Etienne, the financial assistance of the ill-fated Union Générale, and the vast natural resources of a Ural magnate. The properties of Prince Serge Golitsyn were a small kingdom of one-half million hectares of forests and iron deposits exploited by three small ironworks. Annual output, however, was only 5,000 tons of puddled iron. On the basis of reports by an engineer from the Ecole Centrale in Paris named Delmont, who was associated with Petin et Gaudet of Lyons, the new firm planned new works capable of producing an additional 20,000 tons of steel rails per year.[4]

---

nicians in A.N., F 12, no. 7175, Rapport sur l'industrie métallurgique en Russie, 22–10–1892.

3. A.N., 65 AQ, K 4, Annual Report, 22–10–1882.

4. See A.N., 65 AQ, K 164, Articles of Incorporation, and various brochures and articles cited in chapter 11.

This was one of the first attempts to make steel rails in the Urals. By 1900 four charcoal blast furnaces of fifteen tons each, equipped with the still-unusual hot blast, were smelting 42,000 tons of pig iron. Well-run mills rolled 29,000 tons of high-quality steel products. Thus pig-iron production increased more than eightfold, as opposed to a threefold increase for all Ural producers from 1879 to 1900. The reorganized firm also had the lowest costs of production in the Urals, and it offered, by way of contrast, clear evidence of the well-known inadequacy of entrepreneurs and managers in the Urals.[5]

These efforts at implanting more advanced technology were the dress rehearsal for foreign activity in the South Russian steel industry after 1884. The Englishman John Hughes had of course already pioneered there with modern mills, beginning in 1870. His ultimate success, however, like that of those who followed in the late 1880s, was not assured until the long-discussed Catherine Railroad linked Krivoi-Rog iron and Donets coking coal in 1884. Afterward, foreign domination of this new investment opportunity was almost total. Between the founding of the all-important South Russian Dnieper Metallurgical Company in 1888 (see chapter 9), and the end of the period of company formation in 1900, there was only one completely Russian southern steel maker in operation.[6] That was the Sulin (or Pastukhov) firm,

5. C.L., Aciéries de la Kama, various studies. For the backwardness of Ural producers in the nineteenth century and the factors in their entrepreneurial failure see below, and M. Tugan-Baranovskii, *Russkaia fabrika v proshlom i nastoiashchem* (St. Petersburg, 1899), pp. 299–304; Khromov, *Ekonomicheskoe razvitie*, pp. 195–96; Brandt, *Inostrannye kapitaly*, 2:89–106; R. S. Livshits, *Razmeshchenie promyshlennosti v dorevoliutsionnoi Rossii* (Moscow, 1954), pp. 123–29, 209–17.

6. C.L., La Métallurgie dans le Midi de la Russie, Etude Géné-

which had the double distinction of being the oldest (1876) and the least significant southern steel producer. (Even Sulin had a French technical director most of the time and some French foremen.) Thus foreign technology and southern technology were synonymous for all practical purposes.

Foreigners had little trouble convincing themselves that there was a technology gap in the steel industry. In the first place, the relative stagnation of both technique and production in the steel industry of the Urals was well known. The very slow diffusion of the highly economical hot blast in blast furnaces, a Scottish advance dating from 1829, is a striking example. Thus an Austrian traveler in the Urals saw no evidence of this technique in 1870, while an English manager of Russian ironworks at the same time said that "the cold blast is invariably used throughout much of the Urals."[7] Here was a serious failure which the alibi of inadequate coking coal and poor transportation could not excuse. As Glivits shows, the cold blast held on tenaciously: in 1880 there were 110 Russian furnaces working with cold blast and 90 with hot blast; in 1890 there were 69 with cold and 145 with hot; and in 1908 there were still 16 cold-blast furnaces out of a total of 185. Mechanization in general was limited in the Ural industry. The use of energy in steam and electric engines per steel worker, for example, was twenty

rale, April 1905. (Hereafter cited as C.L., Métallurgie dans le Midi, April 1905.) This very long and extremely detailed study, apparently written by Mr. Blanc, sums up the findings of numerous on-the-spot investigations of all the major producers over a period of years. This chapter is based primarily upon the wealth of material on Donets metallurgy at the Crédit Lyonnais.

7. Brandt, *Inostrannye kapitaly*, 2:95; Herbert Barry, *Russian Metallurgical Works* (London, 1870), p. 23.

times as high in the southern areas as in the Urals in 1890.[8]

In the second place, the achievements of steel fabricators outside the Urals, like the Huta-Bankova in Poland, or the Alexandrovskii Company at St. Petersburg, were stopgaps. The logic of modern steel making demanded an integration of smelting, refining, and processing for optimal efficiency. Such integration was clearly feasible in the Donets after 1884, when the Catherine Railroad assured the success of Hughes's integrated steel mill, which then served as a model to emulate and surpass.

Did foreigners use really advanced technology in southern mills after 1885? If so, how advanced was it? Was there a common strategy and an average performance, or were there great differences among firms? To answer these questions one must examine in detail those southern steel companies founded in our period.

The uniformity of foreign behavior in the southern steel industry was striking. Whatever the source of initial interest, or the timing of active foreign involvement, foreign entrepreneurs dominated the crucial period of the investment process for any given firm. In every venture they were present by the time of the all-important detailed technical study, and they remained in control at least until the plants they conceived and built achieved normal operation.

These technical studies followed the usual pattern discussed in the previous chapter. Usually the analysis of raw materials was related to specific available concessions of individual Russians or foreign

8. I. Glivits, *Zheleznaia promyshlennost' Rossii* (St. Petersburg, 1911), p. 113.

promoters. On the basis of these and other inputs the foreign engineer estimated production costs for some or all the products of a modern steel mill. Then he analyzed rapidly, sometimes too rapidly, the market for steel goods. After thereby establishing a wide spread between selling prices and production costs, he figured the estimated annual return on the investment required to build the new plant. Then the final investment decision was made on the basis of these data.

What is particularly significant is that the complete "modern steel mill" appeared as a given in these calculations. Foreign engineers had, it seems, a fixed conception of rational steel making, and this conception could be modified only within narrow limits. Thus foreign entrepreneurs built plants embodying standard, completely proved techniques. This meant that, on the one hand, they strictly limited their concessions to Russian backwardness and that, on the other, they ruled out innovations or experiments, which they felt were best confined to their home plants. Engineers and entrepreneurs were of course aware that modern plants would cost more in Russia, and they did their best to calculate this difference, piece by piece, division by division. Costs would be different, therefore, but techniques would be almost identical.

Analysis of integrated steel mills by their three major divisions—blast furnaces, steel refining, and finishing mills—shows this was the case. Although blast furnaces were unquestionably modern, they were of only average dimension in comparison with *new* furnaces in construction in western Europe in the 1890s.[9] Of the fifty-six operational furnaces com-

---

9. C.L., Métallurgie dans le Midi, April 1905.

pleted in southern Russia by 1901, almost all produced from 120 to 180 tons of pig iron every
twenty-four hours, or 50,000 annually.

There were no really small blast furnaces in
southern Russia, with the exception of those of the
Krivoi-Rog Iron Company and one at Hughes, all of
which had been built before 1888. The first two furnaces of the Dnieper Company in 1888 and 1890
produced approximately 130 tons in twenty-four
hours, while those of the Donets Steel Company
built in the early nineties produced 150 tons. At the
end of the boom a few larger furnaces were built.
The Briansk, Kramatorskaia, and Nikopol-Mariupol
Companies each built a furnace to produce at least
300 tons, and the Russo-Belgian Company built four
with a capacity of 250 tons each. But the new furnaces at Makeevka, Donets-Yur'evka, and Olkhovaia
Companies in the late 1890s produced 180 to 190
tons, or only moderately more than the new furnaces
of the early 1890s.

Production figures are, of course, also dependent
upon the quality of iron ore used: the richer the ore,
the greater the output in a given furnace for a given
period of time. Russian ore from the Krivoi-Rog
averaged 60 to 65 percent pure iron. It was much
richer than the iron ore in the Lorraine field serving
much of western Europe, which averaged between
30 and 40 percent pure iron. Therefore Russian furnaces required on the average only 1.7 tons of ore
for each ton of pig iron, as opposed to 2.5 tons of ore
throughout most of western Europe.[10] This also
meant that the output of identical furnaces in west-

10. S. G. Strumilin, *Chernaia metallurgiia v Rossii i S.S.S.R.*
(Moscow, 1935), pp. 257–59; T. H. Burnham and G. O. Hoskins,
Iron and Steel in Britain, 1870–1913 (London, 1943), pp. 111–12,
295–99.

ern Europe and Russia would normally vary considerably, and in Russia's favor.

All equipment being equal, it seems the greater richness of iron ore gave south Russian blast furnaces about 40 percent more output in a given time span. This may be seen to some extent in table 10. More specifically, it is clear that in about 1903 recently constructed blast furnaces in Lorraine (French and German) had a volume of 500 to 550 cubic meters and produced 180 to 200 tons in twenty-four hours. At the same time the Briansk Company's very up-to-date number 5 blast furnace, completed in 1900, had a volume of 550 cubic meters. It averaged 260 tons of pig iron daily between 1901 and 1903 with ore 58 percent pure, and attained a maximum output of 300 tons.[11]

The difference in ore may account for the erroneous impression sometimes conveyed that new blast furnaces were bigger or more advanced in Russia than in western Europe. True, production per furnace was higher in Russia, as table 10 shows, but the size of new furnaces was similar. Russia itself had such differences in output related to the quality of iron ore. The furnaces on the Kerch Peninsula of the Kerch Metallurgical Company were large and extremely efficient, and they would have produced from 250 to 300 tons in twenty-four hours with Krivoi-Rog ores. Instead they produced 150 to

11. E. Lamoureux, "Gesichtspunkte beim Bau moderner Hochöften," *Stahl und Eisen,* 10:1 (1904) : 390; Modeste Pierrone, "Résultats pratiques de la marche des hauts-fourneaux d'Ekaterinoslaw (Société de Briansk) de 1887 à 1903," *Revue de Métallurgie,* 2 (1905): 678–79. Also, the same author's "Diagramme comparatif des hauts-fourneaux de la Société de Briansk et divers hauts-fourneaux," *Revue Universelle des Mines,* 3d ser., 39 (1897) : 81.

175 tons in a like period with the poor, Lorraine-like ore of Kerch in 1900.

One should also note the widespread gradual increase of furnace size after 1900 shown in table 10. The furnaces of the early nineties were about 20 meters high with a volume of 340 cubic meters and produced 150 tons in twenty-four hours (for example, furnaces 3 and 4 at Briansk). Those of the late nineties were about 22 meters high with a cubic volume of 400 meters and produced 180 tons (Ma-

Table 10

AVERAGE YEARLY OUTPUT PER BLAST FURNACE
IN SELECTED AREAS
(In Tons)

	1880	1890	1900	1910	1913
All Russia	2,300	4,300	9,600	19,500	28,000
South Russia	6,900	15,500	47,000	59,000	63,000
Great Britain			22,500	30,000	
Germany			31,000	49,000	
France			21,000	34,500	
Belgium			27,000	46,000	
United States			56,000	100,000	

SOURCES: S. G. Strumilin, *Chernaia Metallurgia v Rossii i S.S.S.R.* (Moscow, 1935), pp. 245, 247, 252; Glivits, *Zheleznaia promyshlennost'*, p. 114; T. H. Burnham and G. O. Hoskins, *Iron and Steel in Britain, 1870–1930* (London, 1943), p. 145.

keevka, for example), with a few as large as Briansk's number 5 mentioned above. By 1914 most furnaces had been reconstructed with a height of at least 24 meters, volume of 470 cubic meters, and daily productive capacity of at least 250 tons. In these progressive enlargements Russian furnaces again reflected the level of proved metallurgical techniques in western Europe, without in any way going beyond it. In 1913 annual output of pig iron per worker was 294 tons in southern Russia, as opposed to 205 tons per worker in Russia as a whole, and 239 tons in France, 356 in Great Britain, 404 in Germany, and 811 in the United States.[12]

All furnaces were well equipped with proper accessories. There was none of that mindless technical negligence of the Ural producers. Four towering Cowpers surrounding each furnace heated air several hundred degrees before it was then pushed by powerful steam-driven blowers of leading makers (Cockerill, Le Creusot, Klein) into the fiery inferno of the blast furnace. Each firm invariably converted heat from gases escaping from the blast furnaces into useful energy according to standard practice in western Europe. These gases were first used to generate steam for steam engines, then for steam turbines at the central electrical station by 1900, and finally by 1914 directly in gas-driven turbines producing electricity. Thus Mr. Blanc, the Crédit Lyonnais's engineer, who knew both south-Russian and Western practices as very few did, estimated in his 1905 study that the blast furnace divisions of southern producers were generally very satisfactory. His major regrets concerned the medium size of the average furnace and the slow diffusion of the advanced, difficult-to-master, gas-driven turbine.

Pig iron from the blast furnace division was refined in Bessemer, Martin, and Thomas steel-making facilities. These followed Western techniques closely without improving upon them. Bessemer and Thomas steelworks had two or three converters of eight to ten tons each arranged in line, and these converters, like those of the Dnieper Company in

---

12. Strumilin, *Chernaia metallurgiia*, p. 281; Khromov, *Ekonomicheskoe razvitie,* p. 327.

1898, had "nothing exceptional." Nothing exceptional, that is, in comparison with the modern Western steel mills after which they were modeled.[13] Martin works were less uniform. Even in 1904 only Ural-Volga and the Dnieper Company charged ore and scrap iron mechanically—standard practice in western Europe—and only Donets-Yur'evka refined pig iron solely with raw ore and without adding expensive scrap iron, in accordance with the so-called ore process, a difficult but growing practice in western Europe.[14] Hearth capacity of Martin furnaces almost doubled from the late nineties to 1913. The normal twenty-ton hearth was rebuilt with thirty-ton capacity, while new hearths of forty to fifty tons were being installed before the war. Unquestionably, southern Russia remained in the mainstream of world progress in steel making.

The finishing division consisted of a variety of rolling mills. Almost every plant had numerous mills, generally constructed in the following order: the rail mill; mills for girders, beams, and other structural shapes; then two or three mills for sheets of varying gauge. After 1900 mills for corrugated roofing steel, long a specialty of producers in the Urals, were also added by several southern firms. All these rolling mills were generally good, and they did not suffer in comparison with those of western Europe. They were in no way spectacular, however. For instance, in 1904 only Donets-Yur'evka among southern producers had a small mill for structural pieces driven by electricity. Donets Steel was also considering a similar system. Steam-powered rolling mills also predominated in western Europe at

13. C.L., Dniéprovienne, Etude, December 1898; Métallurgie dans le Midi, April 1905.
14. Ibid.

the time, but there was an increasing use of and experimentation with electricity as a power source.[15] On the eve of the First World War, however, when electricity was commonly used for small rolling mills in western Europe, there were several electric mills in southern Russia. Once again the Russian industry followed closely behind proved Western practice.

In short, the Russian steel mills, installed by foreign engineers, ''are well-conceived and follow the plans of great German, Belgian, and French enterprises. . . . The general layout is almost always good.''[16] This was less true of the earlier factories than the later ones. The earlier companies grew a trifle haphazardly, while those between 1895 and 1899 were built as a single piece. There were some differences between plants. Yet these differences also show that Western engineers built their Russian plants primarily as copies of those at home. This may be seen by an examination of machinery, such as steam engines. Generally the Belgians used engines from Cockerill, the French those of Le Creusot or the Cie Alsacienne, and the Germans those of Klein or Fitzner-Gamper. Familiar names aided in the duplication of familiar practice in an alien land.

Likewise, key innovations in the Russian steel industry were usually associated with innovations at some firm's home plant. The pattern of parallel technical change at both parent and affiliate, of which the Terrenoire-Alexandrovskii combination was an example, was widespread. Thus the South Russian Dnieper Company was apparently the first Russian firm to harness the escaping gases of blast

15. Ibid.
16. Ibid.

furnaces in gas turbines to generate electricity. This had occurred by 1904, six short years after the parent firm, Société John Cockerill, had successfully introduced this technique to Western metallurgy.[17]

At Donets-Yur'evka the German engineers from the Friedenhütte of Upper Silesia tried, unsuccessfully, to employ the Witkowitz process, first developed in their area.[18] This remarkable process combined Bessemer and Martin steel production. Bessemer converters removed part of the impurities in pig iron, and then the Martin open-hearth furnace completed the process. This process permitted production of the complete gamut of Bessemer and Martin steels without two separate divisions, and therefore saved considerable capital. The process failed in Russia. Yet according to the Crédit Lyonnais's engineer, the German engineers of Donets-Yur'evka were nonetheless the most skillful producers of Martin steel in Russia.[19]

The Nikopol-Mariupol Company showed the preferences of its American constructors. Both "remarkably installed" blast furnaces (1898) were equipped with the first automatic hoists on inclined planes (the Duquesne system) ever used any place in Europe, according to the Crédit Lyonnais's engineer. This "very ingenious" system eliminated the

17. C.L., Dniéprovienne, September 1904; *110ᵉ Anniversaire de la fondation des usines Cockerill, 1817–1927* (Brussels, 1927), p. 46. Previously these gases heated boilers to create steam for steam engines. Gas engines recovered more of the heat energy of escaping gases than did boilers.

18. C.L., Donetz-Yourievka, Etude, December 1900; *L'Information,* 30–4–1908.

19. C.L., Métallurgie, April 1905; for complete plant description see *Société Métallurgique du Donetz-Yourievka,* a pamphlet presented at the Paris World's Fair of 1900, in the Crédit Lyonnais dossier.

elevator and replaced three workers on the platform next to the cone of the furnace with a single skilled mechanic overseeing the automatic operation. Each of Nikopol-Mariupol's blast furnaces had poured as much as 350 tons of pig iron in twenty-four hours, which was probably the record in Russia before 1900. Production of 300 tons per furnace was normal. A metallic skirt around the furnaces, apparently rare in western Europe, minimized heat loss, and "very handsome" powerful blowers contributed to this impressive output. Nikopol-Mariupol was primarily a tube producer, having bought an entire tube plant secondhand in America.[20]

Similarly Makeevka Steel, always French to the core, was apparently the first company to adopt the Hérault electric furnace in Russia, which it did by 1910. The electric furnace was probably the key French metallurgical innovation in the years before 1914.[21] These idiosyncracies of innovation reflect the foreigner's attempt to reproduce familiar techniques in Russia.

Foreign entrepreneurs also copied the structure of their own firms. With few exceptions they built large, completely integrated, and diversified steel producers which worked toward perfect balance between the three different divisions—blast furnaces, steelworks, and rolling mills. The assumption was simple. Firms with such structures had proved most satisfactory in Europe and America; a priori Russia too would follow the same pattern, and in fact it did.[22] Thus every firm needed at least two blast fur-

20. C.L., Nikopol-Mariupol, Etudes, November 1901, February 1904.

21. Glivits, *Zheleznaia promyshlennost'*, p. 126; *Science et Industrie* 8 (April 1924) : 69.

22. Glivits, *Zheleznaia promyshlennost'*, pp. 48 ff.

naces capable of producing 100,000 tons of pig iron annually, a Martin steelworks, a Bessemer steelworks, at least three or four mills for all shapes of structural steel and rails, and at least three rolling mills for heavy, medium, and thick sheets. Only by observing such technical indivisibilities could the right steel be used for the right finished product at the lowest cost.[23] Only such a large integrated producer could respond flexibly to shifts in demand and profitability. Thus firms in the late 1890s built the obvious rail facilities, but they also moved quickly into the rapidly expanding and more profitable (from 1896 to 1899) private market.

Integration also meant control of raw materials, particularly Krivoi-Rog iron ore. The early pioneers obtained these wonderful ores with minimal difficulty. By 1895, however, widespread fears of rapid exhaustion of Krivoi-Rog deposits and very high prices for those ores encouraged foreign engineers to seek alternative supplies. The price of Krivoi-Rog ore, which oscillated from four to six kopecks per pud (6.5 to 9.7 francs per ton) until 1895, doubled to nine or ten kopecks per pud by 1898. This increase was due mainly to higher royalties for Russian owners, which soared from between one-half

23. The second blast furnace was essential, for instance, to assure continuous output of pig iron. Similarly, Bessemer steel is normally cheaper than Siemens-Martin steel, since the process of decarburization in the converter occurs rapidly in ten to twenty minutes as opposed to several hours in the open hearth. The quality of Bessemer steel is inferior for many products, but it was ideal for rails and government demand, as Martin steel was ideal for sheets and the private market. Thus the need for both facilities and the balance between them. See David S. Landes, "Technical Change and Industrial Development in Western Europe," in H. J. Habakkuk and M. Postan, eds., *The Cambridge Economic History*, vol. 6: *The Industrial Revolution and After* (Cambridge, 1965), pp. 477 ff.

and three-quarters kopecks per pud in the early 1890s to three kopecks per pud after 1895.[24]

This challenging situation provided the incentive for one foreign technical achievement seldom even mentioned in the literature on Russian development —the *mise-en-valeur* of the iron ores of the Kerch Peninsula on the Sea of Azov. Two Belgian firms, the Société des Forges de la Providence and the Société Ougrée-Marihaye, both experts in Thomas steel production with low-grade phosphoric ores from Lorraine, focused on the enormous and completely neglected low-grade Kerch ores as an alternative to the dwindling supplies of Krivoi-Rog in 1896. With reserves estimated at 700,000,000 tons in 1903, or ten times those of estimated Krivoi-Rog reserves at the same time, the poor Kerch ores resembled those of the Luxemburg field.

Kerch ore was actually inferior to Luxemburg ore. It was only 33 to 35 percent pure, phosphoric, very humid, and granular. Worse, the phosphorus content of 1 percent was insufficient for the Thomas process without the addition of phosphates; but it was too much for normal Bessemer methods. Manganese varied irregularly from 1 to 4 percent, with pockets holding up to 20 percent. This posed the greatest problem of all.[25] Yet with open-pit mining and a royalty of one-quarter kopeck per pud, this ore cost an average of 1.5 kopecks per pud—about 15 to 20 percent as much as Krivoi-Rog ore per pud, or 30 to 40 percent as much per unit of pure iron.[26] Here was a possible saving on the principal input

24. C.L., Société des Mines de Krivoi-Rog, September 1912. To convert kopecks per pud to francs per (metric) ton, multiply by 1.62.

25. See C.L., Métallurgie dans le Midi, April 1905, and various studies there on the Providence Russe and Taganrog.

26. C.L., Doubovaia-Balka, Etude, August 1899; C.L., Métallurgie dans le Midi, April 1905.

worthy of great efforts, and the calculated gamble of dynamic entrepreneurship.

The efforts of the Russian Providence, the Taganrog, and later the Kerch, companies to use Kerch ores were eventually successful. But this result came only after a long series of experiments, experiments necessary to convert success in the laboratory into success on an industrial scale. The Kerch Metallurgical Company eventually grilled its ore and then agglomerated it into briquettes. Grilling removed water and some impurities, which raised the iron content, while briquettes did not clog the blast furnace as did untreated Kerch ore in its powdery form. This also permitted the furnaces of this company to use only Kerch ore. The Russian Providence Company had also intended to utilize only Kerch ores initially, but without grilling or briquetting. Technically successful, this method consumed 50 percent more coke than did Krivoi-Rog ores, halved production, and occasionally clogged furnaces. The Luxemburg experts who ran the firm finally mixed 25 percent of the lumpy Krivoi-Rog ore with the untreated Kerch ore to alleviate these problems. In 1909 financial resources for the installation of grilling and briquetting were found, and afterward only Kerch ore was used. Taganrog originally planned to use one-third Krivoi-Rog ore, and thereby apply the Bessemer process. The successful use of Kerch ores by foreign entrepreneurs was a very impressive technical achievement of great potential significance. It meant that had Krivoi-Rog ores become exhausted, or had Ural iron deposits never been linked with Siberian coal, Russia still could have produced pig iron and steel in any necessary quantity at moderate cost.

Perhaps there is some fatal flaw in this picture of advanced foreign technology. Specifically, one might ask if the application of advanced techniques for massive production also gave satisfactory costs of production. One acid test involves a comparison with the steel producers of western Europe. One finds that costs of production in the mills of southern Russia were not greatly higher than those in western Europe, although the more highly finished products compared less favorably, as one might expect. The best comparison is probably with Belgian producers, who paid almost exactly the same amount as Russian producers for raw materials.

In Belgium the cost of raw materials (*lit de fusion*) in a ton of Thomas steel averaged 53.3 francs per ton in 1903.[27] In early 1905 Russian producers also paid, on the average, 53.3 francs per ton (32.8 kopecks per pud). (At that time Russian raw materials were as cheap as they ever were after 1894.) From this equality in the cost of raw materials one finds considerable variation among Russian producers in their costs of smelting these materials into pig iron. These costs ranged from four to 6.5 kopecks per pud (6.5 to 10.5 francs per ton), while averaging 5.5 kopecks per pud, or 8.9 francs per ton, as opposed to six francs per ton in Belgium. Thus the engineers of the Crédit Lyonnais estimated the cost of pig iron at about sixty francs per ton in Belgium and sixty-two francs per ton (38.8 kopecks per pud) in Russia. (Overhead and depreciation were carried on the final finished products, since both Russian and Belgian producers wished to avoid selling intermediary goods.)

A comparison of semifinished goods, the next step in the production process, adds further light. Refin-

27. C.L., Société John Cockerill, Etude, September 1903. By Belgian companies we refer to Cockerill, Ougrée-Marihaye, Angleur, Providence, and Marcinelle-Couillet.

ing costs in Russia averaged about seventeen kopecks per pud (27.5 francs per ton). Thus Bessemer
steel in ingots varied in cost from fifty-one to fifty-
eight kopecks per pud (82.6 to ninety-four francs
per ton), Martin steel from fifty-five to sixty-three
kopecks per pud (89.1 to 102.1 francs per ton), while
the major Thomas producer had a cost of fifty-seven
kopecks per pud (92.3 francs per ton). Here direct
comparison is difficult, since Western producers
were abandoning the acid process for the basic process in order to use Lorraine ores. Note, however,
that Bessemer ingots at Cockerill, the lone Belgian
producer of acid steel from Spanish ores, cost
eighty-eight francs per ton to produce, while
Thomas ingots suitable for rails (*acier dur*) cost
eighty-six francs per ton, on the average, in other
plants. The cost of refining steel in the best Russian mills was less than 10 percent more than in
Belgium.

It comes as no surprise therefore that the costs of
finished products for the better Russian producers
were fairly close to those for the Belgian steelmak-
ers. The cost of rails at the best Belgian mills
ranged from 105 to 110 francs per ton at the plant;
in Russia they ranged from 113 to 154 francs per ton
(70 to 90 kopecks per pud). In 1905 the best Russian
plants were indeed close to their Belgian counterparts in the costs of production of rails, all expenses
and depreciation included: the Russo-Belgian Company produced rails for 113 francs per ton (70 kopecks per pud); the Dnieper Company for 121
francs per ton (75 kopecks per pud); and Donets
Steel and Hughes for 125 francs per ton (77 kopecks
per pud).[28] The Russian disadvantage was due pri-

28. C.L., Métallurgie dans le Midi, April 1905 and other studies
on the individual firms. These very detailed studies on the cost

marily to the poorer quality of Russian labor, which was felt particularly in the highly skilled work of the rolling mills. A plant would reach Western costs only as the quality of this human ingredient was gradually improved.

Costs of production in 1905 represented a considerable reduction from those in 1899. According to the Crédit Lyonnais reports, the average cost of production of 48.8 kopecks per pud (75.4 francs per ton) for pig iron in 1899 was unnecessarily high because of inexperienced personnel and the complacency of boom times. In the next five years mills realized their potential, and the average cost of production of pig iron was reduced by 10 kopecks to 38.8 kopecks per pud—a reduction of 20 percent. Half of this decline was attributed to a 50 percent decrease in fabricating costs; 35 percent came from cheaper raw materials; and 15 percent came from the abolition of the 1.5-kopeck per pud excise tax.[29]

Cost reductions attributable to lower manufacturing costs were also sizable for steel ingots and rolled products, as the 1899 estimates of a careful Russian observer show. In 1899 the costs of production for pig iron, Martin steel, and large sections were respectively 45.6 kopecks per pud, 105 kopecks per pud, and 171 kopecks per pud.[30] Fitting these estimates to those of Blanc for 1905, one sees reductions of 6.8 kopecks per pud for pig iron, 50 kopecks per pud for Martin steel, and 90 kopecks per pud for

structures of Russian (and Belgian and French) steel producers may very well be unique. Then, as now, no secret was more carefully guarded than costs of production, which determined per unit profits and market power.

29. C.L., *Métallurgie dans le Midi*, April 1905.

30. I. A. Time, *Spravochnaia kniga dlia gornykh inzhenerov i tekhnikov po gornoi chasti,* 2d ed. (St. Petersburg, 1899), pp. 701–11.

rails and large sections. The mastering of excellent equipment enabled entrepreneurs to reduce their costs significantly during the depression years after 1900.[31]

What about general gains for the Russian economy? Did foreign entrepreneurs in the steel industry make a powerful impact and thereby contribute to development? The answer is an unequivocable yes. First, previously underutilized, or for the most part unutilized, resources were turned to productive purposes, just as Brandt had argued at the turn of the century in his spirited defense of foreign capital in Russia.[32] Russian output and Russian income were thus raised because foreign funds and foreign entrepreneurship permitted a higher level of investment.

Second, foreigners did succeed in their attempts to establish a modern steel industry. Productivity of workers in southern mills was much higher than in the Urals: in 1890 southern metallurgical workers were five times as efficient as those in the Urals; in 1900, they were 5.6 times as efficient; and in 1909, ten times.[33] More importantly, southern mills were comparable to those in western Europe, as we have seen. Blast furnaces in the South, for example, were as large as in western Europe, and because they were newer and used better ore, they produced more.

Third, foreigners' advanced technology resulted in lower production costs, and this permitted an almost continuous fall in steel prices. As a primary industrial good, cheaper steel meant cheaper inputs for the entire economy, and consequently new investment opportunities. This important contribu-

31. C. L., Métallurgie dans le Midi, April 1905.
32. Brandt, *Inostrannye kapitaly,* 2:203–5.
33. Glivits, *Zheleznaia promyshlennost',* p. 114.

tion has often been overlooked—and no wonder, in view of the attacks ad nauseam on monopoly capitalism in Russia. Whatever else may be said about the informal and formal (after 1903) selling agreements, they did not stop the steady drift toward lower prices from 1890 to 1910. Glivits's invaluable list of selling prices at the mill for a major southern producer, apparently the South Russian Dnieper Metallurgical Company, shows this very clearly. (See table 11.)

Table 11

PRICES OF A LEADING SOUTHERN STEEL PRODUCER
(Kopecks per Pud)

Year	Rails	Merchant Iron	Steel Wheels
1889–1890	156	195	277
1899–1900	117	173	178
1909–1910	109	115	148

SOURCE: Glivits, *Zheleznaia promyshlennost'*, pp. 94–95.

From Glivits's prices for these and other steel products, one scholar has constructed an unweighted price index for finished products in southern Russia. This index shows a decline of 22 percent from 1889–90 to 1898–99, and a further decline of 30 percent from 1899–1900 to 1909–10.[34]

It is true that prices rose after 1910, the last date covered by Glivits in his 1911 publication. But judging by the movement of prices for sheets and girders on the St. Petersburg Metal Exchange, which moved in harmony with Glivits's index before 1910, prices for finished goods apparently rose by only 10 per-

34. Abraham Burnstein, "Iron and Steel in Russia, 1861–1913" (unpublished Ph.D. dissertation, New School for Social Research, 1963), pp. 263–64.

cent between 1910 and 1913.[35] The desire to put the
phenomenon in a traditional language is irresisti-
ble: after 1900, during the period of imperialism, the
highest stage of monopoly capitalism, foreign steel
companies ruthlessly exploited Russia—and lowered their selling prices by about 20 percent.

Fourth, development of the steel industry made
Russia self-sufficient in basic metallurgical products. The long-standing goal of policy makers was
attained. Whereas domestically produced pig iron
accounted for only 67 percent of Russian consumption of pig iron in 1883, it represented 89 percent of
Russian consumption in 1888 and continued to rise
while demand soared. In 1893 local production accounted for 90 percent of consumption; in 1898, 95
percent; in 1903, 99 percent; in 1908, 100 percent;
and in 1913, 99 percent.[36]

A continuing trickle of imports was due primarily
to costs of transportation to St. Petersburg and the
Baltic provinces from the Donets. (Southern producers paid eighteen kopecks to transport a pud of
pig iron to St. Petersburg by rail in 1904; whereas it
cost English coal producers only six kopecks to put
their coal in at St. Petersburg by ship.) [37] These
imports were offset by exports, primarily of rails,
through the Black Sea to a number of countries in
the Balkans, the Mediterranean, and South America. Self-sufficiency in basic steel production was
also achieved for the foreseeable future. Indeed, the
foreign response in the late 1890s was so great that
steel mills operated at only 50 to 60 percent capacity

35. Ibid., pp. 264–65.

36. Gornyi Departament, *Obshchii obzor glavykh otraslei
gornoi i gornozavodskoi promyshlennosti* (Petrograd, 1915), as
quoted by Burnstein, "Iron and Steel," p. 211.

37. C.L., Laminoirs de St. Petersburg, Etude, December 1904.

from 1900 to 1909. This excess capacity permitted southern producers to increase their production by 50 percent between 1910 and 1913 with ease, and with profound relief.[38] As the industry moved toward full capacity in 1913, further expansion through new investments posed few serious problems.

There was, lastly, a favorable impact upon attitudes and talents necessary for domestic investment capacity and entrepreneurship. This may well have been the most important result of all, as we shall see in the following chapters.

Did most foreign enterprises in the southern steel industry earn the high profits they sought? Generally they did not. This is what one might expect, from the data of Ol', which was analyzed in chapter 1. Those figures show that the rate of return on all foreign paid-in capital varied from 3.8 percent to 7.8 percent between 1885 and 1914 (1895 excepted). What these data only imply, however, is the decline in the rate of return for steel producers. This decline is seen in table 12.

There was considerable recovery after 1910. The Crédit Lyonnais calculated that during its last complete fiscal years before the outbreak of war fifteen major south Russian steel producers earned net profits of 12.0 percent on their nominal capital. This permitted dividends and *tantièmes* equaling 7.2 percent on nominal capital, while 4.8 percent was ploughed back into the industry.[39] The market value of this nominal capital of 842,000 francs was

38. Glivits, *Zheleznaia promyshlennost'*, pp. 118–19; Jules Cordeweener, *Contribution à l'étude de la crise industrielle* (Brussels, 1902), pp. 257–58; Livshits, *Razmeshchenie*, p. 280.

39. C.L., Intérêts Français dans la Métallurgie Russe, 6–2–1922 (Etude, no. 5345).

1,045,000 francs on 30 June 1914, when shares were well below their highs of the preceding year.[40] Yet in spite of great improvement this 12.0 percent return on nominal capital was below the all-Russian average net return of 15.8 percent on capital engaged in industry in 1913.[41]

Table 12

FINANCIAL RESULTS OF STEEL PRODUCERS
IN SOUTHERN RUSSIA

Year	Total Nominal Capital (In Millions	Total Dividends of Rubles)	Dividends as Percentage of Capital
1895	24.50	4.30	17.50
1896	36.90	5.60	15.18
1897	58.75	6.45	10.98
1898	75.98	4.71	9.75
1899	91.51	5.20	5.68
1900 a	133.30	6.34	4.76
1901 a	127.97	5.36	4.19
1902 a	126.66	4.90	3.87
1903 a	124.03	4.98	4.01
1904 a	124.30	4.57	3.68
1905 a	110.91	4.41	3.98
1906 a	143.57	4.20	2.87
1907 a	149.09	4.02	2.70
1908 b	147.08	4.04	2.75
1909 c	143.71	3.39	2.36

SOURCE: Glivits, *Zheleznaia promyshlennost'*, pp. 44–49.
a. One company not reporting.
b. Two companies not reporting.
c. Three companies not reporting.

Foreign gains in the Russian steel industry followed very closely the Schumpeterian model of business profit. A few creative innovators, like John

40. Ibid.
41. S. G. Strumilin, *Ocherki sovetskoi ekonomiki* (Moscow, 1930), pp. 72–73.

Hughes with his New Russia Company (1870), and the South Russian Dnieper Metallurgical Company (1888), made very large entrepreneurial gains. Most followers did not, although they did force profits down to a normal rate. In 1897, of forty-five steel and metal fabricating companies paying an average return of 6.1 percent on invested capital, only three paid more than 20 percent (including South Russian Dnieper's 40 percent). Three other firms paid from 12 to 16 percent; twelve paid from 6 to 10 percent; and two paid less than 5 percent. In all, twenty of the firms paid dividends, and twenty-five paid nothing at all, although nine of these were at least two years old.[42]

Another calculation by the influential Belgian financial paper, the *Moniteur des Intérêts Matériels,* also showed the importance of a few very successful firms in the average return of metallurgical firms operating in Russia and quoted on either French or Belgian exchanges. The average return on the nominal capital of forty-one such firms was 7.71 percent in 1899, and 5.21 percent in 1900. However, only thirteen of the forty-one companies paid any dividends in 1899, and only ten did so in 1900. These fortunate dividend-paying firms averaged an impressive 20.25 percent return on par value in 1899, and 13.63 percent in 1900.[43] A few did very well; the rest struggled along.

2

Rapid industrialization in southern Russia created a new situation that led to profound transformation of the Donets coal industry in a single decade. The quantitative increase of 400 percent from

42. Brandt, *Inostrannye kapitaly,* 2:232–33.
43. *Moniteur des Intérêts Matériels,* 2–9–1900.

2.2 million tons in 1888 to 11.0 million tons in 1900 suggests only one aspect of the challenge to the coal industry in those years.[44] Perhaps more important was the greatly altered structure of the industry's market. Whereas before 1888 Donets coal served mainly as fuel for the railroad system and southern sugar mills, afterward the metallurgical industry came to be the principal consumer of coal, both as fuel and as a raw material. By 1905 metallurgy consumed 35 to 40 percent of total coal production, as opposed to almost nothing twenty years earlier.[45]

Table 13

PRINCIPAL CONSUMERS OF DONETS COAL, 1880–99
(As a Percentage of Coal Marketed by Rail)

Consumer Group	1880	1885	1890	1895	1899
Railroads	60.0	47.1	31.1	28.0	22.6
Steamboats	5.9	5.6	6.8	8.2	4.0
Gas works	0.8	0.7	1.5	1.5	0.8
Sugar mills	17.7	13.0	9.9	8.2	6.7
Steel mills					
South	—	—	17.1	23.3	32.5
Elsewhere	0.6	0.1	0.7	0.2	1.9
Other manufacturing	—	0.2	—	—	1.1
Domestic	15.0	33.5	33.0	30.5	29.9

Source: D. I. Shpolianskii, *Monopolii ugol'no-metallurgicheskoi promyshlennosti iuga Rossii v nachale XX veka* (Moscow, 1953), p. 26.
Note: Does not include coal consumed at the mine or contiguous factory, such as in Hughes's works in the 1880s.

Fully one-half of this metallurgical consumption was in the form of carefully processed coke, which with its rigorous technical specifications was absolutely indispensable for modern steel making. Mar-

44. See Livshits, *Razmeshchenie*, p. 276, for time series of coal production by region for the entire period.
45. C.L., Métallurgie dans le Midi, April 1905.

ket and technical considerations linked the steel and coal industries closely together in a reciprocally dependent situation. Metallurgy provided the coal industry with its most promising market, and the new metallurgical industry was only secure with a transformed coal industry with adequate coke-making capacity. Such complementarities led foreigners to play the key role in the transformation of the coal industry, where they sought large profits through superior technology.

Foreign entrepreneurs played a small role initially in the Donets coal industry, which antedated the southern steel industry. With the major exceptions of the French Société Générale's Rutchenko mine, which was opened in 1873, and the mines of John Hughes's New Russia Company of the same period, all the large foreign coal companies dated from the 1890s. During that decade many foreign companies were formed to purchase existing operations or to develop completely new mines.

The first step was the purchase by the Banque Internationale de Paris of a controlling interest in Lazare Poliakov's South Russian Coal Company in 1891, nineteen years after that pioneering Jewish railroad builder had opened these mines to supply his southern railroads with fuel.[46] The following year the Société de Rive-de-Gier and capitalists from Lyons followed with the Berestov-Krinka Coal Company. In 1894 Cockerill of Seraing, Belgium, made its second bid in southern Russia with the Almaznaia Coal Company. In 1895 the Bonnardel

46. C.L., Société de l'Industrie Houillère de la Russie Méridionale, Etude, January 1899; *Société de l'Industrie Houillère de la Russie Méridionale* (Paris, 1900), brochure prepared for the Paris Exposition of 1900; *Science et Industrie* 8 (April 1924) : 84–86.

interests formed the Ekaterinovka Coal Company, while Franco-Belgian interests founded the Makeevka Coal Company. (See chapter 9 for Almaznaia and chapters 10 and 11 for Ekaterinovka).

There were a number of important coal companies founded by Belgian and French entrepreneurs between 1895 and 1900. The Prokhorov Coal Company (1895), the Varvaropol Coal Company (1895), the Belaia Coal Company (1896), the Rykovskii Coal Company (1898), the Gosudarev-Bairak Coal Company (1899), the General Coal Company (1900), and the Irmino Coal Company (1900) are particularly noteworthy. (The Rykovskii firm is examined in detail in chapter 10.) In addition, Sinçay's South Russian Rock Salt Company, founded in 1883, changed its name to South Russian Rock Salt and Coal Company as it expanded into coal mining in 1896, and the Russo-Belgian Metallurgical Company copied Hughes's original steel-making strategy of self-sufficiency in raw materials by placing its mills on its own coal supply.

Fifteen companies, each producing more than fifteen million puds annually (245,000 tons), accounted for 75 percent of all soft coal mined in southern Russia by 1899. Ten of these fifteen firms were then foreign, and they accounted for one-half of the 531.5 million puds of coal produced by the leading eighty-eight mines producing all but about 5 percent of Donets soft coal.[47] Two of the five Russian-owned mines stood first and fourth respectively, but the other three ranked thirteenth, fourteenth, and fif-

---

47. *Trudy 23 S"ezda gorno-promyshlennikov Iuga Rossii,* as quoted by Brandt, *Inostrannye kapitaly,* 2:116–18; Livshits, *Razmeshchenie,* p. 276. Brandt has not noted Rykovskii as foreign, as I have done in the figures above. Rykovskii was clearly foreign after 1898.

teenth in 1899. The largest Russian-owned company, the Alekseev Mining Company, was dependent upon the Russo-German Donets-Yur'evka Company, while fourth-ranked Golubovka-Berestovo-Bogodu-khovo was eventually largely owned by the Bonnar-del Group's Donets Steel Company. If smaller foreign companies producing less than fifteen million puds are included, one may estimate that at least 60 percent of all coal was produced by foreign firms in 1899.[48] Weak in 1890, foreigners were unquestionably the leaders in 1900.

To understand this surge of foreign participation, one must trace the dimensions of the Russian-owned coal industry at about 1890. Quite striking was the low level of mining technology. This conclusion is indicated by both statistical data and by the testimony of foreign engineers and businessmen, who were quick to note deficiencies by comparison with west-European practices.

Technical backwardness was most striking in the tiny peasant mines. These peasant mines still abounded in 1890, although admittedly their quantitative importance was small. Whether on gentry or communal lands, they were actually little more than small vertical holes a few meters deep. A hand-operated windlass raising and lowering a bucket of coal, just as in a well, was the most sophisticated device. Quite often these mines were family operations: the father and adult sons dug coal in the pit; the good woman or a younger son wound the windlass; and the younger children removed stones and sorted the coal.[49] Since the coal deposits of the Donets were

48. Brandt, *Inostrannye kapitaly,* 2:116–18.
49. This description of the peasant family coal mine is based primarily upon incidental remarks in various studies at the Crédit Lyonnais; Lauwick, *L'industrie,* pp. 92 ff.; Cordeweener, *Contri-*

enormous—at least five hundred million tons of proved reserves in 1905 by the most conservative estimate, and as many as fourteen coal-bearing strata with numerous outcroppings—there were many possibilities for such small surface mines, and they were scattered throughout the region. These mines were worked irregularly in conjunction with the seasonal demands of agriculture.

The bulk of production came from permanent mines with year-round operations on fee-simple lands belonging to either corporations or gentry proprietors.[50] In 1890 the largest producer was apparently the Société Générale's Rutchenko Company, with an annual production of 362,000 tons.[51] In that same year Poliakov's South Russian Company extracted 137,000 tons, while the Makeevka property accounted for 273,000 tons in 1893 when it was still Russian-owned.[52] These figures show that the larger companies had little in common with the peasant mines by 1890, since a peasant mine produced at the most a thousand tons yearly. Yet a closer examination of representative larger firms on the eve of foreign ascendency reveals that techniques were generally quite inadequate, and that larger mines followed certain aspects of traditional peasant mining in modified form.

Basically, the larger operations obtained their production with a series of small mines, which often began on the outcroppings and then worked to a

---

bution; Vladimir Islavine, Aperçu sur l'état de l'industrie de la houille et du fer dans le bassin du Donets (St. Petersburg, 1875), pp. 73 ff.

50. For early developments see the valuable study of Islavine, Aperçu, particularly pp. 1–9, 71–88.

51. C.L., Routchenko, Etude, January 1899.

52. C.L., Société de l'Industrie Houillère, Etude, January 1899; Vie Financière, 14–10–1905.

depth of perhaps sixty or seventy meters before being abandoned. Invariably extraction at such a mine was confined to one underground level, and often only one seam of coal was worked, either because that seam was easily exploited or was of superior quality. Ventilation systems were natural, that is, nonexistent. This in itself prohibited deep-level work. Power equipment at the pit head was limited; horse-powered windlasses were giving way to steam-driven cranks by 1890, but these could slowly lift only one small bin at a time. Thus the productive capacity of individual mines was small.

For instance, the lands of what became the Belgian Prokhorov Coal Company in 1895 produced 134,000 tons of coal from ten different mines in 1894. Three of these mines still used horse-driven windlasses, while small steam engines powered the other seven. Output had skyrocketed from 25,000 tons in 1889, but only as a result of sinking additional dispersed shafts, each of which averaged a mere 13,000 tons per year.[53] Likewise, Colonel Rykovskii's production of 244,000 tons in 1897 came from nine different individual shafts with minimal equipment. A modern mine with twin shafts was in construction, but far from complete.[54] A final example was the Korenev and Shipilov Coal Company, which was purchased by a Belgian portfolio corporation, the General Coal Company. Yearly production of 120,000 tons came from six mines—four others having been previously abandoned—sunk to an average depth of seventy-five meters. Four were powered by steam and two by horses. Horses and engines lifted

53. Undated published notice, circa 1895, found in C.L., Prokhorov.

54. C.L., Rykovskii, Etudes, May and December 1901; also published brochure, circa 1900, in A.N., 65 AQ, L 386. See chapter 10.

with equal efficiency—one small bin at a time.[55] Surface installations were absolutely minimal at Korenev and Shipilov. Sorting equipment was particularly needed, as it was throughout the Donets. In 1894 only 20 percent of Donets coal was sorted and graded, as opposed to 97 percent in Germany.[56] In short, all information seems to confirm the opinion of the Crédit Lyonnais's engineer, who judged almost all mines primitive and poorly equipped before 1896.[57]

Given the foreigner's predilection for familiar techniques, a considerable influx of foreign investment was bound to change this pattern of mining. True, there were certain advantages in the unsophisticated Russian system. Production was flexible, because new mines could be developed quickly to increase output. And the capital requirements of such mines were quite limited, as were demands upon the hard-to-train, itinerant labor force. (See chapter 7 for a detailed discussion of the labor force.) Nor were costs of extraction high, at least for the smallest mines working outcroppings.

But there were serious disadvantages, even when coal was used primarily for fuel. Time and again foreign engineers noted that such haphazard exploitation was wasteful and often compromised future mining of all strata. In addition, the quality of the product was low. Sorting, for instance, was essential for grading and optimal pricing of different varieties.[58] More importantly, the fabrication of high-

55. *Rapport sur les Mines Zolotoié et Bokovsky*, in C.L., Cie Générale de Charbonnages.

56. Brandt, *Inostrannye kapitaly*, 2:118.

57. C.L., Métallurgie, April 1905. Brandt, *Inostrannye kapitaly*, 2:116–22, agrees completely.

58. C.L., Société Française et Italienne des Houillères de Dombrowa, Etude, September 1902.

quality metallurgical coke demanded careful sorting, cleaning, and washing that took into consideration small but significant chemical variations in coking coals. Such demands surpassed the capabilities of small mines with minimal installations.

Thus the subtle technical demands of coke production, the foreigner's primary concern within the coal industry, strongly reinforced his basic preference for advanced methods. An anonymous writer summed up the entrepreneurial strategy of the Société des Houillères Unies de Charleroi through its Russian subsidiary, the Lugan Coal Company. "It did like everyone else; that is, it bought coal properties equipped *à la russe,* in the crudest possible manner, and then applied techniques used in western Europe, just like all the French and Belgian companies on the steppe." [59] To be sure, some foreign entrepreneurs continued past practice, but the leaders implanted prevailing Western standards and set the tone for the industry.

What were these Western methods applied in southern Russia? Essentially they consisted in working integrated, centralized mines of large capacity. This meant a labyrinth of underground tunnels and numerous accessories at the surface. It was the substitution of large, fully rationalized, deep-level mines and modern coke-making facilities capable of unlimited production for small, hit-and-miss, temporary operations. As the Crédit Lyonnais's engineer put it, "One may compare the major mines since 1896 with those being built in the Pas de Calais region circa 1900. Donets mines now work regularly below three hundred meters, and some mines have an annual capacity of 600,000 tons." [60]

59. *Vie Financière,* 7–9–1905.
60. C.L., Métallurgie dans le Midi, April 1905.

This was the maximum capacity of the most modern mines, with a range of about 250,000 to 600,000 tons annually for the leaders. It contrasted sharply with the 15,000 to 20,000 tons of the permanent mines of Russian firms examined above and with the annual production of not more than 1,000 tons of the peasant mines. Here indeed was a sharp break with past practice. No wonder the Crédit Lyonnais's engineer sharply criticized the old and poorly equipped mines of the Berestov-Krinka Company in 1901: "One must remember that there are already many companies with modern and powerful installations which are only slightly inferior to the very best installations of western Europe."[61] The remainder of this chapter will focus on major characteristics of these modern mines by examining some of these major producers, and then it will assess the success and appropriateness of these new techniques.

Foreign engineers sought to combine primitive dispersed mines into from one to three large-scale, deep-level mines. Most of these mines (*sièges*) had two closely coordinated shafts (*puits jumeaux*). Each shaft, separated by a few yards, was equipped with its own metal superstructure and accessory equipment. One shaft served to extract coal. It required above all a very powerful engine, usually steam-driven, to lift quickly the multileveled cage containing either two or three wagons. By 1899 machines capable of lifting more than two tons (one of coal and one of dead weight) per lift were in use at leading mines.[62] The nearby twin shaft serviced the underground operations. It lowered miners and ma-

61. C.L., Berestov-Krinka, December 1901.

62. *Société d'Industrie Houillère de la Russie Méridionale;* C.L., Société Métallurgique Russo-Belge, Etude, January 1900.

terials (wood, fill, tools, etc.), permitted an extensive ventilation system, and occasionally was used for extraction. The ventilation system in turn demanded powerful compressors, ventilators, and tubing to carry the air. Such a system was essential to large-scale, deep-level mining. Pumping equipment was placed at this second shaft.[63]

Near the pit head were the centralized boilers to provide steam for the various machines. There were also loading platforms and large storage bins, an essential annex of all Russian mines because of the frequent and occasionally prolonged interruptions in rail transport due to the chronic lack of rolling stock. Then there was the equipment necessary for proper processing of coal, the lack of which the foreigner always noted and attempted to remedy: mechanical sizers to sort and classify coal; washing equipment absolutely essential for the removal of sulphur from even the best Donets coking coals; and (sometimes) mechanical loaders or conveyor belts. All this equipment came late to the Donets, and foreign companies led in its adoption.[64]

The change in the strategy of extraction was almost as striking as the equipment used. Small mines, often beginning on outcroppings, usually mined only some of the coal-bearing strata at a given location. The large foreign mines anticipated working all strata, not just skimming the cream off the top. Work was therefore conducted at either two or three

63. The above discussion is based upon a multitude of dossiers at the Crédit Lyonnais, and various brochures and annual reports of the companies involved which may be found either at the Crédit Lyonnais or the 65 AQ series at the National Archives.

64. E.M., A. Pourcel, Mémoire sur les récentes développements de l'industrie houillère au Donetz et la mine de Shcherbinovka, November–December 1897; C.L., various dossiers, particularly Routchenko, January 1899; Brandt, *Inostrannye kapitaly*, 2:120.

levels to a depth of three or four hundred meters in order to get all coal to that level. This desire to exploit systematically gave each mine a very long life and encouraged geological investigations to ascertain peculiarities of a given property. (The French director of Rutchenko, Barbier, was noted as one of the first to sink exploratory shafts before 1897.)[65]

Perhaps nowhere were the professionalism and sophisticated manner of foreign mines more clearly seen than in coke production, a foreign specialty. In addition to the costly (500,000 francs and up) washing installations, proper coking demanded carefully constructed ovens. A battery of twenty-four ovens was apparently the minimum number. With each oven costing about 20,000 francs, technical indivisibilities clearly favored large and modern installations. By 1900 there were about four thousand coke ovens in southern Russia, most of which were of either the Coppée or Carvès types.[66] These ovens of the Donets were replicas of the leading types in Belgium and France.

A few large foreign producers—Ekaterinovka, South Russian Coal, South Russian Rock Salt and Coal, Rykovskii, Almaznaia, and the steel producers Hughes and the Russo-Belge—dominated this market. They accounted for most of the sevenfold increase in coke production from 308,000 tons in 1895 to 2,238,000 tons in 1900.[67] The South Russian Coal Company, which was producing no coke when purchased from Poliakov in 1891, was making 300,000 tons in 1898. With 346 ovens in action and another

65. C.L., Routchenko, Etude, August 1897.

66. Jules Cordeweener, *Contribution*, p. 263; personal communication from Baron Coppée, 6–1–1966.

67. C.L., Métallurgie dans le Midi, April 1905.

30 scheduled, it was reportedly the largest single coke producer in Europe.[68] All this in the course of a single decade.

The rapid expansion of coke production followed the signals of the market economy. Profits, either as a percentage of sales or a return on investment, were considerably higher on coke than on coal in the late 1890s, although not after 1901.[69] Even smaller foreign firms, like the Lugan, Varvaropol, and Gosudarev-Bairak companies, built at least one battery. Part of the reason was also the logic of advanced technique. The capture of escaping gases from the coke ovens provided heat and therefore energy for the power-hungry centralized equipment. In the 1890s boilers and steam engines were the converters. During the following decade gas turbines for electric generating equipment spread, and electric motors replaced the cluster of small steam engines at the pithead. This seems to have followed Western technical developments. One may also note that foreign firms completely dominated the production of coal tars obtained from recuperating coke ovens. The South Russian Salt and Coal Company installed the first such oven in Russia in 1897.[70] Coke production, profit maximization, and modern equipment for quality control were all related in the 1890s.

Analysis of comparative costs of production provides strong evidence that technical rationale and economic rationale coincided from the point of view of the individual enterprise. Large modern mines, like those of the Ekaterinovka Company or the Russo-Belgian Metallurgical Company, attained significantly lower costs of production than their medium-

68. C.L., Société de l'Industrie Houillère, Etude, January 1899.
69. Ibid.
70. E.M., Pourcel, Mémoire; C.L., Sels Gemmes, January 1899.

sized, more rudimentary counterparts. Exactly how much lower is hard to say, since natural conditions varied considerably from mine to mine. Nevertheless, uniform reports by the Crédit Lyonnais's engineers provide a general indication. They calculated the costs of extraction, processing, preparatory works, sales, and management in the total average cost of each firm. (Interest on debt and amortization varied widely and were therefore omitted.)

In 1899 three leading mines averaged production costs of about five kopecks per pud: the South Russian Rock Salt and Coal Company, five kopecks per pud; the Rutchenko Coal Company, 4.8 kopecks; and the South Russian Coal Company (Gorlovka), 4.7 kopecks. Three unmodernized mines were more than a kopeck higher on average: the Lugan Coal Company, six kopecks per pud; the Rykovskii Coal Company, six kopecks per pud, and (in 1901) the Berestov-Krinka Company, 6.8 kopecks per pud.[71] Six years later, in the midst of depression and revolution, the cost situation was worse, but it still favored the modern producers. The best-equipped mines averaged 5.5 kopecks per pud, while six kopecks per pud was average, and 6.5 common.[72]

Comparisons omitting interest and amortization do not prejudice the case in favor of the more modern mines, as one might think. On the contrary, as far as foreigners were concerned, large centralized mines generally had *smaller* investment per pud of coal mined than small, inefficient mines. A careful calculation of original investment in land and equipment for selected mines shows this clearly.[73] In the

71. For all these cost figures see the dossiers of these firms at the Crédit Lyonnais.
72. C.L., Métallurgie dans le Midi, April 1905.
73. C.L., Berestov-Krinka, Etude, April 1912.

central region of the Donets coal field the modern
Russo-Belgian Metallurgical Company had the lowest investment per pud of coal mined (14.8 k/pd). In
the northeastern region the small Varvaropol Coal
Company, which had long concentrated all production in a single mine, was lowest (16.7 k/pd). In the
southwestern region, where investment was highest
because of extensive coking equipment, the modern
mines of Rutchenko (26.0 k/pd) and Ekaterinovka
(29.6 k/pd) had less invested than backward producers like Berestov-Krinka (63.0 k/pd) and the Russo-
Donets and Markov Company (39.9 k/pd). Clearly,
given the possibility of large production, centralized
and efficient mines saved capital as well as labor.
Again advanced technology paid, as the foreigner
had anticipated.

There is an important qualification, however. It
does seem, in retrospect, that a few foreign mines
tried too sophisticated a set of techniques in the late
1890s, just as others, like Rykovskii or Berestov-
Krinka, were laggards in meeting minimal requirements. One example must suffice. The South Russian
Rock Salt and Coal Company's Shcherbinovka mine
was equipped in 1898–99 as perhaps the most advanced mine in the South. All parts of the equipment were superb: a single large shaft (with only a
small accompanying shaft for ventilation); engines
capable of lifting five tons at a time; electric motors
for small engines and ventilation; and mechanical
sorting and sizing machinery. The mine had a scheduled annual capacity of 500,000 tons, and was completed by its coke division which used recuperating
ovens. This mine was the first in the Donets to experiment with mechanical mining underground as
opposed to tools of the pick and shovel variety.[74]

74. C.L., Sels Gemmes, Etude of Mr. du Marais, January 1899.

A year after operations began, an observer noted that "the mine contains many remarkable parts. The main shaft has very great capacity and *everything* is conceived in accordance with the most modern ideas." But "this ensemble, which would be very well adopted in France or Germany, may be the object of justified criticism in the Donets. . . . Some equipment is too highly perfected for the miners, who are newcomers from agriculture."[75]

The directors of the company evidently reached the same conclusion. The original French director who had equipped the mine was replaced by a Polish mining engineer who intended to use less advanced, more easily understood practices. Specifically, the mechanical mining underground was discarded, and two new smaller mines were sunk. These changes fitted the labor force's skills, desires, and itinerent character.[76] The original, clearly defined strategy of "attempting to reduce the labor force to the absolute minimum and therefore to use mechanical processes whenever possible" was greatly modified.[77]

This limited retreat was indicative of increased technical conservatism among foreign coal companies after 1901. At that time the practices of the better mines were evolving rather slowly. Soviet scholars are correct, for example, to point out that underground mechanical mining was not adopted before 1914. And the productivity of coal miners, which had risen in the 1890s, was unchanged between 1900 and 1914.[78] What Soviet authors fail to

75. C.L., Sels Gemmes, Etude of Mr. Waton, January 1900.

76. Ibid.

77. See the excellent detailed study by A. Pourcel at the Ecole des Mines, Paris.

78. Khromov, *Ekonomicheskoe razvitie*, pp. 203–7, 321–25. British coal mining followed the same pattern of a slow technical change in this period, and thus Russia was not unique. See R. S.

note is that such behavior intelligently followed relative factor prices. After 1901 unskilled labor was more readily available at reasonable prices for southern mines (see chapter 7), while capital was certainly dearer (see chapter 6). Under such conditions the fairly advanced mining techniques of the late 1890s seemed adequate. This does not lessen the foreign technical achievement in coal mining. In fact, it keeps that achievement in clear perspective. Within the framework of capitalist enterprise foreigners were technocrats for personal profit, and not for the sake of technology per se.

As far as profits were concerned, foreigners were distinctly less successful in coal than in steel. Whereas Brandt's data indicates that forty-five steel and metal fabricating producers paid 8.6 percent on their par value in 1896, and 6.1 percent in 1897, fifteen coal companies with heavy foreign participation paid 3.8 and 4.2 percent respectively.[79] In 1899 and in 1900, sixteen predominantly foreign coal companies paid 3.4 and 4.2 percent.[80] Both calculations include three or four well-established Polish mines, which were more successful than their southern counterparts. Thus they actually overstate southern profitability. In the twentieth century the situation deteriorated. Of the major foreign coal companies in southern Russia, only the Ekaterinovka Coal Mining Company did not reduce the value of its shares and force shareholders to accept large losses.

The problem was that foreigners paid dearly for basically undeveloped properties and then floated

Sayers, *A History of Economic Change in England, 1880–1939* (Oxford, 1967), pp. 86–90.

79. Brandt, *Inostrannye kapitaly*, 2:232–35.

80. *Moniteur des Intérêts Matériels*, 2–9–1900.

bonds to construct and build modern mines. This saddled the average firm with high fixed costs of interest and amortization. These costs dragged firm after firm into reorganization after 1901. Reorganization was all the more difficult to escape because overcapacity kept constant pressure on selling prices, a pressure which the coal syndicate reduced but could not remove. Even after extensive recovery the industry was operating at only 74 percent of capacity in 1913.[81] Even so, foreign entrepreneurs as a group derived at least one important benefit from their efforts. In breaking the bottleneck of fuel and coke supply in southern Russia they assured related ventures in the steel industry profitable operations under normal conditions.

81. Eventov, *Inostrannye kapitaly,* p. 46.

5

PATTERNS OF MANAGEMENT

In previous chapters we have seen that different types of foreign entrepreneurs had a common investment strategy—the pursuit of large profits through advanced Western technology. This common strategy also united these entrepreneurial types functionally, although not of course in every venture. The individual promoter sketched the outlines of an investment possibility; a leading foreign firm analyzed this outline in detail from a technical point of view, estimated costs and profits, and made the final investment decision; and the informal group grew from successes and needs for complementary investment.

Analysis of the southern steel and coal industries has shown that in at least two very important cases advanced technology was established, and that this was logical, while the initially large profits of pioneers declined rapidly. More generally, it is safe to say that impressive technical success often failed to bring comparable financial success. This suggests that implementation of the general strategy was difficult and far from automatic. One suspects that the foreigner had special problems and disadvantages which complicated his plan and diminished his effectiveness, and that modifications were therefore required. This involves the entire question of effective management of foreign entrepreneurial investment, which is our concern in this chapter.

The efforts of top decision makers in western Europe and of their delegates in Russia may be divided into two periods. In the first they carried out the original plan upon which the specific Russian venture was based. They constructed a large industrial plant from scratch, or profoundly modified one in operation, and then they proceeded to iron out the inevitable difficulties of starting up new productive facilities. This period of installation was clearly defined, since major foreign newcomers after 1885 did not evolve gradually from modest beginnings through long-term reinvestment of profits, as most enterprises in western Europe or northern Russia had done, but rather sprang fully grown into existence.

After this period of installation each firm entered, with varying degrees of ease, the second period of normal and increasingly routinized operation. Although the chronological break for each firm was related to when it began, the years from 1885 to 1900 may be considered the period of installation for foreign firms in general. Those after 1900 were years of normal operation through long depression (1900–1910), and vigorous expansion (1910–1914). Differences in the supply of factors for foreign entrepreneurs also helped separate the periods and fostered different styles of management. Until 1900 capital was readily available, profits were fair for most and excellent for a few, and public and private confidence ran high. Large-scale investment was continuous. And until 1900 even well-established companies like Dnieper Metallurgy or Rutchenko Coal remained in the period of installation to a considerable extent. After 1900 profits and fresh capital vanished, and the foreign entrepreneur was forced to concentrate on whatever plant his engineers had managed to build. The anxieties of his accountants had come to dominate his decisions for more than a decade. Both periods posed great problems for effective management.

1

Effective decision making was one serious problem. How was a corporation owned predominantly by foreigners to build and then to manage a factory fifteen hundred miles away, especially since both the home office and the plant needed to function together smoothly as a single unit? This problem was particularly acute during the period of installation, when unforeseen pressing difficulties were sure to arise.

The normal organizational response was to appoint a single, clearly designated general director (*administrateur-délégé*) at home and a single plant superintendent, or director for Russian operations, abroad. As top man in Russia, the plant superintendent was given considerable discretionary power to cope with his many tasks. But he was also required to communicate constantly with the general director through a stream of reports or emergency telegrams. Responsibility was clearly defined at both ends of the communications pipeline, and only major decisions were referred to the board of directors. This basic organizational framework lasted until World War I. It is hard to imagine a better system, which is not to say it worked perfectly.

The same individual was often the general director of the parent company in western Europe as well as the Russian affiliate whose creation he had fostered. Léon Hiard, for example, was general director of the Cie Centrale de Constructions at St. Pierre, Belgium, and the affiliated Donets Stamping Company, which he helped found. His Russian plant superintendent was Hector Evrard, a Belgian engineer who oversaw installation and then directed op-

erations until 1913.[1] Similarly, the general director
and important stockholder of both the Société
Métallurgique Espérance-Longdoz (Liège) and its
affiliated Russian venture, the Tula Blast Furnaces
Company, was Armand Stouls. Stouls, a highly competent metallurgist, exchanged a progressively dis-
heartened correspondence with his plant manager,
Pierre Ries. Ries, previously an engineer at the
Belgian Société Angleur, devoted "great attention
to the Russian company and even more to its quotation on the stock exchange."[2] The parent firm often
supplied the plant manager in Russia as well as the
general director in western Europe. The Belgian
Providence Company placed the director of its
smaller, upstream plant, Beduvé, in Russia, and
named its chief technical administrator, Hovine,
managing director in Belgium.[3]

The top personnel at the Taganrog Metallurgical
Company on the Sea of Azov were representative.
The general director of this Russian venture was
Gustave Trasenster, who held the same position
with the parent firm, the Société d'Ougrée, a leading
steel producer in the Liège Basin. Trasenster was
the Russian company's "most active promoter and
its key man." He exercised "preponderant influence, which has been good in general." The only
drawback was that Trasenster went to Russia rarely

1. C.L., Société Métallurgique d'Estampage, Etude, August
1904; A.N., 65 AQ, K 70, Report to Shareholders, 20–11–1913;
Annexe du Moniteur Belge, 7–10–1895.
2. C.L., Hauts Fourneaux de Toula, Etude, December 1898.
Fragments of Stouls's correspondence with Ries are in the archives
of the Société Espérance-Longdoz, Liège, Belgium, and may be
consulted with the firm's permission. Also see L. Willem and
S. Willem, "Espérance-Longdoz," 2 :379–86.
3. C.L., Providence Russe, Etudes, December 1898 and June
1900; P.R. MSS, Délibérations du Conseil d'Administration de la
Providence Russe, 13–12–1897.

because of his extensive business activities and his professorship in the engineering section of the University of Liège.[4]

Trasenster's plant superintendents were Belgian engineers from a variety of backgrounds. The first director, Dutaille, was an engineer from the parent Ougrée Company. He was succeeded by Jules Herpeignes, one of Taganrog's founders, who died suddenly in 1900, and then by Albert Nève. This engineer from Liège had founded and then managed on land of the Taganrog Company a Russian subsidiary of Wilde, Nève et Cie of Liège, appropriately named Wilde, Nève et Cie, à Taganrog. This subsidiary made boilers and metallurgical accessories, exactly like the parent company at Liège, and was closely allied to both the Ougrée and Taganrog metallurgical firms. Trasenster, for example, was a board member of both Wilde, Nève companies. Nève, who had previously specialized in equipment construction and not metallurgy, exercised "a very favorable influence" on Taganrog because of "very great administrative qualities, commercial abilities, and deep understanding of the country."[5] When Nève decided to return to Liège after ten years in Russia, he was replaced by another old Russian hand, Olinger, who had been technical director at the Russo-Belgian Metallurgical Company from 1897 to 1906.[6]

General directors from the home office normally traveled to Russia regularly. Roger Douine, cotton

4. C.L., Taganrog, Etudes, November 1900 and October 1901.

5. C.L., Taganrog, Etude, November 1900; A.N., 65 AQ, K 236, Annual Reports and press clippings. A distant relative of Albert Nève, X. Nève de Mevergnies, who encouraged me in this study, is today managing director of Société John Cockerill.

6. Ibid., Annual Report, 1905–6; C.L., Société Russo-Belge, Etude, November 1911.

spinner at Troyes and founder of the Russo-French Cotton Company, conferred several times a year with his plant superintendent, Léon Kessler, formerly a mill owner in Alsace and manager in Russia from 1898 to 1908.[7] General directors, at home and abroad, often held their posts for many years and gave the better firms managerial continuity, as the example above suggests. The Sinçays, first Ludovic (1883–1905), then his brother Edgar (1905–17), led the South Russian Rock Salt and Coal Company as general directors for more than thirty years in close collaboration with the director in Russia, Etienne de Manziarly (1887–1905), who moved to the Paris office to aid Edgar in 1905.[8]

It was obviously essential that the two directors work together harmoniously. Mutual confidence was essential to split management. Therefore changes in the locus of control for a certain firm usually saw closely related home and foreign managers replaced simultaneously. When Fernand Schmatzer surrendered leadership of the Rykovskii Coal Company to the new managing director (Lauras), Schmatzer's friend the Belgian engineer Tonneau was also dismissed at the mine in Russia. The new mine manager, Franclieu, had previously worked closely with Lauras when both were at the Blanzy mines in France.[9] Emile Delloye-Orban and Georges François, founders of Nikolaev Shipyards, alternated as general directors until both resigned in 1908 when control passed to Franco-Russian interests.[10]

The plant superintendent in Russia was usually

---

7. C.L., Société Cotonière Russo-Française, Etudes, 1906 and 1910; ibid., Annual Report for 1899.

8. C.L., Sels Gemmes, Etude, August 1912.

9. C.L., Rykovskii, Etude, May 1901.

10. A.N., 65 AQ, M 332, Articles of Incorporation; Annual Reports; *Belgique financière*, 3–10–1909.

flanked by two directors, one for technical questions and one for administration and sales. Each director had several assistants. At first, almost all these top directors and many assistants were foreigners, and it was upon their shoulders that crucial administration in Russia rested. They shared common characteristics with such regularity that one may rightly distinguish a typical foreign top manager.

In the first place, as some of the foregoing illustrations suggest, almost all these managers were engineers who had learned their trade at leading schools and firms in western Europe. One may also note that most managers, particularly top managers, received an important promotion in taking their latest positions. Third, foreign managers had often worked their way up the managerial ladder within Russia, and they had gained with time broad knowledge of Russian business and cultural conditions. In short, the ideal top manager was a graduate of a leading European engineering school who had recently gained an important promotion after several years of experience in Russia. Capsule biographies of a few such executives will give life to this abstract average foreign manager.

Take the engineer Linder. Linder, a graduate of the Ecole des Arts et Manufactures in Paris, began his working career as engineer at the Huta-Bankova Company in the early 1890s. He then served the Russo-Belgian Metallurgical Company in its first five years (1896–1901) before moving up to the position of technical director at the Ural-Volga Metallurgical Company for five more years. All three of these large firms were built by different groups of capitalists. Linder then returned to his original employer's southern subsidiary, the Donets Steel Company, where he stayed until at least 1911 and where he was charged with a complete technical reorganization. There he "succeeded in re-establishing order and discipline, which had suffered greatly during the troubled years from 1905 to 1907."[11]

Linder was seconded in his efforts by a Mr. Hilléraux, another graduate of the Ecole des Arts et Manufactures. His career showed the same mobility. After being at the Bonnardel Group's Kama Steel Company in the Urals, Hilléreaux moved to manage the nearby Russian-owned Alapaevsk Company of the heirs of S. S. Iakovlev and P. S. Iakovlev. After a number of years at Alapaevsk, Hilléraux returned to work in France until he was recalled to Russia at the age of fifty-three to help right the listing Donets Steel Company.[12]

A Belgian engineer named Pellérin began his career in Luxemburg before taking a post at this same Donets Steel Company in about 1895. He moved to the new Russian Providence firm in 1899 as chief of the steel division when he was under thirty years of age. The following year he was appointed managing director, a post he held for seven years. He was reputed to be an excellent technician.[13]

These synoptic sketches suggest two further points. First, one notes again and again that top metallurgical directors, who often had Russian experience, often worked first at Huta-Bankova in Poland, or, less frequently, at Kama Steel or Donets Steel. All three firms were founded at an early date, the earliest the Huta-Bankova Company (1876). That firm, which always also employed a large num-

11. C.L., Aciéries du Donetz, Etude, March 1911; C.L., Oural Volga, Etude, December 1910.
12. C.L., Aciéries du Donetz, Etude, March 1911.
13. C.L., Providence Russe, Etudes, June 1900 and November 1901.

ber of French-speaking technicians, served as a seedbed whence plant managers and their associates sprang at the end of the century. It thereby facilitated greatly the efforts of foreign follower companies.

In a similar fashion many foreign directors of coal companies began as engineers at the pioneering Rutchenko or Gorlovka firms, which also provided followers with experienced personnel. Arsène Lebrun, for example, a graduate of the Ecole des Mines at Paris, began as an engineer at Gorlovka early in the 1890s. He then moved to the Russian Providence as director of the firm's Donets coal mines, and finally to the Lugan Coal Company as top director in Russia. Lebrun made his entire career in Russia, spoke Russian fluently, and had a good reputation.[14]

Second, while Russian experience was invaluable, there was no rigid bureaucratic-crawl pattern of advancement. On the contrary, careers were made (and unmade) very quickly. One has the definite impression that, as far as foreign managers were concerned, southern Russia was a land for aggressive, competent, tough-minded young men.

Foreign directors and their top assistants received high salaries to go "to the lost country of the Tartars."[15] During the 1890s foreign directors of metallurgical works in Russia received from 50,000 to 80,000 francs per annum, and the highest paid directors earned 100,000 francs. Principal engineers earned from 20,000 to 25,000 francs, and even neophyte graduates of Western engineering schools re-

14. A.N., 65 AQ, L 130, Lougan, Annual Report, 1903; C.L., Lougan, Etude, September 1904.
15. Lauwick, *L'industrie*, p. 178.

ceived about 15,000 francs.[16] The archives of the
Russian Providence Company, for example, show
the director of blast furnaces, a Mr. Lambert from
Liège, pressuring the directors to match an offer of
35,000 francs per annum plus bonuses which he had
received from another company in southern Russia
in 1899. With one furnace just lighted and with another almost completed, the directors reluctantly admitted they had no alternative.[17] The following year
the new commercial and administrative director, a
German from Westphalia with experience in the Donets, was also engaged at 35,000 francs yearly plus
1.5 percent of all profits above 5 percent.[18] After a
slight tendency to decline between 1900 and 1908, the
salaries of top managers at Russian Providence and
elsewhere regained the levels of those of the late
1890s. The French plant superintendent of the Russian Providence Company from 1907 to 1914 received, for example, 20,000 rubles in basic salary,
plus 2 percent of all net profits with 10,000 rubles
guaranteed, or 30,000 rubles (80,000 francs) in all.[19]

Managing directors of coal mines earned between
10,000 and 15,000 rubles (26,666 and 40,000 francs)
in the late 1890s. Subsequently there was a trend
toward lower salaries after 1900. At the Makeevka
Coal Company the first mine director, Olivier Piette,
was guaranteed a minimum of 15,000 rubles (40,000
francs) in 1899. His successor, L. Eloy, was reportedly engaged for only 7,500 rubles (20,000 francs).[20]

16. Ibid.
17. P.R. MSS, Délibérations du Conseil d'Administration, 6–
3–1899.
18. Ibid., 5–6–1900.
19. B.U.P., Russie, Providence Russe, no. 371, List of Personnel.
20. A.N., 65 AQ, K 71¹, Annual Meetings, 2–12–1898, 11–12–
1901.

When a French engineer stepped up from chief engineer to mine manager at the Golubovka-Berestovo-Bogodukhovo Coal Company in 1904, his guaranteed salary rose from 10,000 to 12,000 rubles. This firm's Russian engineer in charge of sales at Kharkov (Knote) drew the same amount. The mine manager's assistant, a Frenchman, was paid 8,500 rubles per annum.[21] The contracts of mining personnel contained bonuses like those of metallurgical directors. Bonuses were based upon profits until 1900, and usually upon reduction of production costs afterward. Thus at Makeevka Coal Piette stood to gain 1 percent of profits in excess of 500,000 francs and 2 percent of those above 700,000 francs in 1898; in 1901 Eloy's bonus was to be calculated upon reduction of costs and increase of output.

The great demand for managers and engineers in the 1890s meant that some mediocre or inexperienced men found their way to Russia at this time.[22] The Ural-Volga Metallurgical Company, which complained publicly of difficulties in recruiting top employees, was a case in point.[23] In 1898 the director of this firm's plant in the Urals, Gouvy, an engineer from the Ecole des Arts et Manufactures, who had worked first in Austria and then as assistant director at Huta-Bankova, was appraised as competent and able to handle the bureaucrats well. But his assistant, an Englishman named Simpson born in Russia, was "lazy and wasteful with the company's money." Two young French engineers, each about twenty-nine years of age, completed the staff. Neither was well suited for his job. Grossot was "seri-

21. A.N., F 30, no. 340, Rabut to Delcassé, 6–5–1904.
22. Lauwick, *L'industrie*, p. 305.
23. A.N., 65 AQ, K 168, Special Shareholders' Meeting, 23–2–1899.

ous, hard-working, and intelligent," but he was a "Parisian with a weak constitution" in a harsh country with a rigorous climate. Jourde had left the Ecole Centrale without his diploma in 1890 and had begun his Russian career at the Almaznaia Coal Company in 1894. He then floated on to other firms. "He is certainly a bit mad and he will do nothing good, though he may well do something bad." [24]

Foreign managers received certain fringe benefits in addition to their high salaries and important bonuses. Employers provided housing and heating without charge, and extended annual or biannual paid vacations to western Europe.[25] The cost of living in Russia was therefore quite low, and this permitted frugal employees to save much of their salaries. This was a powerful attraction. "Young couples leaving on their honeymoon for the steppe can return home after ten or twelve years with small fortunes, which enable them to provide their children with excellent educations as they themselves return to the less lucrative positions of our old countries." [26] And there were exceptional opportunities for rapid advancement, as the evidence on career mobility showed.

In sum, high salaries, large fringe benefits, and career opportunities more than compensated for the monotonous life of Russian industrial towns.[27] No wonder the French consul at Warsaw noted in 1908,

24. C.L., Oural Volga, Etude of Mr. Marais, August 1898.
25. P.R. MSS, Délibérations du Conseil, 22–1–1900, 5–6–1900; A.N., 65 AQ, K 117, Forges de la Kama, Annual Meetings, 21–4–1904, 24–4–1913; Lauwick, *L'industrie,* pp. 297–98.
26. Lauwick, *L'industrie,* p. 305.
27. Waton, an engineer attached to the Crédit Lyonnais at St. Petersburg, wrote in 1900, for example, that "in comparison to the Donets, St. Petersburg, which is itself very disagreeable because of the extreme temperature changes, is a terrestrial paradise." C.L., Cie Générale des Charbonnages, Waton, 27–3–1900.

with a trace of envy, that French directors and engineers in French textile mills in Poland had "very handsome situations," and that "ordinary French foremen earn the pay of high ranking officers in the French army." Similarly, he found that many managers and engineers remained indefinitely with the Huta-Bankova Steel Company and then passed their jobs on to their children as prized possessions.[28] Nor is it surprising to find that the dossiers of the Russian Providence Company at the Banque de l'Union Parisienne contain many letters written in 1918 and 1919 by former French and Belgian employees who were ready, even eager, to return to their old jobs.[29] In spite of war, revolution, and despoliation, top jobs in Russian industry were still considered excellent positions by foreigners. Foreign managers were expensive, but they were always available.

2

It was all well and good that foreign directors and their assistants could proudly point to degrees on the wall as they built large enterprises. But the crucial question for foreign shareholders and Russian development was how they did their jobs. What was their performance rating? In an attempt to answer this question, it is necessary to focus on the average manager during the period of installation and to determine his normal pattern of error and achievement in the exercise of technical and administrative functions.

In the technical domain the average foreign manager installed his firm's physical plant with a high degree of competence. Advanced techniques were in-

28. A.N., F 12, no. 7275, d'Anglade, consul de France, Voyage d'étude dans les centres de Pologne, June 1908.
29. B.U.P., Russie, Providence Russe, no. 371.

troduced successfully, and below-average costs of production for Russia were attained as foreign managers implemented the basic investment strategy. As we have seen, metallurgical managers performed excellently, and coal-mine directors satisfactorily, in establishing their plants. Detailed evidence on plants in other industries corroborates the conclusion that foreign managers built well technically.

None of the major railway-equipment firms founded in the 1890s—Upper Volga, Southern Ural, Bouhey at Kharkov, Hartmann—lacked modern equipment. The factories of the Upper Volga Railway Equipment Company were laid out rationally and were spacious and well equipped. This excellent situation, which gave costs of production for freight cars as low as any in Russia, was due to the engineers of Dyle and Bacalan who planned and constructed the plant.[30] The Hartmann Machine Company's locomotive plant at Lugansk, which was founded in 1896 by Gustav Hartmann, Krupp's son-in-law and Witte's personal friend, had excellent and perfectly maintained equipment, originally furnished and installed by Hartmann's company in Germany. Work was well directed, resulting in the lowest costs and highest profits per locomotive in Russia.[31] An exporter of locomotives to eastern Europe from 1907 to 1910, Hartmann in Russia was first in its field and unquestionably one of the leading firms of all Europe.[32]

Hartmann's countrymen in the organic chemical industry applied the same techniques in Russia as in

30. C.L., Haut Volga, Etude, May 1901.

31. C.L., Hartmann, Etudes, December 1898 and January 1904; A.N., F 12, no. 7175, Locomotives, Moulin to the minister of war, 1–1–1896.

32. *L'Information,* 8–1–1908, 23–8–1910, 7–2–1911; *Revue Minière.* 9–11–1911.

Germany for simpler products, although they imported intermediaries for complex fabrications. Some of the German electrical-equipment producers were largely assembly plants, but they were very well run.[33] A last example might be the colossal shipyards at Nikolaev, where Belgian engineers and managers successfully built works as large and as modern as any in western Europe.[34] As the capsule biographies suggested, top managers in both western Europe and in foreign plants in Russia had the same background, and given adequate resources, they built similar plants in both places. This was a tremendous achievement.

A second key aspect of management's technical function was evaluating and securing adequate raw materials, particularly mineral resources. Here foreign technical experts turned in a lackluster performance, which deteriorated with time and with increased competition for resources. A major protion of blame lay with original promoters and appraisers, the Schmatzers and the Bormettes upon whom the Rykovskiis and the Podvinstevs unloaded properties. Such promoting appraisers tended to pay too much on the basis of haphazard studies in their preoccupation with the speculative fever in western Europe for all things Russian. But engineers in Russia, who had often participated in the preliminary studies, often compounded original

33. For German technical excellence in these industries see Levin, *Germanskie kapitaly*, p. 73; Zak, *Nemtsy*, pp. 20–24; Eventov, *Inostrannye kapitaly*, pp. 26–27; V. S. Diakin, "Iz istorii proniknoveniia inostrannykh kapitalov v elektropromyshlennost' Rossii," pp. 209–10, in Akademiia Nauk SSSR, Trudy Leningradskogo otdeleniia instituta istorii, *Monopolii i inostrannyi kapital v Rossii* (Moscow, 1962); Haber, *Chemical Industry*, pp. 140–42.

34. C.L., Chantiers Navals de Nicolaev, Etude, September 1904.

errors. Four examples of foreign firms in iron mining in southern Russia show the dimensions of management's technical capacity in this area.

The four polytechnicians who founded the Dubovaia Balka Mining Company (1892) owed part of
their success to their excellent timing, but careful
examination and correct evaluation of the properties involved also played a key role.[35] The founders did not rush impetuously forward in their negotiations with the Pol' heritors. Instead, they
dickered tenaciously an entire year, and made several long trips to Russia, before they finally purchased the plot of 500 desiatinas (545 hectares) for
1,250,000 francs in cash, or 2,500 francs the desiatina—a marvelous price. They then chose, as one
might expect, an excellent manager, a graduate of
the Ecole des Mines of St. Etienne named Vincens.
Vincens, who had been at the Tonkin Coal Company
in Indo-China until 1893, had "learned the mining
practices of new countries." He was reputed to understand completely the habits, law, and language of
Russia six years later. "He is known by all as the
most competent director in the Krivoi-Rog region,
and he conducts all operations rationally and with
order."[36]

35. Their initial studies analyzed carefully the three types of
ore found: the occasional white, almost pure quartzites; the normal red veins; and the "pure" (70 percent) blue-black powdery
crystals. This last type presented difficulties in blast furnaces, according to the polytechnicians, because it filtered too rapidly and
stuck to the furnace's inner lining. But it worked satisfactorily
when mixed with less rich chunk ore. A conservative evaluation
estimated reserves at twenty-five million tons to a depth of only
fifty meters. All this ore could be mined by cheap open-pit methods. A.N., 65 AQ, L 807, *Notice sur les Mines de la Doubovaia
Balka.*

36. C.L., Doubovaia Balka, Etude, August 1899. Cordeweener
(see below) concurred with this judgment. *Contribution,* p. 186.

At the other end of the scale the Rakhmanovka-
Krivoi-Rog Mining Company (1898), of which Felicien Maes was a founder and the French Société
Générale an active supporter, combined poor preliminary studies and unsatisfactory technical management. The original concessions were of little
value and hastily negotiated. One that was purchased for 80,000 rubles was later sold for 5,000.
Another one, for which Maes received all the founders' shares, was abandoned in 1903 after consistent
losses. A third was bought from the Rakhmanovka
peasants after incorporation for 160,000 rubles, or
more than it was ever worth.[37] As was often the case,
founders and managers were of the same caliber.
The first manager, Jules Cordeweener, a Flemish
mining engineer from the Ecole des Mines at Brussels, was ''intelligent, energetic, and likable. But he
was in no way suited for his post. He knew nothing
of the language, laws, or customs of the country and
had to serve a veritable apprenticeship. An experienced director would have saved the company many
losses of time and money.'' [38]

A poor evaluation of iron ore deposits was made
at both the Tula Blast Furnaces Company and the
Ural-Volga Metallurgical Company by groups of engineers who installed excellent plants and overcame
serious technical problems. The chief engineer of
Espérance-Longdoz estimated that the concessions
in central Russia upon which the Tula Blast Furnaces Company was based contained 10,000,000 tons
of 55 percent pure iron ore—enough for three blast

37. C.L., Rakhmanovka-Krivoi-Rog, Etude, March 1903.
38. Ibid., August 1899. Cordeweener later wrote his interesting
Contribution à l'étude du Donetz (Brussels, 1902), apparently
while looking unsuccessfully for another job in southern Russia.

furnaces for one hundred years. Yet after two years the company had been unable to find 100,000 tons of that grade and used ore that was 42 percent pure.[39] The Ural-Volga Company did not find sufficient ore on its concessions in the Urals to produce the pig iron needed by its modern steel mill at Tsaritsyn. Subsequently the company gave up pig-iron production entirely, sold off its Ural properties, and bought all its pig-iron requirements for the mill at Tsaritsyn from Donets producers. One suspects that mines were salted for cocksure foreign experts.[40] Or perhaps honest mistakes were made. Foreign engineers did poorly in either case. This, unfortunately, was all too common in mineral evaluation and purchase after 1894.

The mixed performance of foreign management in the face of technical problems also existed in the administrative realm. Generalization is difficult. Yet on the basis of enterprises examined it seems that the major pluses were satisfactory accounting methods, the ability to determine costs precisely, and a fairly high level of honesty among generally conscientious executives. The French consul's coupling of technical prowess and managerial rectitude in 1892 was typical and significant. "All of these firms under foreign control [at St. Petersburg] have ex-

39. C.L., Toula, Etude, December 1898.
40. Waton of the Crédit Lyonnais wrote while on mission in the Urals in August 1900 of the difficulties of proper evaluation and foreign over-confidence. "I am horribly tired. These long horseback trips from plant to plant in the southern Urals under a driving rain for three weeks are very hard. But I know the region well and the very difficult conditions of its industry—better, I hope, than the learned French engineers set down at Ufa on a bright spring morning." C.L., Sud-Oural, Waton, August 1900. Waton is apparently referring to the engineers from the Société de Châtillon-Commentry who planned the Ural-Volga Company.

cellent expensive equipment. They are generally well-managed, which is not the case for plants run by Russians."[41]

As this comment suggests, foreigners were certain that their methods of business administration surpassed those of Russian managers, who coupled mismanagement and malfeasance with distressing regularity. "It is time," wrote the newly appointed French consul Rabut at Odessa in 1904, "to put an end to the extraordinary waste—to be polite—that reigns among the Russian administrators of mining companies in southern Russia, to stop squandering materials, and to begin to maintain equipment properly."[42] Almost twenty years earlier the need to bribe railroad officials had immediately struck a touring student.[43] And if some foreign managers and directors also exhibited these bad habits, particularly the exaggeration of fees and commissions, one nevertheless has the distinct impression of generally superior conduct.[44] For the foreigner, the adminis-

41. F 12, no. 7175, Rapport sur l'industrie métallurgique en Russie, 22–10–1892.

42. A.N., F 30, no. 343, Cie Minière de Gouloubovka, Rabut to Delcassé, 28–4–1904.

43. E.M., Chapuy, Journal de Voyage, 1887.

44. Documents on many firms, such as Briansk, Putilov, Baranovskii Powder, at the Crédit Lyonnais and the Banque de l'Union Parisienne, as well as French and Belgian consular reports, and even the financial press, show that this was what foreigners emphatically believed. The evidence is biased of course, but I have found nothing to contradict it in the literature deploring prerevolutionary business ethics. For short but stimulating remarks on their low level see A. Gerschenkron, *Economic Backwardness*, pp. 126, 130; C. Joubert, *Russia as It Really Is* (London, 1905), pp. 42–51; as well as Richardson Wright, *The Russians: An Interpretation* (New York, 1917), pp. 136 ff.; L. Tikhomirov, *Russia, Political and Social*, 2 vols. (London, 1888), 1:253–56; Harold W. Williams, *Russia of the Russians* (New York, 1915), pp. 383–87.

tration of public corporations was a profession, not a fief to be plundered.

But honesty is one thing, success another, and foreign managers had numerous problems. Few foreign managers were able to avoid costly, time-consuming legal conflicts with previous owners, peasants, or customers. This was a serious matter. Key contracts selling or leasing properties, for example, were often improperly drawn. The successes of the Bonnardel Group in this field were all too rare, and the misfortunes of the Rykovskii Coal Company all too common.[45] The French Société Générale's Rutchenko Coal Company, for instance, worked a thirty-year lease which included options to buy. Yet for many years it was uncertain whether these options would be upheld by the Russian courts if contested, as the Rutchenko heirs threatened to do.[46] Fears concerning these options encouraged the Société Générale to hustle Rutchenko into that strange ark, the Omnium Russe, in 1897, and to wait, in vain, for the rising tides of speculation to carry it away from the Société Générale. The Russian Providence Company found itself in 1898 with a plant site on the Kalmius River near Mariupol without secure water rights, which it was forced to purchase (for a second time the company believed) from Mariupol's city council.[47]

Leases with peasant communes were particularly difficult to negotiate. They were even harder to renew, since Russian law stipulated that upon expiration after not more than thirty years, all property

45. See chapters 10 and 11.
46. C.L., Routchenko, Etude, August 1897.
47. P.R. MSS, Délibérations du Conseil, 21–2–1898.

and fixed equipment reverted to the commune free of charge.[48] As one observer put it, the "purchase of a mining concession is difficult and complicated, particularly if a Russian commune is involved. The concession must be approved by two-thirds of the peasants, and the methods needed for such consent require operations which are little related to the engineer's art."[49]

Provisions for hauling were often considered a right to supplementary peasant income, and these contracts could also present difficulties. The Tula Blast Furnaces Company, for example, built a second and third blast furnace on the assumption that traditional rates for peasant hauling would remain unchanged. But in fact they soared, doubled the cost of ore, and contributed to the firm's eventual failure.[50] No wonder foreigners tried to deal with peasants indirectly through Russian haulage contractors whenever possible. There were enough problems with peasants anyway, such as right-of-way easements over peasant lands, which had a curious way of snarling in their transfer from Russian proprietors to foreign firms. Thus after the Lugan Coal Company began its eight-kilometer railroad spur to a nearby station, the peasant commune involved challenged the company's allegedly imperfect right-of-way. A long legal dispute was finally settled through the good offices of state officials—and a payment of 260,000 francs.[51]

Another problem was that foreign management often made costly mistakes through its sales organization. The worst mistake was inaccurate appraisal

48. C.L., Sels Gemmes, Etude, August 1912.
49. A. Pourcel, Mémoire, November 1897, E.M.
50. C.L., Toula, Etude, January 1905.
51. C.L., Lougan, Etude, December 1898.

of credit risks, which led to waves of bad debts after 1900. Another was the overextension of credit facilities. Jeunehomme, the commercial director of the Prokhorov Coal Company, was dismissed in 1900 because he had incurred large bad debts. Even Jeunehomme's sure debtor, that notoriously sound but lethargic payer, the Russian state, had obtained credits of 1,550,000 francs, or one-half of Prokhorov's entire funded debt.[52] There is little doubt that foreign entrepreneurs favored syndicated selling arrangements after 1900 not only to raise prices but also to coordinate information on bad debtors and to establish uniform, noncompetitive credit terms.

Perhaps the most serious shortcoming was the underestimation of construction costs.[53] This meant that original capitalizations proved inadequate and that many firms were forced to seek additional capital after 1900 on very disadvantageous terms. Undue haste of construction, inflation in the prices of capital goods, and insufficient allowance for the weight of the Russian tariff were all partly responsible. But perhaps the single most important reason was the underestimation of social-overhead costs. These costs were normally borne by the firm in Russia—and invariably so in the South.[54] Estimates were exceeded on the average by a factor of two. The "very serious" Franco-Russian Cotton Company, for example, spent 1,700,000 francs for housing, baths, hospitals, schools, churches, etc., in place

52. A.N., 65 AQ, L 355, Prokhorov, Annual Meeting, 13–7–1901.

53. Verstraete, "Les capitaux étrangers," *Congrès Internationale* 4, no. 111 :8.

54. C.L., Métallurgie dans le Midi, April 1905; Lauwick, *L'industrie*, p. 31; Olga Crisp, "French Investment in Russian Joint-stock Companies," *Business History* 2 (1960) : 84. See chapter 7 for additional discussion.

of 900,000 francs originally allotted.[55] Most firms could have avoided some of these social expenses if their managers had originally known Russia better.[56]

An examination of a small Belgian metallurgical producer serves as a fitting catalogue of initial foreign management at its worst. The Verkhnii-Dneprovsk Metallurgical Company (Brussels, 1896) began with a good idea—that there was room in the Donets for a specialized foundry producing cast steel pipes.[57] But this plan was "poorly executed. In fact, one cannot criticize the first directors enough." [58] The Krivoi-Rog iron deposits sold to the firm by founders Moses Sinaiskii, a St. Petersburg lawyer, N. Shchedrov, a gentleman from Odessa, and Firmin Bruckert, a Belgian industrialist, were simply worthless.[59] Thus a lack of iron ore forced the company to purchase its pig iron after 1900, while its two large blast furnaces stood idle.

In order to produce quickly, the firm imported "delicate" foundry equipment over the enormous Russian tariff (3 rubles per pud, or 486 francs per ton). This equipment never functioned properly and was eventually broken up and used for scrap. The 1903 reorganization even instituted traditional hand casting, "the prevailing Russian practice everywhere." The machinery then used was worth but

55. C.L., Société Cotonnière Franco-Russe, Note, February 1906; ibid., Annual Report, 1906.

56. C.L., Hartmann, Etude, December 1898.

57. C.L., Cie Métallurgique de Verchny-Dneprovsk, Etude, August 1904.

58. Ibid.

59. Russians subscribed 20 percent of the capital shares, probably the quid pro quo for the sale of their very poor ore concessions. A.N., 65 AQ, M 483, Verchny-Dneprovsk, Articles of Incorporation, 15–10–1896; C.L., Verchny-Dneprovsk, Etude, August 1904.

80,000 francs, "since the major equipment in a hand-operated foundry is insignificant." [60] No wonder twelve of thirteen million francs were lost by 1904.

Finally, inexperienced foreign managers were terrible. "It is difficult to estimate the number of faults and defects, large and small, committed in constructing the plant; the first two managements showed a total absence of all reason and good sense." [61] The third manager was a retired French foreman named Bodin, who was recalled from France to salvage the firm. For many years chief of pipe casting at Pastukhov's works, the second oldest if least significant metallurgical plant in the Donets and the only all-Russian firm, Bodin was a "very good pipe specialist. . . . If the plant can be saved, he will do it." [62] He did not, and in 1909 Verkhnii-Dneprovsk received its just reward—bankruptcy.

In summary, the performance of foreign management in the period of installation was spotty. Technically, foreign engineers built modern plants competently, but they did poorly in appraising and securing raw materials. Administratively, managers were adequate when dealing with internal problems, but their difficulties with units external to the firm were numerous. On a high level of generalization, it seems that foreign managers were successful when they could exercise their authority unimpaired in command situations over men and material within the firm, but that in bargaining situations with independent groups their skill and experience were often surpassed. Excellent plants and proper internal

60. C.L., Verchny-Dneprovsk, Etude, August 1904.

61. Ibid. The first was Bruckert who sold the initial ore concessions that were to provide ore 60 percent pure for 120 years. *Lettres d'un capitaliste,* 9-9-1899.

62. C.L., Verchny-Dneprovsk, Etude, August 1904.

management tended to be offset by costly debits arising from bargaining situations. Such a balance sheet was promising, but unsatisfactory.

3

That the initial performance of foreign managers was extremely uneven is one important conclusion thus far. Equally striking was the clear trend toward russification of management as individual firms began to operate more or less normally. Immediately questions arise. How did this russification take place and what caused it? Was there a connection between it and the early inconsistent pattern of foreign management?

The first fact to note is that a number of firms were explicit partnerships between foreign and Russian entrepreneurs, with each side supplying directors and managers. Russification of such firms often proceeded very quickly, especially if the initial foreign role was limited. For example, the South Russian Soda Company, the first firm to challenge successfully Lubimov-Solvay's Russian monopoly, was a cooperative venture of businessmen in the chemical industry from Lyons and the Russian Private Commercial Bank through its French associate, the Banque Privée Industrielle et Commerciale de Lyon et Marseille.[63] The principal plant was built from French plans under French supervision, but when it was completed in 1899 a Russian engineer was appointed plant manager. One percent of the firm's total capital was set aside for this key employee. The only French employee of importance at the plant for the next fifteen years was the technical director.[64]

63. A.N., F 30, no. 328, Verstraete, 9–3–1898.
64. C.L., Société Sud-Russe pour la Soude, Annual Meeting, 2–12–1899; Annual Reports, 1914, 1915.

Other partnerships that russified quickly included the South Russian Dnieper Metallurgical Company, Bouhey's locomotive producer, and the Kachkar Gold Company. This last firm used several technically oriented foreign directors from 1897 to 1901. Their proposed changes upset workers, however, and in 1901 a Russian engineer took control. The Russian was not a specialist in gold mining, but he was a good administrator. By 1902 only one employee of this Franco-Belgian firm was French.[65]

Since enumeration of quickly russified partnerships would only hint at the process involved, a rather detailed look at one such firm, the Nikopol-Mariupol Metallurgical Company, is rewarding. Incorporated under Russian law in May 1896 with a capital of 4,500,000 rubles in 24,000 shares, Nikopol-Mariupol's Russian and American founders planned to mine manganese deposits belonging to Grand Duke Michael near Nikopol, to refine that ore into ferro-manganese pig iron, and then to export the semifinished product to the United States.[66] After incorporation, detailed investigation proved the ore deposits average and the venture mediocre. But with their combination of unrivaled influence in Russia and great technical renown, the partners

65. C.L., Katchkar, Etude, September 1902. Material in Brandt, *Inostrannye kapitaly*, 2:267–77, on russification of management is confirmed in the different Crédit Lyonnais studies.

66. The founders reflected the two interests: Adolphe Rothstein, director of the St. Petersburg International Bank, represented his bank, a grand duke, and the cream of the Russian elite; Edmond Dutil Smith represented American (apparently Carnegie) interests. See A.N., 65 AQ, K 156, Articles of Incorporation; C.L., Nikopol Mariupol, Etude, December 1898. The Banque Internationale de Paris and its general manager, Théophile Lombardo, subscribed 1,600 shares but played no entrepreneurial role. See Iu. B. Solov'ev, "Mezhdunarodnyi bank i frantsuskii finansovyi kapital," p. 386, in Akademiia Nauk, *Monopolii i inostrannyi kapital*.

shifted gears. They sought and won a government order for 150 versts of eight-inch steel pipe valued at 2,100,000 rubles for the long-debated Baku-to-Batum pipeline.[67]

Since the beneficent state also demanded rapid delivery and imposed exacting technical conditions, the company bought an entire functioning pipe plant in America and then reassembled it in Russia beside the ultramodern American-style blast furnaces. The director of this ambitious undertaking was Harry Loud, twenty-eight years old and previously engineer at Carnegie's Illinois Steel Company. "Loud remains completely American in Russia. He is intelligent and has tremendous energy, qualities absolutely essential for this affair."[68] Loud was seconded by other Americans. The Crédit Lyonnais's engineer believed that in spite of Loud's energy the new company would give only mediocre results. The early changes in program and the ensuing excessive haste had added up to enormous fixed investment. Furthermore, the company was completely dependent on the government.[69]

Within three years the American technical experts had packed their bags, and management at the plant was composed almost exclusively of Polish engineers, a very important if neglected group in southern Russia's industrial development. The American capital participation had apparently disappeared, probably by way of the Paris and Brussels Exchanges. The company was directed completely by the International Bank of St. Petersburg and "very important people" who managed to secure additional pipeline orders from the government

67. C.L., Nikopol-Mariupol, Etude, December 1898.
68. Ibid.; also, a printed note dated 1899.
69. C.L., Nikopol-Mariupol, Etude, December 1898.

in 1900 at very favorable prices.[70] After a reduction of capital in 1907, capital was raised to 15,100,000 rubles in 1913 to permit expansion into the production of heavy armor plate for battleships. Predictably, the firm had secured a government order for 24,000,000 puds of deck armor in the new naval program. "Influence" remained the firm's greatest asset. Interestingly enough, the directors called upon the foreign expertise of Krupp for these new installations. Decision makers and managers were unquestionably Russian.[71]

Occasionally partnerships planned specifically for the training of native management, either in western Europe or Russia, and the withdrawal of the foreigner. The machine-tool company serving as technical consultant for the South Russian Mechanical Engineering Company provided plans and also trained necessary Russian engineers and foremen in its French factories.[72] Thus the original management team was almost entirely Russian. In 1911 the firm of Emile Crumière furnished the Myszkov Rayon Company with crucial patents and foreign engineers until Russians could be trained at the home plant in France.[73] The Société Normand was also to supply its own engineers for the Crichton Shipyards while training Russians in France. In-

70. C.L., Nikopol-Mariupol, Etude, November 1901. The syndicate of five other pipe producers had competed for the order but had received nothing.

71. *Cote de la Bourse et de la Banque,* 5–7–1913. Ol', *Inostrannye kapitaly,* p. 12, estimates that one-third of all capital was in French hands in 1916. This seems almost certainly an overestimation, since the shares were traded inactively and had no following. But even if Ol' were correct, Russians could hardly complain. Dividends were slim and foreign influence was negligible.

72. C.L., Constructions Mécaniques, Etude, May 1895.

73. A.N., 65 AQ, H 190, Articles of Incorporation.

deed, the obligation of foreign technical consultants to help train Russians abroad was widespread in the defense industry.[74]

Normally, however, when foreign entrepreneurs clearly controlled their firms they gradually increased their local personnel, but without any systematic plan to meet problems as they arose. The appointment of Russians with position and influence to the board of directors was often the first step. Entrepreneurs with Russian experience, like the Bonnardel Group, did this automatically when they incorporated, and overconfident newcomers in the 1890s learned to follow suit.

The reason was simple. Foreign entrepreneurs needed Russians for effective negotiations with units outside the firm, in which foreign managers often made serious mistakes as we have seen. Negotiations with the government for contracts was probably the single most important area—witness Nikopol-Mariupol—but there were many others. For example, since all corporations, foreign or domestic, required specific authorization from the tsar in a separate decree, foreigners could find themselves waiting months or even years to obtain official permission, if Russian knowledge (and perhaps foreign money) were not judiciously supplied.[75] And since every change in capital or bonded debt also required state authorization, knowledgeable Russian board members were indispensable.

Within the daily operations of the firm, commer-

74. See C.L., Etude sur le chantier Crichton; B.U.P., Russie, Société Baranovsky, nos. 148, 261, 317–18; Chantiers Nevsky, nos. 317–19; René Girault, "Usines Putiloff," pp. 217–36.

75. See P.R. MSS, Délibérations du Conseil, 6–2–1898; A.E., Brussels, no. 2818, Tramways d'Odessa; C.L., Charbonnages de Sosnowice, Note Annexe, 1902.

cial personnel were russified most completely and most rapidly. Not only did foreign commercial managers occasionally make bad errors, as we have seen, but local personnel performed better for less cost on routine tasks.[76] One careful observer noted that after twenty years of operations the Sosnowice Coal Company of Poland had a serious competitive advantage because all members of its sales force were either Russian or Polish.[77] To help guard against embezzlement, however, foreigners invariably kept a foreign accountant to check the books.

Since superior technology was at the heart of foreign entrepreneurship, it is understandable why the use of Russian technical men was less widespread. Yet careful investigation shows numerous foreign firms using Russian engineers as either plant managers or technical directors by the early years of the twentieth century. Some of these came from that small group of Russian engineers who had worked or studied in western Europe. From the outset they were brought back from western Europe to assume high posts in Russia. One metallurgical engineer named Kravtsov, with several years of experience in France, returned to Russia with the Russo-Belgian Company, and he was the highly satisfactory general plant manager of the Olkhovaia Steel Company shortly thereafter.[78] Julien Couharévitch, a graduate engineer of the University of Liège with "all necessary professional experience" in Bel-

76. Lauwick, *L'industrie*, p. 179.

77. C.L., Mines de Czelade, Etude, September 1902. In the same year the Belgian Gosudarev-Bairak Coal Company noted with satisfaction that finally all its commercial personnel were Russian. A.N., 65 AQ, L 187, Special Shareholders' Meeting, 14–3–1902.

78. C.L., Olkovaia, Etude, August 1904. Kravtsov was particularly good from a commercial point of view.

gium, was the first director of the Prokhorov Coal Company.[79] When Couharévitch proved unsatisfactory, the directors turned momentarily to an old Belgian engineer who proved no better. After 1900 all mine directors were apparently Russian.[80] Finally, when the Belgian Blast Furnaces Company of Ufa was reorganized in 1913, the principal director was Peter Il'in, a Russian engineer who had been worked in Belgium for several years. Il'in had an excellent reputation and a fortune of about one hundred and fifty thousand francs.[81] There were undoubtedly other Russian engineers from western Europe who returned home as managers for foreign businessmen.

More frequently, Russians rose through the ranks in Russia. Thus the engineer-in-chief of Gorlovka in 1899, who was promoted to administrative director in 1902, was a Russian named Knote, the best engineer in the south Russian coal industry according to a Crédit Lyonnais report.[82] The plant director of the Nikolaev Shipyards after 1900 was a Russian Jew named Kanegisser, who replaced the first director, an Englishman.[83] Russian engineers replaced French mining directors at the South Russian Salt

79. A.N., 65 AQ, L 355, Annual Reports, April 1895, October 1896. Couharévitch was the author of an interesting article, "La Russie industrielle (Région Ouest)," *Revue Universelle des Mines,* 3d Ser., 19, 36th year (1892) : 265 ff.

80. Annual Report, October 1900; C.L., Prokhorov, Etude, January 1899.

81. A.E., Brussels, no. 2902, sec. 1, Société des Hauts Fourneaux, Laminoirs et Fonderies de Ufa; A.N., 65 AQ, K 162.

82. C.L., Société de l'Industrie Houillère, Etude, January 1899.

83. C.L., Chantiers Navals, Etude, September 1904; ibid., Annual Report, 1900; A.E., Brussels, no. 2902, sec. 1, note of 27–7–1897.

and Coal Company by 1901 at the latest, and at
Irmino Coal by 1905.[84] These cases of top Russian
technical personnel were exceptional, but they show
that even in the foreigners' key posts substitution
by local personnel tended to take place.

How does one account for this general trend toward greater use of Russian personnel? Initial mistakes and failures of managers without any Russian
experience was only one cause.[85] A second one was
the need to cut the very high costs of management
and administration when profits fell after 1900.[86]
High costs were in part due to the "Russian national habit of waste," which the foreigner was always quick to decry,[87] and in part to high salaries
for foreigners themselves. Most of Rutchenko's
profits were consumed by high-priced management
for many years, Gorlovka paid outlandish salaries,
and Ural-Volga reported enormous managerial expenses.[88] In the Donets, the foreigner's chosen field,
there were "far too many directors, commissioners,
comptrollers, revisers, sales agents, and secretaries
who did little or nothing," even in 1904.[89] Since Russian managers often cost less, their substitution was
rational and helped cut costs. Equally important, a
concentration of management in the Donets, with a
corresponding scaling down of expenses at St. Petersburg and Paris or Brussels, eliminated a certain

84. C.L., Sels Gemmes, Etudes, January 1899 and June 1912;
Irmino, Etude, February 1905.

85. Lauwick, *L'industrie*, pp. 29–31.

86. Ibid., p. 179.

87. A.N., F 30, no. 343, Rabut to Delcassé, 8–5–1905.

88. C.L., Routchenko, Etude, January 1899; Société de
l'Industrie Houillère, Etude, April 1903; Oural Volga, Etude,
August 1898.

89. A.N., F 30, 343, Rabut to Delcassé, 6–5–1904. Also, ibid.,
Rabut to Delcassé, 28–4–1904.

number of foreign positions in many firms, as the use of cartels for selling also did.[90]

But perhaps as important as any factor was the existence of two particularly capable indigenous minorities with whom foreign entrepreneurs could and did work well. Polish engineers and technicians, who were normally Russian citizens, were widely used in foreign firms in the Donets. And the contemporary observer Lauwick is correct in saying that Polish engineers and managers conquered "technical and administrative positions in the South as southern metallurgical products conquered Poland."[91] Both the famous Dnieper and Nikopol-Mariupol metallurgical firms had exclusively Polish managements after 1900. Firms with German participation in the Donets, like Fitzner and Gamper, or the Sosnowice Pipe Company, both of which had migrated from Poland, relied heavily on Polish managers.[92] And one finds individual Polish engineers in high positions in many firms: the engineer replacing the Frenchman at Gorlovka in 1900 was Polish; in 1905 the local directors of the South Urals Railway Equipment Company, the famous Krivoi-Rog Iron Company, and the Prokhorov Coal Company were all Polish.[93] The relative decline of Polish mining and metallurgical industries in the 1890s supplied foreign entrepreneurs in southern Russia with invaluable human capital.

90. For example, the Ural-Volga Company, which at one time had four managements—Paris, St. Petersburg, the Urals, and Tsaritsyn—eliminated the superfluous Paris office and sold the small and time-consuming Urals plant after 1900.

91. *L'industrie,* p. 179. He gives no examples.

92. A.N., F 30, no. 342, letters from the director general of the Union Minière et Métallurgique, Makeevka, to the French ambassador at St. Petersburg, 25–6–1916 and 28–6–1916.

93. See dossiers at Crédit Lyonnais.

What Polish engineers were to technical positions, Jewish tradesmen were to commercial positions.[94] Experienced in commerce, numerous, and discriminated against in Russian-owned firms, Jews were natural auxiliaries for foreign businessmen.[95] In 1914, for example, the branch of the Crédit Lyonnais at Odessa had 6 Frenchmen out of 100 employees. The vast majority was Jewish at all levels.[96]

A detailed example from the streetcar industry is indicative. The Otlet Group of tramways—Odessa, Kharkov, Rostov-on-the-Don, and Tiflis, among others—was directed in Russia almost exclusively by Russian Jews, men like J. Fain, one of the group's top officers and director of the Rostov company. Each individual firm had only one or two Belgians, like Wolthers, the manager of the Kharkov Streetcar Company, who married the sister of a Jewish board member and assimilated completely.[97] After persistent difficulties between these companies and the respective municipal administrations, the exasperated Belgian consul in Tiflis asked in 1910 why foreign companies employed so many Jews in Russia, since it displeased the authorities and infuriated the nationalists.[98] Ten years earlier another

94. Lauwick, *L'industrie*, p. 179.

95. The French consular correspondence noted with regularity that German industry worked closely with Russian Jews, who were allegedly strongly pro-German. See, for example, A.N., F 12, no. 7176, consul at Warsaw to Quai d'Orsay, 25–6–1884; ibid., 20–2–1895; F 30, no. 340, Provodnik, letters and notes.

96. A.N., F 12, no. 7173, consul at Odessa to the Quai d'Orsay, 15–3–1912.

97. A.E., Brussels, no. 2818, Tramways de Kharkov, Boeye, consul at Kharkov, 3–1–1910. This dossier is exceptionally full and informative.

98. Ibid., Tramways de Tiflis, De Waepenaert, consul general at Ekaterinoslav, 23–1–1907.

Belgian consul reported a conversation with the minister of war, General Kuropatkin. Best known for his nefarious role in starting the Russo-Japanese War, Kuropatkin linked Jews and foreigners in a typical violent outburst against both. "He [Kuropatkin] is very much against the invasion of the country by foreigners who . . . exploit natural resources Russians themselves can develop, even if they must first wait for centuries. He says he will oppose foreign companies, particularly if they employ Jews." [99]

Such Russian antipathy toward Jews placed them apart from the Russian population by necessity, and perhaps by choice. It was probably the same for Poles in the Donets. Significantly, in 1901 Polish and foreign workers were housed together, apart from Russian workers, at Konstantinovka Glass in an unsuccessful attempt to prevent friction with Russian workers.[100] The Crédit Lyonnais engineer in Poland noted that Great Russians could never be used to solve the occasional problem of labor supply in Polish coal mines because of the "terrible hatred of the two races." [101] Natives, yet outsiders, Jews and Poles furnished the more rational foreign businessmen with an excellent intermediary group of managers.

Lastly, foreign managers were replaced because they found it increasingly difficult to direct Russian workers, particularly after 1904, when the revolutionary movement of fact and fable mixed xenophobia and anticapitalism in a violent concoction. Dorizon, the director general of the French Société

99. Ibid., Tramways de Rostov-sur-le-Don, embassy at St. Petersburg, 17–1 and 6–2–1899.

100. A.E., Brussels, no. 2904, Konstantinovka.

101. C.L., Czelade, Etude, 1902.

Générale, struck a common note in explaining why (in part) French personnel were lacking at the Briansk Metallurgical Company in 1907. This interesting statement pinpoints the dual problems of russification and effective management and is worth quoting in full.

> One must remember that the mass of workers has been heavily indoctrinated in these last years and their nationalism has been over-excited. The consecutive assassinations of several plant managers have shown this all too clearly. In such conditions one cannot even dream of directing Russian workers except with their countrymen, or with French engineers understanding completely their very special mentality. Such men are very rare, and when found they very often draw back from the grave personal risks involved. We can do little, then, but give them temporary missions of inspection which do not put them in direct contact with the working class.[102]

The Kostroma Cotton Company provided a vivid example of labor problems between foreign managers and Russian personnel. This firm was at the outset a joint effort of two textile manufacturers on the one hand (Jules Gratry of Lille who specialized in producing heavy linen duck, and Firmin Gérard of Brussels, who owned cotton spinning and weaving mills in Belgium and France) and the Banque Privée of Lyons (and in turn the St. Petersburg Private Commerce Bank) on the other.[103] The two industrialists had examined the widow Mikin's small linen factory, taken an option to buy, and organized their firm at Brussels in 1899. The Russian bank was im-

102. A.N., F 30, no. 340, Société Briansk, Dorizon to Sallandrouze de Lamornaix, Directeur du Mouvement des Fonds, 25–11–1907.
103. A.N., 65 AQ, H 153, Articles of Incorporation; ibid., *Notice* (1900).

portant in negotiations and underwriting—the Banque Privée of Lyons subscribed one-third of the capital—but Gratry and Gérard were Kostroma's decision makers.

They chose Henri Fleury, "who has already built several important spinning mills [in western Europe] and who is extremely competent," to be managing director at Kostroma. Fleury's task was "to organize the same productive conditions existing in our country" in both the old linen factory and in the new model cotton mill "in order to compete advantageously with the very best mills in Russia." [104] Using the most modern foreign equipment, the new firm seemed to have bright prospects.

They soon turned dark, then black. A harassed and very sick Fleury returned to France to die in late 1902 after serious labor problems. Then Gratry and Gérard took turns as managing director at the town of Kostroma's first and only cotton mill. They had a terrible time.

> The workers showed themselves hostile to all progress, and never succeeded in reaching normal production. We vainly tried to introduce piece work to stimulate their ardor; yet this only increased their dissatisfaction. We returned badly disillusioned, if not completely disheartened. We decided that the only solution was to send teams of experienced foreign workers to train Russian workers and stimulate production.

> Events decreed otherwise. Shortly after our return a strike followed persistent agitation and after three weeks rioting broke out. The mills were stormed three times by the rioters in May 1903. The entire French and Belgian personnel fled for

104. C.L., Kostroma, Annual Reports, 3–11–1900 and 12–11–1901.

their lives, and left the government to protect the mills. . . .

This time all our organization was completely overturned; no part of it remained in Russia because, knowing their lives in danger there, our *chefs de service* refused categorically to return to Kostroma.

After such an adventure there was no question of using foreigners to reform our top management; we needed Russians for our top personnel at any price, and above all a Russian managing director. Constant Wemaere [director and linen merchant at Lille] took this delicate mission, and after a series of extended Russian trips, we have chosen Morganov, a Russian engineer who has been well recommended. Let us hope he has what we desire— that he combines honesty and unwavering energy with technical skill.[105]

As this remarkable quote suggests, there was never afterward the slightest question of reversing the policy of Russian management, although labor problems certainly did not disappear. In 1908 Morganov was replaced by Ramberg—"a technical man of the first order who has already reorganized two Russian cotton mills." This fitted with the decision to discontinue the consistently unprofitable linen operations and concentrate on cotton. Initial losses were recouped slowly, and all profits were reinvested. Cotton spindles thus increased from 23,000 in 1900 to 27,000 in 1905 and then tripled to 75,000 by 1911 as the linen factory was reequipped for cotton spinning. By 1913 the company was certainly viable, although not more than 3 or 4 percent was being earned on the 10,000,000-franc capitalization, and no dividends were paid.

105. Ibid., Annual Report, 10–11–1903.

It was a rare management that admitted its failures so honestly, or even mentioned them to shareholders. The Russo-French Cotton Company, for example, noted only that its first director, Zunzer, previously a teacher in a textile trade school at Mulhouse, was replaced by another Alsacian with eight years of Russian experience. "Zunzer failed to get the best from his workers . . . who must be treated with firmness, but also with prudence, in view of their present spirit which complicates our task." [106] Similarly the board of directors of the South Russian Mechanical Engineering Company was dismissing the last of their foreign personnel in 1906 because of the "difficulties inherent in the Russian situation." [107] In the early twentieth century the problems of labor-management relations replaced those of labor recruitment. These new difficulties proved much harder to resolve.

Dorizon was also right about assassinations. Recurring waves of revolutionary terrorism killed, maimed, and threatened top foreigners repeatedly, particularly between 1904 and 1908. Georges Raymond, a thirty-two-year-old engineer from the Ecole Centrale, was a typical victim. After beginning his career at Gorlovka, he had worked in the Urals and then directed the Nikitovka Coal Company. In 1906 he was charged with completely reorganizing the Donets Steel Company. He was murdered shortly thereafter. Of prominent family, he received a high mass at Notre Dame in Paris.[108] No wonder top engineers from western Europe, highly productive and employable members of society whether at home or

106. A.N., 65 AQ, H 258, Annual Reports, 1899 and 1901.
107. A.N., 65 AQ, M 387, Special Meeting, 20–1–1906.
108. *Bulletin de la Chambre de Commerce Russe* 5 (1906) : 38; Comité pour l'étude des questions d'intérêt commun des mines et usines du midi de la Russie, *Circulaire,* no. 179, 1907.

abroad, demanded hardship premiums for work in Russia. The boredom of the Donets was one thing; a bullet in the back was another.

How far had russification of management progressed by 1914? Apparently quite far, although comprehensive global data are lacking. According to the Association Nationale, twenty-three predominantly French companies employed only 328 Frenchmen in 1915, or 14 per company.[109] A 1908 census of French personnel in five French-owned coal companies in Poland employing approximately 16,000 workers turned up only 30 French employees. At that time eleven French-owned factories in Poland employed 10,000 workers and had 130 French employees, 54 of whom were at the Huta-Bankova Steel Company.[110]

One has the impression that metallurgical firms also retained their foreign personnel longer than coal companies in southern Russia, just as in Poland. The Société Générale's Rutchenko Coal Company normally had a French technical director, but its commercial director was Avdakov, who was very prominent in the coal syndicate. As early as 1898 all the engineers at this coal company except the technical director's top assistant were Russian. Thus there must have been only a small French staff left in 1912, when Briansk purchased the company and "drove them out with unforgettable brutality."[111]

109. A.N., F 30, no. 340, Sociétés constituées avec des capitaux français exploitant en Russie.

110. A.N., F 12, no. 7275, Voyage, d'Anglade, June 1908. Whereas 4 percent of the Huta's workers were French in 1897, only 2 percent were French in 1911. A.N., F 30, no. 340, De Coppet, consul in Warsaw, 18–2–1911; also Brandt, *Inostrannye kapitaly*, 2:270.

111. See A.N., F 30, no. 328, Verstraete to Delcassé, 26–2–1898; ibid., no. 342, L'Union Minière, letter from the director general, 28–6–1916; M. Zbyszewski, *L'Exposition nationale russe de Nijny-*

Sinçay's coal companies were equally dependent on Russians. In metallurgy, one suspects that the Russian Providence Company's forty foreign employees in 1913 were probably close to the maximum; half of these were foremen.[112] German companies employed Germans, or naturalized Germans, in greater number.[113]

But it is important to note that foreign entrepreneurs never desired, and seldom if ever permitted, total russification. The main reason was that they viewed all-Russian management with the same distaste in 1912 as in 1892. The Belgian consul urged his countrymen in 1909 always to choose Belgian or French directors, because "the Russian is a waster and experience shows that, in general, his administration is ruinous for our companies."[114] The Banque de l'Union Parisienne's representatives were strongly against long-term financial involvement in the Briansk Company, precisely because foreign managers would not be top decision makers at the plant.[115] Major German chemical firms like Badische Anilin always had a sizable proportion of Germans as top managers in their Russian subsidiaries.[116] Some foreign management was indefinitely necessary, for watching the Russians, if for no other reason.[117]

Novgorod et l'industrie russe (Paris, 1897); C.L., Routchenko, Etudes, January 1899 and May 1901; Briansk, Note, 4–1–1913.

112. B.U.P., Russie, no. 53, Providence Russe, List of Personnel, 1–7–1913.

113. Crisp, "French Investment," p. 87.

114. A.E., Brussels, no. 2818, 15–11–1909.

115. B.U.P., Russie, no. 47, Briansk, Darcy and Lombardo to B.U.P., 12–7–1906.

116. Badische Anilin, personal communication, 11–5–1966.

117. A number of Russian-owned firms, like the metallurgical firms of Alapaevsk in the Urals, Sulin in the Donets, and the Tula Cartridge Company, apparently agreed. They all used foreign engineers for directors at times, at least until 1905.

Remaining foreign managers were, however, a very special group: in a real sense they were largely assimilated into Russian industrial life. "Old Russian hands" all, they were almost invariably technical men with great Russian experience, a profound knowledge of the country, and a mastery of the Russian language. The capsule biographies at the beginning of the chapter focused on some of these men. There were others, like the engineer from the University of Liège, the long-time Russian resident Henkart, who was director of the Pobedenko Coal Company from 1905 to 1914 and who had both technical competence and complete knowledge of Russia.[118] Such men learned to solve, or had solved, serious managerial problems, such as the treacherous renegotiating of mining leases with peasant communes, with aplomb. "We believe we have the right to fill our mines and to destroy our machinery," said the experienced representative of the Ciselet Group's Gosudarev-Bairak Coal Company in 1912. "That is a quite sufficient arm for eventually successful renegotiations with the peasants." And indeed it was.[119]

As Dorizon pointed out, these bicultural Western technicians were rare.[120] Thus foreign entrepreneurial groups often learned to spread their talents thinly by attaching them to leading firms or banks, either in the Donets or at St. Petersburg, from which they traveled for investigations or emergency consultation. These men could also effectively screen new entrepreneurial opportunities at minimal cost. The Bonnardel Group used Motet in this way at an early date for the examination of possible shipyards

118. A.N., 65 AQ, L 344, Pobedenko, Annual Report, 1905.
119. A.N., 65 AQ, L 187, Special Meeting, 14–6–1902; *Belgique financière*, 30–10–1913.
120. See above quotation of Dorizon.

at Nikolaev in 1897 and for negotiations concerning the Kerch Metallurgical Company in 1900. Pierre Darcy represented the Banque de l'Union Parisienne at St. Petersburg, where he alternately helped direct the group's three functioning metallurgical firms and searched for new affairs. Similarly the Société Générale's Russian subsidiary, the Northern Bank, had three extremely knowledgeable men after 1901 to oversee the group's affairs: Maurice Verstraete, the former French consul in St. Petersburg; the engineer Waton, who had been well trained at the Crédit Lyonnais's Etude Financières in St. Petersburg; and Théophile Lombardo, who, as director of the Banque Internationale de Paris, had been active in Russian industry since 1891—first in the Gorlovka Coal Company, then in the Ural-Volga Metallurgical Company, and finally in the Société Générale's Northern Bank. These experts could back up and check up on the few foreign engineers actually managing plants in the Donets.

By 1914, then, the solution to the challenge of effective management was widespread use of Russian personnel under a tiny handful of experienced top foreign directors. This gave the foreign firm the necessary balance. While Russians handled commercial affairs and bureaucratic negotiations, in which they were superior, it was hoped that the foreign but acculturated engineer would assure the honest direction and the technical expertise which remained essential to the whole general strategy of entrepreneurship. Of course some experienced entrepreneurs knew from the very beginning that such a balance of foreign and domestic managers was necessary, and they were usually well rewarded for their insight. But generally this effective balance, which definitely prevailed in the prewar years, was achieved with difficulty over a period of time.

6

THE MOBILIZATION OF CAPITAL

Implantation of advanced techniques for entrepreneurial profits by well-paid foreign managers demanded effective mobilization of large-scale capital. Despite some failures foreign entrepreneurship generally met this challenge successfully. So successfully, in fact, that foreign investment in Russian industry has sometimes been explained in terms of the availability of capital to different groups of businessmen. According to this argument, which is often used as an explanation of foreign investment in general, as we saw in chapter 1, foreigners had an unbeatable advantage in their vastly superior capital resources. Thus local entrepreneurs were bound to do less well, and foreign leadership in new expensive industries was completely predictable. Although this explanation contains an element of truth, it must be rejected. The ability to mobilize capital was itself only one important aspect of general entrepreneurial ability. This ability could evolve, and it was never a complete or inherent monopoly of foreign businessmen.

1

The foreigner's first important asset was his capital structure. Capital structures of most foreign firms founded in the 1890s were remarkably similar and well adapted for businessmen seeking large gains. With the major exception of wholly owned subsidiaries of German chemical and electrical-equipment companies, each company operating in Russia was publicly owned and usually had three classes of corporate securities. First, there was common stock representing various types of real resources: cash, technical studies, patents, options, mineral deposits, etc. Common stock was in turn often divided into capital shares, which represented hard cash, and *apport*—or vendor—shares, which were exchanged for nonpecuniary contributions such as land, mines, initial studies, etc., at the time of incorporation. Both categories were usually quickly assimilated and were indistinguishable after the formalities of incorporation. Second, behind the common stock came founders' shares, also known as participating shares or parts. These founders' shares represented payment for intangibles such as the original idea, good will, and general business or technical skill. Founders' shares normally received 15 to 30 percent of any dividends in excess of a stated 5 or 6 percent payable to capital shares. Finally, each firm normally had long-term bonded debt with a privileged fixed claim on earnings and assets. All three forms of securities were marketable and were actively traded on European exchanges.

This common capital structure gave businessmen great leverage that maximized potential profits and minimized possible losses as a percentage return on initial investment. Seldom mentioned in the literature, this leveraged capital structure seems to me to have been of great importance to the whole process of foreign investment in Russian industry.

Consider the following hypothetical but quite representative case. An enterprise that requires 10,000,000 francs is founded with 6,000,000 francs of common stock, founders' shares are entitled to 25 percent of all dividends after a 5 percent dividend to the capital shares, and the bonded debt is 4,000,000 francs. The group of entrepreneur-founders initially takes none of the bonded debt, one-half of the capital shares, and all the founders' shares. Within a year or two the entrepreneurial group sells two-thirds of its initial investment on exchanges at a 20 percent profit for 2,400,000 francs. This reduces the group's initial cash outlay to 600,000 francs, which is backed by shares with 1,000,000 francs par value, or one-sixth of the total capital. This is sufficient for controlling interest in normal circumstances.

Now suppose the new firm makes a moderate *gross* return of but 10 percent on total investment, or 1,000,000 francs. Of this, 250,000 francs go for interest and amortization of bonded debt, leaving a net profit of 750,000 francs. The firm may then pay a first dividend of 5 percent (300,000 francs), a second dividend of 5 percent (300,000 francs) on common stock, a dividend of 100,000 francs to founders' shares, and allot 50,000 francs to reserves. The entrepreneur thus gains 200,000 francs (100,000 francs in ordinary dividends and 100,000 francs on his founders' shares), or 33⅓ percent on his remaining investment of 600,000 francs.

A little juggling and this handsome return would be much higher. Significantly, founders normally paid in only a fraction of par value at the time of incorporating. This added greatly to their leverage and potential rate of profit. Similarly, none of the subsidiary sources of income from the firm has been included.[1] Three carefully chosen examples of creative, mediocre, and parasitic businessmen show specifically how highly leveraged capital structures were used.

---

1. Russian corporations almost never had founders' shares. In them, as well as in foreign companies, unfortunately, the entrepreneur would probably allot himself, say, 1,000,000 francs of capital shares for his "preliminary studies and aids."

Joseph Ciselet, a wealthy industrialist from Antwerp, and his associates, the directors of the Tôleries de la Louvière (Alexis Isidore and Alfred Piérart), used the capital structure of the Konstantinovka Sheet Mills Company with the same finesse they subsequently displayed in managing this specialized steel fabricator. Of the initial (1896) capital stock of 2,500,000 francs, 350,000 francs and all founders' shares went to Ciselet and Piérart. This was "remuneration for contracts, experience, plans, technical studies, and work done," as well as for a vacant factory site of twenty desiatinas purchased from the Santurinovka Glass Company, which Ciselet had helped found the year before.[2] Ciselet, Piérart, Isidore two shipbuilders, and a stockbroker then subscribed 5,000 of the 8,600 capital shares of 250 francs each, paying in 20 percent at the moment of incorporation, or 50 francs per share. The remaining shares were taken in blocks of 20 to 200 shares by forty original subscribers, who described themselves mainly as merchants, industrialists, and engineers, with a sprinkling of lawyers, doctors, and *propriétaires* owning urban or rural real estate.

Capital was increased twice to 4,000,000 francs by 1900, when shares sold well over par. In addition 2,000,000 francs of twenty-seven-year bonds bearing 4 percent were floated at 98.5 percent in 1899 as the plant was being completed. This firm, a member of Prodameta after 1909, produced high-quality steel sheets exclusively for the private market and became highly successful. By 1914 dividends of 15 per-

2. A.N., 65 AQ, K 58, Société Belge des Tôleries de Constantinovka, Articles of Incorporation; A.E., Brussels, no. 2902, sec. 2, Société des Verreries du Donetz, à Santourinovka; *La Cote Libre*, 27–8–1897.

cent were being paid on share capital of 10,000,000 francs (with a market value of 25,000,000 francs). Founders' shares stood at 2,300 francs each and were worth a total of 5,000,000 francs.[3] One suspects that founders were somewhat overpaid for their initial contributions, that they sold some capital and founders' shares quickly and recouped a large portion of their initial investment, and that they then let profits run on their considerable holdings. These profits yielded a very handsome, if unknown, rate of return. The directors were always the same group of founders.

The Bonnardel Group's worst creation, the South Russian Mechanical Engineering Company, was founded in 1895 with 4,000,000 francs and founders' parts entitled to 25 percent of all dividends in excess of 5 percent. In 1897 the company issued 4,000,000 francs of 4.5 percent bonds repayable over fifty years.[4] Although this firm eventually failed, insiders and entrepreneurs probably lost little, and they may well have gained. From 1897 to 1899 the well-placed 500-franc par value shares (on which only 25 percent had been paid in initially) fluctuated from 800 to 1,100 francs, and founders' shares were above 700 francs, as dividends of 35 francs and 25 francs respectively were paid.[5] The Crédit Lyonnais's engineer believed that the company never made

3. A.N., 65 AQ, K 58, Annual Reports; *Lettre Hebdomadaire,* 8–2–1911; *Le Globe,* 22–12–1901; *Courrier de la Bourse et de la Banque,* 3–8–1902; *L'Information,* 8–1–1906.

4. C.L., Constructions Mécaniques, note, undated [October 1906?]. See chapter 11 for a complementary discussion of this firm.

5. Ibid., Etude, September 1904; *Le Pour et le Contre,* 23–1–1898; A.N., 65 AQ, M 387, Articles of Incorporation. The dividend of 7 percent on captal shares was important to insiders, since only with dividends above 5 percent would founders' shares receive dividends and definite value.

industrial profits and that the directors' "deplorable" dividend policy merited "more than severe criticism." [6] Entrepreneurs clearly unloaded both their capital shares and their founders' shares unscrupulously with the help of the kept press as their optimistic expectations soured. Thus in addition to leverage entrepreneurs had the means to cut their losses quickly in large, but manipulated, capital markets—and *sauve qui peut!*

The Nikolaevka Mining Company (Brussels, December 1899) is perhaps the limiting case of leverage of entrepreneurial commitment. A Hamburg merchant named Rose exchanged a twenty-six year lease on the manganese ore properties of a peasant commune and a *verbal* contract to supply an Antwerp steel company with 300,000 tons of ore per year for 4,000,000 of the firm's 5,000,000 francs of capital shares and all its founders' shares. The million francs of capital shares subscribed in cash were only 10 percent paid up initially. These shares could then be paid in full and sold by founders to the extent that the public's interest could be focused on this obvious fraud. Unscrupulous brokers touted these shares at 112 percent of par in July 1900 and promised dividends of 15 percent. If even 2 percent of the total capital of 5,000,000 francs was sold to the public, Rose and his associates recovered most of their initial investment.[7] And a large projected bond issue might have actually produced hard cash for productive investment. Such an issue would at the least have provided funds for bogus "divi-

6. C.L., Constructions Mécaniques, Etude, September 1904. Capital increases to 12,000,000 francs by 1901 helped pay dividends.

7. A.N., 65 AQ, L 2334, Société Minière de Nikolaievka, Articles of Incorporation, and various circulars.

dends'' and permitted insiders to unload common stock for large profits.

That a Hamburg merchant used a Belgian vehicle in his search for Russian profits was due not only to great Belgian interest in Russian investment, but also to the ''great facilities'' of Belgian corporation law, which was as free as any in the world.[8] Whereas French law stipulated that *apport* shares for nonpecuniary contributions remain nonnegotiable for two years, such shares in Belgian companies could be sold immediately after incorporation. This accounts for the fact that some predominantly French companies, like the Omnium Russe or the Kachkar Gold Company, chose the Belgian form.[9] Under Belgian law as little as 10 percent of capital could be paid in for legal constitution. Thus promoters paying down 50 francs on 500-franc shares doubled their money on any shares sold at 100 francs before the first capital call. Many did.[10]

2

Given this highly leveraged financial structure so conducive to entrepreneurship, what were the sources of capital for foreign firms? Rich, active founders were themselves a key source of capital. The fully developed capitalistic society of late nine-

8. A.N., F 12, no. 7173, Bonnet to the Quai d'Orsay, 31–12–1900; Verstraete, "Les capitaux étrangers," *Congrès internationale* 4, no. 111:6; B.S. Chlepner, *Belgian Banking and Banking Theory* (Washington, D.C., 1943), pp. 5–8.

9. As one would suppose, the French law could be bent, if not broken, by clever promoters. *Semaine Financière*, 16–9–1899, pp. 750–51.

10. The popular bearer shares had to be paid in full. But entrepreneurs needed only to pay in full (liberate) those shares being sold, and could leave the rest as partially paid nominative shares. This is of course another aspect of borrowed money for entrepreneurial leverage.

teenth-century western Europe had great dispari-
ties of wealth and income. It is estimated that the
top 5 percent of tax or income units in western
Europe received roughly one-third of total income
during this period.[11] Such concentration of income
gave the economic elite direct command over large
sums of risk capital. A graphic example from this
study was the group of wealthy men clustered
around Jean Bonnardel of Lyons, which is discussed
in detail in chapter 9. This group founded, directed,
and invested heavily in nearly a dozen of the largest
and most profitable French firms in Russia.

The leaders of the Bonnardel Group were part of
a small, active peer group. Adolphe Greiner, general
director of the John Cockerill Company, gives an
indication of his financial resources in a biting re-
tort to critics of Cockerill's management of its ill-
fated associate, the Almaznaia Coal Company.
"Rather than laugh [at Almaznaia's plight], I
should rather cry, for I *still* hold 350 shares [with a
par value of 500 francs each]." [12] Remember that
Cockerill's Belgian workers earned an average of
about three francs per day, or a thousand francs per
year to be generous; therefore Greiner's investment
in a single Russian venture equaled 175 man-years
of ordinary labor.[13] Other metallurgical directors
were capable of similar investments. Armand
Stouls, the general director of Espérance-Longdoz,
subscribed 217,000 francs in the Tula Blast Fur-

11. See Simon Kuznets, "Quantitative Aspects of Economic
Growth of Nations: VIII. Distribution of Income by Size,"
Economic Development and Cultural Change 11, no. 2, pt. 2
(1963): 58–67, for a summary of various estimates on income
distribution in different countries.

12. A.N., 65 AQ, L 139, Special Meeting of Shareholders, 9–10–
1903.

13. C.L., Société John Cockerill, Etude, September 1903.

naces Company. Tula's other directors (a banker, a professor, an industrialist, and an engineer) subscribed another 500,000 francs, or 10 percent of the total capital.[14]

Or consider another major investor in Russian enterprises, Emile Delloye-Orban. His hyphenated name reflected the merging of two important Belgian bourgeois dynasties, and he was in a "brilliant financial situation" in 1912, according to a confidential note from the Belgian Ministry of the Interior. Little wonder then that with presidencies or directorships in sixteen "very serious" firms, including South Russian Dnieper Metallurgical, Varvaropol Coal, and General Coal in Russia alone, he might almost routinely subscribe 100,000 francs in a new Russian rayon venture capitalized at 3,000,000 francs in 1912.[15] Less fortunate was his countryman Eugène Carez, "who did have a certain fortune and even passed for being very rich at one time." Carez was the principal founder and director of the group of companies at Belaia, and later he was an important shareholder in the Donets Stamping Company. By 1910 his financial position had been badly shaken by Russian reverses, and he had no resources other than his Russian shares.[16]

Such wealthy businessmen might quickly sell part of their investment, but they retained considerable holdings necessary for the control they rarely relin-

14. A.E., Brussels, no. 2902, sec. 2, Haut Fourneaux de Toula, Articles of Incorporation.

15. A.E., Brussels, no. 2902, sec. 2, Société des Soies Artificielles de Sokhatchev, confidential note, 1912.

16. In 1910 the fifty-five year old engineer was still grasping for the brass ring in Russia, this time with Emile Wolthers, the streetcar director at Kharkov, in a sulphur mine in the Crimea. A.E., Brussels, no. 2901, sec. 3, confidential note on Carez, 23-3-1910.

quished. The Antwerp industrialist Joseph Ciselet, for example, founded and directed a small group of firms in which he always held a substantial interest. In addition to investing in the Konstantinovka Sheet Mills, which was discussed above, he subscribed 500,000 francs in the Santurinovka Glass Company to complement the 750,000 francs of capital shares and founders' shares he had received for his studies and concessions. Three Ciselets subscribed 15 percent of a small Odessa tile company, which they then directed.[17] Ciselet also founded and controlled the medium-sized Gosudarev-Bairak Coal Company, in which he retained an important stock participation.[18] Ciselet worked with a small number of associates and apparently unified an informal group much as Bonnardel had. This suggests correctly that rich men had rich families to draw upon and that their affairs thrived on nepotism. Wealthy entrepreneurs shared their profit possibilities with their business associates and employees, and this was another aspect of their ability to mobilize personally large sums of capital.

An examination of the initial subscribers of the Nikolaev Shipyards Company illustrates several aspects of the process. This great overambitious firm, the first modern shipbuilder on the Black Sea as well as a major railway equipment producer, was founded primarily by the directors of the Société John Cockerill in 1895. Nikolaev Shipyards was well equipped and was "without doubt one of the very best installations of its kind anywhere in

17. A.E., Brussels, no. 2902, sec. 3, Verreries du Donetz à Santourinovka, Articles of Incorporation; ibid., sec. 4, Tuileries d'Odessa, Articles of Incorporation.
18. C.L., Charbonnages de Gosoudariev-Bairat, Note, 1911.

Europe."[19] Of the initial capital of 12,000,000 francs, which was raised to 20,000,000 by 1899, 1,400,000 francs went to founders Emile Delloye-Orban, Cockerill director and banker, and Georges François, director of an engineering company in Belgium that became part of the new firm, for their nonpecuniary contributions. Eighteen of the 317 original subscribers took one hundred or more of the thousand-franc shares. Several of these larger subscribers were Cockerill directors: Emile Delloye-Orban (319); Baron F. de Macar (100); R. Suermondt (300); Armand Sadoine (100). One may also note other original subscribers from Liège, like Stouls, Lambert, Piérart, and Nagelmackers, who had gone or would go to Russia. Second, counting families' names, one sees the bourgeois dynasties in action: four Delloyes, five Françoises, three Orbans, and five Thoumsins. Third, one has a roll call of the prosperous investing bourgeoisie by profession: forty-eight industrialists, forty-six proprietors, thirty-six bankers, thirty-three directors, twenty-six rentiers, nineteen agents de change, eighteen merchants, fourteen lawyers, six notaries, six doctors, and, last and almost least, two professors and two Cockerill foremen.[20] Here is the profile of the passive investor indispensable for the entrepreneur's work in Russia.

The second key source of capital was the bold, often unscrupulous speculator, like Maes or Schmatzer, whom we have considered elsewhere. He subscribed large blocks initially and often sold them

19. C.L., Chantiers Navals de Nicolaiev, Etude, September 1904.
20. A.N., 65 AQ, M 332, Chantiers Navals de Nicolaiev, Articles of Incorporation.

at wholesale prices to stockbrokers or bankers who had numerous retail outlets.[21] The essential difference between the speculators and the rich founders discussed above was that the large financial (and managerial) commitments of speculators were usually temporary because their primary concern was to sell their shares quickly. Their firms accordingly did much more poorly than those dominated by rich entrepreneurs, who made long-term investments and provided permanent leadership.

It would be a serious though common mistake to assume that foreign entrepreneurs raised their initial capital exclusively in western Europe. For it is a surprising fact that a significant portion of initial financial resources was mobilized effectively in Russia. Russia itself, then, was a third major source of capital for foreign entrepreneurs.

Thoroughly acculturated "foreign" businessmen, whom we discussed in chapter 2, naturally invested in foreign firms which they helped to found. In a similar way, well-paid foreign managers and engineers in Russia supplied a sizable if unknown quantity of capital to new undertakings in the 1890s. In doing so they ploughed back part of their large salaries into Russian industry.

It is striking that almost every list of original subscribers examined reveals investment by this group of foreign personnel working in Russia. When Manziarly used a portion of his sizable income as managing director of the South Russian Salt and Coal Company to found the Irmino Coal Company, or when Bouroz, the manager of the Berestov-Krinka Coal Company, became Bouroz the entrepreneur at the Ekaterinovka Coal Company,

21. See chapter 10 for the quite typical case of the Rykovskii Coal Company.

they were only following the general pattern on a grand scale.[22]

The high-ranking Russian and Polish counterparts of these foreign managers also participated extensively in new foreign affairs. In doing so they joined other Russian businessmen and promoters who also appear time after time as original cash subscribers on these subscription lists.

The Donets Stamping Company (Brussels, 1895) was an excellent example of an undeniably "foreign" firm with large Russian participation from all of the above sources. Two Belgian industrialists, R. Vignoul of Liège and Léon Hiard, the managing director of the Cie Centrale de Construction à Haine St. Pierre, were the driving force in this firm. The founders planned to produce specialty metal products (screws, bolts, clamps, and railway switches) at Ekaterinoslav, just as they did in Belgium. Vignoul

22. Some examples show the pattern. Two foreign metallurgical directors, the Frenchman Verdié of the Donets Steel Company and the German Kamp of the Ekaterinoslav Steel Tube Company, were deeply involved in the Nadine Ceramic Company of Ekaterinovka (1895), one of three such Russian ventures of the Belgian Ceramic Company of Seilles-lez-Ardenne. Six foreign engineers subscribed approximately 5 percent of the second affiliated firm of Grigorievka. They included: Modeste Pierronne, both the father and the son, who were key technical personnel at the Briansk Company; Isidor Brichant, one of the last Belgian engineers of the Dnieper Metallurgical Company; and Charles Vincens, director of Dubovaia Balka Company. Three foreign engineers and directors, Modeste Pierronne, Charles Plumier of the Gorlovka Coal Company, and Raoul Hennig, chief accountant at a small mine, were medium-sized original subscribers in the Ekaterinovka Steel Company. Similarly Eugène Poncelet, the director general of the Almaznaia Coal Company, Arthur Brichant, a Belgian industrialist at Ekaterinoslav, and Mathieu Dubois, alternatively of the Société Marihaye of Belgium and its Taganrog affiliate, subscribed almost 10 percent of a small kitchen utensil company in 1896 (Sté Emaillerie et Lampisterie de Lougansk.) For the original subscription lists of these and several other firms, see A.E., Brussels, no. 2902.

and Hiard received all the founders' shares for their studies and processes, but they subscribed only 180 of the 2,500 shares of 500 francs each. Perhaps the fact that the plant would fill a real need in southern Russia accounts for the fact that nine Polish or Russian directors of the nearby South Russian Dnieper Metallurgical Company took 9 percent of the total capital stock. Similarly 9 percent was taken by top-ranking Briansk engineers (including Alexis Goriainov, who was so often interested in foreign firms, and the Frenchman Modeste Pierronne); other Russians subscribed another 8 percent. The ubiquitous Fernand Schmatzer of Prokhorov Coal subscribed 4 percent. Thus 30 percent of total capital was raised in Russia. The remaining shares were subscribed by thirty-four Belgian industrialists, bankers, stockbrokers, engineers, and landlords.[23] The company was fairly successful under its Belgian managers until 1901, paying 8 percent on its capital. The Russian subscribers had ample time to sell at a handsome profit.

An equally important source of paid-in capital, or perhaps more accurately underwriting support, was the Russian banking system. The St. Petersburg International Commercial Bank, under its aggressive general director Adolph Rothstein, was interested in working with French groups to found industrial affairs or to float shares in Western markets. With this in mind, this Russian bank joined with the Paris-Holland Bank and the (unrelated) Banque Internationale de Paris to found the Russian Gold Mining Company in 1895.[24] Subsequently, the St.

---

23. *Annexe du Moniteur Belge,* 7–6–1895; C.L., Société Métallurgique d'Estampage du Donetz, Etude, August 1904.

24. See Iu. B. Solov'ev, "Mezhdunarodnyi bank," in *Monopolii i inostrannyi kapital,* p. 385.

Petersburg International Bank and the Banque International de Paris under the direction of Théophile Lombardo developed a working relationship in underwriting some ventures. Accordingly, the Paris bank took 1,600 of 24,000 shares in the St. Petersburg bank's Nikopol-Mariupol Company, and the Paris bank gave 4,000 of 36,000 shares in the Ural-Volga Metallurgical Company to the St. Petersburg bank in 1895.[25] Elaborate plans for a joint venture in the railway-equipment industry were also discussed at length, but they never materialized. The St. Petersburg International Bank, closely tied to leading German banks, was even more active in German companies in Russia.

Similarly the St. Petersburg Private Commercial Bank helped form and direct the Banque Privée Industrielle et Commercial de Lyon et Marseille. These banks were then the principal underwriters of several joint ventures.[26] The profitable South Russian Soda Company was one such firm. A less successful company was the Kostroma Cotton Company, and a third enterprise was Bouhey's locomotive works.[27]

In short, foreign entrepreneurs found a substantial portion of their hard cash in Russia in the 1890s. This is a significant and perhaps unexpected discovery. How are we to account for the paradox of poor Russia having a pool of untapped savings? Hirschman's thoughts on the ability to invest suggest part of the answer. In an underdeveloped country, like Russia in the 1890s, the link between savings

25. Ibid., p. 386.

26. A.N., F 30, no. 328, Verstraete, 9–3–1898.

27. A.N., F 30, no. 340, Construction de Locomotives et Mécaniques [Bouhey], Minister of Foreign Affiairs to Director of the Movement of Funds, 12–12–1900 and 16–2–1901.

and investment is far from automatic. Inadequate entrepreneurship lacks this ability to invest, and thereby to link existing or potentially existing savings with investment opportunity. The result is frustrated savings which only await some agent to put them to work. Something of the sort was apparently the case in Russia. Foreign businessmen found bankers and earners of high incomes in Russia eager and able to invest when presented with promising ventures. Entrepreneurship, not capital, was the crucial deficiency.

But this is not all. Both Russian and foreign sources supplied needed capital because many "foreign firms" were cooperative efforts, or partnerships. Both partners supplied some portion of capital as a matter of course, and for neither partner was capital the distinctive contribution. Here we come full circle to one of our major themes. The foreigner's distinctive contribution *during his period of dynamic entrepreneurship* was his technical expertise. This was what he gave that Russia lacked. Secondarily, and largely because of his justly deserved reputation for outstanding technical prowess at home, the foreign entrepreneur provided access to small, passive investors in western Europe. Le Creusot, Hartmann, Châtillon-Commentary, Cockerill—these were names to open the rentier's pocketbook. Russian partners, on the other hand, brought equally essential, nontechnical contributions—natural resources, large government orders, certain managerial abilities discussed in the last chapter—along with their capital.

Attentive readers will recall various firms with these elements of partnership. A look at three major railway-equipment producers dating from the 1890s and not previously examined in detail furnishes additional support.

The Hartmann Machine Company of Lugansk (1896) was underwritten by Gustave Hartmann, son-in-law of Krupp of Essen, and Rothstein's St. Petersburg International Commercial Bank, one of the most German of Russian banks. This bank had every reason to buy shares, since it had been instrumental in obtaining locomotive orders for the new firm worth 5,500,000 rubles for the first two years.[28] The joint venture was reflected in top management: Gustave Hartmann was president; and Adolph Rothstein of the St. Petersburg International Bank was vice-president. All equipment, which was of extremely good quality, was furnished by Hartmann and was subsequently perfectly maintained.[29] Profits were excellent, but Gustav Hartmann came to feel excessive dividends were being paid. In 1908 he resigned to mark his disagreement.[30] Management was then almost completely Russian, and it remained so.

The Russian Locomotive and Construction Company, nicknamed Bouhey in France, was a similar partnership. Here, however, the foreign element provided less capital, although as much technical aid was forthcoming. In 1895 Philippe Bouhey, a French industrialist and major shareholder in the Bouhey Company of Paris, provided plans, models, and equipment for a new locomotive company which was later only slightly inferior to Hartmann's.[31] By 1900 the French minister of finance concluded that

28. C.L., Hartmann, Etudes, August 1898 and June 1904.
29. Ibid., June 1904.
30. *Revue financière*, 22–10–1908; *L'Information*, 23–8–1910.
31. C.L., Construction de Locomotives et Mécaniques [Bouhey], Etude, February 1904.

not more than 10 percent of the company's shares were in France, since arduous attempts to sell shares to the general public in France had failed.[32] Bouhey was even reported to have sold all of his shares in Russia (apparently on the St. Petersburg exchange), in spite of his promise to retain his shares until his Russian partners had sold theirs.[33]

The South Ural Metallurgical Company, a leading constructor of freight cars incorporated in 1898, was a partnership of Belgian industrialists and Russian nobility. Prince Belosel'skii, the company's president, and Emile Digneffe of Liège, vice-president and representative of the technical consultant (Ateliers Germain), first paid themselves 2,000,000 francs in 4,000 shares for their *apports*. These *apports* consisted of a small existing factory, plans, and technical information. Belosel'skii also subscribed 2,200 paid-in shares, while the St. Petersburg Discount Bank took 750 and various Russians another 650. Sixty-seven foreigners, from Liège for the most part, subscribed 4,500 paid-in shares.[34] The new company then transformed Belosel'skii's old foundry in the Urals into one of the first producers of tubular freight cars in Russia. (Cars of this construction cut dead weight markedly and were therefore a notable innovation.)[35] No doubt Russians participated financially because a signed and sealed government order for 2,000 freight cars at the time of incorporation seemed to promise large profits. The prince himself, a very rich man, apparently

32. A.N., F 30, no. 340, Construction de Locomotives [Bouhey], note, 2–8–1900.

33. A.N., F 30, no. 340, letter, Minister of Foreign Affairs to Director of the Movement of Funds, 12–12–1900.

34. *Annexe du Moniteur Belge,* 31–7–1898.

35. Verstraete, *L'Oural,* p. 129; A.N., 65 AQ, K 165, Annual Reports, 1899, 1900.

made no effort to sell his shares. Instead he tried to sell the company an adjoining property of 400,000 hectares producing forty tons of pig iron daily in seven scattered Petrine blast furnaces for more shares.[36] The firm was not very successful, mainly because orders were always much less than originally anticipated.[37]

As the above example shows, Russian landlords and industrialists accepted shares as well as cash for their *apport* of nonpecuniary assets. This was particularly true for mining companies. Rykovskii, Podvinstev, and Prince Dolgorukii acted typically. The well-informed French consul Maurice Verstraete believed that Russians in general sold their vendor shares as quickly as possible, like the good Colonel Rykovskii.[38] Even so, Russians were sharing the risks of initial underwriting. This was another aspect of partnership. Buoyant capital markets encouraged Russians to accept shares, and foreign entrepreneurs willingly issued promises to pay which cost them little or nothing personally. Thus the recurring bane of overcapitalization was in part the result of Russian sharing of the risks of cashing these promises to pay on foreign stock exchanges.[39]

These risks were real. Neither foreign entrepreneurs nor Russian vendors always succeeded in unloading their shares, by any means. (This is one

---

36. C.L., Sud-Oural, Etude, August 1900; A.N., 65 AQ, K 165, Special Shareholders' Meetings, 2–3–1900 and 17–12–1903; *Revue Economique et Financière*, 17–3–1900.

37. The Emperor Nicholas was reported to have denounced Belosel'skii for working so closely with foreigners. T. Von Laue, *Witte*, p. 178.

38. Verstraete, "Les capitaux étrangers," *Congrès internationale* 4, no. 111:8. See chapter 10 for the Rykovskii Coal Company.

39. A.N., F 30, no. 343, Volga-Vichera, Verstraete to Delcassé, 25–3–1901.

reason why most estimates of foreign holdings are probably too high.) The case of the Industrial Platinum Company, founded in Paris in 1899, with the enormous joint-stock capital of 22,000,000 francs and 10,000,000 francs of bonds, is instructive. The original idea of this firm was to group all the Ural platinum producers, who accounted for more than 95 percent of world output, in a powerful trust. This trust could then dictate terms to the very prosperous comonopolist, the Mathey Refining Company, an English firm which refined almost all the world's pure platinum. Of the total capital of 32,000,000 francs, 26,000,000 went to pay for the mines of the Russian owners and the aid of an international syndicate headed by Robert Oppenheim, a Parisian banker.[40] (Shares with a par value of 14,000,000 francs went to Oppenheim, who inflated the affair greatly. Oppenheim in turn ceded an unknown portion of this stock to the Russian intermediaries who secured the original options.) [41] Had this new venture's total capital been 15,000,000 the affair would have been promising. With such an exaggerated capital it was scarcely viable.[42]

What is interesting is that the Russians, who held most of the shares since they were unable to sell at Paris in any quantity, forced Oppenheim to withdraw and then called upon a more reputable foreigner, Jean Bonnardel, to head the company. Their ultimate object, which was never really attained, was still to sell their shares in France. But in the

40. A.N., F 30, no. 345, Société Industrielle du Platine, Verstraete to Delcassé, 24–9–1898, 16–1–1899.

41. C.L., Sté Industrielle du Platine, letters from Baron du Marais with the bank's Etudes Financières in St. Petersburg, 26–10–1900, 31–10–1900.

42. Ibid.; A.N., F 30, no. 345, Société Platine, Verstraete to Delcassé, 16–1–1899.

meantime they needed sound and respectable foreign management to save the company and to keep the door to the passive foreign investor ajar.[43]

This illustration may suggest that the most important ultimate source of capital in the 1890s was the west-European stock exchange. Indeed it was. There foreign entrepreneurs and Russian underwriters enlisted the support of passive sleeping partners who managed their portfolios without thought of management or control. There the entrepreneur sold different types of securities and secured leverage.

Absolutely essential were the bondholders, the most passive of all investors, who stressed safety of principal and accepted low returns stoically when interest rates were very low in the 1890s.[44] Almost every important Russian metallurgical or mining venture obtained one-third to one-half of total capital requirements through publicly held bonded debt. The cost was only 4 to 4.5 percent per annum before 1900.[45] If a high percentage of capital shares was used to pay for existing mines or plants, then bonds might even supply almost all fresh capital, as with the famed Huta-Bankova Steel Company.

One should note that the rate of interest on Russian industrial bonds fell very rapidly from the early 1880s to 1900. The Huta-Bankova Steel Company was able to issue 500-franc 6 percent bonds with a ten-year maturity at an average of 365 francs

43. C.L., Société Platine, du Marais, 26–10–1900; ibid., Etude, 28–2–1911.

44. *Journal des Chemins de fer,* 2–9–1899.

45. For example, three well-secured 500-franc bonds with a 4 percent coupon were the thirty-seven-year first-mortgage bonds of the Russo-Belgian Metallurgical Company emitted at 480 in 1898, the general obligation twenty-seven-year bonds of Konstaninovka Sheet Mills at 492 in 1899, and the thirty-year bonds of the Irmino Coal Company at 470 in 1900. See dossiers at the Crédit Lyonnais and A.N., 65 AQ, K 58, Annual Report, 1899.

in 1880. This provided a yield to maturity of almost 12 percent.[46] By 1890 the Crédit Mobilier was able to place 5 percent first-mortgage bonds of the Briansk Metallurgical Company in the Lyons area fairly close to par, and in 1895 Briansk was seeking Crédit Lyonnais aid to convert old debts into 4 percent bonds with a ten-year maturity.[47] By the end of the decade Russian bonds with 4 percent coupons and thirty-year maturities were common. The abundance of such cheap and tempting long-term capital in the bond market was an enormous asset for foreign entrepreneurs. Similarly, the great difficulty in floating loans after 1900, even at considerably higher rates, was also a factor in the decline of foreign entrepreneurship.[48]

Capital shares were placed with rentiers and speculators alike on west-European exchanges as interest in Russian companies grew into a great speculative boom. Part of the cause was the general promotional campaign of the Russian government, which has been examined. But there was indeed something to promote. Just as entrepreneurs were attracted by individual successes and net profits of 26 percent on invested capital in 1895,[49] so investors were attracted by high dividends. In 1898, for example, Dnieper Metallurgical (1886) paid 40 percent, the Huta-Bankova (1876) 20 percent, Krivoi-Rog (1881) 10 percent, Dubovaia-Balka (1892) 15 per-

46. *L'Information,* 6–12–1899.

47. *Moniteur des Intérêts Financiers,* 9–2–1890; *Economie Revue,* 15–11–1891; C.L., Briansk, Note, January 1895.

48. Some latecomers also failed because they could never float projected loans, or else they limped along for years with a grave capital problem. See the Russian Dynamite Company or the Gosudarev-Bairak Coal Company in A.N., 65 AQ, P 335, and L 187.

49. Glivits, *Zheleznaia promyshlennost',* p. 103.

cent, Sosnowice 7.4 percent, and Gorlovka Coal 8 percent on their respective par values. Nor did well-conceived firms of recent vintage appear less promising. In 1898 the Ekaterinovka Coal Company (1894) paid 5 percent, the Russo-Belgian Metallurgical Company (1895) 10 percent, and the Donets Stamping Company 8 percent.[50]

These dividends were based on rapidly rising earnings.[51] High return on investment, rising earnings, a new field—these were precisely the characteristics of genuine growth industries and growth companies which sophisticated investors wisely sought, and which they often less wisely overevaluated in their enthusiasm, then as now. The best of the Belgian financial journals, the *Moniteur des Intérêts Matériels,* summed up the promising, hazardous investment opportunity very well in 1898. "Enormous profits possible and speculative excesses probable: these are the key facts of Russian investment."[52]

As usually occurs in such cases, there was a good deal of destabilizing speculation in Russian shares, as knowing operators pyramided their original gains with more purchases at ever higher prices. They gambled that they could push overpriced shares still higher. This tactic of course made stock prices particularly vulnerable to rapid cumulative declines, especially since margins of less than 25 percent were common.[53]

In the transition from sophisticated speculation in

50. A useful summary for individual firms is found in *Semaine Financière,* 14–1–1899, p. 23. See table 3 for estimates of Ol' for rates of return over the entire period.

51. See, for example, the profits of the South Russian Dnieper Metallurgical Company, chapter 9, table 10.

52. 21–8–1898, p. 2197.

53. *Semaine Financière,* 1899, pp. 267–68.

growth industries to irrational and even fraudulent promotion at the top of the boom, the financial press played an important role. The financial press, "whose evolution after 1879 was extremely complex," [54] apparently did share a common code of unbridled venality. This was a great aid to entrepreneurs trying to drive up established shares or unload new ones. For example, one of the most reliable papers, *L'Information,* which almost certainly used the invaluable studies of the Crédit Lyonnais's engineers in Russia, would often present detailed, generally accurate examinations which suddenly ended as blatantly dishonest huckstering in the final lines. Thus when Manziarly, Sinçay, and the Länderbank were struggling to obtain official listing at Paris for the overcapitalized Irmino Coal Company in 1904 and 1905, *L'Information* concluded after "impartial evaluation" that Irmino shares, a bit above par, were "certain to climb several hundred francs." [55] *Le Pour et le Contre,* a useful journal on occasion, acted similarly. It is no accident that among the minor participants of the Banque de l'Union Parisienne's underwriting syndicates, one normally finds *L'Information* and Alfred Neymarck of *Le Rentier.* Such participation meant effortless and almost automatic profit.

The economic periodicals of general interest played their part willingly. The Société Générale of France used Edmond Thiéry's prestigous *Economiste Européen* to push its holding company, the Omnium Russe.[56] No wonder Witte's first line of attack against French critics after 1900 was "to pay

54. Bertrand Gille, "Etat de la presse économique et financière en France," *Histoire des Entreprises,* no. 4 (November 1959), p. 58.

55. 11–10–1905. For basic realities, see A.N., F 30, no. 343, Irmino, notes and letters, as well as C.L., Irmino.

56. *Economiste Européen,* 17–2–1897.

the press better." [57] The ceaseless campaigns of the venal financial press meant that even the most conservative strongboxes came to hold a few Russian industrial shares and provide entrepreneurs with capital.

3

If capital was cheap and abundant in boom conditions, it became exceedingly scarce after 1900 when the celebrated peculiarities of Russian factor proportions diminished. The lack of faith of passive west-European investors in Russian companies was probably the principal reason. As one leading Belgian industrialist told his king in 1901, "The fall of certain unviable and poorly-managed enterprises produced an irrational total panic in the public. First distrust, then discredit, has fallen on all firms, good or bad without distinction." [58] In such an atmosphere foreign entrepreneurs largely lost whatever advantage in access to capital they had enjoyed.

Nothing shows this better than the problem of finding working capital. In the best of times working capital for commercial credit represented a large portion of total financial needs in Russia. Vast distances, irregular or seasonal markets, and the practice of extending long credit were all factors. Easily raised before 1900, working capital for foreign firms became extremely hard to come by thereafter. All foreign entrepreneurs agreed on this. [59]

57. Raffalovich, the Russian agent in Paris, was given an extra 300,000 francs for this purpose. A.N., F 30, no. 344, Verstraete to Caillaux, 7–12–1901.

58. A.E., Brussels, no. 2900, Ernest de Moerloose to the king of Belgium, 5–8–1901.

59. Jules Genaert, *Fédération Industrielle Russe* (Brussels, 1901), in A.E., Brussels, no. 2900; A.N., 65 AQ, H 258, Société Cotonnière Franco-Russe, Annual Report, 1902; A.E., France, Russie, N.S., no. 59, St. Petersburg to Quai d'Orsay, 20–2–1907.

In the first place interest rates on working capital were responsive to the less sanguine appraisals of Russian industry by foreign bankers. In 1899 a banking syndicate led by the Banque de Paris et des Pays-Bas advanced the Upper Volga Company 2,500,000 francs at the discount rate of the Bank of France plus 2 percent, or 5 percent in all.[60] After 1903 the Banque de l'Union Parisienne, for which there is good information, supplied steel producers money at a minimum rate of 8 percent.[61] And this seems to have been the standard minimum rate during the depression. The Belgian General Coal Company was advancing its wholly owned Russian firm funds at 8 percent in 1902, "the same rate charged by the Kharkov Land Bank"; and the St. Petersburg International Commercial Bank furnished money at 8 percent to the Tula Cartridge Company, which it controlled.[62] Others paid more. Konstantinovka Sheet Mills, for example, borrowed at 10 percent during "the dark days," and then only after the board of directors (rich men all) gave their personal guarantees for one-third of the principal.[63] Even in the pre-World War I expansion, rates for short-term credit remained near 8 percent for all but the strongest firms.[64]

The need for working capital increased because buyers sought and received longer credit. The Lugan Coal Company lamented typically in 1901 that "our debts are small in comparison to our ac-

60. B.U.P., Russie, no. 17.

61. See dossiers on Donets-Yur'evka and the Providence Russe in particular at the B.U.P.

62. C.L., Cie Générale de Charbonnages, Annual Report, 1902; Toula Cartouches, Etude, August 1903.

63. A.N., 65 AQ, K 58, Annual Report, 1910–11.

64. For example, Nève, Wilde et Cie, Annual Report, 1910–11, at the Crédit Lyonnais.

counts receivable, but those are secured with the very greatest difficulty." [65] Unable to borrow to finance more sales, the company suspended operations from the middle of 1901 to March 1902. State agencies contributed to the problem, since the state, "a sure but very slow payer," continued to demand advantageous credit arrangements. [66] With working capital so scarce bankers could often secure effective control with judicious loans and little or no common-stock ownership. The Société Générale of France (or its Belgian branch, the Banque de Reports et de Dépôts de Bruxelles) retained the direction of some of its firms in this manner, as did the Banque de l'Union Parisienne. [67] Since Russian banks often proved more willing to lend than their foreign counterparts, especially to the small and weak, some firms, like Taganrog or Verkhnii-Dneprovsk, ended by passing into Russian hands in this way.

Another key source of working capital was rich directors. The directors of the Czelade Coal Company, the Belaia Companies, and Tula Blast Furnaces, among others, all advanced money to their firms on occasion. [68] Their willingness to do so was one reason why firms founded by wealthy capitalists weathered the depression better than those founded by speculators.

Some small firms obtained working capital laboriously by reinvesting all profits. This is seen in the history of the Warsaw Hat Company. The leading

65. C.L., Annual Meeting, 10–12–1901.
66. C.L., Société Métallurgique du Donetz, Etude, August 1904.
67. A.N., F 30, no. 343, Cie Minière de Goloubovka-Berestovo-Bogodoukhovo; *Paris-Bruxelles,* 26–2–1914; B.U.P., dossiers on the Russian Providence, Donets-Yur'evka, and Ural-Volga.
68. *Echo de la Bourse et de la Banque,* 28–10–1909; C.L., dossiers on Belaia and Czelade.

Belgian producer of felt and top hats founded this Russian subsidiary in 1898, and it agreed to furnish all patents, processes, future improvements, personnel, and machinery to duplicate production methods in Belgium.[69] In the fifteen years before 1914 demand grew and production went from 40,000 to 175,000 hats. Profits also quadrupled.

The chief problem was always working capital. In 1905 and 1906, for example, interest to Belgian creditors equaled 12 and 16 percent per annum. "If we had our own working capital of 250,000 francs, we would have earned 13 percent [as opposed to 6] on total capital."[70] Presumably Russian bankers demanded even higher rates. Shareholders were fair-weather friends, and two attempts to float preferred shares failed completely. In 1908 improving conditions permitted the company to consolidate all debts, some of which were to directors, in a four-year bank loan. By 1913 perseverance had resulted in adequate working capital, and an initial 5 percent dividend was finally paid. Adequate commercial credit and an agreement with the only other Russian producer of felt hats led management to exult that "our financial results are marvelous and our products excellent." Prospects for expansion in this fast-growing new industry were dazzling. Only 2,000,000 of Russia's 140,000,000 inhabitants had ever bought a felt hat.[71]

The second major manifestation of capital scar-

69. The Société de la Manufacture de Feutres et Chapeaux de Cureghem and the Société de Ruysbroeck were the parent firms of the Société de la Manufacture de Feutres et Chapeaux, à Varsovie (Brussels, 26–2–1898). When the Société de Ruysbroeck was reorganized in 1903 it produced a million hats per year and monopolized the Belgian market. A.N., 65 AQ, M 175, various clippings.
70. Ibid., Annual Report, 1906.
71. Ibid., Annual Meeting, 2–10–1913.

city for foreign firms from 1900 to 1910 may be seen in the common pattern of financial reorganization which few escaped. As cumulative losses depleted reserves and cut off bank credit, entrepreneurs and managers were forced to find new capital. This "fresh" capital invariably demanded and received some privileged position vis-à-vis existing capital, although the details, negotiations, and complexities of even a few such organizations would require many pages. One way was to float an issue of preference shares. Another method was to convert bonds and debts (first-mortgage bonds excepted) into shares, usually preferred. Finally, one might simply reduce the value of the old shares, from, say, 500 to 100 francs, and then float new shares having this reduced value. These new shares might or might not be offered to old shareholders on a prorated basis. Reorganizations of existing companies became the chief field of foreign entrepreneurship after 1900.

This field was particularly promising because of the generous provisions of Russian law on bankruptcy. Foreign owners had every opportunity to salvage something. If a firm was unable to meet its current obligations (first mortgages excepted), and if its total *stated* assets exceeded total debts, the firm might request the judicial administration system. A firm under judicial administration (receivership) was granted an indefinite moratorium on all but first-mortgage liabilities. Court-appointed receivers then tried to earn profits to repay the firm's creditors, whom they represented. Of great importance, the judicial administration could borrow money to operate, and even to reequip the firm, and these debts contracted by receivers stood before all but first mortgages. Thus a firm in receivership could almost always obtain new money and operate.

But the original shareholders remained the owners, and should debts be repaid, or an agreement with creditors be reached, the receivership might be lifted and the original owners might recover full control of their property. It was in this environment of depression and receivership that entrepreneurs sought and brought fresh capital.

Two important reorganizations of two major steel companies by the Banque de l'Union Parisienne are indicative of the intense capital scarcity and the accompanying entrepreneurial opportunity. Successor to the Banque Internationale de Paris as the Ural-Volga Company's banker and with close relations to the Société de Châtillon-Commentry and the Darcy family, as well as with its important shareholder, the Société Générale de Belgique, the Banque de l'Union Parisienne was well situated to undertake reorganizations in Russia. The Russian Providence Company provided the first chance.

This firm near Mariupol, child of the Providence Belge, had shown a fine appetite for capital at an early date. An initial share capital of 15,000,000 francs in 1897 rose to 30,000,000 francs in shares and 20,000,000 in bonds before the plant was basically finished in late 1899, just in time for the depression. Losses followed losses. By 1902, when the company went into judicial administration, it owed another 7,000,000 francs to its original backers (6,000,000 francs to the Belgian Providence and 1,000,000 francs to its directors), 1,000,000 francs to various Russian creditors, and 900,000 francs to Madame Solvay, widow of the famous chemist, as a first mortgage on the entire property.[72]

While sustaining its affiliate with these advances,

72. C.L., Providence Russe, Etudes, December 1898 and March 1901; Note, July 1902.

the Belgian Providence Company looked toward unavoidable financial reorganization. Negotiations for
a reduction of capital and a new first-mortgage bond
issue were undertaken, first with the Crédit Lyonnais, then with the Banque de Paris et des Pays-Bas,
and finally with the Russian State Bank.[73] When all
these proved unsuccessful, the Belgian firm let its
charge go into receivership in 1902. It then began to
work closely with Pierre Darcy and the Banque de
l'Union Parisienne, and after long discussions an
agreement was reached.

The Banque de l'Union Parisienne agreed to advance 3,000,000 francs at 8 percent in return for an
eighteen-month option on a reorganization plan.
Under this plan the B.U.P. would float 6,000,000
francs of new preferred stock upon which it would
receive a 10 percent commission. The initial advance
was crucial, and as improvements continued, the
Banque de l'Union Parisienne exercised its option
in 1905. The Russian firm was reorganized, and the
receivership was lifted. There were then three
classes of shares: the 6 percent A preferred-shares
series with 6,000,000 francs which the Banque de
l'Union Parisienne had underwritten; the B preferred-shares series representing old bonds, bank
debts, and Belgian Providence advances with a face
value of 33,000,000 francs; and finally the C series
without any stated value representing the original
capital shares.[74] The Belgian Providence Company
and its directors retroceded their subscription
rights to the A shares to the B.U.P., which thus
acquired about one-third of the A shares and effec-

73. Providence Russe MSS, Délibérations du Conseil d'Administration for 1901.

74. Ibid., Délibérations du Conseil, particularly 24–7–1905 and
5–11–1906; C.L., Providence Russe, Etude, March 1907.

tive control.[75] This control was then reinforced by the B.U.P.'s role of banker to the Russian Providence.

Darcy, the B.U.P., and Thalmann et Cie also reorganized the Donets-Yur'evka Metallurgical Company. This company had also gone into receivership in 1901, but by 1910 it was ready to seek fresh capital through reorganization. The original capital of 8,000,000 rubles was to be reduced to 3,200,000 rubles, and then immediately increased to 15,200,000 rubles to pay off all old debts. Of the 60,000 new shares, offered to old shareholders at 210 rubles, 24,800 were not subscribed and were purchased by Thalmann, the B.U.P., and Crédit Mobilier syndicate. The syndicate's timing was perfect. Speculation on the St. Petersburg Exchange then pushed the price of the stock over 280 rubles, and all 24,800 shares were sold there by March 1911 for a profit of 75.5 francs per share.[76] So successful was this offering, in fact, that the B.U.P. subsequently had recurring problems in controlling the company. Such control became very important, since the B.U.P. and Darcy wished to lease the Ural-Volga Company to the Donets-Yur'evka Company, and to build thereby a stronger, more viable steel-producing unit which might eventually include the Russian Providence.[77]

4

One more question remains. How did foreign entrepreneurs obtain capital for renewed expansion when prosperity returned in 1910 after a decade of consolidations and reorganizations? Generally this

75. B.U.P., Russie, no. 115, Providence Russe, Option to reorganize the Russian Providence Company.

76. Ibid., note on profits of the syndicate.

77. Ibid., note from Thalmann et Cie; also, note on projected merger (1912).

task presented few difficulties. One reason, of
course, was that profits again provided funds that
could be and were reinvested. Three important
firms, the South Russian Dnieper Metallurgical
Company, the Russo-Belgian Metallurgical Company, and the Krivoi-Rog Iron Mines, for which
there are detailed financial studies, boosted dividends per share by almost 100 percent from 1909 to
1912. Nevertheless, they were paying out to stockholders only 50 percent of net profits for the years
1910–12, as opposed to 76 percent for the years
1906–9.[78] In addition to generating investment funds
internally, increasing profits and dividends permitted foreign entrepreneurs to increase capital stock
easily. Metallurgy was typical. Fifteen major southern metallurgical companies increased their share
capital almost 50 percent from the beginning of 1911
to the beginning of 1914 (from 138,000,000 rubles to
196,000,000 rubles).[79]

Since foreign (and Russian) entrepreneurs
founded few new companies after 1909, capital went
mainly to existing firms. This simplified the underwriting problem. Shareholders were given subscription rights to purchase new stock at a subscription
price below the market quotation. The Russo-
Belgian Metallurgical Company's shareholders, for
example, exercised almost all their rights to subscribe one new share for each old share (666 francs
par value) at 1,150 francs in 1912. Russo-Belgian
shares averaged 1,560 francs for the entire year on
the Brussels Stock Exchange and were never below
1,380 francs. The South Russian Dnieper Metallurg-

---

78. C.L., statistical tables on these three companies, bound together in a separate folio.

79. A.N., F 30, no. 331, Capitaux des Sociétés métallurgiques du
Midi.

ical Company offered new shares with a par value of 666 francs to old holders at 833 francs in 1910, or 200 francs below the year's low. In 1912 the company offered more shares at 666 francs, or 30 francs above the year's low and 400 below the year's average price.[80] Such flotations for well-established companies were secured by underwriting syndicates, but this was mainly a matter of form. Subscription rights were valuable and negotiable, and they were exercised automatically.

For less fortunate firms, whose shares were quoted only a little above par, the underwriting guarantee was important and expensive. But it usually permitted successful flotation of new shares. These new issues were guaranteed by the great Russo-French and Russo-German banking syndicates about which much has been written. Generally discussed in relation to the question of whether or not foreign banking groups effectively controlled and monopolized the Russian economy, these syndicates tell a great deal about the evolving character and contribution of foreign capital and entrepreneurship.

Certain facts seem incontestable. First, foreigners, particularly Frenchmen, owned a great and increasing percentage of the capital stock of Russian banks from about 1907 on. On the eve of the revolution approximately 44 percent of the capital of Russian banks was in foreign hands: the French had 22 percent of the total; the Germans 16 percent; and the English 5 percent.[81] Some Russian banks were

80. C.L., Statistical Tables; B.U.P., Russie, no. 104, Russo-Belge, letter from Société Générale de Belgique to B.U.P., 10–12–1911.

81. Ol', *Inostrannye kapitaly*, pp. 146–250; I. F. Gindin, *Russkie banki*, pp. 371–72.

even reorganized by foreign banks in the early twentieth century. The Parisian banker Joseph Loste, representing himself, the Crédit Mobilier, Thalmann, and Hirsch of London, revitalized the St. Petersburg Private Commercial Bank in 1910 and then placed the new shares in France.[82] The year before, the Banque de l'Union Parisienne and the *haute banque* of Paris fused the three foundering banks of Poliakov into the Moscow Union Bank.[83] Russian bank shares, always popular in Berlin, became a standard commodity on the Paris Exchange. By 1913 nine issues had been introduced there, all of them after 1909.[84] (The Russo-Asiatic and Azov-Don Banks were particularly important to French interests.)[85] Increased foreign investment in Russian banking went with a rapid growth of total capital. Russian commercial banks doubled their share capital from January 1908 to January 1913 (from 352,000,000 rubles to 740,000,000 rubles).[86]

Second, the great Russian banks, following the German model, were the primary force for economic growth in the years before the war, as Professor Gerschenkron and others have pointed out.[87] Their chief tool for supplying funds was the traditional underwriting syndicate, but on a vast international scale. These Russo-foreign syndicates placed Rus-

82. A.N., F 30, no. 336, Convention, 26–12–1909; *Bourse de Paris*, 25–5–1910.

83. A.N., F 30, no. 336, notes of 19–5–1910 and 15–6–1910.

84. S. L. Ronin, *Inostrannye kapitaly i russkie banki* (Moscow, 1926), p. 127.

85. Olga Crisp, "French Investment in Russian Joint-Stock Companies," *Business History* (Liverpool) 2 (1960): 89.

86. A.N., F 30, no. 335, Les banques russes de commerce en 1912, 30–5–1913.

87. *Economic Backwardness* pp. 136–46; Olga Crisp, "Russia, 1860–1914," in Cameron et al., *Banking in the Early Stages of Industrialization*, pp. 225–28.

sian industrial shares simultaneously on several leading European exchanges. In 1914 the Paris Exchange listed shares of 66 companies operating in Russia, Brussels also 66 (with 46 of these incorporated under Belgian law), and London 74, which were almost exclusively oil or gold stocks.[88] But perhaps more crucial was the flowering of the St. Petersburg Stock Exchange, where the number of industrial companies listed jumped from 121 as late as 1912 to 201 in January 1914. Professor Gindin estimates that the St. Petersburg Stock Exchange absorbed one billion rubles of capital stock from 1908 to 1914, while foreign markets absorbed 0.4 billion rubles.[89] And the Russian stock market was certainly a creation of the great Russian banks who subscribed shares and, much more importantly, advanced credit to speculators through margin accounts.[90]

What do these well-known facts suggest about the nature of foreign participation in Russian industry in the years before World War I? Basically, they suggest a decline in active foreign entrepreneurship, with its stress on technical and managerial superiority, and a rise in passive portfolio investment. Whereas foreigners invested directly in their own companies during the 1890s, new foreign investment was now increasingly channelled into the shares of Russian banks. These Russian banks then invested in Russian industry. In these circumstances the key foreign businessmen in Russia were less and less the

88. I. Gindin, *Banki i promyshlennost' v Rossii* (Moscow, 1927), p. 61.
89. Ibid.
90. Ibid. From January 1910 to October 1912 margin account loans to Russians grew from 279,000,000 rubles to 907,000,000 rubles while the Russian banks' holdings of shares grew from 99,000,000 rubles to 244,000,000 rubles. *L'Information*, 14–2–1913.

top managers of increasingly russified industrial corporations, but rather the foreign bankers. These foreign bankers worked with their Russian counterparts in underwriting syndicates to raise capital for the Russian banks and their clients in western Europe. The foreign businessman's emphasis was financial rather than industrial.[91]

It is often alleged that these financial relations represented the final concentration of Russian industry in the hands of foreign monopolists.[92] This is a forced and inadequate conclusion.[93] Russian bankers were strong and opinionated men who worked with foreigners as equals. Nor were foreign holdings of stock in Russian banks closely held. Rather they were widely spread among many investors who sought good-to-excellent returns through a trouble-free, diversified participation in Russian industrial development. In such circumstances the foreign representatives in Russian banks exercised at most a tenuous veto power over Russian decision makers. (See chapter 12 for a rare case study on this whole question of Russo-foreign banking relations within a given firm in this period.) These Russians clearly held the initiative and were the predominating influence.

The passing of foreign business leadership may also be seen in the histories of specific industrial enterprises. There was a tendency for foreign entre-

91. Gindin, *Banki*, pp. 62 ff., 129 ff.

92. See N. Vanag, *Finansovyi kapital v Rossii nakanune mirovoi voiny* (Moscow, 1925), for the extreme and most comprehensive statement of this position. Gindin disagrees sharply in *Banki*, pp. 190–97.

93. This paragraph is based primarily on Gindin's exceptionally fine work, *Banki i promyshlennost' v Rossii*, particularly pages 177–97. My work at the Banque de l'Union Parisienne supports Gindin's interpretation.

preneurs to lose effective control, even as they retained some ownership. Look at the hard-pressed Taganrog Metallurgical Company. It forced its Belgian stockholders to accept a drastic 90 percent reduction of the par value of their common stock in 1905 to avert bankruptcy. The company's creditors in Belgium and Russia then received full payment for their claims in common stock having this reduced par value. The Azov-Don Bank, an important creditor, benefited from this arrangement and became a leading stockholder. Subsequently Taganrog's capital was increased from 7,500,000 to 21,000,000 rubles between 1910 and 1914, and control definitely passed to the Azov-Don Bank.[94] Under this new leadership Taganrog bought from the State Bank in 1912 the bankrupt Kerch Metallurgical Company, with which foreigners had come to grief a decade earlier. In 1913 it was ambitiously creating one of Russia's largest steel companies. If the Azov-Don Bank and its French associates pushed Taganrog's shares to outrageously high prices from 1912 to 1914, there is no doubt that the Russian bank made policy.[95]

Two other examples from metallurgy show the shifting of the entrepreneurial center of gravity. The heirs of the Englishman John Hughes, who had let their New Russia Company decline a bit after 1900, worked untiringly to sell out and withdraw from Russian industry. They finally succeeded in March 1914, when the St. Petersburg International Bank agreed to head a predominantly Russian syn-

94. A.N., 65 AQ, K 236, Annual Report, 1905; *Echo de la Bourse et de la Banque,* 26–6–1904; *L'Information,* 5–1–1913, 9–5–1913; Gindin, *Banki,* pp. 121, 135–38.

95. B.U.P., Russie, no. 219, Affaires Métallurgiques en Russie, Darcy to B.U.P., 4–9–1912, 12–10–1912; *Moniteur des Intérêts Matériels,* 14–11–1912.

dicate which would purchase Hughes's firm for 2,400,000 pounds sterling.[96] The sale was apparently never completed because exchange control established after the outbreak of war made it impossible to meet the adamant demands of young Balfour Hughes for payment in sterling.

The Banque de l'Union Parisienne had difficulties even before the war in retaining control of the Donets-Yur'evka Metallurgical Company, which it had reorganized with Thalmann in 1910. In 1916 a series of panicky telegrams showed that a group of Russians had almost obtained controlling interest. According to Darcy, only a rapid completion of the long-contemplated merger with the predominantly French Ural-Volga Company could assure foreign control.[97] The Banque de l'Union Parisienne had already lost the direction of the recently formed North Donets Railroad Company in 1911, and it knew how quickly this could happen again.[98] These examples show definitely the foreigner's difficulty in maintaining the control necessary for effective entrepreneurship. They help explain the drift toward Russian intermediaries and portfolio investment.

At the same time Russian banks with the aid of their French underwriting partners placed shares of clearly Russian industrial companies on foreign exchanges between 1907 and 1914. Some of the companies were the Maltsov Factories, the Russo-Baltic Freight Car Company, the Sormovo Steel Company, the Kolomna Machine Company, the Hartmann Ma-

96. B.U.P., Russie, no. 228, Affaire Hughes, Darcy to B.U.P., 28–3–1914, 5–4–1914, 8–4–1914.

97. B.U.P., Russie, no. 87, Donetz-Yurievka, Darcy to Thalmann, 15–7–1910; ibid., no. 364, Darcy to B.U.P., 2–2–1917; also, note of November 1922.

98. A.E., Paris, Russie, N.S., no. 60, letters of 2–3–1911 and 7–10–1912.

chine Company, the Putilov Company, and the Stoll Machine Company.[99] These companies all peddled their shares aggressively on French exchanges, where they succeeded in selling minority participations, invariably above the St. Petersburg price.

This was a significant success. Throughout the 1890s Russian businessmen had been generally unable to tap for their own account the funds of the Western passive investor. This had given foreigners one important competitive advantage. Now, as Russian entrepreneurship came of age, the foreign businessman's promotional techniques were emulated and mastered in the foreigner's own backyard. (It is significant that whereas foreigners accounted for almost all fraudulent or shady promotion of companies operating in Russia during the 1890s, Russians were capable of promoting their own frauds and highly questionable speculations in western Europe before the war.) [100] Russia needed only the foreigner's money, and not his entrepreneurship as well as his money.

As for foreign control, the French minister of finance usually required that the Russian firm listed on the Paris Exchange name at least one French member to its board of directors. This was to protect the interests of the French shareholders. These French directors were yes-men, however, and control was always Russian.[101] To the extent that Belgian or English investors bought the shares of

99. See Girault, for the Putilov Company which flirted with French predominance, but which remained firmly Russian. For the others, see the appropriate dossiers in A.N., 65 AQ, and in C.L., Intérêts Français dans la Métallurgie Russe, Etude, February 1922.

100. A.N., F 30, no. 345, Société Neft; F. 30, no. 343, Moulins Oberemchenko and other dossiers.

101. See, in particular, A.N., F 30, no. 340, Société Provodnik.

Russian-managed companies, they were even less able to exercise any influence. Thus passive foreign portfolio investment in Russian industry increasingly replaced the dynamic, technologically oriented, foreign entrepreneurship of the 1890s.

7

THE PROBLEM OF LABOR

Foreign entrepreneurs needed to combine techniques, managers, and capital with the brawn and skill of laboring men to implement their investment strategy. This was no simple task in the 1890s, when the general conditions of Russian economic backwardness complicated the formation of an adequate labor force. In addition to limited industrial development and the corresponding lack of an existing pool of industrial workers, there were also legal and cultural factors which tied the potential factory worker, the Russian peasant, to his village and agriculture. Indeed, the typical factory worker returned periodically to his home village for agricultural work. And even if he did not, he remained psychologically dependent upon the rural environment.[1]

This periodic migration had serious consequences. It postponed the worker's commitment to industrial work, resulted in a widely fluctuating supply of available labor, and hampered the development of

1. For useful discussions of the whole question of labor formation, see Gaston V. Rimlinger, "Autocracy and Factory Order," *Journal of Economic History* 20 (1960) : 67–92, and Theodore H. Von Laue, "Russian Peasants in the Factory, 1892–1904," *Journal of Economic History* 21 (1961) : 61–80. There is a wealth of information in A. G. Rashin's classic, *Formirovanie rabochego klassa Rossii* (Moscow, 1958), which is an expanded version of his earlier *Formirovanie promyshlennogo proletariata v Rossii* (Moscow, 1940).

skilled workmen. The consequences of the unstable and variable Russian work force have even led to the ingenious hypothesis that in spite of rural over-population and poverty,[2] labor was nonetheless the "expensive" factor and capital the "cheap" one in Russia's great push of the 1890s.[3] According to this reasoning, one might argue that the rapid rate of population increase [4]—more than 1.5 percent per annum from 1885 to 1913—created the famed "land hunger," but it did not produce cheap and plentiful labor for industry.

With these general considerations in mind we may examine foreign entrepreneurs faced with the difficult task of forming their labor force. The primary focus is again the typical entrepreneurial experience, which was defined by three basic boundaries: chronologically, from the late 1880s to approximately 1904; geographically, the new southern industrial region; and by industry, primarily metallurgy, machinery, and mining.

2. Gaston V. Rimlinger, "The Expansion of the Labor Market in Capitalist Russia, 1861–1917," *Journal of Economic History* 21 (1961) : 211, believes Russian conditions throughout the period after emancipation "turned peasants into wage laborers at a much faster rate than the still small industrial sector could absorb them."

3. Alexander Gerschenkron, *Economic Backwardness*, pp. 126–28. A lack of entrepreneurs and managers is partly responsible for the relatively expensive character of the labor factor, of which factory workers are only one component.

4. For Alexander Baykov "much more rapid" growth of population in Russia than in western Europe was one of two primary differences in the economic history of Russia and the West from the middle eighteenth century to the early twentieth. The other was Russia's slower industrial development. See "The Economic Development of Russia," *Economic History Review*, 2d ser., 7 (1954) : 137–49. The two best works on Russian population in this period are A. G. Rashin, *Naselenie Rossii za 100 let* (Moscow, 1956), and E. Volkov, *Dinamika narodonaseleniia SSSR* (Moscow, 1930).

1

Foreign businessmen generally agreed that labor was initially a serious and vexatious problem in southern Russia for four main reasons. First of all, much of the area, and particularly the Donets Basin, was a thinly populated, recently settled, frontier region. In population density the Don Territory was among the lowest ten of the fifty Russian provinces from 1863 to 1914.[5] After a tour through the future industrial heartland of the Donets region in 1882, the French consul at Odessa warned his countrymen that "there are only a few isolated sprawling villages . . . with low, poorly constructed huts which clearly show the misery of the inhabitants. . . . The region has great promise, but it is poor and almost deserted now."[6]

The rapid increase of population in the area suggests how sparsely settled the region was on the eve of industrialization. The Don Territory had the highest rate of population growth of all fifty provinces between 1863 and 1914, an enormous 308 percent; the province of Ekaterinoslav was fifth highest with an increase of 187 percent.[7] Industrial towns grew more rapidly. From 1887 to 1897 the provincial capital, Ekaterinoslav, grew from 40,000 to 160,000; Krivoi-Rog grew from 6,000 to 17,000; Kamenskoe (the Dnieper Company) from 2,000 to 18,000; and Druzhkovka (the Donets Steel Company) from a few dozen railway employees to 6,000.[8] It is significant that the first two pioneering met-

5. Rashin, *Naselenie,* pp. 78–79.

6. Rapport du Chancelier du Consulat de France à Odessa [Monestier], undated [late 1882], A.N., F 12, no. 7173.

7. Rashin, *Naselenie,* pp. 44–45.

8. A.E., Paris, C. C., Odessa, vol. 13, letter to the Quai d'Orsay, 11–11–1898.

allurgical firms of this period, the Dnieper and Briansk Metallurgical Companies, did not follow Hughes's lead and locate on Donets coal in the vacant steppe. Both chose sites near the city of Ekaterinoslav in hopes of obtaining labor more easily and avoiding Hughes's serious initial difficulties of labor recruitment.[9] Thinly settled population also meant that peasant landholdings in the Donets were relatively large for Russia and that the peasantry was normally self-sufficient. The pressure of numbers did not compel peasants in the area to seek industrial work.[10]

It is against this background that one must place the fivefold increase of industrial laborers (from 76,000 to 392,000) in the New Russian area from 1881–90 to 1913.[11] (The New Russian area includes five provinces: Kherson, Ekaterinoslav, Tauride, Bessarabia, and the Don Territory.) For the years 1863–1913 the industrial work force of the Don Territory increased sixty times (from 1,500 to 92,000), while that of Ekaterinoslav increased forty times (from 5,200 to 211,000). Of all the other provinces Kherson was next highest with a ten-fold increase.[12] It seems clear that the recruitment of labor in this new industrial area would have presented problems of large-scale in-migration even if Russian labor had been highly mobile and adequately trained, which of course it was not.

Second, foreigners noted with regret that the lack of population in general and the absence of urban

9. C.L., Briansk, Etude, April 1900.
10. I. M. Lukomskaia, "Formirovanie promyshlennogo proletariata Donbassa," p. 301, in Akademiia Nauk SSSR, *Iz istorii rabochego klassa i revoliutsionnogo dvizheniia* (Moscow, 1958); Lauwick, *L'industrie,* p. 136; Rimlinger, "Labor Market," p. 212.
11. Rashin, *Formirovanie,* pp. 189, 192.
12. Ibid., p. 193.

centers in particular entailed a corresponding deficiency in the necessities and amenities of industrial
civilization. Roads, railroad sidings, houses,
churches, hotels, parks, hospitals, libraries, police
departments—none were ready and all were expensive. This leitmotiv runs through contemporary reports and commentaries with regularity.[13] And the
cost of all these facilities fell upon private enterprise. "No [Russian] speculator appeared in those
solitary areas to construct houses to let for high
rents."[14] Little wonder the southern industrial centers were often company towns.

Ecclesiastical authorities were no more enterpris-
ing, and they left the building of churches to the
firms. The Dnieper Company built two churches, one
Orthodox and one Catholic (for its Polish workers).
The German Donets-Yur'evka cannily built an Orthodox Church and then "a prayer chapel with all
the accessories necessary for either Catholic or Lu-
theran services."[15] Medical expenses were heavy,
since large companies universally provided free
medical and hospital service for all employees and
their dependents.

The response of the Gorlovka Coal Company was
typical. By 1900 the company had built more than
thirteen hundred houses, a hospital with 106 beds
and a medical staff of forty people, six schools, two
churches, a lending library, and a large park. In the
hundred-acre park alone the company had planted
more than one million trees in fifteen years and had

13. For example, the letter of Monestier to the Quai d'Orsay,
15–5–1893, A.E., Paris, C.C., Odessa, vol. 13.
14. Lauwick, *L'industrie,* p. 140.
15. C.L., Dniéprovienne, Annual Report, 1893; *Société Métallurgique Donetz-Yourievka.*

created "a veritable oasis in the middle of the arid steppe."[16] Other firms acted similarly to provide social-overhead capital previously lacking in the region.

Third, foreigners consistently noted the seasonal nature of their migratory labor force and bemoaned the attendant problems. "There are very few fixed workers in the area," wrote the French consul in 1893. "Most workers are nomads alternating between industry and agriculture, and this presents an enormous difficulty."[17] A German investigator of the period reported that he "found many establishments in which the work force changed on the average once a year. It was considered fortunate if one-tenth of the work force formed a permanent core."[18] At least one-half of all coal miners in the area were seasonal employees in the middle 1880s.[19] This same pattern prevailed, to a lesser extent, in metallurgy. Speaking of peasants from Kursk province, one observer noted in 1883 that "many go to Ekaterinoslav province to Mister Hughes's steel mill. They go, if possible, in the fall or winter, after the harvest, from the 15th of September on."[20] At the very least the future was always a bit uncertain with such a labor force. For example, the Gorlovka Coal Company anticipated producing 500,000 tons of coal in 1901 but said this depended on the magnitude

16. *Société de l'Industrie Houillère de la Russie Méridionale*, pp. 3–14.

17. A.E., Paris, C.C., Odessa, vol. 13, Monestier to Quai d'Orsay, 15–5–1893.

18. O. Goebel, *Entwicklungsgang der russischen Industriearbeiter bis zur ersten Revolution* (Leipzig, 1920), p. 13, as quoted by G. Rimlinger, "The Management of Labor Protest in Tsarist Russia," *International Review of Social History*, 5 (1960) : 228.

19. Lukomskaia, "Formirovanie," p. 304.

20. Rashin, *Formirovanie*, p. 444.

of the summer exodus, which was in turn linked to the results of the harvest.[21]

Lastly, if ordinary labor was hard to find and harder to hold year round, it was also largely untrained and inexperienced. This was more serious for metallurgical and machinery producers than for coal companies. Yet even for them this was important. Gorlovka Coal found that "some of its very modern accessory equipment is too intricate for its work force, which is of necessity recently recruited among the agricultural population of central Russia."[22] This lack of experience meant that skilled labor and supervisory personnel, such as foremen and section chiefs, were in extremely short supply, or simply nonexistent.

2

Because of these factors foreign entrepreneurs shared Professor Gerschenkron's belief that labor was relatively expensive at the beginning of the industrial revolution (big spurt, take-off) in southern Russia during the 1890s. Relatively expensive, first of all, in terms of the labor which the foreigner knew best, his own. The real cost of labor was as high or higher in backward southern Russia as in advanced western Europe; all sang this tune, no matter who the audience.

That skillful and generally accurate publicist Marcel Lauwick estimated that the cost of Russian labor in the Donets was approximately equal to that in France or Belgium. Donets coal miners, for example, averaged 1.2 rubles per day plus fringe benefits of 10 percent, or about 3.6 francs in all, circa 1904.

21. C.L., Sels Gemmes, Etude by Waton, January 1900. See additional material in Rashin, *Formirovanie*, pp. 508–11.
22. C.L., Sels Gemmes, Etude, January 1900.

Belgian miners earned 3.9 francs on the average.[23] Nor did the promotional literature of the companies themselves differ. A printed preparatory study of Belaia Coal reached the customary conclusion that wages were as high in Russia as in Belgium.[24]

The highly confidential studies by the engineers of the Crédit Lyonnais concurred. The average Russian steelworker, earning two rubles per day during the period 1900–1904 (including fringe benefits), was paid only slightly less than his counterpart in western Europe.[25] It might be noted, however, that the average cash wage of 1.8 rubles per day (4.8 francs) at Dnieper Metallurgical in 1904 compared favorably with the average wage in the Liège area of about 3.6 francs daily, which was admittedly low —25 percent below Westphalia and French Lorraine.[26] At Taganrog Steel at the turn of the century, for example, "workers are recruited with difficulty, as in all of southern Russia. They are also inexperienced and expensive (2 to 3 rubles per day, or 5.62 to 8.0 francs). . . . Only unskilled labor has a low salary (.75 to 1 ruble, or 2 to 2.67 francs)."[27] In short, "labor must be considered fairly expensive" in southern Russia.[28] The implication was clear; foreign engineers needed to economize on expensive labor with advanced, capital-intensive technology. This they did, as we have seen.

Foreigners also believed labor was relatively expensive in southern Russia for another reason, a reason historians have generally ignored. It seemed clear to them that the real cost of labor was signifi-

23. Lauwick, L'industrie, pp. 129–31, 147.
24. Rapport par Hardy et Michot.
25. C.L., Métallurgie dans le Midi, April 1905.
26. Ibid.; C.L., Société Cockerill, September 1903.
27. C.L., Taganrog, Etude, June 1900.
28. C.L., Hartmann, Etude, January 1904.

cantly higher in southern Russia (and in western
Europe) than in northern Russia. Therefore the
price of labor in southern Russia was atypically
high in the early stages of industrialization as far as
Russia itself was concerned.

Both the leading northern cities—Moscow, St. Petersburg, Riga, etc.—and the small northern factory
towns contained a better labor supply, although for
somewhat different reasons. The worker in the large
city was often skilled and permanently settled, and
he was no better paid than his southern
counterpart.[29] The peasant worker of small company towns was cheap and easily recruited, which
compensated for his seasonal migrations and low
level of skills.[30] During the 1890s foreign businessmen believed they had the worst of both systems in
the Donets Basin of southern Russia. Labor was
unskilled and migratory, as in small northern towns,
and as expensive as in the large northern cities.

In detailed studies comparing the competitive
positions of shipbuilders on the Baltic and Black
seas the engineers of the Crédit Lyonnais noted that
the labor force at the southern naval yards was
more expensive and less competent. Nikolaev Shipyards, for example, was clearly at a considerable
disadvantage in comparison with St. Petersburg
shipbuilders as far as labor was concerned.[31] Rail-

29. Four-fifths of the 2,000,000 workers in the Moscow industrial area, for example, were working year round by 1893, according to a survey by the minister of finance in that year. See A. M.
Pankratova, ed., *Rabochee dvizhenie v XIX veke; Sbornik docu-
mentov*, 3, pt. 2 (Moscow, 1952) : 591.

30. Rashin suggests that informed opinion believed that, unless
one needed skilled labor, it was best to put factories in northern
rural areas where labor was cheap and abundant. *Formirovanie*,
pp. 206–11.

31. C.L., Chantiers Navals de Nicolaiev, Etude, September
1904. See also the Etude on the Usines Franco-Russes, January
1905.

way-equipment producers like Bouhey at Kharkov and Hartmann at Lugansk also faced the challenge of less efficient and more expensive labor.[32]

Metallurgy followed the same pattern. A detailed study of the Moscow Metallurgical Company in 1904 noted that the work force, exclusively Russian except for foremen, was "good and not at all expensive in comparison to other steel companies. The rolling mill workers are particularly skillful and they work as quickly as any in Russia."[33] Similarly there were few, if any, complaints by foreign businessmen in the many documents examined concerning the quality of steel workers in the old decadent Ural region.

Quite the contrary. In evaluating the Ural-Volga Company's first plant in the Ufa region, Du Marais of the Crédit Lyonnais voiced the general sentiment. "Workers are abundant . . . and cheap. The company is assured of finding all the ordinary workers it could possibly need within the region."[34] Similarly, Bonnardel's Kama Steel Company had a "well-disciplined, modestly paid work force," which contributed to the intelligent choice of labor-intensive techniques.[35] A general appraisal sums up the consensus of foreign entrepreneurs at about the turn of the century. "Labor at St. Petersburg is superior in quality to that found in all other Russian industrial centers, Moscow excepted. As for price, labor at St. Petersburg and Moscow is considerably cheaper than in southern Russia."[36]

32. C.L., Construction de Locomotives et Mécaniques [Bouhey], Etude, February 1904; Hartmann, Etude, February 1904.

33. C.L., Usines Métallurgiques de Moscou, Etude, February 1904.

34. C.L., Oural Volga, Etude of du Marais, August 1898.

35. C.L., Kama, Etude of Waton, November 1900.

36. C.L., Laminoirs de St. Petersburg, Etude, December 1904. The leading Soviet authority also agrees that wages were "some-

Nor was this all. In addition to that of St. Petersburg and Moscow, there was the excellent labor of the Baltic cities (particularly Riga), which was probably the best in Russia. The Crédit Lyonnais's studies laud this labor consistently. A study on the Russo-Baltic Company, a railway-equipment producer, noted in 1898 that the Lithuanian or Lettish laborer under the direction of German foremen was vastly superior to his Russian counterpart in both skill and perseverance. Wages were not high, and they had a tendency to decline.[37] Riga developed rapidly as a major-equipment and rubber producer after 1890 with this superior labor pool, which was often directed by German entrepreneurs and foremen. The three Baltic provinces constituted in fact the second most rapidly developing industrial region in Russia after 1890.[38]

These regional differences in the quality of the labor force had two consequences for foreign entrepreneurs. First, they explain why these entrepreneurs generally preferred to locate in northern areas (or Poland) if the price of raw materials was not a decisive factor. In the continued expansion of old industries, such as textiles, or the elaboration of new ones, such as electrical equipment or chemicals, foreigners did not stray from proved ground. Textile producers like the Russo-French Cotton Company, or Kostroma Cotton, followed the general movement to northern rural areas. German chemical and electrical-equipment producers chose either Moscow or St. Petersburg almost exclusively. And

what higher" in the South than in other industrial regions from 1890 to 1914. Rashin, *Formirovanie*, p. 445.

37. C.L., Russo-Baltique, Etude, July 1898. See also Haut-Volga, May 1904, and the entire Provodnik dossier.

38. Rashin, *Formirovanie*, pp. 190–91.

when a Belgian company challenged (unsuccessfully) this preeminence, it chose Moscow, even though more than half the sales were expected to originate in the Donets.[39] Only heavy equipment was on the border line. Here newcomers weighed the superiority of northern labor (South Ural and Upper Volga) against the better source of raw materials (Bouhey and Hartmann).

This brings us to the second point. If one chose to produce equipment, or anything for that matter, in the southern area, one needed very modern and advanced machinery to offset the disadvantage of inferior labor *within Russia itself*. The oft-noted modern character of southern industry was in part necessary for the foreign businessman if he were to compete successfully with established native firms with their much better and cheaper work forces. This was the case even in ferrous metallurgy, in which the eventual rout of older producing regions was far from certain in 1887.

3

Foreign entrepreneurs in southern Russia tried to remedy the deficiencies of their labor force in various ways. The choice of advanced labor-saving techniques was one way. Yet foreign firms were not unwilling to use the traditional work habits of the Russian when feasible, even in southern Russia. The pattern of open-pit mining in the Krivoi-Rog district is an outstanding example.

Technology was limited to traditional hand tools

39. C.L., Cie Centrale d'Electricité de Moscou, Etude, March 1906. The American Westinghouse Company later followed this firm to Moscow in a joint venture, which was also unsuccessful. A.N., 65 AQ, G 470, Articles of Incorporation of the Sté Electrique Westinghouse de Russie, founded in Paris, 12–6–1906, and related clippings.

—pick, shovel, and wheelbarrow—and only dynamite for blasting and steam engines for raising ore provided a touch of modernity.[40] "There is absolutely no problem in mining at Krivoi-Rog. The equipment is always very simple [in 1899]." Consequently "the labor situation is favorable, and charges comparable to those of underground mines and great metallurgical works do not exist. Peasants provide hauling at piece rates and the miners themselves are easily recruited from the overabundant agrarian population."[41] Easily recruited also because the work force could fluctuate harmlessly according to the needs of agriculture, since iron ore was easily stockpiled. And foreign mining companies could normally deal with only a few native subcontractors, who in turn had the responsibility of handling their work gangs and fixing wages.[42] Only after about 1906 did the gradual exhaustion of surface deposits force expensive underground mining of iron at Krivoi-Rog.[43] The Russian pattern of technical backwardness and migrant labor functioned well in these operations, and foreign entrepreneurs were delighted to accept it.

This was an exceptional case, however. It was applicable in neither metallurgy nor coal mining, the two staples of southern industry. Metallurgy and related equipment manufacturing demanded perma-

40. See, for example, *Notice sur les Mines de la Doubovaia Balka.* See Jules Cordeweener, *Contribution à l'étude de la crise industrielle du Donetz* (Brussels, 1902), for pictures and discussion of open-pit iron mining at the turn of the century.

41. C.L., Région industrielle du Donetz, Etude Générale du Bassin ferrifère de Krivoi-Rog, August 1899.

42. *Notice sur les Mines de la Doubovaia Balka.*

43. See C.L., Société de Krivoi-Rog, Etude, September 1912, for a meticulous discussion of such a transformation at the oldest and most famous mine of the region.

nent full-time laborers, some of them highly skilled. Blast furnaces burning twenty-four hours per day seven days a week for years at a time cannot follow the cyclical vagaries of planting and harvesting. Since the total number of metallurgical workers in southern Russia increased more than tenfold from 1885 to 1900—from 3,500 to 39,700—it is easy to see that the formation of a qualified labor force in this industry did indeed present foreign enterprise with "very great difficulties."[44]

This serious bottleneck of permanent and skilled metallurgists was broken in large part through the large-scale importation of foreign steelworkers and foremen, especially for the crucial period of construction and starting-up. The Dnieper Company was built and staffed by men from Cockerill; the Russo-Belgian Company by men under Phillipart, a well-known Belgian engineer; Tula Blast Furnaces by men from Espérance-Longdoz and the shops of Liège. The list might be extended. Construction and start-up posed the greatest demand for experienced men, and it was precisely then that the local labor force was least satisfactory. It is no exaggeration to say that almost all southern steel workers were foreigners at the beginning.[45]

The massive recourse to foreign metallurgists was never more than a temporary expedient, however. The Russian worker may have cost as much as the Belgian or French worker in Belgium or France; he was always much cheaper than the Belgian or French worker *in Russia*. Foreign foremen and highly skilled steelworkers were paid from 300 to 350 rubles per month in the southern area in

44. C.L., Métallurgie dans le Midi, April 1905; Rashin, *Formirovanie*, p. 30.
45. C.L., Métallurgie dans le Midi, April 1905.

the 1890s—very high wages indeed.[46] After 1900 foreign wages fell by at least one-third, but for several
years they continued to stand 50 percent above those
of Russians performing the same jobs.[47] Material
from the Russian Providence Company suggests
that wages for foreign foremen fell to about 200
rubles per month by 1913; foreigners and Russians
were then receiving almost equal pay for equal
work. Thus foreign steel companies anticipated
using imported labor only as long as was necessary
to train Russian workers for these positions.

Three Belgian steel companies started with large
contingents of foreign workers. Yet after twenty
years Dnieper Metallurgical had almost none, while
the Russo-Belgian Company had substituted many
Russians for the initial one hundred fifty foreign
foremen and workers.[48] Taganrog Steel, which
started with more than three hundred foreign workers, had about one hundred in 1907.[49] Management
noted in 1898 that "several special jobs are filled by
native workers we have trained," while the Crédit
Lyonnais's engineer noted three years later that
there was "a very strong tendency to replace Belgians with Russians."[50] The director of Donets-
Yur'evka Steel in 1898 hoped that his powerful and
advanced equipment would permit him to afford to
keep a small number of excellent foreign working-
men, who would slowly upgrade the quality of the
average Russian worker. But there was no doubt
that the vast majority of the workers would be, and
indeed was, Russian.[51] By 1904 foreign workers, for-

46. Lauwick, *L'industrie*, pp. 138–41.
47. Ibid., pp. 142–43, 305–6.
48. Ibid., p. 138; Brandt, *Inostrannye kapitaly*, 2:268–69.
49. Lauwick, *L'industrie*, p. 138.
50. Annual Report for 1898, 65 AQ, K 236; Taganrog, Etude,
November 1901, C.L.
51. C.L., Donetz-Yourievka, Etude, December 1898.

eign foremen apart, were only a "very small minority of southern metallurgical workers."[52] The formation of a native work force was complete.

The inability of foreign and Russian workmen to work well together also encouraged rapid russification of the force. Higher wages and better housing for the large contingent of Belgian and Polish glassworkers, who lived together, aroused the emnity of their Russian counterparts at the Konstantinovka Glass Company. An ugly name-calling incident in August 1900 incited two hundred of the Russians to burn all the possessions and buildings of foreign workers. Sixty thoroughly frightened Belgians fled homeward, and the company's ultimate goal of an all-Russian labor force was precipitously attained.[53] This riot also destroyed part of the housing of foreign workers at the nearby Konstantinovka Steel Company.[54] The following annual report of that firm noted with evident satisfaction "another very substantial reduction of foreign labor" and the existence of a "very satisfactory force of workers which is almost exclusively Russian."[55]

Turning to foremen and highly skilled technicians, a small minority of the total work force in steel mills, we find that almost all of them were also foreigners at the beginning. Again russification progressed, but much more slowly. In fact, from our data it appears that only top technical personnel remained foreign for as long a time.[56]

---

52. C.L., Métallurgie dans le Midi, April 1905.

53. A.E., Brussels, no. 2904, Conflict entre ouvriers belges et russes, Société de Konstantinovka.

54. A.N., 65 AQ, K 58, Tôleries de Konstantinovka, Annual Report, 1899–1900.

55. Ibid., 1900–1901.

56. There is similar evidence in Brandt, *Inostrannye kapitaly,* 2:270–72, as well as in John F. Fraser, *Russia of To-day* (New York, 1916), p. 183.

At Taganrog Steel most of the foremen were Belgian in 1901; Makeevka Steel always had numerous French foremen.[57] But the most telling example is the Russian Providence Company, for which a personnel list in 1913 exists. It clearly shows that this leading producer retained a high percentage of foreign foremen. Of the thirty-five foremen, or *chefs de service,* earning salaries of from two to three thousand rubles per annum, ten were Russian and two were Polish, while sixteen were Belgian and seven were French.[58]

This continued use of foreign foremen also apparently existed in the older metallurgical companies outside the Donets. Goujon and his French managers at Moscow Steel continued to use French foremen almost exclusively in 1904 after more than twenty years of operations.[59] Old German metallurgical firms in the North did likewise. The German-owned St. Petersburg Iron and Wire Company, founded in 1883, was using predominantly German foremen to direct its Russian workmen in 1904.[60] This suggests that competent native foremen requiring long years of on-the-job training were in even shorter supply than native engineers, and certainly than native commercial experts. Such engineers and salesmen were more easily found among the local privileged classes, having been formed by the existing system of higher education or trade, and they

57. C.L., Taganrog, Etude, November 1901; C.L., Makeevka, various studies.

58. B.U.P., Russie, no. 53, Providence Russe, List of Personnel, 1-7-1913.

59. C.L., Usines Métallurgiques de Moscou, Etude, February 1904.

60. C.L., Laminoirs de St. Petersburg, December 1904. This company (Obshch. St. Peterburgskikh zhelezoprokatnogo i provolochnogo zavodov) shared the leading role among specialty producers in central Russia with Goujon's firm.

were rapidly employed by foreign firms, as we saw in chapter 5.

The formation of coal miners fell somewhere between the patterns in iron mining and metallurgy. Coal companies desired skilled and permanently settled miners working year round. This was not absolutely imperative, however. They could follow Russian procedure, which concentrated production in the winter months and struggled along with perhaps half the normal work force from May to October.[61]

As in the case of metallurgical workers, the vast majority of coal miners in the Donets came from other regions, a fact which the investigations of recent Soviet scholars have clearly shown.[62] According to information based on the census of 1897, 70 percent of the workers in mining and manufacturing in both the Don Territory and Ekaterinoslav province were born in other provinces.[63] N. C. Avdakov, commercial director for the Société Génrale's Rutchenko mine, estimated that an enormous seven-eighths of all Donets coal miners came from other provinces, principally Tula, Smolensk, Orel, Riazan, Tambov, and Kursk—all to the North.[64]

Listen to one such worker from Orel province recount his experience. "I was earning little, and I worried and worried about it. Finally after collecting nine rubles I decided to go [south] in search of a

61. *Trudy XVIII s"ezda gornopromyshlennikov Rossii, byvshego v Khar'kove s 1 po 14 dekabria 1893 g.* (Kharkov, 1894), pt. 1, pp. 337 ff.

62. See Lukomskaia, "Formirovanie," p. 298, for references to these studies, of which Rashin's *Formirovanie* is the most important. Contemporary foreign observers certainly would have agreed. Note for the moment only Marcel Lauwick's contention that "most workers in the Donets come from Central Russia." *L'industrie*, p. 139.

63. Rashin, *Formirovanie*, p. 356.

64. *Trudy XVIII s"ezda gornopromyshlennikov*, p. 334.

living. . . . I went on foot—840 kilometers in twenty-three days. I left New Year's Day and on the 23rd of January 1884 I arrived at the mine."[65] Others came in artels or groups after recruitment by special agents who then often directed the artel at the mine or steel mill.[66] Few workers came from the local population, and those that did maintained the closest ties with agriculture and were the most certain to leave in the summer.[67]

Until the early 1890s most foreign firms throughout Russia followed Russian custom and housed their workers in large, rather crude dormitories. There the men, married and unmarried, slept and ate in the male environment of the artel, detached from their families to which they periodically returned.[68] Little wonder they did so. The Bayer Chemical Company described the quarters of its workers, which were built at Moscow between 1894 and 1904, as a great two-story dormitory in which 200 and later 250 men slept. Simple iron bedsteads with straw mattresses were provided, in accordance with existing police regulations.[69] Conditions at Bayer were certainly no worse than average. Such rough barracks minimized the cost of lodging irregular furlough-prone recruits on the industrial frontier in southern Russia, and they fitted with existing

65. Recollection of K. I. Rusanov, Donbass living-history expedition (GIM), no. 28. Quoted by T. S. Vlasenko et al., "K voprosu o formirovanii proletariata v Rossii v kontse XIX—nachale XX v.," in *Iz istorii rabochego klassa i revoliutsionnogo dvizheniia* (Moscow, 1958), p. 282.

66. Ibid., Lukomskaia, "Formirovanie," pp. 300–301.

67. Ibid., p. 304; *Trudy XVIII s"ezda,* p. 334.

68. See, for example, Lauwick, *L'industrie,* pp. 158–59.

69. A. Blank and W. Löw, "Geschichte und Entwicklung der Farbenfabriken vorm. Friedrich Bayer & Co. Elberfeld in den ersten 50 Jahren," unpublished internal history [1909?], p. 268. I wish to thank the Bayer company for a copy of the interesting chapter in this history on the firm's Russian branch, pp. 265–88.

social patterns. But they certainly did little to create a permanent industrial population.

Foreigners were unanimous in their belief that such a population was necessary. They were well aware that long summer sojourns to native villages weighed heavily on foreign firms with their high fixed costs. Interest on expensive machinery and salaries of management continued independently of output. And in the boom years of the late 1890s existing firms fought to fix their workers and prevent their being enticed away to the new mines or steel mills.

The Rutchenko Coal Company voiced the common problem. "Until now we only worried about the long absence of workers for four or five months in the summer. But today [1899] considerable industrial development, with steel mills, new mines, and new railroads, makes labor scarce until January." [70] Another coal company noted at the same time that "the Russian worker has become more demanding since industrial development began in the Donets, and it is necessary to provide living conditions very different from those which satisfied him a few years ago." [71] Consequently both companies decided on special measures to settle their workers permanently. Like other foreign firms, they also believed that only if miners—like metallurgical workers—were fixed and sedentary would they gradually acquire the skills of their counterparts in other Russian areas and in western Europe.

4

This desire to settle Russian peasants from the distant central provinces in the Donets as perma-

70. C.L., Routchenko, Annual Report, 1899.
71. A.N., 65 AQ, L 3221, Sels Gemmes, Annual Report, 28–6–1899.

nent workers led foreign entrepreneurs to a crucial innovation in the 1890s. Or more properly, it led to the general diffusion of an innovation first successfully introduced at the great pioneering foreign steel firms of southern Russia. Foreign companies, which had from the beginning provided their permanently employed managers and foremen with attractive cottages or duplexes suitable for family living, extended similar housing to their skilled and unskilled workmen. These workmen were encouraged to leave artel, dormitory, and the high road south, and to live with wife and child in company-owned cottages or apartments at nominal rent. Foreign managers came to see such adequate housing as the key to turning long-distance wandering into permanent settlement. They were not disappointed. This is the picture that emerges from company records, as well as from recent Soviet documents.

As the oldest firm, Hughes's New Russia Company led the way. By 1905 almost all workers—5,000 in the steel mills and 4,500 in the coal mines—had houses and families. They were permanently fixed, and this meant that Hughes was in a favored position vis-à-vis his competitors.[72] Other metallurgical firms—the Russo-Belgian Company, for example—proceeded similarly and built housing at an average cost of 200 rubles per worker.[73]

The Gorlovka Coal Company was a pioneer in the development of family housing for coal miners. Originally the company allowed miners to build their own traditional one-room huts, half dug into the ground, on company land.[74] But the company had

72. C.L., New Russia Iron Co., Etude, 1905.
73. C.L., Métallurgie dans le Midi, April 1905.
74. *Société d'Industrie Houillère de la Russie Méridionale*, pp. 4–7.

already built 10 decent stone houses as an experiment by 1893, when it decided to construct 470 more cottages for its miners.[75] Each of these wooden cottages contained a medium-sized general living room, a kitchen with stove and baking oven, and an antechamber. Total living space exceeded seven hundred and fifty square feet. There was also a cellar and a yard, where miners "with a sense of proprietorship" planted trees and flowers. In 1896 the company added 55 cottages of the same type, and in 1898 and 1899 769 improved cottages were built. Ceilings were raised to eight and one-half feet, and roofs were now made of galvanized iron. Costs per new house had risen to 550 rubles—almost two years of a miner's pay—as opposed to 300 rubles in 1893. "These cottages are provided without charge to each married worker, who is, however, required to deposit a guarantee against damages of eighty rubles, payable in ten monthly installments after moving in."[76]

Other firms proceeded similarly. Almaznaia Coal built 300 small wooden houses for its miners in its first full year (1896), and only three dormitories. Two years later the company noted that production depended upon the recruiting and then the housing of workers.[77] Housing was so important that it was the best single indicator of a coal company's productive capacity, according to the Crédit Lyonnais's engineer.[78] Thus some firms, such as the ill-fated Uspensk Coal Company (1896) near Lugansk, never even tried dormitories. In 1899, 90 percent of its 584

75. Ibid.; A.E., Paris, C.C., Odessa, vol. 13, Monestier to Quai d'Orsay, 15–5–1893.

76. Société d'Industrie Houillère de la Russie Méridionale.

77. A.N., 65 AQ, L 139, Annual Reports, 1895–96, 1897–98.

78. C.L., Rykovskii, Etude, May 1901.

housing units were units for families.[79] When struggling Pobedenko Coal was unable to expand production in 1913, it blamed a lack of funds for housing construction, which was "necessary to attract and to hold workers." Sometimes dormitories were built only to be converted to apartment buildings.[80]

Housing also provided a means of holding workers in a highly competitive labor market, and of limiting wage increases. "Briansk Coal was very wise in establishing a sufficient number of remarkably comfortable houses for its miners [in the late 1890s]. That is the only way to draw and to hold Great Russians from the interior and to pass through a period of prosperity, a so-called 'coal crisis,' without raising salaries too much."[81] This correctly suggests that despite the rapid increase of suitable housing, the problem of adequate labor remained serious until 1900. Rutchenko was typical both in ascribing lower production in 1899 "almost entirely to the exceptional rarity of man power" as well as in building more houses, which the optimists hoped would eventually solve the problem.[82]

In fact it was the darkest moment before the dawn as far as a permenent labor supply was concerned. As business slowed after 1900, it became clear that improved housing had gone far toward creating a sedentary work force. The engineers of the Crédit

79. A.N., 65 AQ, K 167, Annual Report for 1899.
80. C.L., Donetz-Yourievka; Providence Russe, Annual Report, 1898–99.
81. Houillères de Briansk, Etude, April 1900, C.L. Also see P. P. Semenov-Tian'-Shanskii, ed., *Rossiia: Polnoe geografiches-koe opisanie nashego otechestva.* Vol. 14: *Novorossiia i Krym* (St. Petersburg, 1910), p. 372.
82. C.L., Routchenko, Annual Report, 1899; also, Etude, May 1901.

Lyonnais were emphatic. "The experience of 1900 conclusively shows that the northern provinces hold inexhaustible man power, which is recruited with astonishing ease if the question of [family] housing is adequately resolved." [83]

Confidential reports from another private source provide corroboration. In October 1901 the engineer at the Comptoir National d'Escompte de Paris noted that a very detailed report from Lauras, President of Rykovskii Coal, contained absolutely nothing on labor, "an extremely serious question in Russia." In reply Lauras noted that labor had never been a problem, partly because Yuzovo, a town of 40,000, was on the firm's doorstep. More generally, he noted that "the fears that existed three years ago have simply vanished. Workers come easily from great distances to work in the mines." [84] After 1900 the summer exodus of miners continued, but at an ever decreasing rate. "The construction of houses for families, as opposed to barracks for men, has had very favorable effects and has led to the fixing of a considerable working class population in the South." [85]

Foreign coal companies, like their metallurgical brethren, were within sight of a permanently settled work force by the first Russian revolution of 1905. During the next ten years the goal was almost fully attained. Whereas there were 82,000 coal miners in the Donets in December 1904 and 201,000 in December 1913, there were populations of 118,000 and 374,000, respectively, living in the coal-mining towns

83. C.L., Rykovskii, Etude, May 1901.
84. C.N.E.P., Rykovskii, Note récapitulative, 11-10-1901; ibid., Lauras to Comptoir d'Escompte, 5-11-1901.
85. C.L., Sels Gemmes, Etude, January 1901.

of the Donets Basin on these dates. The number of miners doubled while total population tripled as women and children moved in.[86]

This is no place to examine in detail the condition of the working class in Russia in regard to housing. We did note, however, the common practice of lodging married and unmarried male workers in dormitories away from their families. This practice was widespread. Indeed, if we may accept the considered judgment of a non-Soviet authority who states that low wages and the dormitory system normally meant that "a family in his home was apparently an unattainable luxury for the average worker," [87] then it is clear why decent housing provided Russians with an enormous incentive to settle in the new southern industrial area. There, at large foreign firms, the unattainable luxury became part of the standard wage. With such a wage foreign entrepreneurship successfully recruited and formed its labor force.

5

The foregoing considerations apply most forcefully to the period from about 1890 to about 1904. During this period the foreign impact was greatest, and foreign entrepreneurs were most intimately involved in the task of forming a labor force in southern Russia. After 1904 the recruitment and formation of labor was a minor concern standing low on the foreigner's list of anxieties. Then the crucial labor problem was the relations between an existing and often hostile working class and an increasingly Russianized management, Russianized in part because of this very problem, as we saw in chapter 5.

86. Rashin, *Formirovanie*, pp. 511–12.
87. T. von Laue, "Russian Peasants in the Factory," p. 65.

In this situation the typical firm found itself with too much hard-to-fire labor rather than with too little hard-to-hold labor. And since capital was much harder to come by, the peculiarities of Russian factor proportions, which probably never really existed outside the atypical southern frontier area in the 1890s, disappeared.

To summarize, it is clear that the formation of an adequate labor force was a vexing challenge to foreign companies in southern Russia. But it seems equally clear that foreign entrepreneurship successfully met this challenge fairly quickly. Foreign metallurgical workers trained native newcomers and were replaced by them. Coal miners and metallurgical workers migrated from great distances to work in modern collieries and steel mills. For both groups of workers adequate housing, particularly family housing, was crucial. Such housing provided a powerful incentive for permanent migration which decisively broke the bottleneck of labor supply in the new industrial area. Then Russia, long a poor and overpopulated country, revealed that its central provinces held inexhaustible man power only waiting to be tapped.

8

RELATIONS WITH STATE
AND SOCIETY

The nature of relations between the Russian state and foreign enterprise is of great interest because so much of Russian economic development after 1885 was due to their combined efforts. Were relations generally good? If so, does this mean Russia's elite simply sold out its country to foreigners, as Soviet historians sometimes charge? Or in fact, were foreigners tricked into investment and then partially expropriated by politically contrived collapse, as certain disillusioned businessmen suspected in the early twentieth century? In broader perspective, what do relations with the state, as well as with various groups of Russian society, suggest concerning the possibility or desirability of less advanced areas emulating late nineteenth-century Russia, and thereby giving foreigners a basic role in their development schemes? These are some of the questions to be considered in this chapter.

1

The first thing to note is that relations between government and private enterprise were close and continuous in Russia. Therefore, these relations were of greater significance to the individual business enterprise than those in western Europe, and they had to be taken seriously.

One aspect of this intimate connection stemmed

from the importance of the state as a purchaser of industrial goods. At first glance this may appear to contradict our discussion in chapter 1. There we noted that the positive contribution of state orders in the rapid development of the economy has sometimes been exaggerated. Yet the minute part of the state's budget expenditure specifically directed toward developing industry could be absolutely crucial for any given firm. This was the case mainly because government purchases were distributed very unevenly. Some favored producers became major suppliers; other identical competitors were almost completely neglected. It all depended on the administrative decisions of key officials.

These decisions of Russian officials were not based primarily upon cost or quality considerations. Everyone understood this. "As you know, state contracts are bid upon only as a matter of form. To obtain a contract, it is necessary to ask, to solicit, and to make certain types of sacrifices on the spot."[1] The French consul's euphemism for widespread bribery and corruption, wherein officials saw their positions in part as opportunities for personal profit, suggests how crucial relations were.

It was the pursuit of this personal profit and control of markets that placed Russian bureaucrats and financiers in so many foreign firms initially. In essence, foreigners supplied technology and managerial skills, and Russian bureaucrats supplied markets through long-term contracts. And, as seen earlier, both gladly contributed capital to firms whose success seemed inevitable.

This was certainly the basic pattern among lead-

1. A.N., F 12, no. 7176, Consul at Odessa, note, 13–3–1897. See also Josef Melnik, ed., *Russen über Russland* (Frankfurt am Main, 1906), pp. 226–27.

ing metallurgical and railway-equipment producers before 1900. It is extremely significant that the very successful metallurgical firms—the Huta-Bankova, South Russian Dnieper, Donets Steel, and Russo-Belgian companies—all had bureaucrats involved initially, either directly or indirectly, who had secured or could secure large government contracts. At the same time the less profitable Makeevka, Donets-Yur'evka, Taganrog, Russian Providence, and Kerch companies either lacked official support or were positively discouraged by the government.[2]

Among railway-equipment producers top officials were connected with the large orders upon which the Hartmann, Bouhey, and South Ural firms were based. Hartmann, Krupp's son-in-law, was allegedly a close personal friend of Witte.[3] One incident concerning the Bonnardel Group was typical. When the group was considering entering this field in 1897, it was working closely with Russian "intermediaries" whom the group tentatively agreed to pay one million rubles in cash, and an additional 4 percent commission on an enormous anticipated twenty-year contract for freight cars worth 280,000,000 rubles.[4] Such an order was unthinkable without influence, bribes, and kickbacks.

Other industries which were dependent on government demand, such as munitions or shipbuilding, were similar. The Belgian consul noted propheti-

2. In studying a possible merger of the Russian Providence and the Taganrog Steel companies the Banque de l'Union Parisienne's mission in Russia noted in 1905 that "it is not a secret for anyone that the minister of finance, on whom rail orders depend, was not pleased to see these two firms established." Thus the chances of increasing very small state rail orders were slight. P.R. MSS, Rapport sur une mission dans le Sud de la Russie, p. 163.

3. C.L., Hartmann, Etude, August 1898.

4. C.L., Kama, Projet, June 1897.

cally that Nikolaev Shipyards' uncertain future depended "entirely upon the orders the Naval Ministry will decide to give."[5] Streetcar and electric concessions were completely dependent upon government support purchased at the local level. The *St. Petersburg News* charged in early 1911 that Belgian entrepreneurs had only followed their normal pattern in expending one million rubles to obtain a major streetcar concession for St. Petersburg.[6] Certainly an examination of the detailed negotiations for that same line of an unsuccessful competitor, the Banque de l'Union Parisienne and its associates, indicates that competition was intense and bureaucrats expensive.[7]

Widespread bureaucratic participation in firms in leading industries dependent upon the state's monopsony power suggests that in backward countries operating in the capitalist framework, as in Russia in the 1890s, bureaucrats may initiate and encourage economic development to capitalize their offices fully. Since the drawbacks of such a system are obvious, it is worth noting its highly dynamic growth-oriented character. Bureaucratic opportunities are great with rapid economic advance, and slight with stagnation.

Bureaucratic protection and patronage of individual entrepreneurs explain in part the state's notorious and determined favoritism. In the southern steel industry there were not only privileged firms based on large initial rail orders, in sharp contrast to those without such an assured market, but these initial advantages hardened into permanent inequi-

5. A.E., Brussels, no. 2902, sec. 2, Chantiers Navals de Nicolaiev, letter, 7–2–1897.
6. 14–6–1911. Copy in A.E., Brussels, no. 2900.
7. B.U.P., Russie, no. 142, Tramways de St. Petersburg.

ties. In 1902, for example, the government gave all its rail orders to only six firms (Hughes, Donets Steel, Russo-Belgian, Briansk, Dnieper, and Taganrog, in order of the size of these sales), while other firms producing just as satisfactorily received nothing. After consistent pressure the state decided in 1903 to begin competitive bidding on rails—in 1906.[8] In the meantime the government's purchase price of 1.15 rubles per pud, which gave privileged producers a handsome gross profit of at least 20 percent on sales, enabled those subsidized companies to sell other steel products to the private market well below cost and forced nonprivileged producers to accept losses in their only market.[9]

This was part of the state's overall policy of regulated noncompetitive markets, which harmonized well with the syndicates subsequently formed.[10] Thus it is possible to understand the state's refusal of the Russo-Belgian Company's offer for 200,000 tons of rails at 0.95 rubles per pud, as well as its continued subsidization (through large, noncompetitive orders) of very expensive and illogical pig-iron production for finished products in St. Petersburg and other northern towns (outside of the Urals) after 1900.[11] No wonder high-ranking Russians sat on foreign boards at the outset, or shortly thereafter. No wonder that the quality of a firm's "relations" and "influence" was so systematically appraised in the voluminous reports on Russian firms

8. A.N., F 30, no. 344, Veillet Dufrêche, Consul in Moscow, to Delcassé, 19–3–1903; ibid., Boutiron to Delcassé, 14–5–1903.
9. C.L., Métallurgie dans le Midi, April 1905; see also n. 8 above.
10. Olga Crisp, "Some Problems," p. 228.
11. C.L., Briansk, Etude, January 1903; A.N., F 30, no. 344, Théodore Motet to Caillaux, copy of undated letter [1901].

by the engineers of the Crédit Lyonnais's St. Petersburg branch.[12]

Really promising ventures with apparently secure state demand, such as rail production in the 1890s or shipbuilding before the war, were fiercely disputed within the bureaucracy by different officials or ex-officials turned entrepreneurs.[13] And to the extent a promising venture was cornered effectively, it was submitted by individual bureaucrats and their associates to a highly competitive bidding system to secure the greatest benefit, howbeit for themselves for the most part and not for the state.

For example, when the Russian navy sought an entrepreneur to build shipyards worth 30,000,000 francs in 1897, it negotiated with Cockerill, a logical choice, while seeking other entrepreneurs in France and Belgium.[14] Similarly, French industrialists seeking large locomotive orders (to be fulfilled in Russia) were warned to expect "bitter competition from German industrialists who have superior sources of action, information, and of course corruption."[15] They were advised to work, if possi-

12. A superficial sounding of Crédit Lyonnais reports on French and Belgian steel producers significantly reveals that this question is almost entirely ignored.

13. For light on this bureaucratic competition in the naval armaments industry, see René Girault's interesting study on French involvement with the Putilov Works, in *Revue d'histoire moderne et contemporaine* 13 (1966) : 217–36. Dossiers on the North Donets Railroad Company, the Company for Railroad Sidings, and the Syndicat des Affaires Russes at the Banque de l'Union Parisienne provide additional insights into the complexities of bureaucratic competition and the entrepreneur's relation to it.

14. A.E., Brussels, no. 2902, sec. 1, Projet de création d'un grand établissement métallurgique en Sibérie, letters from consul in Berlin, 6–2–1897, 8–2–1897, and notes.

15. A.N., F 12, no. 7175, Locomotives, copy of a dispatch from Moulin, French naval attaché at St. Petersburg, 1–1–1896.

ble, with Russian industrialists who had already built up these bureaucratic relations out of necessity.

Were these evidences of intense competition among both bureaucrats and foreigners of any real significance? Orthodox Marxists since Lenin have said no. They have generally concluded that foreign investment did quicken the pace of Russian industrialization, but only at the expense of Russian political independence. Foreign competition was a sham. One recent Soviet scholar states typically that "the bourgeoisie was not able to promote industry without destroying by its support of foreign capital the very basis of the existence of an independent state."[16] In the final analysis, then, foreign capital was harmful primarily because of its political implications, and not because of its economic performance. As was noted in the introduction, this is probably the most damning indictment possible. Factories are never worth the price of foreign bondage, especially since there are many paths to industrial society.

Part of this argument rests upon alleged Russian subservience to foreign bankers and their loans. As Lenin sarcastically said at the time, "The economy of the 'great Russian state' under the control of the henchmen of Rothschild and Bleichröder: this is the bright future you open before us, Mr. Witte!"[17] The political implications of foreign loans lie well beyond the scope of this study. Two points should be

16. Iu. B. Solov'ev, "Protivorechiia v praviashchem lagere Rossii po voprosu ob inostrannykh kapitalakh v gody pervogo promyshlennogo pod"ema," p. 388, in Akademiia Nauk SSSR, Trudy Leningradskogo otdeleniia instituta istorii, *Iz istorii imperializma v Rossii* (Moscow-Leningrad, 1959). Also see, among others, Khromov, *Ekonomicheskoe razvitie*, p. 385.

17. Lenin, *Sochineniia*, 5:307.

made, however. First, only France made large loans to the Russian government before 1914, and thus only she held this leverage to compromise independent Russian policy. Loans to the Russian government were largely irrelevant for other countries. Second, according to the most recent and exhaustive study of the interplay of finance and politics in the Franco-Russian alliance by Professor Crisp, the loss of Russian sovereignty due to French financial pressure was "not very significant." [18] Professor Crisp believes that the minor infringements upon complete independence (which no nation ever possessed) were amply compensated by the positive contribution loans made to overall economic development. In broader perspective the loan question was but one aspect of alliance diplomacy wherein the creditor (France) was as much a captive of the debtor (Russia) as vice versa.

But let us leave this ground ploughed to exhaustion and return to the foreign businessman. What was his effect on Russian sovereignty? On the basis of documentary evidence it seems that the Russian state was generally able and willing to regulate foreign business. Of course foreign businessmen tried to gain favors, like most businessmen anywhere and particularly those in Russia. But such efforts were effective within a limited range of possibilities. Foreigners could on occasion bend Russian law and administrative rulings, but they could not make or break these codes. This was clear to most foreign businessmen and to Russian authorities. Both groups acted accordingly, as the following evidence suggests.

18. Olga Crisp, "The Financial Aspect of the Franco-Russian Alliance, 1894–1914" (unpublished Ph.D. thesis, University of London, 1954), p. 519; ibid., chap. 2.

It is well known that the Russian government maintained a rigorously independent commercial policy in these years. For example, in 1890 when a French silk merchant complained of a projected tariff increase on silk articles to his diplomatic representatives, he was told that it was inconceivable that diplomatic pressure would have the slightest effect, since Russia had always been "extremely independent in her tariff policy."[19] The grandiose tariff war of 1892–94 with Germany, which ended in a draw (with each side naturally claiming victory), was the most vivid example of independent commercial policy.[20] Even during the agonies of 1905 French negotiators received with great difficulty small, almost token concessions on wines and spirits, key French exports to Russia.[21] Fiscal independence in the form of a progressive corporate income tax, one of the first in Europe and hardly popular with foreign businessmen, complemented commercial independence.[22]

Central administrative control of foreign businessmen manifested itself in many ways. All joint-stock companies in Russia operated under a permissive rather than a declaratory corporate system. Each company, foreign or Russian, needed permission not only to incorporate but to make any major changes in its structure, such as increasing capital, floating bonds, or entering a new line of business.

19. A.N., F 12, no. 6600, letter from P. Roux et Cie, 27–10–1890, and undated answer.

20. A.N., F 12, no. 7176, consul at Warsaw, 29–10–1896; Von Laue, *Witte*, pp. 109–10.

21. For these negotiations, see A.E., Paris, N.S., Russie, St. Petersburg, no. 69.

22. The corporate income tax ranged from 3 percent on profits of 3 to 4 percent on total capital to 6 percent on profits of 9 to 10 percent and 5 percent on anything above. A.N., F 30, no. 328, Verstraete to Delcassé, 23–6–1898.

Witte himself came to feel that "under such circumstances one should rather speak of an excess of control of foreign capital, which takes its chances in going to Russia, and of unnecessary limitation imposed upon its freedom of investment." [23] The effect of all these "difficulties and tribulations" for the foreign entrepreneur—to use Witte's straightforward language—was effective control and regulation. "Russia is not China!" said Witte in his highly secret memorandum to the tsar in 1899.[24] "We are neither in Turkey nor in China," echoed the government-inspired English-language *Russian Journal of Financial Statistics* in explaining, a bit proudly, Russia's administrative supervision.[25]

But jingles and bold phrases are the cheapest of commodities. What of the state's deeds? One indication of the reality of these claims of independence is the fact that only one foreign bank, the Crédit Lyonnais, was ever permitted to establish a branch in Russia. This was despite numerous requests by foreign banks as powerful as the Deutsche Bank and the Dresdner Bank, which unsuccessfully applied their considerable powers to obtain such authorization on more than one occasion.[26]

Certainly the Belgian Jules Nagelmackers, an important banker at Liège, Taganrog Steel Company director, and founder-director of the international Société des Wagons-lits, would not have doubted the state's power. In 1903 he went to St. Petersburg to see Minister of Finance Witte concerning the total

23. Sergei Witte, "Secret Memorandum to the Tsar," February 1899, as translated by Von Laue, *Witte*, p. 181.

24. Ibid., p. 182. See this entire fascinating document in Akademiia Nauk SSSR, *Materialy*, 6:173–95.

25. *Russian Journal of Financial Statistics* 2 (1901) : 676.

26. A.E., Paris, N.S., Russie, St. Petersburg, no. 60, report, 8–6–1912.

nonpayment by the Russian government of postal fees due his company in relation to a weekly sleeping car and restaurant service from Moscow to Vladivostok. The French ambassador Bompard looked at Nagelmackers's contract and agreed that his claim was just. Nonetheless, Bompard counseled prudence and moderation with Witte. Later a furious Nagelmackers recounted that when he presented his case to Witte, Witte asked to see the contract, read it, and then "carefully taking it between thumb and forefinger, tore it to pieces and threw it in the wastepaper basket without adding a word of explication or justification." Nagelmackers left St. Petersburg that evening in a hopeless rage, "vowing never again to return to this country of savages."[27]

Similarly the French diplomats and businessmen who struggled (unsuccessfully for the most part) in the late 1890s for "French influence" in the Russo-Chinese Bank—initially 62 percent French-owned—lost any illusions concerning effective control of Russian policy through financial pressure. This bank became purely and simply an instrument of Russian economic penetration into China and Manchuria, quite independent of French ownership or diplomatic pressure.[28]

Perhaps the acid test for the independent state was whether it could control foreign businessmen when they combined forces. The cartels, or marketing syndicates, about which much has been written,

27. Maurice Bompard, *Mon ambassade en Russie, 1903–1908* (Paris, 1937), pp. xxx–xxxi.

28. This instructive chapter in financial diplomacy may be studied in detail in A.N., F 30, no. 337, in the dossier appropriately entitled "La Banque Russo-Chinoise: La Lutte pour l'établissement de l'influence française." Also see W. Langer, *The Diplomacy of Imperialism*, 2d. ed. (New York, 1951), pp. 397 ff., 407 ff.

are frequently mentioned in the case for domination by foreign businessmen. The work of Olga Crisp and other sources, however, suggest that this was not the case. The syndicates facilitated state regulation of industry, they did not act as monolithic blocs, and they were not feared by the government.[29] Witte therefore did not oppose the metallurgical cartel, but he warned industrialists against shortsightedly taking undue advantage of their position.

This was what his successors felt foreign metallurgists were attempting to do when they sought to form an American type of steel trust in 1908. This proposed trust, scarcely mentioned in the literature, was to merge leading southern steel producers into a gigantic firm with a share capital of 100,000,000 rubles and 50,000,000 rubles of funded debt. After eight years of depression and disappointment the trust's promoters claimed, perhaps in good faith, that a trust would aid them without injuring the Russian economy. All but the most efficient plants would be closed, the remaining plants would operate at optimum capacity, and reduced costs would give much higher profits with little or no price rise.[30]

Under the terms of the proposed trust this technocratic solution was particularly advantageous for the weaker French-controlled producers like Makeevka, Russian Providence, and Ural-Volga. These firms were to save much of their stock capital and all of their bond capital. Therefore the interested patrons, and particularly the Société Générale of France and the Banque de l'Union Parisienne, sponsored the project enthusiastically.[31] And because of the pressure of these banks, which were important

29. Crisp, "Some Problems," pp. 224–32.
30. A.N., F 30, no. 344, Bompard to Pichon, 24–12–1907.
31. For example, C.L., Aciéries Makeevka, Etude, August 1910: "The trust would be extremely favorable for Makeevka."

sellers of Russian government bonds in France, French diplomatic observers favoring the plan believed that the Russian government would eventually accept the trust. It would do so in spite of violent public hostility and the problem of laying off some Russian steelworkers.[32]

The French were wrong. After considering the matter at length the government refused to ratify the trust. The status quo in metallurgy, so distasteful to foreign industrialists, remained unchanged.[33] This significant refusal also shows incidentally why there was never any need for antitrust legislation in Russia. The middle class had never become dominant in the Russian state, as it had in western Europe, and unfettered capitalism had never existed to require subsequent regulation.[34]

There was also control over local operations by mining and factory inspectors and other administrative officials. Relations with local officials at the plant were thus as important as those with top authorities in the capitals. One of the highest compliments that could be given a foreign manager was that he knew "how to treat officials correctly."[35] The delicacy of this correct treatment goes far to explain the general tendency of seasoned firms to choose either Russians or "old Russian hands" for administrative functions, as we saw in chapter 5.

An interesting example of control at the local

32. A.N., F 12, no. 7273, consul at Moscow, 27–7–1908.

33. A.E., Brussels, no. 2902, sec. 2, Projet pour un trust, notes, 27–4–1908, 23–7–1908.

34. The refusal to permit the merger of two railway producers, Kolomna and Sormovo, in 1913 was a good example of administrative antitrust measures. See A.N., 65 AQ, K 231; *L'Informa-tion*, 3–8–1913.

35. Appraisal of Mr. Gouvy, director of Ural-Volga's plant in the Urals. C.L., Oural Volga, Etude, August 1898.

level was the experience of the Odessa Tramway Company in a strike situation in 1903, as confidentially reported by the vice-director, J. Cambier, son of the first president of this firm.

> At one point [as the strike was just beginning] the chief of the secret police of Odessa told me almost word for word: "You must accept all the strikers' conditions. If you do not, I shall have you led immediately to the border by two gendarmes, and we shall seize the company which will be lost to you in any event." I said this was ruin, to which he replied, "It is of no importance to us if all your Belgian millions are lost; our only concern is that no Russian blood is shed in the streets." I then agreed to sign, but said we would go back on our word when order was re-established.
>
> Soon after the strike spread to other firms and disorder rose. It was now impossible to say that only our company was at fault. As the state of siege was proclaimed, we knew we were saved.[36]

Such dramatic clashes and less striking continuous supervision left foreign businessmen with few illusions concerning their strength vis-à-vis the state in any showdown confrontation.

The evident power of the Russian government also fostered the feeling among some foreign capitalists after 1900 that their investment was being expropriated gradually as the state consciously made the foreigner's position untenable.[37] This feeling was strongest among industrialists in heavy industry in southern Russia between 1900 and 1902. In those years government demand declined considerably, favorites were protected, and the fate of the

36. A.E., Brussels, no. 2818, Tramways d'Odessa, Cambier, 25-7-1903.

37. A.N., F 30, no. 344, Boutiron to Delcassé, 8-10-1901; ibid., Motet to Caillaux, n.d. [1901].

proposed syndicates was uncertain.[38] Foreigners
and the foreign press pointed out then that Witte
had always sought the reduction of prices and profits through more investment and greater competition, and they hinted that the bankruptcy of foreign
enterprise was his ultimate goal.[39] When the French
Société Générale's distraught representative wrote
bitterly at one point in his negotiations with the
ministry of finance concerning the Briansk Company that "they want to push us out, and then have
us pay the bill," he was only voicing a widespread
foreign anxiety.[40] This feeling subsided afterward,
but there was always a certain suspicion regarding
state power and policy.

Were these suspicions justified? Certainly one
may understand the foreigner's frustration. The
market value of the shares of ninety-eight Russian
industrial enterprises, primarily metallurgical and
coal mining, fell 59 percent from the middle of October 1899 to the middle of October 1901.[41] The economist Paul Leroy-Beaulieu caught the general tone of

38. It was estimated that whereas the state rail orders equaled
the equivalent of 60 and 62 million puds of pig iron in 1898 and
1899, they represented only 58 and then 47 million puds in 1900
and 1901. A.N., F 30, no. 344, Verstraete to Delcassé, 13–3–1901.

39. A.N., F 30, no. 344, Delcassé to Caillaux, 24–3–1902; A.E.,
Brussels, no. 2902, sec. 4, Henin, 1–7–1903; *St. Peterburgskie
vedomosti,* 27–11–1901 (old style); *Novoe vremia,* 12–3–1899 (old
style), Witte to commission on grains.

40. A.N., F 30, no. 343, Société Briansk, correspondence of Société Générale, Rocherand to Dorizon, 14–9–1902. The year before
this same complicated affair brought this ominous note from Caillaux, the French minister of finance: "There is an implacable desire to ruin the industries in which French capitalists are interested. Thus some Russians want the metallurgical situation to
worsen." Ibid., Société Briansk, Caillaux, undated note following
conversation with Motet [October] 1901.

41. A. Finn-Enotaevskii, *Kapitalizm v Rossii, 1890–1917 gg.*
(Moscow, 1925), p. 95.

pessimism: "This is a real debacle, a real financial crash."[42] And of course Witte desired lower prices in the 1890s, and he got them. But every competent foreign entrepreneur was also expecting prices and profits to continue their downward drift, which had already begun in metallurgy about 1895. What was equally surprising, and perhaps equally distressing, to both foreigners and the state was the magnitude of the price decline. That decline approached 50 percent in steel and coke products, as we saw in chapter 4. Confronted with such an unexpectedly severe depression, Witte and his successors did not attempt to take advantage of the foreigner's misfortune. Rather they tried to help them surmount their difficulties. In doing so, Russia remained, a little grudgingly perhaps, what it had been: a good host that extended to foreign businessmen "a sympathetic welcome for the most part."[43]

Sanctioning the foreign-dominated syndicates in metallurgy and coal was the most significant aid after 1900, just as profitable government orders were of greatest assistance previously. The French ambassador noted appreciatively in mid-1902 following the formation of the metallurgical syndicate that "some enterprises almost dead last year have begun to breathe a little."[44] The Crédit Lyonnais's mission in Russia estimated that the metallurgical syndicate had raised prices about 10 percent by 1904 from the low point in 1901, while the coal syndicate had raised prices 5 percent. These modest increases saved several foreign firms from falling under the auctioneer's hammer.[45]

42. Ibid.
43. Genaert, *Fédération Industrielle Russe.*
44. A.N., F 30, no. 344, Montbello to Delcassé, 9–5–1902.
45. C.L., Métallurgie dans le Midi, April 1905.

There were many other smaller aids to foreign businessmen both before and after 1900 which added up to the sympathetic welcome. These aids were quite compatible with, and were indeed an exercise of, full national sovereignty. Until 1899 the statutes of all foreign corporations stipulated that they could be dissolved at any time. To increase investor confidence foreign companies were required only to abide by Russian laws after April 1899.[46] Foreign personnel were also permitted to import their personal belongings duty free, a small but useful favor. In 1901 the excise tax of 1.5 kopecks per pud of pig iron was abolished, and that same year the 5 percent income tax on industrial bonds sold outside Russia was waived.[47] In addition, the State Bank reluctantly agreed to advance loans to foreign companies, as it had long done for Russian capitalists.

The crucial aid, however, was to extend the facilities of the generous Russian law on receivership to firms owned by foreigners or incorporated abroad. Firms in receivership were spared bankruptcy, as we saw in chapter 6, since there was an indefinite moratorium on all claims and charges (interest on first mortgages excepted). Generally speaking, Russian and foreign creditors of firms in receivership were treated equally, which was only fair, as the state concluded, but which was vigorously opposed by some Russian bankers and businessmen.[48] Had the administration decided differently a great deal of foreign capital would have been washed out completely in the years from 1901 to 1909. In fact, almost all foreign firms compromised in the depression had recovered part of their losses by 1914.

46. A.N., F 30, no. 344, undated note.
47. Ibid., note 14–3–1900.
48. See A.N., F 30, no. 343, Oural Volga, Verstraete to Delcassé, 3–1–1901, 8–2–1901; Lauwick, *L'industrie,* pp. 34–36.

In summary, relations between state and foreign entrepreneur were basically satisfactory. Both parties realized that foreign participation in Russian industry was mutually advantageous, although they might dispute the division of gains from investment. In the steel industry, for example, foreign businessmen wanted the monopoly of a trust; the government wanted free competition for most and privileges for a few, but both came to accept as satisfactory a uniform syndicated market. It was this mutually advantageous character of foreign entrepreneurship that has made the whole question so fascinating.

Why was this so? The real key, it seems to me, was the political independence of the host state, Russia. This unquestionable political independence meant effective control over the foreigner, control which the state exercised both directly through law and indirectly (and as effectively) through the discipline of a relatively free market economy. Thus the entrepreneur from abroad worked within the state's broad developmental scheme and was never permitted to use his technical and financial superiority to drain the country through contracts or relations implicitly or explicitly based on constraint rather than consent.

This was crucial. Even if one feels (rightly in my opinion) that many attacks against nineteenth-century economic imperialism are unbalanced and exaggerated, careful studies of foreign businessmen in backward areas during the period do show that there was all too often more exploitation (for want of a better word) than mutually advantageous development.[49] Perhaps there is a lesson here. For-

49. See, for example, David S. Landes, *Bankers and Pashas: International Finance and Economic Imperialism in Egypt* (London, 1958), pp. 319–27 in particular.

eign investment is predictably most rewarding for poorer areas when they have effective political independence. Given such independence and coherent development plans (like Witte's), the foreign businessman is perhaps more wisely sought than feared. Domestic political power is sufficient to counterbalance foreign technical and financial superiority.

2

Thus far we have considered relations between the state and foreign business and noted the views of orthodox Marxists concerning that relationship. In fact, most groups in Russia had a strong opinion on foreign capital, particularly in the 1890s. In those years the whole question became a burning issue. Three general positions stand out. They add further light on the power of foreign business in Russia and its impact on economy and society.

As a group the landed nobility hated foreign capital and led a spirited attack against it.[50] Part of this attack came from within, since the landed nobility still dominated the upper bureaucracy and the tsar's entourage. Another front was a violent press campaign between 1896 and 1900 in periodicals identified with the noble cause. These periodicals included the *St. Petersburg News* (*St. Peterburgskie vedomosti*), the *Moscow News* (*Moskovskie vedomosti*), *New Times* (*Novoe vremia*), and *Russian Labor* (*Russkii trud*). In this last journal Sergei Sharapov

---

50. Von Laue, *Witte,* pp. 177–88; Brandt, *Inostrannye kapitaly,* 2:211; Solov'ev, "Protivorechiia," pp. 373–76. Landed families with natural resources needed by foreign industrialists were apparently an exception. In every instance (which we uncovered) gentry landowners were delighted to sell such properties to foreigners. No doubt the windfall profits of this tiny minority of landowners excited first the avarice and then the envy of the bitter majority.

grouped several particularly determined, if not fanatical, conservative foes of foreign capital, such as P. V. Ol', G. Butmi, and Lev Rafalovich.[51]

In these private and public attacks critics of Witte's scheme of industrialization argued that Russia was losing forever her own resources. This was in itself shocking. But worse, foreigners were indeed speeding up the entire industrialization process, and thereby destroying old social and economic patterns.[52] As the *Moscow News* put it, foreign capital was forcing Russia to become an exclusively industrial country. Such a development could gladden only dreamers striving for the subsequent socialization of a capitalist Russia.[53] Of course the landed nobility and its supporters posed as patriots defending the country against exploitation. In reality, their motives were less pure. The conclusion of a Soviet scholar is harsh, but basically just. "The campaign of the landowners should be considered within the context of their general struggle for the preservation of the vestiges of feudal society."[54] Their opposition was part of their reactionary outlook.

A second view was that of the Legal Marxists.[55] These Russian revisionists agreed with the landowners that foreign capital was quickening the development of Russia and breaking up the old agrarian society. But instead of deploring this movement the Legal Marxists welcomed it and cheered it on.

51. Solov'ev, "Protivorechiia," p. 375.
52. Von Laue, *Witte,* pp. 284–87.
53. *Moskovskie vedomosti,* 24–1–1899, p. 1, as quoted by Solov'ev, "Protivorechiia," p. 375.
54. Solov'ev, "Protivorechiia," p. 388.
55. See Richard Kindersley, *The First Russian Revisionists* (Oxford, 1962), as well as J. L. H. Keep, *The Rise of Social Democracy in Russia* (Oxford, 1963).

Industrialization was one aspect of Westernism, which Legal Marxism supported completely.[56] According to Bulgakov, a leading spokesman:

> Every new factory, every new industrial concern leads us forwards, increasing the number of people capable of intellectual Europeanization. . . . For Russia there is only one way of development, inevitable and undeniable: it is the way from East to West. It is high time![57]

At the height of the campaign against foreign capital in 1899, the leading Legal Marxist, Peter Struve, concluded that "the flow of foreign capital into our country is certainly desirable."[58]

The Legal Marxists, who almost without exception followed Struve into the liberal Kadet Party, did not waver in their defense of foreign capital. This may be seen by examining a short essay by Mikhail Tugan-Baranovskii on this question written in 1912.[59] One of Russia's greatest economists and economic historians, Tugan-Baranovskii presented the position of the moderate Left with clarity and vigor.

Tugan-Baranovskii began by noting that the 1912 meeting of the representatives of the Congress of Trade and Industry had agreed that foreign capital was not only desirable, but absolutely indispensable for significant industrial progress. This was so, according to Tugan-Baranovskii, because the domestic market for industrial goods remained weak. Demand was in turn weak because of Russian poverty

56. Kindersley, *Russian Revisionists*, p. 218.

57. Nemo [Bulgakov], *Novoe slovo*, June 1897, pt. 2, p. 57, as quoted by Kindersley, *Russian Revisionists*, p. 218.

58. P. S., *Nachalo*, 1899, no. 3, pp. 232–33, as quoted by Solov'ev, "Protivorechiia," p. 378.

59. M. Tugan-Baranovskii, *K luchshemu budushchemu* (St. Petersburg, 1912), pp. 201–4.

and slow capital accumulation. Since demand and capital accumulation were thus interdependent, the inadequacies of both closed tight the circle of backwardness.

But there was hope.

The enormous growth of the market in the countries of the West creates the colossal growth of society's savings and capital. Capital in the West accumulates at such a rate that it not only abundantly nurtures its own internal market, but also flows abroad in an uninterrupted stream. . . . This golden torrent, pouring out from countries with old capitalist cultures, is an extremely important factor in the development of capitalist industry throughout the world. Without the flow of capital from abroad young countries would not be able to develop their own capitalist industry by themselves, since the capital in these countries is inadequate for this. . . . As far as Russia is concerned, she is to the last degree poor in domestic capital. The accumulation of our own capital does not exceed a few hundred million rubles per year, and this is absorbed by government borrowing to a large extent. Therefore, without the aid of foreign capital, it is useless to hope for the development of our industry.[60]

Tugan-Baranovskii went on to anticipate the opposition's normal line of attack. Russian poverty would not hold back foreign investment as it did local investment, because foreign investment on a massive scale created its own effective demand. This occurred directly through the purchase of capital goods in Russia, and indirectly through newly created purchasing power among all classes of Russian society.

As for the hoary assertion that foreign capital was destroying agriculture, the opposite was more

60. Ibid., pp. 202–3.

accurate. Industry gave peasants a supplementary source of income which they could invest in agriculture. This was all the more important since the government continued to drain away a large portion of the meager investment sums generated by agriculture, in part through the cooperative credit societies themselves.[61]

The alleged seizure of natural resources and the payment of colossal dividends were dismissed with the argument used a decade earlier by Witte's best publicist, B. F. Brandt.[62] Only a small portion of the total income created by foreign investment left the country as profit, since most of that income stayed in Russia as wages, royalties, taxes, etc. And the popular mind exaggerated the size of foreign profits and dividends. Foreign capital was worth its price. "What can possibly be accomplished there [in the Urals] without the aid of foreign capital? . . . All of our industry in recent years has developed on the basis of foreign capital."[63] Thus the Legal Marxists were among the firmest advocates of foreign investment and its consequences.[64]

In the light of the gradual shift from foreign to Russian entrepreneurial leadership, the views of Russian businessmen are especially significant. These views were highly diverse. In the first place, one finds many established Russian industrialists growing increasingly hostile to foreign investment during the 1890s. This feeling was strongest among industrialists of the Moscow region and the Urals. These businessmen understood perfectly that foreign enterprise's superior technology and lower

61. Ibid., p. 203.
62. Brandt, *Inostrannye kapitaly,* vol. 2, chap. 4.
63. Tugan-Baranovskii, *K luchshemu budushchemu,* p. 204.
64. Solov'ev, "Protivorechiia," pp. 378–79.

costs of production posed an extremely serious competitive threat. Therefore they formed an incongruous alliance with the landed nobility to campaign against foreign capital at the end of the century.[65] The Committee of the Moscow Stock Exchange charged in December 1898, for example, that foreign capitalists were responsible for an excessive increase in the price of oil, the basic fuel of the Moscow region.[66] A month later this committee passed a resolution warning the government of the dangers of foreign enterprise to Russian independence and Russian interests. The conservative periodicals of the agrarian interest were quick to publicize this resolution and agree with it.[67]

These assaults were beaten off by Witte in a vigorous counterattack. First in a private memorandum to the tsar, and then in a widely quoted public speech, Witte charged that local businessmen were hiding their fears of foreign competition under the cloak of patriotism. These industrialists quite simply wanted no intruders at the golden table of Russian protectionism.[68] Yet it was precisely because of the competitive effects, which resulted in lower prices and profits, that foreign enterprise was needed and could form the basis of Witte's system.

Other big businessmen and bankers, men like Alchevskii and Rothstein, whom we have observed in this study, had a different view. They collaborated with both state and foreigners in new ventures in southern Russia, and they were, like Witte, enthu-

65. Ibid., pp. 376, 382–87; Von Laue, *Witte,* pp. 167–94.
66. *Russkii trud,* 5–12–1899, pp. 12–13, in Solov'ev, "Protivorechiia" p. 382.
67. Solov'ev, "Protivorechiia," p. 383. Also see "Russkaia promyshlennost' i inostrannye kapitaly," *Torgovo-promyshlennyi iug,* 1–2–1912, pp. 1–12.
68. Akademiia Nauk SSSR, *Materialy,* 6:172–95.

siastic supporters of foreign capital.[69] The *Gazette of Trade and Industry* (*Torgovo-promyshlennaia gazeta*) represented this group and defended foreign enterprise in early 1899.[70] At the same time the annual Congress of Southern Coal and Steel Producers concluded categorically that there was no harmful foreign influence in southern mining or metallurgy.[71] Thus the views of Russian big business depended mainly on whether foreign enterprise meant increased competition or increased opportunity.

Small businessmen were also undecided and opportunistic.[72] They agreed that foreign capitalists were remaking Russia, but they were uncertain whether this was for good or for evil. On the positive side there was the prospect of lower prices, more rapid growth of large industry, use of idle resources, and new employment opportunities. On the other hand there were fears that emerging foreign monopolies and a growing proletariat would eventually crush the small businessman.

The members of this group also felt a sharp sense of injured pride. The Brussels correspondent of *This Week* (*Nedelia*), which spoke for the small bourgeoisie, showed this clearly in an 1897 dispatch. He was pained to see "Russian poverty running after Belgian gold" and chagrined to hear a respectable Belgian lady say, "All Russia is for sale, isn't it?" The fervor with which high officials and bankers pushed such transactions led to a bittersweet conclusion. Russia was indeed entering into a "new era. All of our unused national resources will

---

69. Solov'ev, "Protivorechiia," pp. 378–79.
70. *Torgovo-promyshlennaia gazeta*, 29–1–1899, p. 1.
71. *Vestnik finansov*, 17–2–1899, p. 302.
72. Solov'ev, "Protivorechiia," p. 379.

be worked, industrial development will move forward with giant strides, towns will result in a cultivated outlook and social system—and all this on the
basis of French and Belgian money.''[73]

A more somber report from *This Week*'s Ekaterinoslav correspondent was dominated by this same
wounded self-view.[74] Life in the burgeoning town
was frightening and abnormal. Foreigners set the
tone, and life was as expensive as in the capital
cities. The proletariat grew, the local middle class
declined, and the Russian population resembled the
poor Afrikaners of South Africa.[75]

This Week eventually took a position in 1898 that
probably reflected the views of the middle strata of
urban Russia. The usefulness of each foreign company had to be judged separately, since variations
in behavior were very great. A willingness to develop local human resources, to employ Russian
administrators, to create new industries, and to loan
to Russian businessmen were seen as indicators of
proper conduct.[76]

In summary, the conflicting views of landowners,
businessmen, Legal (and orthodox) Marxists were
united by a common theme: foreign enterprise was
speeding up industrialization, and industrialization
was transforming society. This consensus is a significant finding. It offers unmistakable proof that
foreign enterprise had a powerful impact upon Rus-

73. *Nedelia,* 9–2–1897, p. 185, in Solov'ev, "Protivorechiia," pp.
380–81.
74. I owe this piquant phrase to Professor Dawn. The reactions
of the Russian petite bourgeoisie and the Arab nationalist to foreign impact and its demands seem to have much in common. See
C. Ernest Dawn, "Arab Islam in the Modern Age," *Middle East
Journal* 19 (1965): 435–46, particularly 442–43.
75. *Nedelia,* 10–8–1897, p. 1011.
76. Ibid., 28–6–1898, pp. 819–20.

sian backwardness. The indolent were challenged, the aggressive stimulated, and the modernizers encouraged. Thus the important and potentially beneficial lessons of direct foreign investment were taught—and learned, as the Russian-directed spurt after 1909 showed.

Part II

Case Studies and Conclusions

9

A PIONEERING INNOVATOR:

THE JOHN COCKERILL COMPANY IN SOUTHERN RUSSIA

1885–1905

The total foreign contribution to Russian economic development reflected the efforts of many individual enterprises. The celebrated John Hughes, the Welsh ironmaster who began smelting iron at Yuzovo in 1870, was only the forerunner of a whole group of foreign businessmen who contributed to the establishment of a modern metallurgical industry in southern Russia between 1885 and 1900.[1] In 1900 foreign entrepreneurs were present in sixteen of the eighteen steel producers in this new industrial region, and foreign capital accounted for an estimated 78 percent of total investment in the steel industry of southern Russia.[2] Foreign companies were also responsible for 60 percent of total production in the allied south-Russian coal industry.[3]

Of all the foreign enterprises participating in this development none was more important than the John Cockerill Company of Seraing, Belgium. From its head offices in the ancient summer residence of the bishops of Liège, Cockerill founded and man-

1. See J. N. Westwood, "John Hughes and Russian Metallurgy," *Economic History Review*, ser. 2, 17 (1965) : 564–69.
2. C. L., Métallurgie dans le Midi, April 1905.
3. Brandt, *Inostrannye kapitaly*, 2 :116–18.

aged two major companies which played a large part in Russian growth and which produced highly contradictory results for their foreign creator. Brilliant success and abysmal failure—that, in a word, is the intriguing history of this company in southern Russia between 1885 and 1905.

The South Russian Dnieper Metallurgical Company (Yuzhno-Russkoe Dneprovskoe Metallurgicheskoe Obshchestvo), a Russian corporation founded in 1888, was both a pioneering leader and the most consistently successful and profitable Russian steel company during the late nineteenth century and the early twentieth century. An unprecedented record of unbroken and often very high dividends (40 percent on par value, 1896–1900) from creation to Revolution made Dniéprovienne, as it was called by Belgian and French investors, "the marvellous affair that all the world knows."[4]

Cockerill's second venture was the Almaznaia Coal Company, a Belgian firm incorporated at Seraing in September 1894.[5] Originally a coal and coke producer, Almaznaia quickly expanded into metallurgy as a pig-iron producer. Almaznaia was initially fairly successful and paid 5 percent dividends from 1895 to 1900 (1896 excepted), but in 1904 it ended its activities in a disguised bankruptcy that meant a 90 percent loss for its shareholders.

Like the little girl, Cockerill was either very good or simply horrid in its Russian undertakings. This

4. Marcel Lauwick, *L'industrie,* p. 13.
5. The full name was S. A. belge pour l'exploitation des Charbonnages du Centre du Donetz à Almaznaia, which was known as Almaznoe Kamennougol'noe Obshchestvo in Russia. Most Russian firms were named after the locality in which they operated. Perhaps this is a reflection of the evanescent character of the private entrepreneur in Russia and the recurring periods of state ownership or control of many enterprises.

great variation in financial success plagued the whole group of foreign entrepreneurs, who generally, if not always, came from the west-European business elite. Blue-ribbon Cockerill's triumph and defeat was all foreign entrepreneurship in Russia in miniature. A case study of this single firm thus focuses on many of the major problems of foreign enterpreneurship in Russia, and by extension it contributes to the formation of hypotheses concerning direct private investment in general.

1

Belgian steel and equipment makers, constrained by their small national market, turned to foreign areas for markets and investment opportunities early in the nineteenth century. The John Cockerill Company was a leader in this general movement and thus was naturally interested in Russia. Unsuccessful in his attempt to furnish rails for the French portion of the Paris-Brussels railroad, John Cockerill himself had sought alternative markets in Poland without results before he died in Warsaw in 1840.[6] In 1864 the John Cockerill Company built a small shipyard near St. Petersburg to assemble small cannon boats for the Russian navy from material produced in Belgium. Five years later, after all the ships had been assembled and sold, this shipyard with its dry docks, workshops, and equipment was sold to Prince Tenishev, who later became the driv-

6. Société John Cockerill, *110ᵉ Anniversaire de la fondation des usines Cockerill, 1817–1927* (Brussels, 1928), p. 35. Almost all the archives of the Société Cockerill have been destroyed; only the minutes of the board of directors remain. Although I was kindly received by the firm, it was impossible to consult these minutes. Some duplicates are to be found at the Ministère des Affaires Etrangères in Brussels, and they have been used in this study.

ing force in the Briansk Ironworks Company.[7] Cockerill's investment in a Russian shipyard had served to facilitate a large export sale, and the shipyard was unneeded when this sale was completed.

Another indication of the importance of the Russian market was the appointment of Eugène Sadoine, formerly chief engineer of the Belgian navy, as Cockerill's managing director in 1867. Sadoine had represented the firm in Russia for many years and was thoroughly familiar with Russian business conditions.[8]

The thoroughly extroverted Cockerill was thus vitally concerned when Russia turned sharply toward high tariff protection after 1877. The lucrative Russian market simply vanished, and Cockerill's annual Russian sales dropped from five million francs in 1877 to three hundred thousand francs in 1886.[9] Direct foreign investment then seemed to be a possible solution to the problem of impending total exclusion from the Russian market.

In 1883 the board of directors sent directors and engineers to Russia to investigate Krivoi-Rog iron deposits and on the basis of their reports decided to buy mining concessions.[10] Investigation and negotiation were skillfully conducted and were crowned with complete success in 1885. The cautious Monsieur Blanc of the Crédit Lyonnais's St. Petersburg branch stated that the "richness and abundance [of these concessions and others secured in 1889] are

7. Ibid., p. 39.

8. Ibid.

9. A.E., Brussels, no. 3646, sec. 3, letter from Adolphe Greiner, managing director of Cockerill, to the minister of foreign affairs, 30–11–1886.

10. Ibid., Extrait du procès-verbal de la Société Cockerill, 27–9–1886; Cockerill, *110ᵉ Anniversaire*, p. 40.

completely unique in Russia."[11] With high-grade (65 percent) iron ore assured for at least forty years, Cockerill decided on a great Russian subsidiary which would combine large steel mills and a great naval shipyard at Nikolaev on the Black Sea. This was to be a centralized duplication of Cockerill's two divisions, the steelworks at Seraing near Liège and the naval shipyard at Hoboken near Antwerp. The Russian plant was to be owned and operated exclusively by Cockerill and foreign capitalists.[12]

The Belgian company's projects were quite unwelcome in Russia. The depression of the 1880s had meant excess capacity and hard times for Russian metallurgists, and in 1882 they had formed the first Russian syndicate, with the state's active support, to share orders and hold up prices.[13] Cockerill's ambitious plans threatened to shatter this fragile arrangement. Therefore one of the first of periodic campaigns against rapacious foreign capital was launched: the *Odessa Messenger* reported with alarm that Cockerill's shipyard would completely monopolize all construction connected with Russia's Black Sea fleet; and the *Moscow Gazette* bitterly attacked the "invasion by foreign industry" and condemned an alleged desire of the state to protect foreigners.[14] After half a century of business in Russia Cockerill read the signs correctly. The foreigner in Russia needed indigenous state and business sup-

11. C.L., Société Métallurgique Dniéprovienne du Midi de la Russie (henceforth Dniéprovienne), Note, December 1898.

12. Cockerill, *110° Anniversaire,* pp. 39–40.

13. See I. F. Gindin, *Gosudarstvennyi bank,* pp. 254–69, for an excellent discussion.

14. A.E., Brussels, no. 2908, sec. 3, report from St. Petersburg, 17–7–1886.

port, and a go-it-alone policy in the face of such opposition was foolhardy. Only an active partnership with Russian businessmen would secure support and neutralize opposition.

Cockerill found such a partner in the Warsaw Steel Company, one of the two or three leading Russian steel producers in the middle 1880s, and from their union of forces came the South Russian Dnieper Company.[15] Each partner brought many elements of success to their joint enterprise; between the two of them it was truly the case of the perfect partnership. The Warsaw firm brought three crucial factors. First, it agreed to subscribe one-half of the five million rubles of original capital. In the second place, as one of the leading steel producers in Russia entitled to a 25 percent share in the rail producers' syndicate of 1882, the Warsaw Company was able to transfer this allotted share to the proposed company. It thereby assured large rail orders.[16] Lastly, the Russian partner had an already formed management capable of running the projected plant. These three contributions insured excellent relations with the state and neutralized Russian xenophobia.

The contributions of Cockerill to the new venture were different. Its capital participation was much less; although entitled to 50 percent of the new company's shares, Cockerill's management judged it prudent (and perhaps advantageous) to subscribe

15. The Warsaw Steel Company, or Praga Company, incorporated in 1880, was the steel-making division of Lil'pop, Rau, and Levenstein—an equipment producer of German origins founded in 1873. Gindin, *Gosudarstvennyi bank*, pp. 201–2. W. E. Rau, president of the Lil'pop, Rau, and Levenstein, and Dnieper founder, was a German citizen.

16. See Gindin, *Gosudarstvennyi bank*, pp. 238–47, for the profitable domination of the bankrupt Putilov Company by the Praga-Briansk syndicate.

only 16 percent (800,000 rubles) and to distribute the remainder among its friends and directors.[17] The Cockerill Company also provided its ore contracts. This was not its primary contribution, however, since the Warsaw firm also brought another excellent ore contract as well as the factory site at Kamenskoe near Ekaterinoslav on the Dnieper. Cockerill's primary task was to provide the technical know-how required to build and assemble the new firm's capital equipment, most of which came from Cockerill's Belgian factories. This technical excellence was as necessary for the Warsaw Company as that company's Russian relations were for Cockerill.

Cockerill clearly anticipated large entrepreneurial profits on its invested capital. Baron Macar, one of the company's directors, told the Belgian foreign minister that detailed preliminary studies in Russia and an analysis of Hughes's New Russia Company promised profits of 20 to 30 percent on invested capital.[18] Almost as important, however, were anticipated sales of at least three million francs of machinery, which would exceed Cockerill's investment in the new firm by 50 percent. In fact, the new firm marked "the establishment of a very important agency in a rapidly growing industrial area that will be able to recommend more efficaciously Seraing products."[19] Cockerill was also to receive 15 percent of all profits in excess of 6 percent as special remuneration for its technical aid. Lastly, there was a slight hope that the new firm would

17. A.N., 65 AQ, K 51, Société John Cockerill, Annual Report, 1887.

18. A.E., Brussels, no. 3646, sec. 3, undated note from Baron Macar.

19. Ibid.

facilitate eventual installation of the originally projected shipyard on the Black Sea. Such a shipyard would unquestionably purchase considerable quantities of naval equipment from Cockerill. Thus exports and the capitalization of advanced techniques were apparently as important as an anticipated high return on investment.

In 1889 the first rails rolled off the mills, and by the end of the year management could honestly boast that the smoothly functioning plant produced the best-quality pig iron in southern Russia.[20] With surprising candor, Rau, the firm's president, estimated that with two blast furnaces and a yearly production of 80,000 tons, a pud of pig iron would cost thirty-five or thirty-six kopecks and would sell for seventy kopecks.[21] These projections were quite accurate. In the next ten years sales, profits, and dividends soared upward, as table 14 shows. Here indeed were entrepreneurial profits of fable and theory.

Three factors seem to have been of particular importance in this phenomenal success. First, the technical problems were consistently handled well. For example, Donets coal provided excellent coke, but only after careful sorting and washing, just as the preliminary reports of Cockerill's engineers had foreseen. Thus sorting and washing installations were added immediately to complete the modern coke ovens, which then gave good results.[22] In 1898 the Dnieper Company had, without question, the

20. Gindin, *Gosudarstvennyi bank,* p. 259; C.L., Dniéprovienne, Special Meeting, 1889. The Crédit Lyonnais's engineer often noted in his reports the excellent (and superior) quality of the company's products, which initially gave an important competitive advantage.
21. C.L., Dniéprovienne, Special Meeting, 1889.
22. Ibid.

best equipment for special products in southern
Russia.[23] Good techniques meant low costs; in 1903
only the Société Générale de Belgique's Russo-
Belgian Company among southern producers had
significantly lower costs of production.[24] And in 1904
new well-installed Bessemer works "put the com-

Table 14

GROWTH OF THE SOUTH RUSSIAN DNIEPER METAL-
LURGICAL COMPANY
(In Thousands of Francs)

Year (Ending June 30)	Sales	Gross Profits (Overhead Costs Deducted)	Gross Profits as Percentage of Sales	Dividends as Percentage of Par Value
1889–1890	10,413	2,595	25.9	5
1890–1891	16,446	3,776	23.0	10
1891–1892	19,536	4,021	20.6	10
1892–1893	20,883	4,261	20.4	12
1893–1894	26,296	7,587	28.8	20
1894–1895	29,046	10,144	34.8	30
1895–1896	34,475	11,024	31.8	40
1896–1897	38,880	11,339	29.1	40
1897–1898	39,392	10,539	26.9	40
1898–1899	43,745	11,061	25.2	40
1899–1900	46,187	9,896	21.5	40
1900–1901	48,129	10,440	21.6	30
1901–1902	38,648	9,059	23.2	20
1902–1903	35,899	5,931	16.5	12

SOURCE: Crédit Lyonnais, Dniéprovienne, August 1904.

pany back on top as far as the equipment of Russian
steel producers is concerned." [25] In 1911 the new
mills for merchant iron were "the most modern and
powerful in Russia." They filled out "the entire

23. C.L., Dniéprovienne, Etude, December 1898.
24. Ibid., Etude, August 1903.
25. Ibid., Etude, August 1904.

group of mills and accessories which are satisfying to the very highest degree in both force and organization." [26]

Excellent management was a second factor in continuing success. After Cockerill had completed installation, Polish directors and engineers from the Warsaw firm directed daily operations. From 1889 to early 1914, Jasiukowicz, who had worked earlier at Warsaw Steel, was the able managing director. "In Russia they universally attribute the largest part of the success of the Dnieper Company to Mr. Jasiukowicz, whose competence, administration and strength of direction are without equal in Russia." [27] Jasiukowicz was seconded by management and technical personnel which were also Polish and highly competent. [28] The technical director in 1903, for example, was Guchevski who had earlier been chief of Dnieper's rolling mills, and then managing director of a small Polish steel company before returning to the Dnieper Company. [29] Most of the foremen were also initially Polish. And the situation changed little to 1914. Other foreign entrepreneurs in the Donets also called upon experienced Polish technicians, but none so successfully: "The Dnieper Company's management, engineering per-

26. Ibid., Etude, July 1911.
27. Ibid., Etude, December 1898.
28. In 1916 the general director of the French L'Union Minière, a major south-Russian steel producer, wrote Halgonet, the commercial attaché of the French mission in St. Petersburg, that "everyone knows that in Polish factories [in southern Russia] there is no place for either Russians or French. The Dnieper Company, for example, which is owned by Belgian and French capitalists, does not have a single French, Belgian, or Russian engineer or manager outside of those sitting on the Board of Directors." A.N., F 30, no. 343, L'Union Minière (Makeevka), letter of 28–6–1916.
29. C.L., Dniéprovienne, Etude, August 1904.

sonnel, foremen, and workers are very superior to those in all other Russian plants."[30]

Finally, the firm's market strategy was excellent. As is well known, Donets steel companies were primarily rail producers initially, and Dnieper Metallurgical was no exception. But this firm was an aggressive leader in the development of other products destined for private consumption. Whereas rails accounted for two-thirds of finished products from 1890 to 1895, they declined rapidly in relative importance to represent only one-quarter of finished products during 1899–1900 and subsequent years.[31] These important investments in new mills and products from 1895 to 1900 provided diversification and insulated the firm from fluctuations in government demand. In fact, with the new rail producers competing for government orders after 1894 and with the investment boom in private construction, the private market was more profitable than the government one from 1896 to 1899.[32]

It is fitting to close our analysis of the South Russian Dnieper Metallurgical Company with a detailed appraisal by an extremely demanding and shrewd capitalist—the famed president of the Crédit Lyonnais himself, Henri Germain.[33] Germain noted in 1901 that the firm was assured of iron ore for at least twenty-five years. Should the recently purchased coal concession provide adequate coking coal, the firm would enjoy a "privileged position," since production costs of pig iron would be lowered by 11 percent. Equipment was excellent,

30. Ibid., Etude, December 1898.
31. Ibid., various studies.
32. Ibid., Métallurgie dans le Midi, April 1905.
33. Ibid., Dniéprovienne, Observations de Monsieur le Président, September 1901.

and financial analysis showed fixed investment per unit of capacity to be fairly low. With evident satisfaction Germain noted that all new investments were financed by reinvested profits—the approved policy of conservative and prosperous European companies at the end of the nineteenth century, particularly in France, and a policy rarely followed in Russia. The financial situation was good, and management was prudent and intelligent. "All in all, it is a serious company [the ultimate compliment] able to pay handsome dividends, especially if it succeeds in producing its own coke. In this condition it merits a good credit and its shares—not counting the price —can be the object of a solid investment."[34]

2

In 1894 there were four major steel producers in southern Russia. In 1900 there were at least eighteen major steel producers, and this does not include several firms whose plans or installations were cut short by the crisis of 1900, or certain coal companies planning to become metallurgical firms. The success of the pioneers, particularly the Dnieper Company, drew many imitators—including Cockerill itself.

In September 1894 Cockerill founded the Almaznaia Coal Company, incorporated under Belgian law and domiciled at Seraing. Almaznaia was in fact complementary investment for the existing Russian affiliate. It was to mine coal and manufacture coke primarily for the Dnieper Company, which lacked its own mines in 1894.

The close ties between the foreign entrepreneur and his Russian partner continued in the new venture. Dnieper agreed to purchase all of the new

34. Ibid.

firm's coke for three years.[35] Almaznaia's capital of 6,000,000 francs, completely subscribed in cash, was again taken by both partners. This time, however, Cockerill subscribed 1,675,000 francs—more than a quarter of the total—whereas the Dnieper Company itself took only 675,000 francs.[36] The relative shares of the partners were almost exactly reversed in this new firm, as compared with those of the Dnieper creation six years earlier.

Cockerill was to handle all the complex technical problems of installation and was to receive for its technical aid and preliminary studies one-fifth of all profits in excess of 5 percent for ten years—again terms much like those of the Dnieper Company contract. And again Cockerill saw advanced techniques as the key to success.

On Almaznaia's mining property of twenty-five hundred desiatinas (2,700 hectares) in the extreme eastern section of the Donets coal basin, Cockerill projected "one of the best equipped mines in the Donets—quite capable of competing with the best mines of Western Europe."[37] All operations would be concentrated on the unique mine capable of producing fifteen hundred tons of coal per day. A powerful (600-horsepower) engine from Cockerill would raise coal, while the mine's steel superstructure would come from the Dnieper Company. Washing and sorting equipment and 180 of the "most perfected" coke ovens were to complete the installation.[38]

35. A.N., 65 AQ, L 139, Almaznaia, Articles of Incorporation; ibid., Annual Report, 1894–95.

36. *L'Information*, 27–7–1902.

37. A.N., 65 AQ, L 139, Almaznaia, Annual Report, 1894–95.

38. Ibid.

These plans were well executed. According to the Crédit Lyonnais's engineer, the installation of the mine was "excellent," an evaluation he seldom bestowed on Russian coal mines.[39] Almaznaia was also the first coke producer in the Donets to harness escaping gases from coke ovens to drive gas motors.[40] As table 15 shows, production increased rap-

Table 15

GROWTH OF ALMAZNAIA COAL COMPANY

Year	Coal (In Tons)	Coke (In Tons)	Profits (In Francs)	Dividends (%)	Percentage of Net Profits Paid as Dividends
1894–1895	53,000		236,000	5	95
1895–1896	95,000	12,000	122,000		
1896–1897	163,000	58,000	596,000	5	51
1897–1898	226,000	117,000	463,000	5	65
1898–1899	291,000	138,000	805,000	5	75
1899–1900	347,000	113,000	876,000	5	74

SOURCE: A.N., 65 AQ, L 139, Annual Reports.

idly, from nothing to almost three hundred fifty thousand tons in six years, and in 1900 it was approaching the originally projected capacity of four hundred thousand tons per year. It was then the second- or third-largest single mine in the Donets.

There was, however, a serious technical problem which the early annual reports scarcely mention. This was the problem of producing a top-grade metallurgical coke as opposed to one of average quality. The coal at Almaznaia was rich in volatile materials (20 to 24 percent).[41] Such coal made fair but

39. C.L., Almaznaia, Etude, February 1899.
40. Brandt, *Inostrannye kapitaly*, 2:120.
41. A.N., 65 AQ, L 139, Almaznaia, Annual Reports, 1902, 1908.

not excellent coke, since it was less compact and therefore friable. True, Almaznaia's product met all minimum requirements for metallurgical coke. But in the years immediately following Almaznaia's creation, a number of mines—those of the Russo-Belge, Ekaterinovka, and Rykovskii in particular—developed to produce coke from coal with less volatile materials (18–20 percent) which gave a perfect coke.[42]

It was this gradual upgrading of the quality of metallurgical coke in southern Russia that provided the drama for Almaznaia. The crucial year for the company was 1898. The Dnieper Company refused to renew its coke contract, which was Almaznaia's raison d'être. I. Jasiukowicz, Dnieper's Polish managing director, also left the board of Almaznaia for "reasons of personal convenience."[43] Almaznaia lost in one swoop its major customer.

How is one to understand this canceled contract, which even in the boom years 1898–99 seriously threatened the firm's existence? Why did Cockerill and Dnieper jeopardize a large investment to secure for Dnieper a better coke, a coke facilitating production but not essential to it?

Apparently the key is that although Cockerill's directors were well represented in the Dnieper firm, since Cockerill continued to hold its original 16 percent of the affair, the real locus of decision-making power rested with the Polish-Russian group, and

42. Ibid., Annual Report for 1902, and report of Paul Trasenster to the Special Meeting of 3–10–1903. Blanc's studies for the Crédit Lyonnais on the Russo-Belgian Metallurgical Company and the Rykovskii Coal Company frequently stress the superior quality of coke obtained from the coal of the Kalmius Basin. Hughes's New Russia Company at Yuzovo was centered on this superior coking coal.

43. *L'Information*, 27–7–1902.

particularly with the energetic general manager. This group's investment in Almaznaia through the Dnieper Company was also small. And when Almaznaia shares went to 200 or 300 percent of par in 1894 and 1895, they may have taken their windfall profits.[44] Thus Cockerill could not force Dnieper to take small losses to assure Almaznaia continued prosperity. From the Dnieper Company's point of view, Almaznaia's coke was inferior and the contract was an unnecessary liability, especially since powerful new competitors were arriving in the Donets to nibble at Dnieper's profits and to gnaw at its preeminence. The decision to cancel the contract with Almaznaia is indicative of the increasing competition in Russia before 1900.

Perhaps Cockerill could have forced renewal of the coke contract if renewal had seemed a life-or-death matter. But in the optimism of the late 1890s this seemed hardly the case. In September 1895 Cockerill's directors—Fernand Macar, Emile Delloye-Orban, and R. Suermondt—and managing director Armand Sadoine had ambitiously founded the long-contemplated shipyards at Nikolaev with a capital of twelve million francs.[45] And although Cockerill held none of the shares, Cockerill's administrators provided all plans and equipment, plus experience and entrepreneurship. This exclusively Belgian enterprise, "equipped in a remarkable manner to build machinery, ships, and railroad cars," was going forward without the aid of either a Russian partner or the certainty of a dependable customer.[46] No doubt Almaznaia could pursue a similar course.

44. A.N., 65 AQ, L 139, various clippings from 1894 and 1895.
45. C.L., Chantiers Navals de Nicolaiev; A.N., 65 AQ, M 332, Chantiers Navals de Nicolaiev, Articles of Incorporation.
46. C.L., Chantiers Navals de Nicolaiev, Etude, September 1904.

Cockerill therefore decided to transform Almaznaia into a metallurgical firm concentrating on the production of ferro-manganese pig iron.[47] Ferro-manganese pig iron presented special technical problems and was generally imported from England; only Hughes produced the product in Russia in quantity. Thus technical prowess again offered possibilities of large profits.[48]

As in the past, skilled engineers and workmen from Seraing oversaw installation of the two blast furnaces, which were begun in 1898 and 1899 respectively. But now all the equipment was furnished by the Dnieper firm with the exception of two blowing machines from Cockerill.[49] In 1889 Cockerill's Belgian factories had supplied Dnieper with most of its capital equipment. Such was the growth of industrial capacity and sophistication in southern Russia in a single decade.

Once again equipment was admirably installed. The Crédit Lyonnais's engineer noted, for example, that escaping gas from coke ovens was being used to heat hotter and cleaner air for the hot blast than would have otherwise been attained from the use of escaping gases from the blast furnace. Those gases were more suitably used to heat boilers.[50]

Almaznaia was much less successful in securing adequate iron ore deposits—a common experience among latecomers to the Donets. One of its two concessions was poor and the other had an excessive royalty of three kopecks per pud, which equaled the highest royalties ever paid for Krivoi-Rog ore. Moreover, only a small portion of the concession could be mined by the cheap open-pit method. Forty

47. C.L., Almaznaia, Etude, February 1899.
48. Ibid.
49. A.N., 65 AQ, L 139, Almaznaia, Annual Report, 1897–98.
50. C.L., Almaznaia, Etude, February 1899.

meters of earth and rock overlaid the iron ore, which could only be reached by mines costing two million francs.[51] Expensive, hastily assembled ore contracts saddled Almaznaia with high costs and left the firm dangerously exposed to depression.

In 1900 depression struck Russian metallurgy, and by late 1903 Cockerill had disposed of its Almaznaia shares with a 90 percent loss.[52] Space limitations prevent us from tracing this denouement in detail, but three points can be made.

First, Cockerill, like other foreign entrepreneurs, completely misread its market. Everyone expected prices to decline in 1899, but not by 50 percent. Inaccurate market predictions contrasted sharply with generally correct evaluations of technical possibilities.

Second, it became impossible in the pessimism of depression to obtain fresh capital from the Belgian investing public. At first this public had shared Cockerill's enthusiasm: four weeks after incorporation Almaznaia shares were introduced on the Brussels Stock Exchange at 1,700 francs (240 percent of par), and they soon went to 1,950 francs. And when capital was doubled to 12,000,000 francs in 1898 to expand into metallurgy, small investors cheerfully subscribed the new shares at 150 percent of par (750 francs). The augmentation to 15,000,000 francs in early 1900 was more difficult, however, and it marked the end of investor confidence. Afterward, several reorganizations proposed by Cockerill, all involving fresh funds from Almaznaia stockholders, were totally unsuccessful. The Cockerill Company,

51. Ibid., Dniéprovienne, August 1904; *Le Globe,* 20–11–1902; *L'Information,* 27–7–1902.

52. See the complete dossier on Almaznaia, in A.N., 65 AQ, L 139.

which had 1,500,000 francs in Almaznaia shares in 1900, found itself forced to lend an additional sum of approximately four and a half million francs by 1902 to prevent immediate bankruptcy. Cockerill's increased participation was even greater if considered in terms of available funds: the 6,000,000 francs invested in Almaznaia in 1902 was five times net profits in 1901-2; the 1,400,000 francs invested in 1898-99 was only 50 percent of net profits in that year.[53]

Third, when it became evident that the crisis would be of long duration, Cockerill's primary concern was to cut its losses by recovering its loans. To do this Cockerill called upon its old partner, the South Russian Dnieper Metallurgical Company, and arranged a complicated contract which guaranteed the recovery of Cockerill's advances and left shareholders (including Cockerill) with a 90 percent loss.[54] The Almaznaia venture thus ended in disaster. It thus shared a common fate with the Nikolaev Shipyards Company, whose demise came gradually, but no less disastrously.[55]

3

What does Cockerill's experience tell us about the problems of foreign entrepreneurship in Russia? Clearly, timing was a crucial factor. Cockerill's interest in southern Russia in the middle 1880s was

53. A.N., 65 AQ, K 51, Société John Cockerill, Annual Reports.

54. Almaznaia shareholders would receive 50 percent of net profits of the Dnieper Company's Almaznaia division for only twenty years after 6 percent was paid to the Dnieper Company on its capital invested in the Almaznaia division. This was estimated as a 90 per cent loss on Almaznaia's original capital at the time. A.N., 65 AQ, L 139, Special Meetings, 28–10–1903 and 5–12–1904.

55. A.N., 65 AQ, M 331, M 332, and M 648.

the interest of an innovating entrepreneur wrestling with a commonly perceived problem whose solution promised the windfall profits of great innovation. By 1894 Cockerill was only a front runner in the small group of technically sophisticated and adequately financed foreign entrepreneurs carrying the industrial revolution to southern Russia. "Normal" profits—Almaznaia's 5 percent a year perhaps— were the predictable results of a well-run coal company. Bankruptcy was only the harsh but normal penalty for overinvestment at the top of the business cycle. The basic innovation of modern steel making in southern Russia, which was shared with other entrepreneurs and which creatively destroyed both Western exports and antiquated Russian producers, reaped profits seldom if ever associated with a successful "follower."

There is a second, equally important consideration. Cockerill's first venture with Warsaw Steel in the South Russian Dnieper Metallurgical Company was the case of the perfect partnership. Cockerill, the foreigner, brought capital, concessions, and crucial technical ability equal to any in Europe. Warsaw Steel also brought capital and concessions, but its key contributions were excellent relations with government and experienced managers. The resulting firm was much stronger than it would have been if either partner had acted alone.

Almaznaia had elements of the original partnership of foreign technique and Russian relations. But basically Almaznaia was, or quickly became, uniquely Cockerill's affair as the extremely exigent Russian partner withdrew and the Belgian investor took his place. The withdrawal of the Russian partner created unavoidable marketing difficulties, since the best technical achievements could not produce coke of the highest quality. To build on a shaky partnership and to continue with increased optimism when that partnership collapsed were Cockerill's fundamental errors in its Almaznaia venture.

The factors which contributed to Cockerill's success and failure also influenced significantly the results of other foreign entrepreneurs in Russia. There is a lesson here that generates a general hypothesis concerning the nature of successful direct foreign investment. The foreigner's key card in the pursuit of entrepreneurial profits is advanced (and superior) technology. But technical expertise must be closely combined with domestic connections and local management in an active partnership for maximum effectiveness. Otherwise the entrepreneur, like Cockerill and many other similar foreigners in Russia in the 1890s, may find he holds an ace singleton and wins only the sympathetic understanding of a future historian.

10

BOOM-TIME SPECULATION: THE RYKOVSKII COAL COMPANY

Individual foreign promoters and speculators provided the initial driving force in many companies, as we saw in chapter 2. Individual promotion was associated in particular with foreign mining ventures, which often originated in negotiations between proprietors of Russian mines and foreign businessmen, as opposed to manufacturing firms, which were founded upon the sophisticated techniques of leading large corporations.

The businessman himself, often also a mining engineer, could take most of the necessary steps of entrepreneurship in this industry. As an engineer he could find out easily enough which properties were for sale, examine them, and project measures for expansion and improvement. As a promoter he could then negotiate a short-term option for the promising concession with the Russian owner and return to western Europe to secure underwriters for a company to exercise the option. Finally, the engineer-entrepreneur could manage his publicly held creation.

In this way foreign entrepreneurship in mining often remained personal, almost artisanal, as opposed to corporate entrepreneurship (direct investment) in metallurgy and manufacturing. In those industries attempts to export complex technology surpassed individual capabilities and required the teamwork of corporate organization. But in mining, particularly coal mining, superior Western technology was the rather unspectacular common knowledge of a whole corps of technicians and promoters. One of these individuals was Fernand-Raoul Schmatzer, an Austrian engineer residing in Brussels. He was directly responsible for two important foreign coal companies, Prokhorov and Rykovskii. An examination of the latter firm provides a rare close look into the art of the individual promoter as well as his relations with Russian landowners and Western bankers.

Schmatzer's success with the Prokhorov Coal Company,[1] and the exceptional interest of foreign investors in Russian industry, encouraged this entrepreneur to investigate more projects on his numerous business trips to Russia. While some promoters, like Manziarly with Irmino or Bouroz with Ekaterinovka, had branched out to form companies based on leases with peasant communes, or developed properties of secondary quality, Schmatzer continued to concentrate on those few remaining fee-simple holdings of great size and of excellent quality. Once again Schmatzer began by negotiating directly with a gentry owner for an almost matchless property, available for an almost matchless price.

From his handsome country home Colonel Rykovskii directed his mining enterprise strewn over his large lands of more than twenty-five hundred hectares.[2] Situated in the center of the Kalmius Basin in the southwestern Donets (Taganrog district, village of Novo-Cherkassk) and in close proximity to Hughes, Makeevka, and Schmatzer's other firm

1. See chap. 2, pp. 60–62.
2. C.L., Société des Charbonnages de Rykovskii, Etude, December 1901.

(Prokhorov), Rykovskii's coal field was excellent in almost every respect. The beds of coal were regular, fairly thick, and contained proven reserves of fifty to one hundred million tons.[3] At least six seams of coal were known, including the Smolianinov seam, which Rykovskii had worked extensively and which unquestionably made the best coke in the Donets. Rykovskii's equipment was poor, however. The Crédit Lyonnais's impartial observer noted that "with the exception of a magnificent [company] hospital and the family chateau, all of the physical plant [in 1898] was of little value. The mines were installed incorrectly, while machines were old and material poor."[4]

Nor could new investment be long evaded. Previously the colonel had skimmed the cream off his field with minimal investment. Following Russian practice he had sunk a number of small mines that attacked the various outcroppings of the Smolianinov seam to a certain depth, and then other shallow mines were sunk elsewhere. Such methods were increasingly unsuitable, for two reasons, as Colonel Rykovskii no doubt knew. First, that portion of the Smolianinov seam near the surface was exhausted, and deeper, more expensive mines were now re-

3. The Crédit Lyonnais's engineer estimated probable reserves of these lands at fifty-five million tons after an on-the-spot investigation of May 1901. In that same year the new president, Xavier Lauras, stated confidentially that proven reserves exceeded one hundred million tons. See the Archives of the Comptoir d'Escompte de Paris, Paris (renamed the Comptoir National d'Escompte de Paris after World War II and hereafter abbreviated C.N.E.P.), the dossier on La Société Anonyme des Charbonnages de Rykovskii (hereafter Rykovskii), Note de M. Xavier Lauras et Observations des Etudes Financières (du Comptoir d'Escompte), 11–10–1901.

4. C.L., Rykovskii, Etude, December 1901.

quired.[5] Second, the installation of modern mines
with their lower production costs posed the threat of
intensive competition for primitive mines. These
problems of inadequate techniques and large investment requirements encouraged Rykovskii, like so
many of his peers, to join the foreign-company
bandwagon if he were paid well to do so.

In late 1897 Schmatzer bought a short-term option
for 30,000 francs to purchase Rykovskii's property
for 11,000,000 francs (8,750,000 in cash and 2,250,000
in shares of a company to be formed), or more than
4,000 francs (or 1,500 rubles) per desiatina. This
was considered a very high price at the time—that
is, at the very top of the business boom—even for
such excellent coal deposits with fine coking coal.[6]
The Crédit Lyonnais's engineer in Russia believed
that this price was "at least 500 rubles per desiatina
too high."[7]

Having outbid other promoters, Schmatzer returned to Brussels to persuade other businessmen to
form a company to exercise the option. Schmatzer
had little trouble in finding support, mainly among
leading industrialists of the Liège region. The first
board of directors included Georges Dewandre, previous director of Les Hauts Fourneaux de Selessin,
who was a rich, aggressive industrialist with many
business connections in Belgium and Russia. He was
the key man in the South Ural Company, and his
brother-in-law, Armand Stouls, was director of
Espérance-Longdoz and Tula Blast Furnaces.
There were also Félix Durieu, the wealthy director
of Les Charbonnages de Patience and Beaujonc,

5. Ibid., Etude, May 1901.
6. Ibid., Etude, December 1901.
7. Ibid., Etude, May 1901.

near Liège, and Hermann Hubert, professor of mining engineering at the University of Liège.[8]

On 24 February 1898 Schmatzer officially ceded his option to the new mining company, incorporated at Brussels with 8,000,000 francs of capital in 16,000 shares, in return for 30,000 francs in cash and 570,000 francs in shares.[9] Most of the shares of the newly formed company were subscribed by Schmatzer, his associates on the board of directors, and a group of Belgian stockbrokers.[10] All subscribers paid in only 20 percent at the moment of incorporation, while agreeing to pay the remaining 80 percent within one year.[11]

There was no doubt that small investors were the promoters' target.[12] By early 1899 10,300 shares apparently remained with the promoters, the rest having been sold to the Belgian public at 600 to 650 francs—or 20 to 30 percent above the original subscription price. Of the unsold portion, Schmatzer and his group held 3,800 shares; the Volga-Kama Bank, which was represented on the original Board of Directors, held 800; and Colonel Rykovskii held 5,200.[13] These shares were then sold off in France during 1899, as were 10,000,000 francs of first-mortgage bonds in 1898.[14]

8. C.N.E.P., Rykovskii, confidential letter to the Comptoir, 6–1–1900.

9. An additional 418,000 francs for "expenses of incorporation" meant a total price of 12,000,000 francs for Rykovskii's rich reserves and miserable mines. It also meant that almost one-half of the 10,000,000 francs of the first-mortgage bonds, which were floated three months later, was taken for the purchase of existing mines, and not their improvement.

10. *Vie Financière*, 4–2–1902.

11. A.N., 65 AQ, L 386, Articles of Incorporation.

12. *Le Pour et le Contre*, 8–1–1899.

13. C.N.E.P., Rykovskii, undated note [early 1899].

14. See the printed notice from Alfred Bonzon, Agent de Change, Lyons [June? 1898], in A.N., 65 AQ, L 386.

The inflated cost of acquiring Colonel Rykovskii's property dictated Schmatzer's market strategy from the beginning. It was absolutely necessary to increase production rapidly from the original level of 244,000 tons to a figure three or four times as high if the new firm's large capital was to be remunerated. Schmatzer's original stated program called for an annual output of 1,000,000 tons of coal and 200,000 tons of coke within four or five years with an investment of 5,000,000 francs in new equipment.[15] If the new company could in turn duplicate other well-run Russian mines and earn 3 francs per ton of coke and 1.5 francs per ton of coal on the greatly expanded output, then total investment of 23,000,000 francs (8 in stock, 10 in bonds, and 5 in working capital) would receive 1,800,000 francs. Interest and amortization of bonds would take 1,000,000, and shares would then receive something less than 10 percent.[16] Thus only intensive exploitation of the property could justify the initial purchase price.[17]

A 300 percent increase in output in four years demanded excellent technical organization and administration at the very least. Schmatzer provided neither. True, the problems were considerable. Tanon of the Comptoir d'Escompte wrote from Russia that "the [original] mines were exploited by Colonel Rykovskii to the absolute limit, and now [May 1899] the company has great difficulty in utilizing the old material effectively in order not to interrupt the extraction before the new mines assure

15. C.N.E.P., Rykovskii, note from Tanon, engineer with the Etudes Financières of the Comptoir d'Escompte de Paris, on mission in Russia at Rykovskii, 3–5–1899. Quoted in Note récapitulative du Service des Etudes Financières, October 1901.

16. C.N.E.P., Rykovskii, note from Lauras, 11–10–1901.

17. Ibid., Lauras to Rostand, director of the C.N.E.P., 5–11–1901.

regular production."[18] There was not only the costly task of installing "two new, modern, and well-equipped mines," but also that of "infusing vitality into the old mines with repairs, excavations, and new equipment."[19] Therefore more than half (2,300,000 francs) of the 3,500,000 francs invested in the first year went toward rejuvenation of old mines, which had higher costs of production and would eventually be abandoned.[20] No wonder Tanon, after a year of operations, concluded in May 1899 that "in place of the pompously announced programs they have scattered their resources in many directions . . . and production is still furnished only by the old mines or temporary arrangements."[21] Construction of the new mines, a long process in any event, lagged dangerously. The old Russian pattern of numerous inefficient mines was perpetuated.

There was a certain limited justification for this shortsighted policy. The company was able to profit immediately from the exceptionally high coal prices of 1898 and 1899 and gain profits of 1,700,000 francs during its first full year in 1899. Schmatzer's conduct as manager was indefensible, however. His main concern was speculation and personal gain at the firm's expense. Ten million francs of first-mortgage bonds, which were placed mainly in France in June 1898, produced only 8,000,000 francs—part of the missing 2,000,000 having stuck in the chief executive's pocket. "The president [Schmatzer] paid the company 400 francs for each 500 franc bond which was bought by a syndicate for more than 400

18. Ibid., letter of 3–5–1899, quoted in the Note récapitulative.
19. Ibid., Lauras to Rostand, 5–11–1901. This very long letter, and Lauras's note of 11–10–1901, are in part a history of the company under Schmatzer's administration by his successor.
20. Ibid.
21. Ibid., letter from Tanon, 3–5–1899.

francs and then placed with the public [at 450 francs]. Thus Schmatzer realized a profit without any real risk from the company he directed."[22]

Schmatzer also returned to France for bank loans in early 1899 to finance continued expansion to the projected capacity of one million tons. At the same time he continued to use his position for personal profit. Throughout 1899 bank loans increased, and they reached 2,200,000 francs by the end of the year.[23] The Comptoir d'Escompte de Paris advanced approximately one-third of these bank loans. Little wonder this bank began to follow the coal company closely from May 1899 at the latest, when the bank sent one of its engineers (Tanon) attached to its Etudes Financières to Rykovskii's mines in Russia for detailed examination.[24] The engineer Tanon was not encouraging, and by late 1899 it was clear that the Russian mining company could not pay its bank loans. These bank loans, it must be remembered, stood *after* 10,000,000 francs of first-mortgage

22. Ibid., letter from Lauras, 11–10–1901. Two prominent brokers in Lyons, Alfred Bonzon and A. Galicier et Cie, placed a large number of Rykovskii bonds in the Lyons area and apparently led the syndicate selling these bonds. The Lyons group received one place on the board of directors as well as the post of technical consultant. Both positions were filled by men from the Dombrowa Coal Company in Poland, a French company founded in 1878 and controlled by this Lyons group since 1891. Rykovskii's new technical consultant, Matheron, the director of Dombrowa, had investigated Rykovskii on the spot in March 1898 in order to judge the security underlying the bond issue. See A.N., 65 AQ, L 386; *Le Pour et le Contre*, 8–1–1899; *Circulaire Galicier;* and Notice from Alfred Bonzon. See A.N., 65 AQ, L 137, for clippings and Annual Reports of Dombrowa.

23. C.N.E.P., Rykovskii, note of Xavier Lauras, 11–10–1901.

24. There are numerous quotes and references to Tanon's May 1899 report in the Note récapitulative (October 1901), although the original report is missing. Tanon continued to undertake numerous missions of inspection and control to the Rykovskii mines until late 1902.

bonds. There was a scent of impending disaster in the air in late 1899 for all concerned.

The market for Russian shares was still strong, however, and the Comptoir saw a profitable exit in Schmatzer's proposal for an increase of capital. There was but one serious roadblock barring escape —Colonel Peter Rykovskii. Colonel Rykovskii, an original member of the coal company's board of directors, was adamantly opposed to an increase of capital. And as the owner of 5,160 shares (almost one-third of the outstanding shares), he was in a position to block the proposal.[25] On the other hand, the Rykovskii Coal Company's debt to the Comptoir of 750,000 francs was due and unpaid. If the Comptoir publicly called this loan and thereby drove down the price of the company's shares, Colonel Rykovskii would lose greatly. The Comptoir believed the best solution would be to use this threat to force the colonel out by buying his shares and selling them to the public. Then the coal company could proceed to the increase of capital needed to bail all insiders out. Schmatzer was in perfect agreement and proceeded accordingly.[26]

From his quarters at the Hôtel de Louvre the colonel acknowledged his capitulation—or more accurately, his final victory. The Comptoir purchased 5,160 shares from Colonel Rykovskii at 550 francs per share. The Comptoir then accepted 750,000 francs in new shares in payment for its previous loans and also bought 750,000 francs of shares at par (500 francs). In addition, the Comptoir took six- and twelve-month options on the remaining 9,000 shares (4,500,000 francs par value), which had been

25. Ibid., Accords avec Colonel Peter Rykovskii, note of 30–12–1899.

26. Ibid., Accords, note of 27–12–1899.

authorized by Rykovskii's Board of Directors. These options opened the door to further profits without risk, provided the market stayed strong after the first blocks of shares were profitably sold.[27] Schmatzer served his personal interest again (for the last time). He obtained 12 percent of the syndicate's total profits on all operations for his pains as "intermediary."[28] The Comptoir apparently ceded about one-half of the interest in this syndicate to friends and associates.

Both the secondary offering of the colonel's shares and the capital augmentation were very successful. The colonel's shares were sold at 620 francs for a profit of almost 70 francs per share. Then the options on the remaining 4,500,000 francs of shares were exercised at par and were quickly sold at an average price of 635 francs by the end of February 1900. This operation gave the Comptoir's underwriting syndicate a net profit of 115 francs per share in two months.[29]

While primarily concerned with their brilliant financial transactions, the Comptoir also tried to make Rykovskii a viable concern. A new management team was an obvious first step. The bank gave Schmatzer notice and named an associate (Adrien Josse, vice president of the Banque Industrielle et Coloniale) to be Rykovskii's president in March 1900.[30] Xavier Lauras, an engineer who was pre-

27. C.N.E.P., Rykovskii, note on the augmentation of capital, 6–3–1900.

28. Ibid., letters with Betzold, Agent de Change, 18–12–1899 and 5–2–1900.

29. C.N.E.P., Rykovskii, note on the augmentation of capital, 6–3–1900.

30. The Comptoir's first choice in January was Ludovic Sinçay, close associate and long-time managing director of the South Russian Salt and Coal Company. Schmatzer had fled Brussels by the

viously secretary general at the Blanzy mines in France, replaced Lambert as managing director. Lauras in turn soon called upon a trusted former associate at Blanzy to replace Schmatzer's original Belgian director in Russia. This was a good decision.[31] Frequent trips of inspection by Tanon were to check continually the competence and rectitude of the new management.[32]

More funds and new management did not solve the company's problems, however. By April 1900 the May 1899 program calling for increased production to a million tons in three years with 5,000,000 francs of investment had been revised downward drastically by Lauras to 600,000 tons with 6,500,000 francs of investment. This also proved too optimistic. By late 1901 Rykovskii had almost exhausted the funds raised in early 1900 and the modified program was still unfinished. The first of the modern wide-

---

middle of August 1900 before "very grave financial difficulties." Letter from the Caisse Commerciale de Bruxelles to Comptoir d'Escompte, 20–8–1900. One might note in closing a last monumental affair of this precocious if unscrupulous promoter. In 1899, while the clouds gathered around Rykovskii, Schmatzer negotiated options to purchase three coal properties belonging to Prince Dolgorukii for almost ten million francs. Then, with his Belgian associates—Durieu, Hubert, Andras, Fontainas, etc.—he formed the Sté des Charbonnages réunis du Midi de la Russie in August 1900. Capitalized at 8,500,000 francs with 8,000,000 francs of bonded debt, the firm failed to pay Dolgorukii all it owed. It eventually went bankrupt in 1905 because Schmatzer and other founders, who paid in only 20 percent upon incorporation, refused to meet subsequent capital calls on their shares. See A.N., 65 AQ, L 381 for this affair.

31. The first director, Tonneau, had previously directed only a very small mine in Belgium and was unproven. C.N.E.P., Rykovskii, note of Griner, [late 1899]. The Crédit Lyonnais engineer later felt he was a "fairly poor director" while Franclieu, Lauras's choice, deserved his good reputation. C.L., Rykovskii, Etude, May 1904.

32. C.L., Rykovskii, Etude, May 1901.

section mines had been completed and was producing at the rate of 250,000 tons per annum. But the second such mine was only half finished, as were most of the coke ovens. These coke ovens would be a total loss if not completed quickly.

Nor was this all. Schmatzer's unintentional (or intentional) negligence in drawing the original option had meant that Colonel Rykovskii had not ceded his rights on adjacent peasant lands which were part of the enterprise. Thus on the last day of December 1899—the day Colonel Rykovskii sold his shares to the Comptoir—Schmatzer had been forced to buy these necessary rights expiring in 1907 from the colonel for an additional 1,250,000 francs.[33] And in 1900 the company's new management had been compelled to buy the colonel's chateau and park for 350,000 francs as the only way of finally freeing itself of the original owner.[34] This meant that 1,600,000 francs from the increase of capital served no constructive purpose. In late 1901 Lauras admitted his desperate need for a new bank loan of at least five hundred thousand francs, which he felt the Comptoir was morally obligated to provide. Could a great bank like the Comptoir forget its stepchild, Lauras asked, after having been joined to it so closely?[35]

This question of the responsibility of the deposit bank toward the Russian company was discussed in detail in an exchange of letters between Rostand,

33. C.N.E.P., Rykovskii, letter from Lauras, 5–11–1901.

34. "The presence of Colonel Rykovskii living in the midst of our operations . . . made management impossible. The only way to finally rid ourselves of him was to buy his chateau and park. The price was very high, but it is probable that his presence at the mines would have cost us even much more in the long run." Ibid.

35. Ibid.

Director of the Comptoir, and Henri Catoire, a French industrialist active in Russian affairs, who had entered Rykovskii's board in July 1900 to aid "my friend Lauras." It shows clearly how industrial considerations were secondary for the Comptoir, which never wished to assume permanent and effective control of the Russian coal company.

Noting that the public always searched for a scapegoat after meeting misfortune, Rostand reminded Catoire of the boom conditions before the Russian collapse and defended his bank in a passage worth quoting.

> All industrial companies, but particularly Russian companies, were in favor . . . and many well qualified people reproached us for a lack of initiative in not seeking a corner of this great country which was insufficiently developed and which awaited an immense economic development. Everyone cited the example of the Belgians, as they continue to do for colonial enterprises because of their results in the Congo.

> It was at that moment that we were presented the Rykovskii project. The company had unquestionable elements of vitality and potential success. The price of coal was very high. . . . Numerous Russian companies paid excellent dividends. Thus with a group of secondary participants the Comptoir undertook a financial operation to guarantee an augmentation of capital and then sold these shares on the stock exchange, since only a few were placed with the clientele. And I must remind you that those who buy on the exchange are not minors. Nor are they usually interested in anything but short-term profits. . . . The excessive markup at the beginning appears to be Rykovskii's only real affliction. The Comptoir knew nothing of these over-evaluations (*majorations*), because no report had indicated them. . . . In short, why should the

Comptoir bear any responsibility for simply buying and selling shares?. . ."[36]

A financial operation was a financial operation, *tout
court.*

Two days later Catoire answered. Contrasting
himself, an industrialist, with the Comptoir's director, a financier, Catoire conceded that the Comptoir
may not have known of the initially exaggerated
price. But that ignorance was precisely the point.
"The Comptoir remained only a financier; everything was examined from the financial side: coal
prices, the craze for Russian shares, nearby examples, etc. and in fact, financially speaking, the operation was a great success. But in all this the mine was
not able to obtain what it might have expected from
the Comptoir's intervention. This is indisputable. If
there was no responsibility towards Rykovskii, then
the Comptoir could disinterest itself completely and
leave others the pain. This is not the case in my
opinion, and Comptoir would honor itself in lending
aid."[37] In answer, Rostand reiterated his position
and asked how, when so many had been carried away
in the Russian boom, the Comptoir could be held
responsible for such a general sentiment and miscal-
culation.[38]

But the Rykovskii shoe fit, or pinched, and the
Comptoir knew it. A "few highly confidential lines"
at this time from Ludovic de Sinçay of the South
Russian Salt and Coal Company showed that the
bank was still considering attempts to salvage Rykovskii. Sinçay noted that Rykovskii's costs were
much too high, and that in fact Rykovskii's anticipated costs equaled Sinçay's expected selling price.

36. Ibid., Rostand to Catoire, 5–10–1901.
37. Ibid., Catoire to Rostand, 7–10–1901.
38. Ibid., Rostand to Catoire, 10–10–1901.

He noted that fixed investment per ton of capacity was much too high—almost twice what it was for his company.[39] In a second letter Sinçay stated that a loan of a half million francs was absolutely insufficient, and that three or four million francs were needed for survival.[40]

A sense of limited responsibility finally compelled the Comptoir to support Lauras. The Comptoir provided a new bank loan of 500,000 francs, but only on the condition that a new issue of at least four million francs of 5 percent cumulative preferred stock be issued and that the expansion program be finished. The Comptoir agreed to underwrite one million francs of the new shares. Lauras was to obtain a similar commitment from Bonzon, Galicier, and other brokers who had shared in earlier operations.[41] Presumably, at least one-half the present stockholders would exercise their rights. After an initially favorable answer, Bonzon backed out, telling Lauras that he had been spoiled by the overly indulgent Comptoir.[42] Bonzon and Galicier had placed the first-mortgage bonds which were still well secured. They apparently wanted a drastic reorganization that would wash out the original shareholders, give the company to their bond-holding clients, and place themselves at the head of the affair.

With shareholders unenthusiastic and with no un-

39. Ibid., Sinçay to Rostand, undated [late 1901]. Rykovskii's investment of 45 francs per ton of coal produced was twice the average of 23 francs per ton at three other foreign-owned mines—Almaznaia, Rutchenko, and Ekaterinovka. C.L., Rykovskii, Etude, September 1901.

40. C.N.E.P., Rykovskii, Sinçay to Rostand, 26–10–1901.

41. Ibid., Rostand to Lauras, 27–11–1901.

42. As Lauras reported his harrowing meeting with Bonzon, Bonzon told him with a fierce air to "look at me well. Do I look like a man to be satisfied with 2% [profit]?" Ibid., Lauras to Rostand, 12–12–1901.

derwriting partner, the augmentation of capital foundered. The Comptoir, which had originally opposed an embarrassing capital reduction—a tacit admission they were linked to Rykovskii—now agreed on a drastic reduction of capital stock (from 14,000,000 to 2,800,000 francs) and the simultaneous flotation of 1,700,000 francs of new preferred stock.[43]

As Sinçay had predicted, this was a halfway measure. It did not provide the funds necessary to concentrate all production in three or four very modern mines—the oft-discussed, never completed technical reorganization that had been imperative since the firm's origin. But with productive capacity of 450,000 tons exceeding sales of 365,000 tons in 1902, opportunities for thorough-going reorganization had been squandered indefinitely. High costs from poor techniques brought losses of 60,000 francs in 1902 and 100,000 francs in 1903 as the depression deepened.[44] By early 1904 another financial reorganization was inescapable.[45]

One possible solution was a merger with a larger, profitable, continuously well-run Russian coal company. One such suitor was the Bonnardel Group's Ekaterinovka Coal Mining Company. This firm differed from Rykovskii in almost every respect.[46] Tightly held, technically advanced, and well managed, Ekaterinovka had limited but excellent coal deposits and was actively searching for additional reserves.

In 1902 and 1903 Ekaterinovka had offered to buy two nearby Donets companies, first Berestov-

43. *L'Information,* 17–2–1903.
44. C.L., Rykovskii, Etude, May 1904.
45. C.N.E.P., Rykovskii, note on visit from Galicier, 23–2–1904.
46. See chapter 11.

Krinka Coal, and then Makeevka Coal. Both firms judged cash-rich Ekaterinovka's propositions insufficient, even unscrupulous.[47] Ekaterinovka then turned its steely eyes toward Rykovskii and proposed a merger on the basis of one share of Ekaterinovka (quoted at 800 francs) for every ten shares of Rykovskii. This offer, worth 80 francs per share, was vetoed by the Comptoir, which demanded that the reduced capital of 100 francs per share they had underwritten be maintained.[48] Ekaterinovka eventually met these demands and agreed to exchange one share of Ekaterinovka for only eight shares of Rykovskii. A syndicate headed by the Comptoir agreed to pay par value of 100 francs to any Ryskovskii shareholder preferring cash to shares in Ekaterinovka. Ekaterinovka also assumed Rykovskii's first-mortgage bonds at par.[49]

When the formalities of merger were completed in February 1905 Rykovskii vanished as a corporate entity. Henceforth Schmatzer's creation and the Comptoir's stepchild was the adopted charge of Ekaterinovka and the Bonnardel Group until war and revolution passed it once again to new hands. These developments lie beyond our purview.

It is significant, however, that Ekaterinovka's engineers once again sought large modern mines that would increase production and lower costs. There was simply no alternative in the long run. Before the merger Ekaterinovka believed two million francs would be needed to complete the second large shaft mine and thereby bring down Rykovskii's costs of production, which stood a full 20 percent

47. *Le Pour et le Contre,* 9–11–1902; *L'Information,* 12–8–1907. See chapter 11 for details.
48. C.N.E.P., Rykovskii, notes of 23–2–1904 and 3–3–1904.
49. Ibid.

above those of Ekaterinovka.[50] The cost of complete technical reorganization was revised upward to three or four million after the merger in 1905. In 1907 the Rykovskii division still needed an additional two million.[51]

Continuing problems were complicated in June 1908 by a fire-damp explosion at Rykovskii's number four mine. This accident claimed 270 lives and turned an expected profit of one million francs—the first real gain in a long time—into a million-franc loss. The accident also led to new regulations for complete filling of all tunnels to prevent a recurrence of such an accident. Such regulations had long been anticipated by the company, but they meant higher costs nonetheless.[52] Even in 1913, the first year profitable enough to permit a dividend payment since 1905, the *combined* operations of Ekaterinovka produced less than the million tons Schmatzer had first promised for Rykovskii in 1899. Yet the competent management of the Bonnardel Group had weathered the storm. In 1914 one could reasonably expect that the worst was behind.

In summary, the Rykovskii Coal Company effectively focuses on several key problems of individual entrepreneurship and the evolution of patterns of investment in Russia.

First, the changing locus of entrepreneurship at Rykovskii was indicative of a general trend. In the boom conditions of the late 1890s talented individuals specialized in transferring the accumulated funds of small west-European capitalists to wealthy Russians, and they called upon willing bankers to aid in the task. In the ensuing depression individual

50. Ibid., 23–2–1904; C.L., Rykovskii, Etude, May 1904.
51. *L'Information*, 12–8–1907.
52. Ibid., 30–9–1909.

entrepreneurs often lost control of their creations in subsequent reorganizations, reorganizations which tended to place their firms in larger, more viable industrial units. Such units might be formal corporations or they might be informal groups.

Second, the Comptoir d'Escompte de Paris became interested in Russian industrial affairs primarily in a financial capacity. It had no desire to control or manage its firm, and did so halfheartedly and reluctantly. The Comptoir's flirtation with investment banking was a by-product of unsuccessful (or too successful) underwriting ventures.

Finally, one notes the problems in increasing production rapidly to reduce the weight of heavy fixed costs which were inherent in the inflated price of coal deposits. Most firms faced the need to increase production, but it posed a particularly grave dilemma for firms purchasing operating mines. Namely, should one continue with the outdated but barely serviceable equipment actually producing, howbeit expensively; or should one simply concentrate on efficient production with new mines?

Because they needed to earn something immediately, Schmatzer and to a lesser extent Lauras tried both strategies. They attempted to salvage old mines temporarily, while sinking new ones erratically. Coal producers like Ekaterinovka, South Russian Salt and Coal, and the Russo-Belgian Metallurgical Company, which began with a *tabula rasa,* were more fortunate. They were freed from the seductions of old mines and methods "in the interim," and of necessity they concentrated effort and resources only upon new modern mines. Shareholders expected to wait before receiving a return, and management was less tempted to fritter away resources mindlessly.

11

THE HUTA-BANKOVA STEEL COMPANY
AND THE BONNARDEL GROUP

In 1897 the annual meeting of shareholders of the Société des Forges et Aciéries de Huta-Bankova, the leading steel producer of Russia's Polish provinces and the pride of French capitalists, was marked by an unexpected incident. For the first time a few shareholders actually criticized the Huta-Bankova's management and its president, Jean Bonnardel, for perpetuating the "dangerous and abusive system of concealing real profits." According to its critics, management's steadfast policy of rapid depreciation and continuous write-offs had become irrational. It only served to limit reported profits, and therefore dividends. Similarly, management's well-known mania for secrecy had ceased to serve a useful purpose. In short, a more generous distribution of dividends and information was long overdue. According to one observer, the president and the board of directors answered these criticisms politely but in "vague generalities, without losing a trace of their Olympian attitude"—or promising the slightest change of policy.[1]

This passing incident of little apparent significance actually highlighted the peculiar trademarks of what was probably the most successful foreign industrial group in Russia before 1914. Self-financing, secrecy, and managerial omnipotence—these

1. *Le Pour et le Contre,* 5–10–1897.

were indeed the firm cornerstones upon which the imposing Bonnardel Group built, and built well. The Bonnardel Group was not sui generis, however. It was instead the chef d'oeuvre of a widespread entrepreneurial type, the foreign group. In spite of its fascinating peculiarities the Bonnardel Group shared with other foreign groups many characteristics in structure and development. An examination in detail will therefore be doubly rewarding.

Before specific ventures and the history of the group's development are discussed, an overview will perhaps be useful. The number of firms associated with the group and their total capital in Russian industry were impressive. The first firm was the Huta-Bankova Steel Company, which was formed at Lyons in 1877 with a capital of 6,300,000 francs. In 1883 Bonnardel and his associates took control of a second enterprise in Russia, and in 1892 a third major venture was undertaken. Then the dam broke. By 1900 the group had founded or controlled a total of at least nine large companies with nominal share capital of 48,300,000 francs and 17,400,000 francs of bonded debt, or 65,700,000 francs in all. Market value of these shares and bonds equaled 185,600,000 francs in February 1900. The group's holdings, which expanded only slightly in the following fourteen years, may be seen in table 16.

The companies of the Bonnardel Group accounted for perhaps 18 percent of the market value of all French industrial investment in Russia in 1900.[2]

2. The best estimate of total French industrial investment in Russian joint-stock companies at the turn of the century (railroads excepted) was made by M. Verstraete, the French consul at St. Petersburg. Verstraete concluded that the nominal, or par, value of French capital stock and bonds in French and Russian corporations in February 1900 was 692,000,000 francs, and that another 100,000,000 francs was held in Belgian corporations op-

Table 16

CAPITAL ENGAGED IN PRINCIPAL FIRMS OF
BONNARDEL GROUP IN RUSSIA, 1900
(In Millions of Francs)

	CAPITAL STOCK Nominal Value (28-2-1900)	Market Value	FUNDED DEBT
1. Forges et Aciéries de Huta-Bankova, French, 1877.	4.8	48.8	—
2. Sté des Forges et Aciéries de la Kama, French, reorganized 1883.	1.0 [b]	28.0	4.0
3. Donetskoe obshch. zhelezodelatel'nogo i staleliteinogo proizvodstv (Forges et Aciéries du Donetz, à Droujkovka), Russian, 1891.	12.0	28.3	6.0
4. Sté des Mines de la Doubovaia Balka, French, 1892.	2.5	12.5	—
5. Ekaterinovkoe gornopromyshlennoe obshch. (Sté Minière d'Ekaterinovka), Russian, 1895.	5.0	12.4	1.9
6. Sté des Constructions Mécaniques du Midi de la Russie, French, 1895.	8.0	15.0	4.0
7. Sté Industrielle et Métallurgique du Caucase, French, 1897.	5.0	13.2	1.5
8. (Sté Minière Franco-Russe), Russian, 1896.	6.7	6.7 [c]	?
9. Sté pour l'Industrie Métallurgique en Russie (à Novoradomsk), French, 1898.	3.3	3.3 [c]	?
Total	48.3	168.2	17.4

SOURCE: Based upon findings of M. Verstraete (cited in n. 2 of this chapter) and my calculations.

a. Six million francs is deducted from the market value of Huta-Bankova shares to avoid double counting, since the Huta-Bankova held 6,000,000 francs of Aciéries du Donetz in its portfolio.

b. This figure is artificially low because the complicated reorganization of the previous firm, the Sté Franco-Russe de l'Oural, substituted shares without par value for all old capital stock and bonds.

c. Unlisted.

In addition to investing capital, this group *conserved* its capital. Only one enterprise was a failure, and only one other firm reduced the par value of its shares after 1900. All these firms were in heavy industry—metallurgy, coal, iron, copper mining, and machine tools. Geographically the distribution was very wide—Poland, the Urals, the Caucasus, and of course the Donets. Even seen in this skeletal form, this was clearly an exceptional entrepreneurial unit. Since there were a number of firms, founded at different times and under different technical and geographical conditions, plus some near misses, it is also a difficult one with which to deal. Since it is impossible to analyze each company in detail, this study will focus on key turning points within the group's general evolution, and a few key enterprises.

The establishment of the Huta-Bankova in 1877 marked the formation of the first major Russian enterprise by capitalists from the Lyons area. There had been a considerable migration of skilled artisans from this region earlier in the nineteenth century which had contributed impressively to the growth of the Russian textile industry, particularly

---

erating in Russia, a total nominal capital of almost 800,000,000 francs. Since the nominal value of the firms in the Bonnardel Group had little meaning, market value is the best measure of the group's relative position. In February 1900 the market value of shares of the majority of foreign-owned enterprises was only slightly above the nominal value, and the shares of some such companies (Ural-Volga, Verkhnii-Dneprovsk, Volga Vishera, Nikolaev Shipyards, Ateliers Franco-Russes, and others) were already quoted well below par. Thus assuming generously that French nominal capital calculated by Verstraete had a market value of one billion francs, one concludes that the Bonnardel Group had fully 18 percent of total French industrial investment. See M. Verstraete, "Les capitaux étrangers," *Congrès International des Valeurs Mobilières,* 4, no. 111:10–28; ibid., no. 115; and 2, no. 44, for French capital in 1900.

in silk.[3] But the export of capital and technique from Lyons to Russia without permanent migration and gradual assimilation began only with the Huta-Bankova. The activities of this firm taught the capitalists of Lyons about the possibilities of Russian investment, as Cockerill's Dnieper Company did later for the citizens of Liège. The Russian enterprises from Lyons, however, were linked more closely with a key man, Jean Bonnardel, and his associates, who first joined together in the Huta-Bankova.

Jean Bonnardel, director (1878–80) and president (1880–1914) of the Huta-Bankova, was the extremely wealthy scion of a bourgeois dynasty that had been active in the commerce of Lyons since the sixteenth century.[4] This family formed the Cie Générale de Navigation, which first monopolized the Rhone River traffic and then grew to be by far the largest French shipping company. This company, of which Bonnardel was a board member at twenty-two and owner of one-fourth of the share capital in 1870, provided a solid base for a varied business career in France and in Russia.[5] This career must certainly have increased appreciably Bonnardel's inheritance of 22,000,000 francs (shared with his brother-in-law) which stood behind his many ventures.[6]

Bonnardel had excellent coworkers in the Huta-Bankova. Gabriel Chanove, an engineer and long-time general manager of the Huta, was also a mem-

3. A.N., F 30, no. 328, Rapport à Rouvier, Ministre des Finances, par Victor de Swarte, payeur général, à la suite d'un voyage en Russie (June 1891).

4. Jean Bouvier, "Une dynastie d'affaires lyonnaise au XIXe siècle: les Bonnardel," *Revue d'histoire moderne et contemporaine* 2 (1955): 185–205.

5. Ibid., pp. 187–93. The only major check in his successful career was his failure to reorganize the Panama Canal Company.

6. Ibid., p. 190.

ber of the board of directors of the Crédit Lyonnais, which would occasionally lend its support to the Huta.[7] The Verdié family, which had built the Aciéries de Firminy into one of the Loire's leading metallurgical concerns, was a second invaluable associate.[8] After François-Félix Verdié's death in 1878 his son, Eugène, an engineer who had examined the Polish works before incorporation and was the Huta's titular founder, was active in the firm. He provided technical expertise with his associates from Firminy Steel.[9]

The Huta-Bankova works near Dombrowa in Polish Silesia on the Warsaw-Vienna line had been founded in 1842 by the Bank of Poland. The Russian government subsequently managed the works with indifferent success until June 1876, when they were sold to a Russian noble and businessman named

7. It is often implied that the Huta-Bankova was an emanation of the Crédit Lyonnais. Actually the Crédit Lyonnais seems to have been only one of the Huta's bankers—the Crédit Industriel et Commercial was another—and little more. In 1881, for example, the Crédit Lyonnais refused to discount letters of exchange from the Moscow-Brest Railroad Company assigned to the Huta in payment for rails on the grounds that the Russian state was not directly obligated. Bouvier, *Crédit Lyonnais,* 1:396, and 2:764.

8. Firminy was the work of François-Félix Verdié, who began as an ordinary metal worker for the Jackson brothers before he founded Firminy in 1854. One of the causes of this company's profitable operations during the railroad boom of the 1850s was a new process for the "fabrication of large objects [mainly rails] with a surface of cast steel and an ordinary iron interior." The simultaneous use and conservation of strong but dear steel before Bessemer's discovery became Verdié's specialty. Verdié remained a first-class technician and was one of the first to sign licensing agreements with Siemens and Martin. See L. J. Gras, *Histoire économique de la Loire* (St. Etienne, 1908), pp. 218–23, 269.

9. Ibid.; A.N., 65 AQ, K 110, Articles of Incorporation of the Société des Forges et Aciéries de Huta-Bankova, Paris, 28–7–1877.

Alexis Plemiannikov.[10] When Plemiannikov, a first captain in the Imperial Navy and a director of the Russian Land Bank, purchased the works and mines it was apparently stipulated that the Huta-Bankova would equip itself to produce at least a million puds (16,000 tons) of steel rails per year. In any event, this obligation was stated clearly in the French firm's articles of incorporation.[11] Undoubtedly the Huta-Bankova already had large orders for steel rails.[12] The Russians provided resources and demand in state rail orders, but they needed technical expertise.

In return for ceding the existing works Plemiannikov received 12,000 shares of 500 francs each, or six million francs at par value, in the new firm; Verdié, Bonnardel, and their associates subscribed an additional 300,000 francs of stock in cash. Thus less than 5 percent of the original capital was new money from foreign sources; the remainder went to Russians in payment for existing factories and guaranteed markets. No doubt Plemiannikov's agent, the state counselor Strzelecki, had contracted with the Lyons capitalists for sale or retrocession of some of the vendor shares. But one suspects that Plemiannikov's 12,000 vendor shares went primarily to Russians initially, especially since those vendor shares were clearly separated from the capital shares: the capital shares were to be amortized as soon as the surplus reached 300,000 francs and then

10. A.N., 65 AQ, K 110, Articles of Incorporation; Kovalevsky, *La Russie*, pp. 667–68; Rondo Cameron, *France and the Economic Development of Europe, 1815–1914* (Princeton, 1961), p. 96.

11. A.N., 65 AQ, K 110, Huta-Bankova, Articles of Incorporation.

12. See below.

replaced by rights entitled to second dividends. Nor was the company legally established until Verdié acknowledged that the 600 capital shares were one-quarter paid.

The French capitalists also leased rather than purchased the Huta complex from Plemiannikov for thirty-six years. Upon expiration of the lease all properties were to revert to Plemiannikov without any payment from either lessee or lessor. In view of the difference between existing iron production (5,000 tons per year) and promised production for steel rails alone (16,000 tons), Plemiannikov obviously could look forward to a large capital gain at the end of the lease.[13]

Thus the contractual agreements embodied in the articles of incorporation bore a striking resemblance to modern management contracts. Russian owners had resources and markets, but they lacked special skills necessary for successful development. They then sought French associates who pledged technical know-how, managerial competence, and (implicitly) access to Western capital markets. The stated investment of the French was very small, almost symbolic; their entrepreneurial role was very large.

The transformation of a small iron producer into a modern steel-making unit was the key problem facing foreign managers and technicians. In 1878 the works consisted of four small blast furnaces, seventeen puddling ovens, nine reheating ovens, and three small mills with their accessories. There were neither Bessemer converters nor Siemens-Martin open-hearth furnaces, and apparently not even coke ovens. In short, equipment existed for small quanti-

13. Huta-Bankova, Articles of Incorporation; *Lettres d'un Capitaliste*, 8–11–1902.

ties of merchant iron and perhaps puddled steel. There were no installations for either modern steel refining, or mills for heavy finished products like rails.[14]

One other participant was required, the small Western investor. Or more exactly, in this instance, it was the Western bondholder. Long on Russian bureaucrats and Western technicians, the Huta was still short on capital, since incorporation had brought only 300,000 francs in fresh funds. Therefore the articles of incorporation authorized an initial bonded indebtedness of 4,000,000 francs. Bonds of this amount were floated at Lyons in 1880. At the time bonds of Russian industrial firms were a novelty and the risk premium proved high. Eight thousand obligations of 500 francs, reimbursable in annual installments within ten years, were floated in two emissions at 350 and then 400 francs. This meant yields to maturity of approximately 12.5 percent and 10 percent for investors.[15] The interest and amortization charges weighed heavily on gross profits and helped explain the absence of any dividends to 1885 as well as the fall of shares to a low of 115 francs in 1882.[16] Whatever initial arrangement was made for Plemiannikov's shares, it is clear that by 1884 almost all the Huta's capital was in the hands of Bonnardel and his group, where it then remained.[17]

Because of the extreme reticence of the Huta-

14. Huta-Bankova, Articles of Incorporation, Inventory of Assets. (Article 6 of the Articles of Incorporation.) The Putilov works in St. Petersburg was the only domestic producer of steel rails in 1876. Gindin, *Gosudarstvennyi bank*, p. 195.

15. *L'Information*, 6–12–1899. After deductions of fees and commissions the firm must have paid a considerably higher rate.

16. *Le Pour et le Contre*, 5–10–1897.

17. *Le Globe*, 3–10–1903.

Bankova it is not exactly clear how initial difficulties were transformed into "marvellous success."[18] Certainly the government's decision of 1876 to establish domestic steel-rail producers and railway-equipment producers was a prerequisite for success as it had been for the initial decision to invest. After 1876 the "protective difference" for domestic rail producers was eighty kopecks per pud (129.6 francs per ton), of which forty-five kopecks came from tariff protection and thirty-five kopecks from direct state subsidy. This protection amounted to fully one-third of the Russian producers' selling price of 2.3 rubles per pud. In just two short years after the government's new policy domestic producers supplied 70 percent of Russia's demand for steel rails.[19]

The Huta-Bankova clearly benefited from these measures. It procured purchases of 2.9 million puds (47,500 tons) of rails from 1876 to 1882, and it averaged 700,000 puds yearly from 1880 to 1882. This amounted to almost 7 percent of Russian rail production.[20] In 1882 the Huta's steel rail capacity was 1.2 million puds, or 10 percent of total Russian capacity. Not surprisingly, the Huta obtained a share of 12.5 percent in the first syndicate of Russian rail producers formed in 1882.[21] All these orders came from private railroad companies in Russia, such as the Moscow-Brest Company. Some of these companies were owned by French capitalists who had been permitted to import rails freely before 1876—in part, no doubt, from the Loire area and the Firminy Steel Company.

18. *Le Pour et le Contre,* 2–10–1900.
19. This is based on the excellent discussion in Gindin, *Gosudarstvennyi bank,* pp. 191–98.
20. Ibid., pp. 260–61.
21. Ibid., pp. 254–58.

The government's tariff protection and premiums were available to all, however. One must look further for the factors in the Huta's success, a success contrasting sharply with the hardships of other producers. For according to a leading authority, "The position of all the members of the rail syndicate of 1882 remained difficult until the beginning of the 1890s, and only the leading firm, Briansk, continued to pay a continually reduced dividend."[22] All the members, that is, except the Huta-Bankova, whose initial dividend of 2 percent in 1885 rose to 10 percent in 1890 (and then skyrocketed to 25 percent in 1899).[23]

Three internal factors seem to have been of particular importance for the Huta's achievement. The technical problems of modern steel making were apparently resolved with ease, primarily by the technicians of Firminy Steel.[24] By 1892 the firm was producing 67,000 tons of steel as opposed to 5,000 tons of iron originally. Production doubled to 125,000 tons in 1902,[25] and at the Nizhnii-Novgorod Fair of 1895 the Huta was understandably awarded the Imperial Eagle, the highest honorific award in Russian metallurgy, which was shared only with Cockerill's

22. Ibid., p. 259. Briansk paid 25 percent in 1881–82, 20 percent in 1883, 15 percent in 1884–85, and 12 percent in 1886–88. N. Pushkin, *Statistika aktsionernogo dela v Rossii*, 3d ed. (St. Petersburg, 1898), p. 280.

23. *L'Information*, 16–1–1910.

24. A.N., 65 AQ, K 110, Huta-Bankova, Annual Reports for 1894 and 1895. Firminy easily found trained engineers and metallurgists in the 1880s. In that difficult decade steel companies of the Loire area stagnated or declined as they struggled to adapt to the competition of Lorraine producers, who were introducing the Thomas-Gilchrist process, and to combat serious general depression in France. Firminy's sales dropped 50 percent from 1882 to 1886. Jean Bouvier, *Le Krach de l'Union Générale* (Paris, 1960), p. 254.

25. *Journal des Finances*, 1–10–1913.

Dnieper Company.[26] The French consul at Warsaw characteristically noted the quality of expertise at the Huta-Bankova in 1908.

> From a financial and technical point of view the Huta-Bankova is managed remarkably well. . . . The [French] personnel is an elite, very carefully recruited in the leading [French] metallurgical centers. Once engaged our countrymen stay with the firm or its subsidiaries, and then place their sons there. They find very handsome situations with the firm and large salaries.[27]

Another aspect of this technical skill manifested itself in a diversified and appropriate market policy. By 1894 the firm was a large producer of sheets— "always the most profitable item"—merchant iron, wire, and railroad accessories, as well as steel rails, the first major product. After 1895 this diversification continued at an accelerated pace.[28]

The extremely disciplined and austere financial policy of French metallurgy, which ploughed back profits into new equipment and built up large reserves, was a second element of success. All investments were treated as costs of production, even when they clearly increased the value of the firm's assets. This meant that the firm's capital stock actually declined between 1878 and 1908, although productive capacity increased twenty or thirty times.[29]

26. *Le Pour et le Contre,* 2–11–1896.

27. A.N., F 12, no. 7275, d'Anglade, Voyage d'étude dans les centres industriels de Pologne, June 1908.

28. See the Annual Reports of the Huta-Bankova from 1895 to 1899, in A.N., 65 AQ, K 110.

29. In large-scale French industry like metallurgy "autofinancing was intense. . . . It formed the leitmotiv of the annual reports of Schneider . . . and it was the rule at Firminy. . . . The Forges de Châtillon-Commentry increased its capital only once in the fifty-eight years from 1862 to 1920." Bouvier, *Crédit Lyonnais,* 1:390.

Nor was this all. Extensive investments in affiliated companies were also financed exclusively from the Huta's profits until 1908. Thus reported profits showed no increase from 1886 to 1900, while the "working capital," which included shares in subsidiaries, went from one to eight million rubles.[30] With very large reserves the group's directors were never embarrassed by depression, bankers—or shareholders.

The expansion of the Huta into other areas and related industries was a third reason for success. The transformation from leading firm to leading group broke bottlenecks in supply, permitted each plant in the group to specialize in its most advantageous product, and secured important economies of scale for management and supervision. Profits from subsidiaries eventually found their way back to the Huta, the nerve center of a vast if informal organization.

The successful reorganization and development of the Kama Steel Company in 1883, in the Ural Mountains near Perm on the Kama River, was the first such step by Bonnardel and his associates. Kama Steel, originally the Société Franco-Russe de l'Oural, was formed in 1879 by Prince Serge Golitsyn and French metallurgists from Lyons to profit from the same protective system that stimulated the Huta-Bankova.[31] Prince Golitsyn leased his prop

30. Nominal capital actually decreased as 3,000 of the original 12,600 capital shares of 500 francs each were repaid by 1900 and replaced by participating shares without par value which shared in all dividends above 5 percent. If there had been no progressive corporate income tax in Russia after 1898, the Huta might have eventually reached the ultimate goal, an enormous industrial enterprise with no stated capital. Annual Reports; *L'Information,* 16–1–1910.

31. "Until now the supply of rails has come almost exclusively from abroad; thus the Russian state, seeing the large importations

erties of 410,000 hectares, and mills that were producing 500 tons of iron yearly, to the new firm for thirty-six years. In return he received vendor shares worth 6,000,000 francs. Two million more was subscribed in cash through an underwriting syndicate headed by the Union Générale.[32]

The new firm intended to transform the existing works to produce a minimum of 20,000 tons of steel rails. These ambitious plans failed, however, partly because of problems of climate and inexperienced management, and partly because the firm's banker, the Union Générale, went bankrupt in January 1882.[33] Shortly thereafter the Ural producer suspended payment on its bonds and tottered toward bankruptcy. At this point Bonnardel and four engineers bought the company's bonds, dissolved the old company, and negotiated a new arrangement with both French shareholders and Prince Golitsyn. This arrangement became the Kama Company in September 1883.[34]

The existing pool of experienced administrators and technicians was an important factor in subsequent success. Jean Bonnardel, Kama's president or honorary president from 1883 to 1914, joined rigorous capitalist orthodoxy with his influence and great personal resources. In 1888, for example, he

---

of rails . . . and desiring a national industry capable of meeting demand, has recently established a highly protective system, like that in the United States. There are also premiums for rails made with local materials." *Création d'une Société Métallurgique Franco-Russe* (Lyons, 1879), in A.N., 65 AQ, K 164.

32. Ibid.; Bouvier, *Krach,* p. 57.

33. C.L., Kama, Etude, November 1900; Bouvier, "Une dynastie," pp. 195–96.

34. A.N., 65 AQ, K 117, Société des Forges et Aciéries de la Kama, Articles of Incorporation, 30–9–1883. Bonnardel's associates were Camille Astier, Louis Neyrand, Etienne Locard, and Joseph Lamaizière.

gave his personal guarantee to the firm's bankers to secure badly needed working capital.[35] A Crédit Lyonnais note dated July 1904 also suggested that perhaps Bonnardel would personally guarantee a loan of one million francs that Kama Steel was seeking for expansion.[36] The man behind the firm was much stronger than the firm itself.

Louis Neyrand, president of the Forges de l'Horme, was either the director-general or the president of Kama until 1914. He picked the engineer Lavizon from his company to direct the Kama works from 1892 to 1902. Lavizon proved to be a very good director according to an impartial source.[37] The group also supplied a Verdié, nephew of Eugène Verdié, the director of Firminy and Huta-Bankova, as chief engineer from 1900 to 1910.[38] Significantly, Verdié was replaced in 1910 by Nothon, his brother-in-law, as part of the group's policy of "periodic rotation of personnel, a necessary consequence of the distance and isolation of our plants." [39]

The reorganized Kama paralleled the Huta in its development. From a rich documentation several key points stand out. First, production of finished products grew impressively from 3,000 tons in 1883 to 10,000 tons in 1893, 34,000 in 1903, and 68,000 in 1913.[40] This compares favorably with the relative stagnation of other Ural producers.[41]

35. Report of management for the year ending 12–10–1890, as quoted in *Bourse de Lyon,* 3–5–1891.

36. C.L., Kama, Etude, July 1904.

37. Ibid., Etude, November 1900.

38. Ibid., Etude, July 1904; A.N., 65 AQ, K 117, Report of the Board of Directors, 10–4–1911.

39. A.N., 65 AQ, K 117, Report of the Board of Directors, 11–4–1910.

40. A.N., 65 AQ, K 117, Articles of Incorporation, 30–9–1883; C.L., Kama, Etude, July 1904.

41. Livshits, *Razmeshchenie,* pp. 171, 210–11.

Second, Kama's management was undeniably excellent. The Crédit Lyonnais's engineer was struck by how well the plant and equipment were adapted to local conditions.[42] In 1900 the old but well-maintained blast furnaces used Cowpers—"still a rarity in the Urals"—for the sizable economies of the hot blast. On the other hand, iron ore was mined exclusively with hand tools by "very modestly paid" miners, and it was then lifted by horse-powered windlasses, the universal elevator in the Urals.[43] The fluvial system of the Kama and its tributaries was also well utilized, as were excellent forest reserves. All these factors help explain why this firm had the lowest pig-iron production costs in the entire Ural region.[44] Sheer technical skill and good management were also responsible for low costs of refining pig iron into steel. In July 1904 the Crédit Lyonnais's engineer concluded that "these costs [of refining] are without doubt the lowest in the Urals."[45]

Lastly, one may note again that initial capital committed by the Bonnardel Group was small, approximately 800,000 francs for new shares plus an undisclosed amount for the previous company's bonds. And, except for 4,000,000 francs of bonds (in 1894 and 1898), share capital was never increased subsequently. In 1904 the Crédit Lyonnais's experts, noting the old machinery, added that "the two last directors who succeeded thus far had only an infinitely small capital for reorganizing an enterprise

42. C.L., Kama, Etude, November 1900.
43. Ibid.
44. One pud of pig iron cost 33 kopecks to produce, not including overhead expenses. "This is an extremely favorable figure, by far the lowest in the entire Ural region. The average cost is 40 kopecks per pud at the least, not including overhead expenses." Ibid.
45. Ibid., July 1904.

which previously gave nothing but losses.''[46] But when profits were made, far more than 50 percent was invariably reinvested.[47] Patience and steadfastness received their reward: in 1913, after all the capital shares had been repaid, the "large parts" representing the first company's 500-franc bonds stood at 1,500 francs each, while the "small parts" representing the original firm's 500-franc capital shares had reached an all-time high of 515. This meant a combined stock market capitalization of more than thirty-five million francs.

The third firm, the Donets Steel Company at Druzhkovka, was initially a branch of the Huta-Bankova. The Huta-Bankova subscribed and subsequently retained one-half of the total share capital of 1,500,000 gold rubles (6,000,000 francs) and offered the other half to Huta shareholders.[48] Founded in the Donets under Russian law in 1891, Donets Steel was the fourth major steel producer to operate in southern Russia. Like other southern rail producers, Donets Steel began with a large state contract, in this case for 100,000 tons.[49] Simultaneously the Huta planned to decrease and eventually to drop rail production in Poland, and to concentrate on merchant steel and specialty products, for which high-quality workmen provided a comparative advantage. The engineers of the Bonnardel Group had little trouble realizing that sooner or later rail production would migrate southward, whether they participated or not.

Construction did not proceed immediately after

46. Ibid.
47. *Bourse Lyonnais,* 19–5–1889; *L'Information,* 21–4–1911; A.N., 65 AQ, K 117, Aciéries de la Kama, Annual Reports.
48. *Le Pour et le Contre,* 9–8–1892; *Circulaire Roumagnac,* 23–7–1905.
49. *Le Pour et le Contre,* 9–8–1895.

incorporation in July 1891. This was probably because of unsuccessful merger discussions with the Briansk Ironworks Company, the only great all-Russian producer that ever moved production of rails to southern Russia.[50] Therefore it was not until May 1894 that the first blast furnace was operational. A year later the Bessemer steel works were producing and rails were rolling off the mills. The board admitted that "difficulties" hindered production and that costs of construction were "very high and greatly exceed our provision"—perhaps by a factor of two, since management reluctantly doubled the share capital by the end of 1895.[51]

The Huta's previous experience in Poland and the Urals had provided intimate knowledge of the Russian metallurgical market. It also provided managers. Both Eugène Verdié and Edouard Pasteur were again founders and administrators, as were Gabriel Chanove and Jean Bonnardel, who seconded Pasteur as vice president.[52] Ventures in Poland and the Urals also provided an invaluable pool of experienced personnel. One financial paper stated that all of Donets Steel's original management came from the Huta.[53] This was quite possible, since more than fifty Frenchmen, mostly engineers, were at the Huta works in Poland in 1907.[54] Certainly two of Donets Steel's managing directors were previously at the Huta-Bankova: Pasquier, "one of the best directors in Russia," was in charge of the steelworks at the

50. *Le Journal Financier,* 31–7–1892.

51. A.N., 65 AQ, K 68, Aciéries du Donetz, Annual Report, 31–5–1895; ibid., Special Report, 10–2–1895.

52. A.N., 65 AQ, K 68, Articles of Incorporation, 5–7–1891; C.L., Aciéries du Donetz, Etude, March 1911.

53. *Le Pour et le Contre,* 9–8–1892.

54. A.N., F 12, no. 7275, d'Anglade, Voyage d'étude dans les centres industriels de Pologne, June 1908.

Huta-Bankova before heading the southern company from 1901 to 1905; Linder began at the Huta in
the 1890s and after extensive Russian experience
returned to the Donets in 1908 as codirector. The
other codirector was Hilléraux, who had been at the
Kama Steel Company for many years. The director
at the iron mines after 1910 had been director of the
mines of the Dubovaia-Balka Company, an associated firm.[55] The group never lacked skilled managers with Russian experience.

Donets Steel was less successful than either the
Huta-Bankova or Kama Steel. Although it lost
money only in 1906–7 and 1907-8, it paid its unique
dividend of but 5 percent in 1913. Profits were always reinvested, primarily to attain a balanced
product mix, and thus to lessen the firm's depend-
ence on rails and state demand. Several times, when
it seemed that the last program of substantial investment was completed, the board would note with
regret the necessity to expand or to redo part of the
plant, and to forego any dividend payment.[56]

This is an excellent indication of the real competi-
tiveness of south-Russian metallurgy; one had to
run hard to keep up. In fact, profits were not adequate, and in 1910 the company was forced to increase its capital from 4,500,000 rubles to 7,700,000
rubles for absolutely unavoidable investments. The
Crédit Lyonnais's engineer believed these important investments had been delayed too long, and that
this put the company in a poor bargaining position
vis-à-vis its competitors in the southern steel syndicate.[57] Obviously the Bonnardel Group was quite

55. C.L., Aciéries du Donetz, Etudes, August 1901 and March
1911.
56. See the company's Annual Reports, A.N., 65 AQ, K 68.
57. C.L., Aciéries du Donetz, Etude, March 1911.

willing to plough back its profits unendingly, but it was extremely reluctant to dig down for new money if that policy was proved insufficient.

The original limited commitment in Russian Poland of leading capitalists from Lyons had expanded by 1891 to become a group of three metallurgical firms, which were all united by common personnel and ownership, and an industrial division of labor. The group was now formed and ready to expand rapidly before the challenges and opportunities of complementary investment during the boom of the 1890s. Like modern planners pursuing a policy of balanced growth, a whole series of investments interacted and made new investments possible and profitable.

The Société des Mines de la Doubovaia Balka was an outgrowth of the problems and opportunities of securing adequate raw materials. Founded by four French polytechnicians—Paul Bayard, A. De Bovet, L. Le Chatelier, and Théodore Motet—and Alexis Goriainov of Briansk, the Dubovaia Balka Company purchased extremely rich Krivoi-Rog iron deposits from the heirs of Alexander Pol'.[58] The company was closely tied to the Huta.[59] The four founding engineers first examined the concession in May 1891 (two months before Donets Steel's founding), but the sale and incorporation of Dubovaia Balka occurred fifteen months later after long negotiations.[60]

The mining company's prospectus stressed repeatedly its close relations with the Huta-Bankova. The Huta-Bankova had agreed in March 1892 to buy

58. A.N., 65 AQ, L 807, Mines de la Doubovaia Balka, Articles of Incorporation.

59. Bayard, *Notice sur les Mines de la Doubovaia Balka.*

60. A.N., 65 AQ, L 807, Articles of Incorporation.

all its iron ore needs for fifteen years from the projected Dubovaia Balka Company.[61] These needs were expected to reach 110,000 tons per annum in for years (30,000 for the Polish plant and 80,000 tons for the southern subsidiary), and to account for seven-eighths of the new mining company's sales.[62] In addition, Donets Steel subscribed at least 5 percent of initial capital of 2,500,000 francs and placed two of its administrators, Chanove and Pasteur, on the board of directors until 1898. With excellent administration, assured markets, and easily mined deposits of great value,[63] Dubovaia Balka sold the parent company ore at relatively low prices and still made excellent profits.[64] The company paid dividends of from 10 to 15 percent from 1894 on, and it always stood with the Krivoi-Rog Iron Company as one of the two leading iron-ore producers in southern Russia.[65]

The mining company also widened the group's entrepreneurial horizon. ''The knowledge that Messrs Le Chatelier and Motet, founders and directors of Dubovaia Balka, have acquired in managing this mining company concerning the state of industrial development in southern Russia showed the urgent need to create a machine tool producer capable of manufacturing in the Donets itself the machines and equipment normally bought abroad. Such equipment is very expensive in southern Russia because of freight costs, tariff protection, and the frequent necessity of bringing skilled foreign techni-

61. *Notice sur les Mines de la Doubovaia Balka.*
62. Ibid.
63. C.L., Mines de la Doubovaia Balka, Etude, August 1899.
64. C.L., Aciéries du Donetz, Etude, September 1904.
65. *La Cote,* 7–9–1912; C.L., Doubovaia Balka, Etude, August 1899.

cians to install it.''[66] Therefore the South Russian
Mechanical Engineering Company, founded with
4,000,000 francs in early 1895, built factories on land
leased for eighty years from the Admiralty at Nikolaev, on the Sea of Azov, to produce machine tools,
as well as steam engines, boilers, and locomotives.[67]
This was the first machine-tool producer in southern
Russia.[68] A leading French machine toolmaker, Bariquand of Paris, was technical consultant and
agreed to furnish all necessary plans and technical
aid for twelve years. Bariquand also agreed to receive and to train Russian engineers and foremen in
its French plants and to send its own staff to Russia
upon request.[69]

This daringly conceived enterprise was eventually
a disastrous failure. It finally merged with hard-
pressed Nikolaev Shipyards in 1906, and its shareholders lost more than 90 percent of their investment. This denouement contrasts so sharply with
other Bonnardel Group enterprises that one must
seek an explanation.

Managerial personnel were in fact almost exclusively Russian from the beginning. This was quite
indicative of the firm's Franco-Russian character,
or specifically its Bonnardel-Briansk character.[70]
For since 1892 the ties between the group and the
Briansk Company had tightened. Now G. Goriainov,
as managing director of the new firm, led the group
of Russian engineers and foremen to France for
training, while Alexis Goriainov, Briansk's manag-

66. C.L., Constructions Mécaniques du Midi de la Russie, Etude,
May 1895.
67. Ibid., Etude, September 1904.
68. Ibid.
69. Ibid.; A.N., 65 AQ, M 453, Constructions Mécaniques, Annual Report, 1895-96.
70. C.L., Constructions Mécaniques, Etude, September 1904.

ing director, sat on the board of directors.[71] Certainly the problems inherent in precision manufacturing with an untrained, expensive labor force, as well as the severe depression in the capital goods industry after 1900, were part of the answer. But there was more than this.

Clearly insouciance and outright mismanagement played their part. The South Russian Mechanical Engineering Company became an engine for unbridled speculation when the Bonnardel Group, or at least some of its members, turned partially from serious industrial effort to windfall gains in speculative promotion between 1897 and 1900. The directors declared dividends of 6 percent in 1897 and 1898 and of 7 percent in 1899 and 1900. This helped push the 500-franc par value shares to 1,100 francs, although "it seems certain that the company never realized real [manufacturing] profits."[72]

Profits came instead from promotion. In 1898–99, 400,000 francs were earned from the sale of shares in the Kerch Metallurgical Company, the large steel company founded in 1899 with old friends from Briansk.[73] Kerch occupied Motet and Gorjeu, who

71. A.N., 65 AQ, M 453, Annual Report, 1895–96. One suspects he used this opportunity primarily to promote other affairs. In any event he proved to be a poor managing director and lived in St. Petersburg, where "he does not apply himself to the company in an effective manner." C.L., Constructions Mécaniques, Etude, September 1904.

72. A study on the Dubovaia Balka, August 1899, noted the same trend. It seemed so easy to make money in Russia in the late 1890s. "Until 1897 management was absolutely prudent; then dividends per share jumped from 25 to 75 francs per share in three years while reserves diminished."

73. C.L., Constructions Mécaniques, Etude, September 1904. When Kerch turned sour in 1900 it almost dragged the all-Russian Briansk Company into bankruptcy or French control. These alternatives were avoided only because of Count Witte's active intervention. See A.N., F 30, no. 343, Société Briansk.

were among the representatives of the Bonnardel Group in Russia and were also directors of the Sté des Constructions Mécaniques, almost continuously throughout 1899 and 1900 before Kerch collapsed.[74] Another 750,000 francs was garnered from a participation in the founding of the affiliated Société Française des Constructions Mécaniques in France, which succeeded the Société des Anciens Etablissements Cail.[75] These are only two examples of general promotional activity which even became the engineering company's stated purpose.[76]

Finally, unlike the shares of the Group's mainstem affairs—Huta-Bankova, Donets Steel, and Kama—the shares were never closely held by owner-managers. Instead they were passed to the public for an immediate profit as quickly as possible. One journal reported that more than five hundred shareholders subscribed to the doubling of capital in 1897 and concluded that "this is an index of the perfect classing of the shares [in many small but sure hands], and proves that the young company has an excellent reputation and already an important following."[77] True or false, this statement clearly reveals the founders' intentions—sell and sell fast.[78]

Two other ventures of the group, founded in part

74. *Paris Bourse,* 11–6–1900 and 25–7–1900; A.N., F 30, no. 343, Société Briansk.

75. C.L., Constructions Mécaniques, Etude, September 1904; A.N., 65 AQ, M 453, Annual Report, 12–12–1898.

76. "Finally we ask you [shareholders] to approve a general resolution authorizing several of your directors to administer along with your company various affairs having connected interests." A.N., 65 AQ, M 453, Annual Report, 12–12–1898.

77. *Le Pour et le Contre,* 23–1–1898.

78. They were all too successful. The founders shares alone, entitled to one-fourth of all dividends above 5 percent, were actively traded in 1898, when they were capitalized at more than two million francs. They were soon worthless.

through the intermediary of the Dubovaia Balka, were more typical. The Ekaterinovka Coal Mining Company (1896), later merged with the Rykovskii Company, was the most consistently successful coal company in the Donets. Again ties with Briansk were close, since the directors in 1897 were Paul Bayard, Dubovaia Balka founder and Ekaterinovka's managing director; Théodore Motet, general director of both the tool company and Kerch; Modeste Pierronne, the technical director at Briansk; Edouard de Billy of the Crédit Lyonnais's Etude Financières in St. Petersburg; and Goriainov.[79] The president was René Raoul-Duval, a Lyons financier and group member. It was completely natural that Donets Steel became a major purchaser of coke and that the Crédit Industriel et Commercial, which was one excellent link to the public (Bonnardel was a board member), underwrote bonds equal to almost half Ekaterinovka's original capital stock and "placed them very rapidly among its clients."[80]

Careful preliminary studies and the economical application of advanced techniques by proved managers successfully met the two key problems of the foreign entrepreneur in the Russian coal industry. These problems were the securing of suitable properties at reasonable cost and the rational development of them. An initial capital of only 375,000 gold rubles (1,500,000 francs) sufficed to secure an 800-hectare mining concession which contained the highest quality coking coal in the Donets.[81] This concession, leased until 1922 from the peasant commune of Ekaterinovka, had been purchased in 1894 by a

79. *Le Pour et le Contre,* 12–10–1897.
80. A.N., 65 AQ, L 151, Société Minière d'Ekaterinovka, Report to the Preparatory Meeting, 28–9–1899.
81. Ibid., Articles of Incorporation.

French mining engineer named Auguste Bouroz while Bouroz was director of the contiguous Berestov-Krinka Coal Company.[82] The following year Bouroz as general manager and Raoul-Duval for the group formed the Ekaterinovka Company to develop the rich and undeveloped leasehold property. The company cleverly planned two large central mines and an annual production of at least 500,000 tons which would largely exhaust estimated reserves of 20,000,000 tons during the course of the lease.[83] The leasehold was thus as satisfactory as fee simple, and much cheaper—an excellent strategy.

There was ample time to find other properties and insure corporate immortality. A first step in this direction was the purchase of an adjoining property of 1,200 hectares from a Mr. Schmidt in 1898. Larger holdings were also investigated continuously. Contiguous Berestov-Krinka was a candidate, and nearby Makeevka was another, while coal-rich, cash-poor Rykovskii was the final choice.[84] Common nationality played a negligible role, unless it meant harder terms because of more accurate information.

Ekaterinovka was the prototype of the centralized, technically advanced foreign mining company. The principal mine on the peasant lands was built to produce 350,000 tons a year. There were also 220 new coke ovens and the necessary accessories.[85] Correct use of advanced technology resulted in one of the lowest fixed investments per ton of coal mined of

82. Ibid.; C.L., Berestov-Krinka, Etude, April 1912.

83. A.N., 65 AQ, L 151, Report to Special Meeting of Shareholders, 15–2–1898 (as quoted in *Circulaire Lyonnaise*, 25–2–1898); ibid., Report to the Preparatory Meeting, 27–10–1898.

84. See chapter 10.

85. A.N., 65 AQ, L 151, Société Minière d'Ekaterinovka, Special Meeting, 15–2–1898; ibid., Report to the Preparatory Meeting, 28–9–1899.

any firm in the Donets, as well as production costs for both coal and coke well below average.[86] It also permitted the highest rate of growth. Standing one hundred forty-first among Russian coal producers in October 1896, Ekaterinovka was seventh in early 1898 with 200,000 tons per year, and second with 600,000 tons for the year ending June 1904 before the Rykovskii merger.[87] After the merger Ekaterinovka was unquestionably the largest coal and coke producer in Russia. Unlike most coal companies, Ekaterinovka never went through financial reorganization, although dividends were omitted from 1906 through 1912.

Through the Dubovaia Balka the Bonnardel Group also entered into the copper industry in the Allah-Verdi region of the Caucasus in October 1897, when it subleased undeveloped properties from a French company dating from 1887.[88] In spite of technical difficulties, strikes, violence, assassinations, and important investment in transport, production of refined copper rose implacably from little or nothing in 1897 to 750 tons in 1900 and 4,100 tons in 1912. After 1906 dividends averaging 6 percent annually were declared on a reduced share capital. The firm employed excellent industrial technology.[89]

86. *L'Information,* 25–10–1902 and 28–5–1903; C.L., Rykovskii, Etude, September 1901.

87. A.N., 65 AQ, L 151, Special Meeting, 15–2–1898.

88. Motet and Gorjeu were the founders, while the original directors included Jean Bonnardel, Motet, René Raoul-Duval, Denis Petitjean, Eugène Fontaine, Joseph Lamaizière, and Félix Block —a roll call of the group's leaders in Russia. A.N., 65 AQ, K 37, Sté Industrielle et Métallurgique du Caucase, Articles of Incorporation; *Cote de la Bourse et de la Banque,* 17–11–1897; *Science et Industrie* 10 (April 1924): 75–76.

89. C.L., Société Industrielle et Métallurgique du Caucase, confidential report from the company to the Crédit Lyonnais, December 1908; ibid., Etude, February 1913; A.N., 65 AQ, K 37, Annual Reports.

It is significant that this firm (the Caucasian Industrial and Metallurgical Company) formed another nodal point for further investment throughout the whole Caucasian area. In 1907 it participated in the Russo-Persian Company to investigate mineral deposits in northern Persia. The following year the firm's principal engineer was sent to examine a property at Zanguezour on the Russian side of the Persian frontier. A favorable technical report led to "a six month legal study by a group of lawyers to determine what was in fact for sale" and the purchase of a year option. Then a second group of engineers, including a French engineer with twenty years of Russian experience, carefully examined the property on the spot and recommended the subsequent purchase.[90] With various other mining concessions (including a renewed lease on the principal mine at Allah-Verdi), a syndicated and heavily protected domestic copper market, and "technical directors who have acquired thorough knowledge of mining conditions in the Caucasus," the group's Caucasian future appeared promising in 1914.[91]

One should not overlook the group's activities in Poland in the 1890s through its original pride and joy, the Huta-Bankova Steel Company. In 1897 the Huta bought most of the German Gesellschaft Graf Renard, one of the largest coal mines (700,000 tons in 1907) in the Dombrowa Basin. It also acquired the accompanying tube factory, also named Graf Renard.[92] In the late 1890s the Huta-Bankova bought four-fifths of the Franco-Russian Mining Company of Dombrowa, a coal company which had passed into

90. Ibid., Report to Special Meeting of Shareholders, 1911.
91. Ibid., Annual Report, 1914; C.L., Etude, February 1914.
92. A.N., F 12, no. 7275, d'Anglade, Voyage, June 1908.

the hands of German and Russian banks. In 1907, 2,000 workers were producing 150,000 tons of coal there in addition to 6,000 tons of zinc. That was half the total zinc output of Russian Poland.[93] Finally, the wholly owned Novoradomsk plant (1898) allowed the Huta to diversify further into specialized steel products, such as nails, wire, and roofing steel.

The Huta's directors and technicians managed these legally separate firms as a single unit to assure continued operations should their original lease not be renewed in 1912. The group saw clearly that the development of alternative producing units would serve as a useful bargaining tool in its lease negotiations. Years of discussions finally met with success, and the Huta-Bankova finally bought its original leasehold property in 1908, four years before expiration of the lease.

After 1900 the Bonnardel Group of associated firms and businessmen entered a period of consolidation and more gradual development of existing firms. The Dubovaia Balka, never as closely held, passed under the control of the French Société Générale's Makeevka Steel Company in 1912. The unfortunate machine-tool company merged with the Nikolaev Shipyards Company. On the other hand, the Berestov-Krinka Coal Company, which had been founded by the Sté de Rive-de-Gier (Loire) at Lyons in 1892, finally passed to the group in 1907 when it was reorganized with the help of the Crédit Industriel et Commercial.[94] In 1910 Donets Steel also bought more than one-half of Golubovka-Berestovo-Bogodukhovo, one of the few remaining major Russian-owned coal producers in the Donets.[95] But

93. Ibid.; *Le Pour et le Contre*, 2–10–1900.
94. C.L., Berestov-Krinka, Etudes, August 1898 and April 1912.
95. Ibid., Aciéries du Donetz, March 1911.

mainly the group expanded through its existing companies.[96]

In summary, the foundations of this prodigiously successful group were laid on a modest scale well before either Franco-Russian diplomatic realignment or Russian take-off in the early 1890s. The gradual elaboration of the original plan served as an invaluable training period during which entrepreneurs acquired Russian experience, contacts, and confidence. When rapid development began these entrepreneurs were well prepared to seize a multitude of interrelated, complementary opportunities without long or costly apprenticeship.

Second, entrepreneurship began with technical contribution. And the group's manager-engineers, formed by Western scientific instruction and Russian experience, continued to respond well to technical and managerial challenges. This accounts for much of the group's success.

Finally, the investment policy of the great French industrial bourgeoisie gave these firms a peculiar stamp. Wealthy but cautious capitalists used the most rigorous autofinancement to expand and retain control. Unloading of shares on the public for quick gain was atypical. Entrepreneurs normally wished to recover part of their initial commitment quickly through public sales. Having done so, however, they were willing to hold controlling interest indefinitely

96. In 1900 Jean Bonnardel and the group reorganized the Sté Industrielle du Platine, Russia's largest platinum producer, which had been founded in 1899 at Paris with a total capital of 32,000,-000 francs (22 in shares and 10 in bonds) by the Oppenheim Group. Bonnardel was chosen by Russian shareholders who held the vast majority of the "scandalously inflated" capital. Letter of 25–10–1900 from Baron du Marais of the Etudes Financières, Crédit Lyonnais, St. Petersburg, in Sté Industrielle du Platine, C.L. See various studies there also.

and allow reinvested profits to carry them for a long ride. Because initial investments were limited, capital increases rare, and dividends small, the group expanded rapidly in prosperity and stagnated in depression. Reinvested profits, or the lack of them, determined the rate of advance.

12

TOWARD PASSIVE INVESTMENT:
THE BANQUE DE L'UNION
PARISIENNE AND THE BOGATYR
RUBBER COMPANY
1910–1914

During the four years of prosperity before the First World War foreign entrepreneurs played a less crucial role than they had a half-generation earlier. Indeed, Russia was close to entrepreneurial self-sufficiency by 1914. She still lacked techniques and capital in comparison with western Europe, but she had businessmen who recognized industrial opportunity and who could draw together the factors of production, including hired foreign technicians and capital when necessary, for dynamic response. And increasingly able to direct their industrial development, Russian businessmen and technicians were quick to chafe at foreign tutelage. So quick, in fact, that in 1910 the French commercial attaché in St. Petersburg might have even considered Russian businessmen all more or less antiforeign, "just like the masses." Therefore he warned French industrialists "to secure all possible guarantees" before investing in Russia.[1] It is against this general background that the reorganization of the Bogatyr Rubber Company of Moscow in 1910 provides considerable insight into the evolving pattern of entrepreneurship in Russia before 1914.

1. A.N., F 30, no. 329, Les capitaux étrangers et l'opinion en Russie, dispatch to the Quai d'Orsay, 13-7-1910.

The Moscow Rubber Company, founded in 1887 by Moscow industrialists with a capital of 600,000 rubles, was bankrupt in all but name by 1910. A large loan of 1,000,000 rubles from the Moscow Union Bank was overdue and repayment was completely impossible.[2] This situation was potentially dangerous because the Moscow Union Bank was itself a bit unsteady. It had been formed only a few months before, in January 1909, as a merger of three faltering banks associated in part with the Poliakov family—the Bank of Orel, the Moscow International Bank, and the Bank of South Russia.[3]

The impending demise of the Moscow Rubber Company was also of considerable interest to a leading French investment bank, the Banque de l'Union Parisienne. The Banque de l'Union Parisienne had taken a large interest in the Moscow Union Bank by purchasing 5,000,000 rubles of common stock in early 1910 when the Moscow Union Bank's capital was doubled to 15,000,000 rubles. The B.U.P. had at that moment placed seven Frenchmen among the Russian bank's top administrators.[4] In doing so the

2. The archives of the Banque de l'Union Parisienne in Paris formed the principal source for this study. The dossiers Russie, nos. 153, 169, and 222, concerning the Société Moscovite de Caoutchouc, were essential. The Banque de l'Union Parisienne remains today, as in 1910, the second-ranking French investment bank after the Banque de Paris et des Pays-Bas.

3. Report of L. S. Poliakov to a special meeting of shareholders of the three banks (middle 1908), in A.N., F 30, no. 336, Banque de l'Union (Moscou), note of 19-5-1910.

4. Ibid., note to the Quai d'Orsay from St. Petersburg, 19-5-1910. Four Frenchmen were placed among the twelve-member Board of Directors (*Sovet*): Octave Homberg, president of the Banque de l'Union Parisienne, was named vice president, while Charles Wehrung, Philippe Vernes, and Brocard became directors. Three Frenchmen were also entered on the seven-man management team (the *Direction*, or *Pravlenie*) which actually directed the Moscow Bank: Paul Giraud, a leading silk manufacturer of long

B.U.P. was applying its policy of building a network
of financial affiliates to search for investment opportunities in poor but developing countries throughout the world.[5] The failing Russian rubber company
now provided—unavoidably—one such opportunity.

The Banque de l'Union Parisienne's first move
was to dispatch a specialist to Russia to examine the
existing plant and evaluate the possibility of complete technical and administrative reorganization.
In the ensuing detailed study the French engineer
Jung noted with satisfaction three positive factors:
the location of the plant ten kilometers south of
Moscow was excellent; the labor force, with low salaries and generally good disposition, was quite suitable; and the factories—one- to three-story brick
buildings—were in good condition. Unfortunately,
this exhausted the assets of the present company.

The level of industrial technology was woefully
low. "All work is done by hand and all the machines
normally used to make galoshes (the main product)
are lacking; a complete reorganization of production would be necessary."[6] Vulcanization, for example, "is carried out in ovens heated directly with
coke—a process that has been abandoned everywhere for a long time." Similarly, the manufacture
of tires for automobiles and bicycles was conducted
in a "very rudimentary fashion."[7]

---

standing in Moscow; Pierre Darcy, president of Prodamet and
Banque de l'Union Parisienne agent at St. Petersburg; and M.
Boutry, previously a ranking employee of the French Société
Générale's Northern Bank of St. Petersburg.

5. Affiliated banks were established in Argentina, Brazil, Cuba,
Haiti, Mexico, Bulgaria, Serbia, and Greece. Edmond Baldy, *Les
banques d'affaires en France depuis 1900* (Paris, 1922), pp. 165–
68; E. Kaufman, *La banque en France* (Paris, 1914), pp. 130–37.

6. B.U.P., Russie, no. 153, Société de Caoutchouc, C. Jung,
Rapport sur la Sté Moscovite pour la Fabrication d'Articles en
Caoutchouc, 17–5–1910.

7. Ibid.

Poor technique resulted in poor quality. Almost one-fourth of all galoshes were of second or third quality. This was an unacceptably high percentage. "With new steam-heated ovens seconds should not exceed 2 percent of total output—the maximum for a well-run production line."[8]

The present managers were obviously deficient in administrative skill. The technical personnel were poorly qualified and lacked energy and ability. Their colleagues in administration and sales were also "quite unable to do their duty," and there was a great deal of waste and petty graft, including undisguised padding of overhead expenses. New management, and particularly a vigorous and honest director, was therefore an absolutely necessary first step in any reorganization. "I shall never advise French capitalists to place one sou in this affair if you do not carry out a complete technical and managerial transformation, or if you fail to find a capable and honest director."[9] Effective investment required effective control.

There was a good possibility of impressive success, since there was no good reason for the many years of "detestable profits."[10] There was strong demand for galoshes—Russia's annual output exceeded thirty million pairs in 1913—and the small market for tires was shooting upward rapidly.[11] Galoshes were, in fact, "the only footwear of the poor classes, not only of Russia, but of all northern Europe. . . . They are the only Russian manufactured product that is exported in any quantity."[12]

There was also no doubt that the other Russian

8. Ibid.
9. Ibid.
10. Ibid.
11. C.L., Société des Usines Russo-Françaises de Caoutchouc "Provodnik," Etude, June 1913.
12. Ibid., Etudes, March and November 1911.

producers were extremely profitable. The older of the two, the Russo-American Rubber Company "Treugolnik," founded in 1860 at St. Petersburg, was paying dividends of 20 percent on its 18,000,000 rubles of capital and was in excellent financial condition.[13] The somewhat smaller Russo-French Rubber Company "Provodnik," founded at Riga in 1888 a year after the Moscow firm, had obtained even better results. Sales and profits had almost tripled over the last seven years, and demand was still unsatisfied as the firm worked at full capacity.[14] According to one excellent observer, Provodnik's equipment was very modern and the workers were competent and well directed.[15] With 5,000,000 francs for new equipment and a good director the Moscow firm might yet take this path.[16]

Following the Banque de l'Union Parisienne's approval by telegraph, Jung went on to negotiate the preliminary terms of the proposed reorganization with the chief creditor, the Union Bank of Moscow.[17] A new firm with a capital of 5,000,000 rubles, the Bogatyr Rubber Company of Moscow (really the Hercules Rubber Company of Moscow), would take all the assets of the existing company, whose shareholders would accept a 90 percent loss. The State Bank would accept 600,000 rubles in shares for its loans, while the Banque de l'Union Parisienne and the Moscow Union Bank would underwrite the bulk

13. C.L., Société de la manufacture russo-americaine de caoutchouc "Treougolnik," Etudes, November 1911 and April 1914.

14. C.L., Société des Usines Russo-Françaises de Caoutchouc "Provodnik," Etude, June 1913. Production of tires for automobiles increased 1,000 percent (to 2,700 tires per year) from 1906 to 1911 at this firm.

15. Ibid., Etudes, November 1911 and June 1913.

16. B.U.P., Jung, Rapport.

17. B.U.P., Russie, no. 153, Procès-Verbal de Séance du Pravlenie de la Banque de l'Union de Moscou, 3–5–1910.

of the new capital issue.[18] The Banque de l'Union Parisienne was guaranteed the right to choose the commercial and technical personnel which Jung had felt was so important for success.

The French bank made serious efforts to improve techniques and to secure capable managers for the reorganized company. It helped negotiate a contract with a Swedish rubber company for technical aid.[19] The Swedish firm agreed to furnish technical know-how for ten years and to install modern equipment capable of a daily output of 12,000 pairs of galoshes. The technical consultant also promised to share all its technical improvements in the future in return for sliding fees based on Bogatyr's production. The processes obtained from the Swedish firm improved quality and cut costs because cheap old galoshes could now be mixed with expensive pure gutta-percha as a raw material.

The choice of a technical director was satisfactory, if less brilliant. A thirty-two-year-old French engineer named Marchandise, previously an engineer at the Société Industrielle des Téléphones of Paris, learned his job quickly. Unfortunately, he lacked previous training in either the rubber industry or Russia. Although initially willing, he was not completely able to infuse the new firm's management with perseverance and dedication.[20]

For the old slipshod habits remained, or so the

18. The final arrangements saw old shareholders receiving 3,310 shares, the State Bank 6,600 shares (guaranteed at par for three years), 1,875 shares each to the Banque de l'Union Parisienne and the National Bank für Deutschland, while the Union Bank of Moscow and associates—including the B.U.P.—took 39,340, of which at least 10,000 were for old debts to the Moscow Bank. B.U.P., Russie, no. 153, report from Kasse, B.U.P. representative on Bogatyr's Board of Directors, 10–4–1912.

19. Ibid.

20. Ibid.

French believed. The Russian commercial director, formerly a rubber merchant, was allegedly unsatisfactory and quite incapable of calculating his costs of production.[21] Yet he remained as director despite French protests. And Russian managers and directors were apparently as prodigal as ever, and they received fees and sinecures three times the necessary amount. This exaggeration of directors' fees reflected upon Count Tatishchev, the president of the Moscow Union Bank, as well as Bogatyr Rubber, and indicated the somewhat strained relations between the French and Russian banks.

There were other sources of friction. The French group preferred large amortizations and no immediate dividends, while Count Tatishchev leaned toward early cash payouts. Thus during 1912 he spread rumors of dividends in 1913 to spur speculation. This drew a sharp rebuke from his stern French associate in Moscow as being "clearly impossible. I told him we must first make large amortizations no matter what the profits might be."[22] At the same time the count himself reproached his French associates for dragging their feet on increases of capital (to 6,500,000 rubles in 1911 and to 10,000,000 in 1913) which he asserted were necessary.

Not least, there was a conflict of wills on daily managerial decisions between Count Tatishchev and Boutry, the B.U.P.'s representative. "Boutry—a nervous type—is too sharp sometimes, particularly towards the count whom one leads more effectively with reasoning and a more cordial exchange of views."[23] In short, this was hardly the way to treat

21. Three penciled exclamation points in the margin of Kasse's report to the Banque de l'Union Parisienne express French financial orthodoxy's horrified reaction to such profane practice.

22. B.U.P., Russie, no. 153, report from Kasse, 10–4–1912.

23. Ibid.

the minister of finance's handpicked choice for the presidency of the largest bank in Moscow,[24] a man who had already made an estimated 400,000 rubles on the rubber company's reorganization for his bank.[25]

Moreover, by 1912 the Banque de l'Union Parisienne had relinquished any effective control or any hopes of effective control over the Moscow Union Bank. While the French bank had sold its shares, worth 5,000,000 rubles, to the French public, the Moscow Bank had raised its total capital from 15,000,000 rubles to 22,500,000 rubles and contemplated yet another capital increase to 30,000,000 rubles.[26] This occurred in 1912.[27] A large part of this capital was raised in Russia, and by the end of 1913 it was authoritatively estimated that only 30 percent of the shares of the Union Bank of Moscow were in France—and few of those were still with the Banque de l'Union Parisienne.[28] This erosion of direct influence undoubtedly reduced the force of French remonstrations concerning Bogatyr.

It was against this background of increasing friction and decreasing influence that Count Tatishchev learned at the beginning of 1912 that the Banque de l'Union had sold on the St. Petersburg Stock Exchange about one-third of its original subscription of Bogatyr at 130 rubles, or 30 percent above the price of subscription.[29] The count, engrossed in

24. A.N., F 30, no. 336, note of 19–5–1910.

25. B.U.P., Russie, no. 153, letter, Kasse to Homberg, 10–4–1912.

26. A.N., F 30, no. 336, notes of 19–5–1910 and 15–6–1910 from mission in St. Petersburg to Quai d'Orsay; note from le Syndic des Agents de Change, 14–4–1911.

27. A.N., F 30, no. 336, note of 20–6–1912.

28. Ibid., Extrait du procès-verbal de la séance du 8–12–1913 de la Commission des Valeurs Mobilières.

29. B.U.P., Russie, no. 153, note of 28–2–1913.

whipping up speculation on the St. Petersburg Exchange, did not appreciate this sale. A bit peevishly he offered to buy the French bank's remaining shares for his bank's account. Kasse, accustomed to working with this strong-minded Russian partner, feared an impending and perhaps inevitable rupture. Therefore he advised Homberg and the Banque de l'Union Parisienne to accept this offer.[30]

They did, and the Paris bank's evanescent leadership of Bogatyr ended. After April 1912 the Banque de l'Union Parisienne's only remaining financial involvement was its 5 percent interest in the Moscow Union Bank's syndicate for the management and eventual sale of Bogatyr shares. The French bank's future role as far as Bogatyr was concerned was clearly that of middleman between the Russian entrepreneur and the French rentier.

In October 1913 the Bogatyr Rubber Company increased its capital a third time, to 10,000,000 rubles from 6,500,000 rubles.[31] The Moscow Union Bank owned approximately 40,000 shares of Bogatyr common stock before this increase, and only 25,000 shares were in public hands. Of the 35,000 new shares offered in October 1913, less than 1,000 were subscribed by old stockholders at 117 rubles per share. Thus the Moscow Union Bank's syndicate was required to take 34,000 shares, which brought its total holdings to approximately 75,000 shares representing an investment of more than 7,500,000 rubles.[32]

This was indeed investment banking, and with a vengeance. The Moscow Union Bank was the only major participant in the underwriting syndicate for

30. Ibid., Kasse to Homberg, 10–4–1912.
31. Ibid., no. 169, note of March 1913.
32. Ibid., no. 222, Augmentation de capital, October 1913.

Bogatyr shares. On the other hand, the Banque de l'Union Parisienne retained only its previous 5 percent share in the future profits and losses of this syndicate. And, as was its practice, the B.U.P. ceded half of this small commitment to closely allied private bankers of the *haute banque parisienne*. The French bank's only active involvement now was the handling of all details required to list and sell Bogatyr shares on the Paris Stock Exchange.

The reorganization of the Bogatyr Rubber Company provides a striking illustration of the evolution of entrepreneurial leadership in Russian industry during the pre-1914 boom. One must conclude that the junior partner, the Union Bank of Moscow, had become the senior partner in this venture in just three short years. The Banque de l'Union Parisienne was apparently decisive in the reorganization of this potentially brilliant enterprise—the third-ranking Russian rubber company—but afterward it was unable to control such elementary matters as the selection of the commercial manager or the firm's financial policy. Thus unable to direct Bogatyr effectively, this second-ranking French investment bank preferred to yield to the independently minded Russians and to liquidate its investment in the rubber company, as in the Russian bank itself. Subsequently the French bank would maximize profits and minimize risks simply as Bogatyr's emissary to the French public.

Two other bits of information indicate that Russian agents were now crucial for Bogatyr's destiny, just as Russian entrepreneurs were increasingly the effective leaders of the Russian economy. First, Count Tatishchev was financing the researches of a Moscow chemist, Professor Ostromyslenskii, who claimed to have been successful in his quest for synthetic rubber. According to this professor, it was only a question of choosing the best industrial method for mass production in 1913. This not only shows that the technology gap had decreased appreciably in twenty years but also that in a few areas Russians were beginning to pioneer in industrial techniques. Naturally most of Count Tatishchev's great interest in Ostromyslenskii's research stemmed from the speculative enthusiasm this carefully leaked news generated on the St. Petersburg Stock Exchange, where Bogatyr was becoming a speculative favorite.

This leads to the second point, which is at least as important as the first. For the first time Russian entrepreneurs had the invaluable aid of highly developed *domestic* financial institutions with their great banks, stock markets, speculators, brokers and rentiers. In such circumstances a Russian entrepreneur could increasingly shrug off the admonishments of the stern old French uncle, while still paying him an occasional visit—with palm outstretched.

13

CONCLUSION

In many ways the most original aspect of the Russian scheme for economic development in the 1890s and after was its emphasis on direct foreign investment. This was the distinctive Russian addition to the standard nineteenth-century mix of railroads, tariff protection, and state patronage shared by continental followers in the industrialization process. From this point of view Russia anticipated some contemporary developing countries, but not in the way usually imagined. The stress on massive inflows of foreign investment had little to do with those contemporary strategies of development based on planning, autarchy, and state production. How successful then was this pioneering Russian experiment, and what conclusions are relevant today?

Our general conclusion is that foreign entrepreneurs played an important and beneficial role in Russia's relatively successful industrialization. One note of qualification is necessary, however. Russian development was essentially capitalistic during this period despite "feudal remnants." Therefore it shared the much-debated general virtues and faults of capitalism, both as an economic system of development and as a basis for a whole society. And one's ultimate judgment of foreign entrepreneurs in Russia is probably closely related to his general conception of capitalism. Perhaps my implicit position should be made explicit.

I began this study with a view of capitalism as an economic system derived largely from Joseph

Schumpeter.[1] I emerged from my efforts more strongly convinced of the essential validity of Schumpeter's analysis of capitalism and of its great ability to develop an economy, when it is permitted to do so. As far as forming the basis for a society is concerned, this requires a value judgment of what Schumpeter called the "civilization of capitalism." As a personal judgment, the civilization of capitalism seems to me to have been superior to most alternative interlocking social and economic systems which have existed historically. As such, it is quite acceptable, although not necessarily always the most desirable by any means. With this in mind, we may group our findings under three specific contributions.

First, foreign entrepreneurs provided and mobilized missing capital needed for industrialization. It would be facetious to suggest that the inflow of foreign capital, which accounted for roughly one-half of all new investment in industrial corporations during this period, was due only to noneconomic deficiencies in Russian business, government, and society. Such deficiencies there were, and in abundance. But contemporary observers were right in believing that Russia was a *poor* country with enormous untapped natural and human resources. And with their capital foreign entrepreneurs could and did hire these resources and put them to work.

Foreign entrepreneurs also mobilized capital to be found in Russia for their ventures, particularly in the 1890s. To exactly what extent, it is impossible to say. But the frequency of this pattern strongly indicates that foreign enterprise served as a useful intermediary between domestic savings and domes-

1. Particularly *Capitalism, Socialism and Democracy*, 3d. ed. (New York, 1950).

tic investment opportunities. By linking savings and investment, foreign entrepreneurs reduced the level of frustrated savings or misdirected savings and developed investment ability.

A second contribution was the implantation of advanced techniques in several key industries. Advanced technology was in fact at the heart of the foreign investment strategy. Foreigners generally had a very low opinion of Russian industrial technique, and they were quick to assume that deviations from accepted practices in western Europe were inexcusable. Retrograde techniques would lead neither to substantial profits, nor would they follow pure engineering rationale calling for the best proved method. Alternative technologies to those in use in home plants were rarely considered. Either technical indivisibilities, or perhaps more importantly, psychological rigidities in the minds of competent foreign engineers, fixed the size and sophistication of the projected plant in the preliminary study. Subsequently a west-European plant, slightly modified at the most, was judged feasible and built, or the entire matter was dropped. After advanced plants were completed in Russia, foreigners did make minor modifications in the direction of economizing on increasingly expensive capital with more intensive use of cheap labor. But they modified their plants only slightly. The Russian experience suggests that most discussion concerning the use of less advanced, and thus more labor-intensive, practices in poorer lands has limited practical significance for foreign entrepreneurs. Their busy engineers simply do not think this way. The best is good enough for them.

This helps explain the excellent technology employed by the average foreign firm. The technology was excellent because it was only slightly inferior to that found in the most modern plants of western Europe and because it surpassed that of native Russian enterprises by a wide margin. The foreign entrepreneur showed this outstanding technology best in metallurgy, especially between the years 1895 and 1900, during which he was far ahead of his Russian counterpart and in the mainstream of west-European achievement. The techniques employed in coal mining were almost as impressive. In washing, sorting, and coking of coal, as well as in ventilation, electrification, and centralization of mines, west-European entrepreneurs were in the lead. The metal-processing plants, like Hartmann or Nikolaev Shipyards, which were built near the new southern steel complexes, were often the leaders in their respective fields. They forced the pace of technical adaptation for established Russian-owned producers in the older industrial areas. The technology employed by foreigners in electrical and chemical industries, in which German entrepreneurship was particularly vigorous, was sufficient for the complete domination of these advanced industries in Russia.

It is significant that foreign businessmen were not necessarily the first to apply a given process or innovation standing on the technological frontier of their particular industry—certain Russian-owned firms like the Briansk Ironworks Company were also on that frontier—but that foreigners as a group applied the advanced techniques universally. The consistency of their adoption meant that what might have remained isolated or exceptional very quickly became the usual situation in industries dominated by foreigners. It seems certain that foreign entrepreneurship thus accelerated the diffusion of advanced technique through key Russian industries.

This accelerated diffusion was one of the foreigner's greatest achievements in Russia.

Perhaps an equally noteworthy achievement was reaching costs of production that compared fairly well with those in western Europe, at least in metallurgy and in coal mining. Modern equipment and competent technical management obtained enviable costs of production in Russia as elsewhere. At the same time foreigners generally used only proved techniques and avoided risky experimentation. They surmised quite correctly that implantation of accepted industrial practice was sufficiently challenging.

Russia lacked adequate entrepreneurship as well as capital and technology on the eve of rapid industrialization. It was in this area that foreign enterprise made its third contribution. With a different mentality, formed by a different cultural and historical experience, foreign businessmen reacted positively to the exciting challenge of economic development in the 1890s. In doing so they helped infuse a missing dynamism and growth outlook into Russia. The concentration upon and creation of a whole new industrial area in southern Russia was one indication of this dynamism. The pioneering role of foreigners in several new industries holding the greatest challenge and growth potential was another. So also was their systematic reinvestment of profits, best seen in the Bonnardel Group, which showed a desirable long-term commitment. The foreigner did not seek simply to milk an enterprise and then run. In short, aggressive foreign entrepreneurship made the Russian government's hope of rapid economic development a reality at the end of the nineteenth century.

Nor was this all. Effective foreign investment

ability helped create a larger and better supply of local entrepreneurship, and the cooperative factors that went with it. In the long run this was probably as important as initial foreign leadership. More and better local entrepreneurship was in part a natural consequence of a larger and more rapidly expanding modern sector. Nothing begets interest in opportunity like opportunity itself. But specific foreign contributions stand out. The formation of local managers who were substituted for foreign executives and engineers provided a pool of ready talent. More rapid formation of a more adequate labor force by means of larger investments in social facilities, notably housing, helped break the bottleneck of labor supply. In the last analysis the ever increasing recourse to local management and labor may be seen as examples of the foreigner's powerful economic rationality. The foreigner's unprejudiced and highly rational employment of Jewish and Polish personnel was only one indication of a more intelligent use of Russia's human resources.

A comparison of the relative performances of foreign and local businessmen in the late 1890s and before World War I shows how rapidly and to what extent foreign enterprise was emulated and even superseded. After about 1908 the great Russian banks took the lead in the investment process. They tracked down opportunities, organized preliminary studies, and tapped foreign capital and technical know-how themselves. At the same time specific Russian-owned-and-operated industrial corporations gave evidence of the same maturity, as their huckstering of their securities in western Europe itself showed. In some cases foreign businessmen were not even sure of maintaining control of their original ventures. In short, the ultimate tribute to foreign entrepreneurs was that they forced and encouraged imitation and bought their own relative decline.

These, then, are aspects of successful foreign impact upon the Russian economy. But in the last analysis how is one to explain this success? Two related underlying conditions provide much of the answer.

In the first place, Russia was an independent sovereign nation. There was never that imbalance of power in the foreigner's favor which Professor Landes argues is the mainspring of imperialism and exploitation.[2] Within Russia itself any imbalance was clearly in the state's favor. In minor skirmishes or major showdowns between the state and foreign business the state ultimately held the whip hand. The state could and did enforce its laws and regulations. In these circumstances economic gain depended upon economic performance. Therefore the looting, exploitation, and draining, which might conceivably have occurred in a politically weak and defenseless Russia and did occur on occasion in colonial areas where European governments and businessmen could use coercion, was simply impossible. On the whole foreign enterprise understood this and acted accordingly. Profit in Russia varied with skill in business, and not with talent for banditry or extortion.

This helps explain why international political factors were always a secondary consideration for foreign businessmen. We noted that the origins of the principal French groups are found well before the Franco-Russian rapprochement. Belgian businessmen quite rightly had no illusions about using diplomatic pressure to control the Russian administra-

2. David S. Landes, "Some Thoughts on the Nature of Economic Imperialism," *Journal of Economic History* 21 (1961) : 496–511.

tion. German investment grew steadily in certain technically advanced industries, independently of the nature of Russo-German relations. The English surge into the petroleum industry in the late 1890s coincided with bitter political quarrels and public recriminations. Effective Russian sovereignty determined and administered fairly uniformly the rules of business activity. Foreign enterprise was never a law unto itself.

The power to control foreign excesses was crucial, but it was negative and static. It does not account for the close ties that existed between foreign and local forces within specific firms. The allegedly foreign firm often concealed active cooperation between foreign and Russian elements at some point. Our analysis of company promotion, management, capital, and state relations uncovered this cooperative effort time and again. Sometimes the foreign firms rested on concessions, projects, or markets presented by a Russian promoter or bureaucrat. Some firms, like the Huta-Bankova Steel Company or the Nikopol-Mariupol Metallurgical Company, were really management contracts under which foreigners furnished skilled management and technical competence while wealthy Russians provided much of the necessary capital. But whatever the nature, chronology, and extent of association, the majority of foreign firms were, or came to be, partnerships. They united foreign and local forces in the pursuit of common objectives.

The existence of this partnership, and the word is used advisedly, is the second reason for the successful foreign impact. A partnership involves cooperation and mutual advantage—the opposite of exploitation with its coercion and injustice. Foreign investment was seldom enclave investment carefully sealed off from the local society and economy. It produced for the domestic market, used local resources, and employed local personnel. This meant that foreign enterprise stimulated dormant Russian potential and then allowed that potential to develop dynamically. This enabled local forces to play an ever larger role and to be graduated from junior to senior partner in some firms by 1914.

Partnership was equally valuable from the foreigner's point of view. In independent Russia, with its own language, customs, and laws, local participation was necessary to cope with a myriad of nontechnical questions. This meant that the foreigner's effectiveness varied more or less directly with his ability to find and create Russian competence to complement his own expertise. The best entrepreneurs knew this from the beginning. The others learned after an expensive lesson or two. Private foreign profit and Russian public benefit were mutually interdependent.

Our findings seem to have relevance to contemporary problems. History is in part didactic. The Russian experience suggests that strategies of development based on market economies can use large-scale private foreign investment to help meet the challenge of industrial revolution. Witte's Russia could do so because the international supply of entrepreneurship, capital, and know-how was very great and highly responsive to new profit opportunities. There are certainly contrary trends in today's world— fears of investing in underdeveloped countries, pressures to limit the export of capital, etc.—and they should not be underestimated. But the development of international corporations, the enormous resources of the world's wealthier countries, and the proliferation of industrialized countries would seem to offset the negative factors. Foreign entrepreneurship is available to aid the development of market economies. Whether it will be allowed to do so is another question.

As far as foreign businessmen are concerned, the Russian experience suggests that partnership is also a profitable, probably the most profitable, arrangement. This enables the direct investor to maximize his technical and managerial advantages, which can bring large entrepreneurial gain, and to minimize the pitfalls of an alien culture. At the same time foreign businessmen are probably wise to avoid forcing their services on hostile governments. (A certain amount of public hostility is probably inevitable, although not particularly important, as the Russian case suggests.) Effective foreign entrepreneurship must probably rest upon a valid if implicit contract involving the consent of both host and guest. Without such an agreement on the rules of the game, neither the dynamic possibilities of relatively free market economies are tapped nor are very good investments made.

In the best circumstances foreign entrepreneurial success has its limitations. Success is based on a definite but clearly limited superiority in industrial technology and in effective organization of that technology. This is both a great deal and very little. The foreign entrepreneur may indeed hasten technical modernization and industrial growth—keys to material abundance. But he has limited influence upon the great options and decisions of a society. The foreigner's feeling of impotence in the face of internal Russian disturbances and conflicts before 1914 is profoundly revealing. Those knotty larger problems of national aspirations and culture, of the just society, and of balanced human progress are not solved by the foreigner's exact science, as the intricacies of blast-furnace construction certainly are.

APPENDIX

Names of most foreign-affiliated enterprises in Russian industry have been translated into English for convenience,
and then often used in abbreviated form. Because of the
number and importance of firms in the steel and coal industries, however, more complete data are required to assure proper identification in the text. The material in the
following list should do this, and it should also aid the interested reader in pursuit of a particular firm in secondary
works and documentary collections. The items given include
full name, year of incorporation, legal corporate nationality,
name of factory or mine, and group affiliation. A good index
of important enterprises is found in Ak. Nauk SSSR, *Materialy*, 6:776–99.

Steel Industry

Briansk Ironworks Company
> Brianskogo rel'soprokatnogo, zhelezodelatel'nogo i
> mekhanicheskogo zavod ob-vo; Russian, 1873. Original
> steel and later railway division at Bezhitsa, Orel prov-
> ince; southern mill (Aleksandrovskii Yuzhno-Rossiiskii
> zavod) at Ekaterinoslav, Ekaterinoslav province, be-
> gan 1887.

Donets Steel Company at Druzhkovka
> Donetskoe ob-vo zhelezodelatel'nogo i staleliteinogo
> proizvodstv v Druzhkovke; Russian, 1892. Steel mills
> at Druzhkovka, Ekaterinoslav province. Subsidiary of
> the Huta-Bankova Steel Company; Bonnardel Group.

Donets-Yur'evka Metallurgical Company
> Donets-Yur'evskoe metallurgicheskoe ob-vo; Russian,
> 1895. Alchev, Ekaterinoslav province.

Huta-Bankova Steel Company
> Société des Forges et Aciéries de Huta-Bankova;
> French, 1877. Steel mill (Dombrovskii zavod) in tsar-
> ist Poland, Pietrkow province; Bonnardel Group.

Kama Steel Company

Société des Forges et Aciéries de la Kama; French, reorganized 1884. Steel works in Urals, Perm province, Ekaterinburg district.

Konstantinovka Sheet Mills Company (Donets)

Société des Tôleries de Konstantinovka (Donetz); Belgian, 1897. Specialized steel and later pig-iron producer; Konstantinovka, Ekaterinoslav province.

Kramatorskaia Metallurgical Company

Kramatorskoe metallurgicheskoe ob-vo; Russian, 1899. Specialized pig-iron producer at Kramatorskaia, Kharkov province.

Krivoi-Rog Iron Company

Société des Minerais de fer de Krivoi-Rog; French, 1880. Purchased concessions from Alexander Pol'; principally mining company, but limited production of pig iron also.

Makeevka Steel Company

Société des Hauts fourneaux, Forges, et Aciéries en Russie, à Makeevka; French, 1896. Steel mill (Makeevskii zavod) at Makeevka, Don Territory. Founded by the Société Générale of France, and key holding of that bank's portfolio company, the Omnium Russe (Société Générale d'Industrie Minière et Métallurgique en Russie [Omnium]). Affiliated with the Makeevka Coal Company. Both Makeevka companies leased to a new holding company, the Union Minière et Métallurgique de Russie, in 1910.

Moscow Metal Works (Goujon)

Moskovskogo metallicheskogo zavoda (Goujon) t-vo; Russian, 1883. Steel producer and fabricator at Moscow.

New Russia Ironworks Company

English; founded by John Hughes in 1870. Steel mill and coal mines (Yuzovskii or Novorossiiskii zavod) at Yuzovo, Ekaterinoslav province.

Nikopol-Mariupol Mining and Metallurgical Company

Nikopol'-Mariupol'skoe gornoe i metallurgicheskoe ob-vo; Russian, 1896. Steel and pipe works at Mariupol, five versts from the Sea of Azov.

Russo-Belgian Metallurgical Company
Russko-Bel'giiskoe metallurgicheskoe ob-vo; Russian,
1895. Steel mill and coal mines (Petrovskii zavod),
Petrovskaia, Ekaterinoslav province. Founded prima-
rily by the Société Générale de Belgique with the tech-
nical assistance of Aciéries d'Angleur and Société des
Outils de Saint-Léonard.
Russian Providence Company
Société de la Providence Russe; 1897, Marchienne-au-
Pont, Belgium. Steel mill (Sartanskii zavod) on the Sea
of Azov at Sartana, Mariupol district, Ekaterinoslav
province. Founded by the Société belge des Laminoirs,
Hauts fourneaux, Forges, Fonderies et Usines de la
Providence; reorganized by the Banque de l'Union
Parisienne.
South Russian Dnieper Metallurgical Company
Yuzhno-Russkoe Dneprovskoe metallurgicheskoe ob-vo;
Russian, 1888. Principal steel mills (Kamenskii zavod)
at Kamenskoe, Catherine Railroad, near Ekaterinoslav,
Ekaterinoslav province. Generally known as Dneprovs-
koe ob-vo in Russian sources and as Société Dniépro-
vienne in French sources. Founded by Société John
Cockerill and the Warsaw Steel Company (also known
as Praga, or Ob-vo Lil'pop, Rau, i Levenstein).
Taganrog Metallurgical Company
Taganrogskoe metallurgicheskoe ob-vo; Russian, 1896.
Steel mill on the Sea of Azov at Taganrog, Ekaterinoslav province; iron mines on the Kerch Peninsula. Purchased bankrupt Kerch Metallurgical Company from
the State Bank in 1913.
Tula Blast Furances Company
Société des Hauts fourneaux de Toula (Russie Centrale) ; Belgium, 1895. Operated blast furnaces in Tula
province; founded by Société Métallurgique
d'Espérance-Longdoz; in administration 1902; bankrupt 1912. Société des Laminoirs en Russie Centrale,
1899, affiliated firm.
Ural-Volga Metallurgical Company
Société Métallurgique de l'Oural Volga; French, 1896.
Steel mill (Tsaritsynskii zavod) on the Volga River at

Tsaritsyn, Saratov province. Original blast furnaces and iron mines in Urals ceded to separate company in 1900; in administration, 1901–11; leased to the Donets-Yur'evka Metallurgical Company with option to buy in 1911; Banque de l'Union Parisienne Group.

Coal Industry

Almaznaia Coal Company
Société pour l'exploitation des Charbonnages du Centre du Donetz (Almaznaia); Belgian, 1894. Founded by Société John Cockerill; first coal mines (Maksimov); pig-iron producer 1898. Leased and then purchased by the South Russian Dnieper Metallurgical Company.

Belaia Coal Company
Société des Charbonnages de Bielaia; Brussels, Belgium, 1896. Mining properties on Belaia River, north Donets, Ekaterinoslav province. Central firm of Carez Group, which included Société des Hauts fourneaux de Bielaia, 1899.

Berestov-Krinka Coal Company
Société Franco-Russe des Houillères de Berestov-Krinka; 1892, Lyons, France. Near Makeevka, Taganrog district, Don Territory. Founded by Société de Rive-de-Gier.

Ekaterinovka Coal Mining Company
Ekaterinovskoe gornopromyshlennoe ob-vo; Russian, 1895. Mines in Taganrog district, Don Territory; Bonnardel Group.

General Coal Company
Cie Générale de Charbonnages; Brussels, Belgium, 1900. Portfolio company holding all shares of Donetskoe kamennougol'noe t-vo Korenev i Shipilov. E. de Sinçay and associates dominant after 1901.

Gosudarev-Bairak Coal Company
Société des Charbonnages, Mines et Usines de Gosoudariev-Bairak; Belgium, 1899. Near Makeevka, Taganrog district, Don Territory; Cislet Group.

Irmino Coal Company
Société Houillère d'Irmino; Belgian, 1900. Northern

Donets, Debal'tsev-Popasnaia Railroad, Irmino stattion. Part of Sinçay's South Russian Rock Salt and Coal Company Group by 1912.

Lugan Coal Company

Société des Charbonnages de la Lougan, Donetz; Belgian, 1895. Northeastern Donets. Became Charbonnages Réunies du Nord-Donetz à Marievka, 1905; liquidated 1908.

Makeevka Coal Company

Russkoe Donetskoe ob-vo kamennougol'noi i zavodskoi promyshlennosti; Russian, 1895. Makeevka, on the Southern Railroad, Don Territory. Founded by the Länderbank with Société Générale of France cooperation. Leased to Union Minière et Métallurgique de Russie in 1910.

Pobedenko Coal Company

Société des Charbonnages de Pobedenko; Belgian, 1898. Mines in Riazan province, south of Moscow; tie to Omnium Russe and Société Générale of France. Largest coal company in Moscow region.

Prokhorov Coal Company

Société des Charbonnages Prokhorov; Belgium, 1895. Founded by F. Schmatzer; reorganized 1906.

Rutchenko Coal Company

Société Minière et Industrielle de Routchenko; Belgian, 1897. Successor to operations begun by Société Générale of France in 1873. Sold by the Société Générale's Omnium Russe to Briansk Metallurgical in 1912.

Rykovskii Coal Company

Société des Charbonnages de Rykovskii; Belgium, 1898. Near Yuzovo, Bakhmut district, Ekaterinoslav province; merged with Ekaterinovka Coal Mining Company in 1905.

South Russian Coal Company (Gorlovka)

Yuzhno-Russkoi kamennougol'noi promyshlennosti ob-vo; Russian, 1872. Korsun mines, Gorlovka, on Catherine Railroad. Founded by Samuel Poliakov; Banque Internationale de Paris controlled after 1891. Known as Société de l'Industrie Houillère de la Russie Méridionale in France.

South Russian Rock Salt and Coal Company
    Société des Sels Gemmes et Houilles de la Russie
    Méridionale; French, 1883. Originally salt producer;
    coal and salt after 1896. Founded and administered by
    the Sinçay brothers.

Varvaropol Coal Company
    Société des Charbonnages de Varvaropol; Belgium,
    1895. In Ekaterinoslav province; merged with contig-
    uous Petro-Marievka Coal Company in 1912; Delloye
    and François families supplied principal founders and
    directors.

BIBLIOGRAPHY

1. Private Archives

Archives du Crédit Lyonnais (C.L.), Paris
This extraordinarily rich source was of the greatest
value for this study. Approximately 125 dossiers were
examined, almost all of which dealt with a single
corporation in Russia. These dossiers contain published
materials—annual reports, press clippings, articles of
incorporation, brochures, etc.—plus unpublished,
highly confidential studies of the Crédit Lyonnais's
Etudes Financières division in Russia centered at St.
Petersburg. (The Crédit Lyonnais was the only foreign
bank ever permitted in tsarist Russia.) These reports
sometimes run to 150 double-spaced typewritten
pages, and the most important firms have several over
a period of years. Almost all of these studies were made
by the engineers Du Marais, Waton, and Blanc. Their
work followed the bank's common, standardized pattern of exhaustive technical and financial probing of
corporations.
Banque de l'Union Parisienne (B.U.P.), Paris
An important source for this study because of its extensive activities in Russia, the archives of the Banque
de l'Union Parisienne contain 381 separate dossiers on
Russian industrial and financial operations. Those concerned with industry were carefully scrutinized; some
of those dealing with financial and underwriting operations were quickly examined.
Comptoir National d'Escompte de Paris (C.N.E.P.), Paris
One important dossier on the Rykovskii Coal Company
was examined in great detail, and it provided key
material for chapter 10. The Rykovskii Coal Company
was apparently this bank's most important Russian
promotion.
Crédit Industriel et Commercial (C.I.C.), Paris
There is probably more material of considerable interest than the two slim dossiers on the Czelade and

Berestov-Krinka Coal Companies which were examined. Apparently most of the old documents still await classification and therefore remain in an almost unusable state.

Forges de la Providence (Providence MSS), Marchienne-au-Pont, Belgium.

The minutes of the Board of Directors of the Russian Providence Company and assorted technical studies were placed at my disposal. The building housing all other records of the Russian Providence Company was blown up during the invasion of 1940. Records at the Banque de l'Union Parisienne stated that all the firm's archives in southern Russia were lost completely; the unused backs of corporate record pages in Russia made ideal stationery during the tragic period following 1917.

2. Public Archives

Archives Nationales (A.N.), Paris
Série AD 21
This series contains annual reports which were used to fill in occasional gaps in the 65 AQ Series.
Série 65 AQ
These archives of the Agents de Changes (Association Nationale des Porteurs des Valeurs Mobilières) were extremely valuable. Dossiers are organized by corporation with annual reports, articles of incorporation, brochures, and press clippings on the given company filed together. The researcher is thus able to cull almost all contemporary articles on more than two thousand companies (I studied about two hundred) drawn from most of the financial presses, great and small. (The more important financial periodicals encountered in this archival source are listed in part 4 of this bibliography.) This archival source complemented that of the Crédit Lyonnais.
Série F 12
These archives consist of copies of dispatches on com-

mercial relations from France's diplomatic representatives. The relevant dossiers were nos. 6351, 6594–6602, 6834[2,3], 7014, 7172–76.

Série F, 30

These archives emanated from the Direction du Mouvement Générale des Fonds, a section of the Ministry of Finance. When a foreign company sought to list its stock on the Paris Exchange, the company was required to furnish this bureau with detailed information on the firm. The opinion of France's diplomatic representatives was also sought. This source contains documents of great value for the economic history of foreign countries. Dossiers utilized were nos. 328–45 and 1091. Nos. 328–29 and 340–45 were particularly valuable.

Archives du Ministère des Affaires Etrangers (A.E., Brussels), Brussels

The relevant dossiers, arranged topically, are:

No. 164/2: Revolutions de 1905 et 1908

No. 2818: Tramways

No. 2900: Placements de capitaux en Russie

No. 2901, secs. 1–3: Chantiers navals, éclairage, gaz, mines

No. 2901, secs. 4–6: Aciéries, charbonnages

No. 2902: Industries diverses

No. 2904: Troubles sociaux, 1900–1908

No. 2905: Commerciale expansion

No. 2906: Syndicats

No. 2907: Mines et usines du Sud URSS

No. 2908, sec. 1–3: Russie: 1838–1908

No. 3646: Sté John Cockerill

Ancien 4417: Rapports des Boursiers

Archives du Ministère des Affaires Etrangères (Quai d'Orsay), Paris (A.E., Paris)

The consular correspondence regarding Russia, which is well catalogued and easily accessible, was carefully skimmed after exhausting the F 12 Series at the Archives Nationales. There is some duplication, but one finds numerous pieces which exist only at the Quai d'Orsay or (apparently) in the F 12 Series. Principal volumes examined included Russie, vols. 12–14, 20–55; Russie, N. S., nos. 51–76.

Ecole des Mines, Paris
  Seven studies by graduating seniors on Russian mining technique were examined. Four were excellent and very helpful.

3. Government Publications and Documentary Collections

FRANCE

Ministère des Affaires Etrangères. *La fortune française à l'étranger en 1902.* Paris, 1903.
Ministère des Affaires Etrangeres, Direction des Affaires Commerciales et Industrielles. *Rapports commerciaux des agents diplomatiques et consulaires de France.* Paris, 1892–1912. Most of the reports concerning Russia may be found unabridged and unedited in A.N., F 12. On several occasions interesting and unflattering information on Russia was carefully omitted from the printed version.
Ministère des Travaux Publics. *Le Développement des Travaux Publics sous la III° Republic; l'Oeuvre des Ingénieurs Français a l'Etranger, 1870–1915.* Paris, 1915.

RUSSIA

Tsarist Publications

Ministerstvo Finansov. *Ezhegodnik Ministerstva Finansov.* St. Petersburg, yearly.
———. Kovalevskii, V. I. *Rossiia v kontse XIX veka.* St. Petersburg, 1900.
———. *Ministerstvo Finansov, 1802–1902.* 2 vols. St. Petersburg, 1902.
———. *Ministerstvo Finansov, 1904–1913.* St. Petersburg, 1914.
———. *Obzory glavneiskikh otraslei promyshlennosti i torgovli.* From 1908 to 1911. St. Petersburg, 1909–1912.
———. *Russia, Its Industries and Trade.* Issued by order of State Secretary S. J. de Witte. Glasgow, 1901.

———. *Vestnik Finansov, promyshlennosti i torgovli.* Weekly. St. Petersburg, 1883–1914.

———. Departament Torgovli i Manufaktur. *The Industries of Russia.* 5 vols. St. Petersburg, 1893. (Published for the World's Columbian Exposition at Chicago, 1893.)

———. ———. *Obzor inostrannykh zakonodatel'stv ob aktsionernykh kompanii.* St. Petersburg, 1896.

———. Osobennaia Kantselariia po Kreditnoi Chasti. *Bulletin russe de statistique financière et de la législation.* St. Petersburg, 1887–1906.

———. ———. *Ukazatel' deistvuiushchikh v Imperii aktsionernykh predpriiatii.* Dmitriev-Mamonov, V. A., ed. St. Petersburg, 1903.

Ministerstvo Torgovli i Promyshlennosti. *Sbornik svedenii o deistvuiushchikh v Rossii aktsionernykh obshchestvakh i tovarishchestvakh na paiakh.* St. Petersburg, 1914.

Soviet Publications

Akademiia Nauk SSSR. Institut ekonomiki. *Istoriia russkoi ekonomicheskoi mysli.* Pashkov, A. I., ed. 2 vols. Moscow, 1955–59.

———. Institut istorii. *Genezis kapitalizma v promyshlennosti Moskvy.* Moscow, 1963.

———. ———. *Materialy po istorii SSSR,* vol. 6, *Dokumenty po istorii monopolisticheskogo kapitalizma v Rossii.* Moscow, 1959.

———. Trudy leningradskogo otdeleniia instituta istorii. *Iz istorii imperializma v Rossii.* Moscow, 1959.

———. ———. *Monopolii i inostrannyi kapital v Rossii.* Moscow, 1962.

Pankratova, A. M., ed. *Rabochee dvizhenie v XIX veke: Sbornik dokumentov.* 6 vols. Moscow, 1950–52.

4. Contemporary Newspapers, Periodicals, and Brochures

GENERAL OR SEMIOFFICIAL

Economiste Européen
L'Economiste français
L'Economiste International

Gornyi Zhurnal
Journal de St. Petersburg
Journal des Chemins de fer
Le Journal des Economistes
Le Messager de Paris
Revue des Deux Mondes
Revue Universelle des Mines
The Russian Journal of Financial Statistics, St. Petersburg,
    1900–1901
Torgovo-promshlennaia Gazeta
Torgovo-promyshlennyi Iug

SPECIALIZED FINANCIAL AND ECONOMIC PRESS

Belgique financière
Birzhevye Vedomosti, St. Petersburg
Bourse de Paris
Bourse lyonnaise
Bulletin de la Chambre de Commerce Russe de Paris, 1902–
    13
Le Bulletin Financier
Le Capitaliste
Comité pour l'étude des questions d'intérêt commun des
    mines et usines du Midi de la Russie. *Circulaire.*
    Weekly. October 1904 to December 1909.
Le Conseiller
Cote de la Bourse et de la Banque
La Cote Libre
Cote lyonnaise
Le Crédit national
Courrier de la Bourse et de la Banque
Echo de la Bourse et de la Banque
Le Globe
L'Industrie
L'Information
Journal des Actionnaires
Journal des Intérets financiers
Journal des Rentiers
Journal du Crédit Public
Lettres d'un capitaliste
Le Monde économique

Le Moniteur de la Bourse
Moniteur des Finances de l'Industrie et du Commerce
Moniteur des Intérêts Matériels
Le Pour et le Contre
La Reforme économique
La Rente
Le Rentier
La Revue économique et financière
La Semaine Financière

BROCHURES

Bayard, Paul. *Notice sur les Mines de la Doubovaia Balka.*
N.d., n.p. [1892–93]. In A.N., 65 AQ, L 807.
Création d'une Société Métallurgique Franco-Russe. Lyons,
1879. In A.N., 65 AQ, K 164.
Etude sur l'industrie cotonnière en Russie. Paris, 1898. In
C.L., Société Cotonnière Russo-Française.
Genaert, Jules. *Fédération Industrielle Russe.* Brussels,
1901. In A.E., Brussels, 2900.
Monin, J. *Notice sur le Bassin Houiller du Donetz (Nouvelle
Russie); Constitution d'une Société pour l'achat des
propriétés et des houillères Ilovaisky.* Paris, 1882. In
A.N., 65 AQ, K 69.
*Rapport sur la mission en Russie par MM Hardy et Michot
en Juin 1896.* Paris, 1896. In C.L., Charbonnages de
Bielaia.
*Rapport sur les Mines de Houille et d'Anthracite "Zolotoié
et Bokovsky" en Russie Méridionale de la Sté Houil-
lère du Donetz, Koreniff et Chipiloff.* Liège, 1900. In
C.L., Cie Générale de Charbonnages.
Société des Sels Gemmes et Soudes Naturelles de la Russie
Meridionale. *Notice.* Paris, n.d. [1894–95]. In A.N.,
65 AQ, L 3321[1].
Société de l'Industrie Houillère de la Russie Méridionale.
Paris, 1900. At C.L. in dossier with this name.
Société Métallurgique du Donetz-Yourievka. Paris, 1900. In
C.L., Donetz-Yourievka.
Zbyszewski, M. *L'Exposition nationale russe de Nijny-
Novgorod et l'industrie russe.* Paris, 1897.

5. Contemporary Books and Articles

Agahd, E. *Grossbanken und Weltmarkt.* Berlin, 1914.

Anspach, Alfred. *La Russie économique et l'oeuvre de M. de Witte.* Paris, 1904.

Barry, Herbert. *Russia in 1870.* London, 1871.

Bloch, J. *Les Finances de la Russie au XIX siècle.* Paris, 1899.

Boustedt, Axel von, ed. *Das russische Reich in Europa und Asien: ein Handbuch über seine wirtschaftliche Verhältnisse.* Berlin, 1913.

Brandt, Boris F. *Inostrannye kapitaly; ikh vliianie na ekonomicheskoi razvitie strany.* 3 vols. St. Petersburg, 1898–1901.

Claus, R. *Das russische Bankwesen.* Leipzig, 1908.

Collas, H. *La Banque de Paris et des Pays-Bas et les émissions d'emprunts publics et privés.* Paris, 1910.

Cordeweener, Jules. *Contribution à l'étude de la crise industrielle du Donetz.* Brussels, 1902.

Couharévitch, J. "La Russie industrielle (Region Ouest)." *Revue Universelle des Mines* 19, 3d ser., 36th year (1892) : 265.

Den, V. E. *Kamennougol'naia i zhelezodelatel'naia promyshlennost'.* St. Petersburg, 1901.

Delage, Emile. *Chez les Russes.* Paris, 1903.

Dillon, E. J. "M. Witte and the Russian Commercial Crisis." *Contemporary Review* 79 (1901) : 472–501 .

Diouritch, Georges. *L'expansion des banques allemandes à l'étranger.* Paris, 1909.

Ditmar, N. F., ed. *Aktsionernoe delo v Rossii.* St. Petersburg, 1900.

————, ed. *Zhelezorudnaia promyshlennost' Iuzhnoi Rossii.* Published by Statisticheskoe biuro soveta s"ezda gornopromyshlennikov iuga Rossii. 1900–.

Egorov, P. I. *Inostrannye kapitaly i russkie tekhniki.* St. Petersburg, 1910.

Fomin, P. I. *Gornaia i gornozavodskaia promyshlennost' Iuga Rossii.* 2 vols. Kharkov, 1915, 1922.

————. *Kratkii ocherk istorii s''ezdov gornopromyshlennikov Iuga Rossii.* Kharkov, 1908.

Glivits, I. *Zheleznaia promyshlennost' v Rossii.* St. Petersburg, 1911.

Gras, L. J. *Histoire économique de la Loire.* St. Etienne, 1908.

Horn, A. E. *A History of Banking in the Russian Empire.* 2 vols. New York, 1896.

Ischchanian, B. *Die ausländischen Elemente in der russischen Volkswirtschaft.* Berlin, 1913.

Islavine, Vladimir. *Aperçu sur l'état de l'industrie de la houille et du fer dans le bassin du Donets.* St. Petersburg, 1875.

Joubert, C. *Russia as It Really Is.* London, 1905.

Kovalevsky, Maxime. *Le régime économique de la Russie.* Paris, 1898.

Kovalevsky, Vladimir. *La Russie à la fin du XIX⁰ siècle.* Paris, 1900.

Lauwick, Marcel. *L'industrie dans la Russie Méridionale, sa situation, son avenir.* Brussels, 1907.

Levin, I. I. *Germanskie kapitaly v Rossii.* 2d. ed. Petrograd, 1918.

Lewin, J. *Der Heutige Zustand der Aktienhandelsbanken in Russland, 1900–1910.* Freiburg im Breisgau, 1912.

Lur'e, E. *Organizatsiia i organizatsii torgovo-promyshlennykh interesov v Rossii: Podgotovitel'nye materialy dlia kharakteristiki predprinimatel'skogo dvizheniia.* St. Petersburg, 1913.

Machat, J. *Le développement économique de la Russie.* Paris, 1902.

Melnik, Josef, ed. *Russen über Russland.* Frankfurt am Main, 1906.

Migulin, P. P. *Nasha bankovaia politika, 1729–1903.* Kharkov, 1904.

————. "Inostrannyi kapital v Rossii, doklad obshchemu sobraniiu Russko-angliiskoi torgovoi palaty." *Novyi Ekonomist,* no. 12, 1913.

Orlov. *Ukazatel' fabrik i zavodov Evropeiskoi Rossii.* 3d. ed. St. Petersburg, 1894.

Pergamainte, Joseph. *De la condition légale des Sociétés étrangères en Russie.* Paris, 1899.

Pushkin, N. *Statistika aktsionernogo dela v Rossii.* 3d. ed. St. Petersburg, 1898.

Rafalovich, Arthur. "*. . . l'abominable vénalité de la presse . . .*" *D'après les documents des archives russes (1897–1917).* Paris, 1931.

Ragozin, E. *Zhelezo i ugol' na Urale.* St. Petersburg, 1903.

Ragozin, Victor. *Neft' i neftianaia promyshlennost'.* St. Petersburg, 1884.

Schulze-Gävernitz, G. von. *Volkswirtschaftliche Studien aus Russland.* Leipzig, 1899.

Sering, Max, ed. *Russlands Kultur und Volkswirtschaft; Aufsätz und Vorträge im Auftrage der Vereinigung für staatswissenschaftliche Fortbildung in Berlin.* Berlin, 1913.

Skalkovsky, C. *Les Ministres des Finances de la Russie, 1802–1890.* Paris, 1891.

Sovet s''ezda gornopromyshlennikov iuga Rossii. *Kratkii ocherk istorii s''ezdov gornopromyshlennikov iuga Rossii.* Kharkov, 1908.

Stevenson, J. L. *Blast Furnace Calculation.* London, 1906.

Théry, Edmond. *L'Europe économique et financière pendant le dernier quart de siècle.* Paris, 1900.

———. *La transformation économique de la Russie.* Paris, 1914.

Time, I. A. *Sovremennoe sostoianie tekhniki na iuzhnorusskikh gornykh zavodakh i rudnikakh.* St. Petersburg, 1897.

———. *Spravochnaia kniga dlia gornykh inzhenerov i tekhnikov po gornoi chasti.* 2d. ed. St. Petersburg, 1899.

Titov, V. I. *Materialy dlia opisaniia proizvoditel'nykh sil zhelezodelatel'nykh i mekhanicheskikh zavodov iuga Rossii.* St. Petersburg, 1898.

Trasenster, P. "L'industrie sidérurgique russe: Etude économique." *Revue Universelle des Mines,* 1899.

Tugan-Baranovskii, M. I. *K luchshemu budushchemu.* St. Petersburg, 1912.

―――. *Russkaia fabrika v proshlom i nastoiashchem*. 2d. ed. St. Petersburg, 1900.

Verstraete, Maurice. *La Russie industrielle: Etude sur l'exposition de N. Novgorod*. Paris, 1897.

―――. *L'Oural*. Paris, 1899.

―――. "Les capitaux étrangers engagés dans les sociétés industrielles en Russie." In *Congrès international des valeurs mobilières*, vol. 4, document no. 111. Paris, 1900.

Voronov, L. *Inostrannye kapitaly v Rossii*. Moscow, 1901.

Zak, A. N. *Nemtsy i nemetskie kapitaly v russkoi promyshlennosti*. St. Petersburg, 1914.

Zak, S. S. *Promyshlennyi kapitalizm v Rossii*. 2d. ed. Petrograd, 1917.

Ziv, V. S. *Inostrannye kapitaly v russkoi gornozavodskoi promyshlennosti*. Petrograd, 1917.

―――. *Inostrannye kapitaly v russkoi neftianoi promyshlennosti*. Petrograd, 1915.

6. Secondary Works

Akhundov, B. Iu. *Monopolisticheskii kapital v dorevoliutsionnoi Bakinskoi neftianoi promyshlennosti*. Moscow, 1959.

Amburger, Erik. "Firmen-, betriebs- und industriegeschichte Literatur Altrusslands und der Sowjetunion (eine Sammelbesprechung)." *Tradition, Zeitschrift für Firmengeschichte und Unternehmerbiographie* 6 (1961) : 225–38.

Bakulev, G. D. *Razvitie ugol'noi promyshlennosti Donetskogo basseina*. Moscow, 1955.

Baykov, Alexander. "The Economic Development of Russia." *Economic History Review*, ser. 2, 7 (1954) : 137–49.

Bill, Valentine T. *The Forgotten Class*. New York, 1959.

Bompard, Maurice. *Mon ambassade en Russie, 1903–1908*. Paris, 1937.

Bouvier, Jean. *Le Crédit Lyonnais de 1863 à 1882*. 2 vols. Paris, 1961.

———. "Une dynastie d'affaires lyonnaise au XIX° siecle: Les Bonnardel." *Revue d'histoire moderne et contemporaine* 2 (1955) : 185–205.

Bovyinke, V. I. "Problèmes de l'histoire de la révolution industrielle, des crises et des banques en Russie." *Histoire des Entreprises,* no. 4 (November 1959), pp. 49–58.

Cameron, Rondo E. *France and the Economic Development of Europe, 1800–1914.* Princeton, 1961.

Cameron, Rondo E., with Olga Crisp, Hugh T. Patrick, and Richard Tilly. *Banking in the Early Stages of Industrialization.* New York, 1967.

Chlepner, B. S. *La banque en Belgique: étude historique et économique.* Brussels, 1926.

———. *Belgian Banking and Banking Theory.* Washington, D.C., 1943.

Clapham, J. H. *The Economic Development of France and Germany, 1815–1914.* 4th ed. Cambridge, 1936.

Crihan, Anton. *Le capital étranger en Russie.* Paris, 1934.

Crisp, Olga. "French Investment in Russian Joint-Stock Companies, 1894–1914," *Business History* (Liverpool) 2 (1960) : 75–90.

———. "Some Problems of French Investment in Russian Joint-Stock Companies." *Slavonic and East European Review* 35 (1956) : 223–40.

———. "Russian Financial Policy and the Gold Standard at the End of the 19th Century." *Economic History Review,* ser. 2, 6 (1953) : 156–72.

Epstein, E. *Les banques de commerce: Leur role dans l'évolution économique de la Russie.* Paris, 1925.

Eventov, L. Ia. *Inostrannye kapitaly v russkoi promyshlennosti.* Moscow, 1931.

———. *Inostrannye kapitaly v neftianoi promyshlennosti.* Moscow, 1925.

Feis, Herbert. *Europe, The World's Banker, 1870–1914: An Account of European Foreign Investment and the Connection of World Finance with Diplomacy before the War.* New Haven, 1930.

Fenin, A. *Vospominaniia inzhenera; K istorii obshchestven-nogo i khoziaistvennogo razvitiia Rossii (1882–1906 gg.).* Prague, 1938.

Finn-Enotaevskii, Alexander. *Kapitalizm v Rossii (1890–1917 gg.).* Moscow, 1925.

Fuks, N. *Iz istorii poznaniia Donetskogo kamennougol'nogo basseina.* Kharkov, 1923.

Gefter, M. Ia. and Sheveleva, L. E. "O proniknovenii angliiskogo kapitala v neftianuiu promyshlennost' Rossii (1898–1902 gg.)." *Istoricheskii Arkhiv* (1960), no. 6.

Gerschenkron, Alexander. *Economic Backwardness in Historical Perspective.* Cambridge, Mass., 1962.

———. "The Rate of Industrial Growth in Russia since 1885." *Journal of Economic History* 7 (1947), Supplement: 144–174.

Gindin, Iosif F. *Banki i promyshlennost' v Rossii.* Moscow, 1927.

———. *Gosudarstvennyi bank i ekonomicheskaia politika tsarskogo pravitel'stva, 1861–1892 gody.* Moscow, 1960.

———. *Russkie kommercheskie banki: Iz istorii finansovogo kapitala v Rossii.* Moscow, 1948.

Gille, Bertrand. "Etat de la presse économique et financière en France." *Histoire des Entreprises,* no. 4 (November 1959), pp. 58–77.

Girault, René. "Finances internationales et relations internationales (à propos des Usines Poutiloff)." *Revue d'histoire moderne et contemporaine* 13 (1966): 217–236.

Goldman, M. "The Relocation and Growth of the Prerevolutionary Russian Ferrous Metal Industry." *Explorations in Entrepreneurial History* 9 (1956): 19–26.

Goldsmith, Raymond W. "The Economic Growth of Tsarist Russia, 1860–1913." *Journal for Economic Development and Cultural Change* 9 (1961): 441–79.

Haber, L. F. *The Chemical Industry during the 19th Century.* Oxford, 1958.

Hausler, E. *Der Kaufmann in der russischen Literatur.* Konigsberg, 1935.

Keep, J. L. H. *The Rise of Social Democracy in Russia.* Oxford, 1963.

Khromov, P. A. *Ekonomicheskoe razvitie Rossii v XIX–XX vekakh.* Moscow, 1950.

———. *Ocherki ekonomiki Rossii perioda monopolisticheskogo kapitalizma.* Moscow, 1960.

Kindersley, Richard. *The First Russian Revisionists.* Oxford, 1962.

Kokovtsov, V. N. *Out of My Past: The Memoirs of Count Kokovtsov, Russian Minister of Finance, 1904–1914, Chairman of the Council of Ministers, 1911–1914,* ed. H. H. Fisher. Stanford, Calif., 1935.

Krimmer, Alexandre. *Sociétés de capitaux en Russie impériale et en Russie soviétique.* Paris, 1934.

Kuznets, Simon. "Quantitative Aspects of Economic Growth of Nations: VIII. Distribution of Income by Size." *Economic Development and Cultural Change* 11, no. 2, pt. 2 (1963).

Landes, D. S. *Bankers and Pashas: International Finance and Economic Imperialism in Egypt.* London, 1958.

———. "Technical Change and Economic Development in Western Europe, 1750–1914." In H. J. Habakkuk and M. Postan, eds., *The Cambridge Economic History,* vol. 6, *The Industrial Revolution and After,* pp. 274–603. Cambridge, 1965.

Langer, W. *The Diplomacy of Imperialism.* 2d. ed. New York, 1951.

Lewery, L. J. *Foreign Capital Investment in Russian Industries and Commerce.* Washington, 1923.

Liashchenko, P. I. *Istoriia narodnogo khoziaistva SSSR,* vol. 2, *Kapitalizm.* Moscow, 1956.

Livshits, R. S. *Razmeshchenie promyshlennosti v dorevoliutsionnoi Rossii.* Moscow, 1954.

Miller, Margaret S. *Economic Development of Russia, 1905–1914.* London, 1926.

Ordinaire, J. *L'évolution industrielle russe depuis la fin du XIX° siècle.* Paris, 1927.

Ol', Pavel V. *Inostrannye kapitaly v narodnom khoziaistve dovoennoi Rossii.* Leningrad, 1925.

————. *Inostrannye kapitaly v Rossii*. Petrograd, 1922.

Pogrebinskii, A. P. *Ocherki istorii finansov dorevoliutsionnoi Rossii, XIX–XX vv.* Moscow, 1954.

————. *Gosudarstvenno-monopolisticheskii kapitalizm v Rossii: Ocherki istorii*. Moscow, 1959.

Portal, R. *La Russie industrielle de 1881–1927*. Paris, 1956.

————. "The Industrialization of Russia." In H. J. Habakkuk and M. Postan, eds., *The Cambridge Economic History of Europe*, vol. 6, *The Industrial Revolution and After*, pp. 801–72. Cambridge, 1965.

Propper, S. M. von. *Was nicht in die Zeitung Kam: Erinnerungen des Chefredacteurs de "Birschewyya Wedomost."* Frankfurt am Main, 1929.

Queen, George S. "The McCormick Harvesting Machine Company in Russia." *Russian Review* 23 (1964): 164–81.

Rashin, A. G. *Formirovanie rabochego klassa Rossii*. Moscow, 1958.

————. *Naselenie Rossii za 100 let*. Moscow, 1956.

Rimlinger, Gaston. "Autocracy and the Factory Order in Early Russian Industrialization." *Journal of Economic History* 20 (1960): 67–92.

————. "The Expansion of the Labor Market in Capitalist Russia, 1861–1917." *Journal of Economic History* 21 (1961): 208–15.

————. "The Management of Labor Protest in Tsarist Russia, 1870–1905." *International Review of Social History* 5 (1960): 226–48.

Ronin, S. L. *Inostrannye kapitaly i russkie banki*. Moscow, 1926.

Rosovsky, Henry. "The Serf Entrepreneur in Russia." *Explorations in Entrepreneurial History* 6 (1954): 207–33.

Science et Industrie, 8th year, no. 121 (April 1924). Issue devoted to a series of articles, "Les Intérêts Français et L'Industrie Russe."

Shpolianskii, D. I. *Monopolii ugol'nometallurgicheskoi promyshlennosti iuga Rossii v nachale XX veka*. Moscow, 1953.

Silly, J. B. "Capitaux français et sidérurgie russe." *Revue d'histoire de la sidérurgie* 6 (1965) : 28–53.

Société Générale [de Belgique]. *La Société Générale de Belgique, 1822–1922.* Brussels, 1922.

Société John Cockerill. *110ᵉ Anniversaire de la fondation des usines Cockerill, 1817–1927.* Brussels, 1928.

Strumilin, S. G. *Chernaia metallurgiia v Rossii i SSSR.* Moscow, 1935.

――――. *Istoriia chernoi metallurgii v SSSR.* Moscow, 1954.

――――. *Problema promyshlennogo kapitala v SSSR.* Moscow, 1925.

Timoshenko, S. P. "The Development of Engineering Education in Russia." *Russian Review* 15 (1956) : 173–85.

Vanag, N. *Finansovyi kapital v Rossii nakanune mirovoi voiny.* Moscow, 1925.

Volkov, E. *Dinamika narodonaseleniia SSSR.* Moscow, 1930.

Von Laue, Theodore H. *Sergei Witte and the Industrialization of Russia.* New York, 1963.

――――. *Why Lenin? Why Stalin?* New York, 1964.

――――. "Factory Inspection under the 'Witte System.'" *American Slavic and East European Review* 19 (1960) : 347–62.

――――. "Russian Peasant in the Factory, 1892–1904." *Journal of Economic History* 21 (1961) : 61–80.

Westwood, J. N. "John Hughes and Russian Metallurgy." *Economic History Review,* ser. 2, 17 (1965) : 564–69.

Wildman, Alan. *The Making of a Workers' Revolution: Russian Social Democracy, 1891–1903.* Chicago, 1967.

Witmeur, E. "Les avoirs et intérêts belges en Russie." *Revue Economique internationale* 2 (1922) : 296–324.

7. General Works on Entrepreneurship and Foreign Investment

There is a vast and growing literature on the problems of economic development in general and on those of foreign investment in particular. The following selected titles are particularly suggestive.

Aharoni, Yair. *The Foreign Investment Decision Process.* Boston, 1966.

Aiken, Thomas, Jr. *A Foreign Policy for American Business*. New York, 1962.

Amsterdam Universiteit. *Management for Direct Investments in Less Developed Countries*. Report submitted to the International Bank for Reconstruction and Development by the Foundation of Economic Research of the University of Amsterdam. Leiden, 1955.

Berrill, K. "Foreign Capital and Take-Off." In W. Rostow, *The Economics of Take-off into Sustained Growth*. London, 1963.

Brannen, Ted R., and Hodgson, Frank X. *Overseas Management*. New York, 1965.

British Institute of International and Comparative Law. *The Encouragement and Protection of Investment in Developing Countries*. London, 1962.

Brown, Wilfred. *Exploration in Management*. London, 1960.

Bryson, George D. *Profits from Abroad: A Reveille for American Business*. New York, 1964.

Daniel, James, ed. *Private Investment: The Key to International Industrial Development*. New York, 1958.

Dobb, Maurice. *Economic Growth and Underdeveloped Countries*. New York, 1963.

Dunning, John H. *American Investment in British Manufacturing Industry*. London, 1958.

Fayerweather, John. *The Executive Overseas*. Syracuse, 1959.

Guth, Wilfried. *Capital Exports to Less Developed Countries*. Dordrecht, Holland, 1963.

Hazlewood, A. *The Economics of "Under-developed" Areas: Annotated Reading List of Books, Articles, and Official Publications*. 2d. ed. New York, 1959.

Heilbroner, Robert. *The Great Ascent*. New York, 1963.

Hirschman, A. O. *The Strategy of Economic Development*. New Haven, 1958.

Johnstone, Alan W. *United States Investments in France: An Investigation of the French Charges*. Cambridge, Mass., 1965.

Kohler, M. *The Common Market and Investments*. New York, 1960.

Lampard, Eric. "The Social Impact of the Industrial Revolution." In Melvin Krangberg and Carroll Pursell, Jr., eds., *Technology and Western Civilization*, 1:302–21. New York, 1967.

Landes, David S. "Some Thoughts on the Nature of Economic Imperialism." *Journal of Economic History* 21 (1961) : 496–511.

Mikesell, Raymond F., ed. *United States Private and Government Investment Abroad.* Eugene, Ore., 1962.

Nurske, Ragnar. "International Investment Today in the Light of Nineteenth Century Experience." *Economic Journal* 64 (1954) : 744–58.

Redlich, Fritz. "Toward a Better Theory of Risk." *Explorations in Entrepreneurial History* 10 (1957) : 33–39.

Robinson, Harry J. *The Motivation and Flow of Private Foreign Investment.* Menlo Park, Calif., 1961.

Schumpeter, Joseph A. *Capitalism, Socialism and Democracy.* 3d. ed. New York, 1950.

Singer, H. W. "U.S. Foreign Investment in Underdeveloped Areas : The Distribution of Gains between Industry and Borrowing Countries." *American Economic Review* 40 (1950) : 473–85.

Spence, Clark C. *British Investments and the American Mining Frontier.* Ithaca, N.Y., 1958.

United Nations. *International Flow of Long Term Capital and Official Donations.* Published intermittently.

8. Unpublished Works

Burnstein, Abraham. "Iron and Steel in Russia, 1861–1913." Ph.D. dissertation, New School for Social Research, 1963.

Crisp, Olga. "The Financial Aspect of the Franco-Russian Alliance, 1894–1914." Ph.D. thesis, University of London, 1954.

Farbenfabriken Bayer. "Geschichte und Entwicklung der Farbenfabriken vorm. Friedrich Bayer & Co. Elberfeld in den ersten 50 Jahren." Internal history [1909].

Herme, Jules. "Livre d'or d'Ougrée-Marihaye." Internal history, n.d. Copy at Société John Cockerill, Seraing.

Willem, L., and Willem, S. "Histoire de la Société Métallurgique d'Espérance-Longdoz." Manuscript. 2 vols. With Mr. Willem, division chief at Espérance-Longdoz, Liège, Belgium.

Yurick, Edward. "The Russian Adventure: Belgian Investment in Imperial Russia." Ph.D. dissertation, Ohio State University, 1959.

INDEX